My Life Story

(1886-1979)

Raja Mahendra Pratap

In 2 Vols.

Vol. 2
(1942-1979)

Compiled & Edited by
Dr. Rajendra Kumar

Originals
Delhi-110052

First Published 2016

ISBN 13: 978-81-8454-161-8
ISBN 10: 81-8454-161-9

Published By
Originals
A-6, Second Floor, Nimri Commercial Centre,
Ashok Vihar Phase-4, Delhi - 110 052 (India)
Tel.: +91 11 2730 2453 Fax: 011 4706 1936
website: www.Lppindia.com
e-mail: info@Lppindia.com

Printed At
D K Fine Art Press P Ltd.
Delhi-110052

PRINTED IN INDIA

Editorial

Raja Mahendra Pratap left India in 1914 and worked for the cause of freedom of India for the next thirty two years in exile. Besides a zealous revolutionary, social reformer and thinker, he was a voracious writer and a dedicated journalist. To inform people about his revolutionary ideology and activities to free the country and to preach and spread his philosophy of love and the realization of healthy, prosperous and peaceful life by every individual in Aryan and the World, he started publishing a periodical, 'World Federation' from September 1929 in Berlin (Germany), which he called a circular. In this paper he used to write by way of diary, his life story, about his 'doings or time wastings'. When he shifted to Japan in 1933, he continued its publication from Japan. But after Japan joined the Second World War on 8th December 1941, he was ordered by the Japanese Government to sit quiet at his World Federation Centre in Tokyo and he had to suspend the publication of this paper. In 1942, he published his life story, 'My Life Story of 55 Years'.

Raja Mahendra Pratap arrived in India on 9th August 1946, after an exile of thirty-two years from his motherland, and the monthly publication of 'World Federation' was resumed in 1948. He also started regular publication of 'Sansar Sangh' in Hindi and 'Ittehaade Duniya' in Urdu. In these papers Rajaji used to write his monthly diary in shape of My Story, as well as his personal views.

Raja Mahendra Pratap's 'My Life Story of 55 Years' was incomplete as he lived a long and active life of 93 years, preaching his philosophy of international fraternity, without giving up caste and community identities, his concept of the originality of Aryan country and religiosity combined with modernity and one-world government, therefore it was necessary to expand his life story.

published in 2004. It was thought to bring out rest of his life story as 'My Life Story,' Volume 2, on the same pattern, as he would have himself collected from the Circular. Dr. Vir Singh wished to publish the Life Story in Hindi, but the task lingered on due to his ill-health and could not be started. Therefore the Society entrusted this responsibility to Dr. Rajendra Kumar, who nicely and adequately fulfilled this difficult task of compiling and editing the book in Raja Mahendra Pratap's style.

Surajmal Memorial Education Society, since its inception in 1972 aimed to provide education facilities to weaker sections of the society, especially those belonging to rural areas. To fulfil its objectives, the Society established professional institutes in its campus at C-4, Janakpuri, New Delhi, two public schools, one each in U.P. and Rajasthan, and is in a process of establishing a new school in Haryana. To undertake the collection, preservation and publication of material on rural heritage, the Society established Maharaja Surajmal Centre for Research and Publication, which has published a variety of books, including research work of scholars, translation of prominent works in Hindi, reprinting of important works related to peasants of North-West India and the proceedings of the National Seminars organised by the Society from time to time.

The Society has always striven for excellence, and in that attempt published more than 28 books, including three books on Raja Mahendra Pratap .'My Life Story' Volume 1; 'Reminiscences of a Revolutionary : Raja Mahendra Pratap'; and 'Life and Times of Raja Mahendra Pratap', proceedings of the National Seminar organised by the Society on 25-26th April, 1998.

An Introduction has been incorporated to provide a glimpse of Raja Mahendra Pratap's early life, his ideas and vision.

I hope the readers would find this book not only interesting but informative and useful. I take the opportunity to appreciate the serious efforts put in by our Honorary Director Dr. Rajendra Kumar, who compiled, edited and brought out this volume with his scholarly Introduction, which has been incorporated to give

a glimpse of Raja Mahendra Pratap's ideas and vision, so that the readers may get the reflections of his versatile and multifaceted personality along with his invaluable contribution to our country, world and mankind as a whole.

S. P. Singh
President
Surajmal Memorial Education Society
C-4, Janakpuri, New Delhi

Foreword

Raja Mahendra Pratap published his life story, 'My Life Story of 55 Years' in 1943. In the Preface of that book he writes, 'I have just collected what I wrote by way of my life story in our circular of World Federation from 1929 to 1941. In 1942 I also published couple of circulars and I can add a bit more of my doings or time wastings, bringing the story up todate, I am writing these lines today on 29th of May, 1943, but I prefer to stop this story at the end of 1941, because if I were to add further, I would have to bring in details of my life which the Japanese Imperial authorities did not like to see in print. Due to official hindrance our circular of April 1942 could not be published and then I suspended it altogether......'

The above-mentioned life story of Raja Mahendra Pratap was incomplete, as he lived hale and hearty for the next thirty-eight years, and engaged in preaching his philosophy of love and international brotherhood through the same circular, 'World Federation', whose publication he resumed in 1948. In this monthly paper he used to write his monthly story. During their visit to Prem Mahavidyalaya, Vrindavan, Late Dr. Vir Singh, Director of Research and Publication and Dr. P.S. Dabas collected the copies of the available issues of 'World Federation' and 'Sansar Sangh', published during last 30 years and brought them to Surajmal Memorial Education Society.

As 'My Life Story of 55 Years' was incomplete and did not depict the later part of Raja Mahendra Pratap's life, Surajmal Memorial Education Society planned to expand his biography based on his diaries published in his circulars. Keeping this object ahead, it was decided to publish 'My Life Story of 55 Years' in shape of 'My Life Story', Volume I and that was

Surajmal Memorial Education Society published 'My Life Story' Volume 1, 1886-1941, in year 2004, and decided to publish rest of his life story as Volume 2, 1942-1979.

I was entrusted this responsibility by the Society. The task was hard and yet difficult, as Rajaji's language and his ideas were to be kept in original, as such, as his life story must speak for him in detail. As mentioned earlier, the main source of this biography is the collection of 'My Story' which Raja Mahendra Pratap used to write in the monthly circular 'World Federation'. I did not change his language, neither the expressions (such as I and Pt. Nehru, instead of Pt. Nehru and I, etc.) are changed nor the spellings of names, places and words. Only some minor mistakes in the language such as use of prepositions have been corrected. Moreover, some contexts have been left due to fear of expansion, but to keep order and consistency some material has been taken from his other publications, specially from 'Sansar Sangh'. However, in translation also I tried to use the same expressions as that of Rajaji though it was quite difficult.

So far as I am personally concerned, it has been my pleasure that I had good fortune of spending some time with Raja Mahendra Pratap, watching him working from pretty close quarters on several occasions, listening him and discussing with him his ideas and every time I have been struck with particular aspect of his personality. A few instances that come readily to my memory, I should mention here. During my stay at the USSR in 1974, I had been to Gorki Leninskiye, the residence of Vladimir Ilyich Lenin. I was astonished to see Mahendra Pratap's book 'Religion of Love' in the Library of Lenin. Coming back to India, I met Rajaji and told him about that, and he narrated the incident of his meeting with Lenin with live demonstration in such a way, as it happened only yesterday. Except my personal visits, I accompanied E. Rumyantsev, editor of Soviet Land magazine in September 1975, G. A. Syomin of Information Department of the USSR embassy in India and E. Artamonov, artist in October 1977 and later, Russian journalists of Novosty Press Agency twice for his interview. I happily used this opportunity in compiling, editing and sharing with the readers this Life Story of Rajaji. I used Rajaji's language and expressions without any change.

I express my sincere gratitude to Shri S. P. Singh, the popular and progressive minded President of the Surajmal Memorial Education Society for his active inspiration, continuous encouragement and support extended to me in compiling this volume.

I am grateful to Shri Ajit Singh Chaudhary, Secretary, Surajmal Memorial Education Society for giving me full cooperation and help. I am thankful to Shri Kaptan Singh, Vice President of the Society and Shri J. S. Dalal, Treasurer, SMES for their continous support. Dr. S.S. Rana stood by me to inspire and support as ever, I convey my heartfelt thanks to him. I may also make a special mention of Shri Dharamvir Singh (Molaheri) Advocate, Muzaffarnagar, who provided some valuable information about Rajaji.

I would not forget to acknowledge the hard work of my Research Associate, Mrs. Monika in publication of this book. I am also thankful to Shri Pradeep Mittal for publishing this book with excellent get-up.

Dr. Rajendra Kumar
Director
Maharaja Surajmal Centre for
Research & Publication
Surajmal Memorial Education Society
C-4, Janak Puri,
New Delhi-110058

Contents

Introduction

There were two ruling families of the Jats in northern side of the Jamuna, Hathras and Sasni. Both were descent of same forefather, Chaudhary Makhan Singh, a Thenua Jat, who appears to have come from Rajputana in the sixteenth century AD, and settled at Aligarh district. They both fought against the British and were defeated. Both remained later on as landlords owning a large number of villages. Sasni family shifted to Mursan in Aligarh district during the last decades of nineteenth century. During 1857 Uprising, Gobind Singh of Hathras and Tikam Singh of Mursan helped the British, so they got the title of Raja and Raja Bahadur respectively. Raja Bahadur Ghanshyam Singh was the ruler of Mursan. He had three sons—Duttaprasad Singh, Baldev Singh and Kharag Singh. Kharag Singh was born on 1st December 1886. In 1889, Kharag Singh was adopted as heir-son by Raja Harnarain Singh of Hathras in Aligarh district and was named Mahendra Pratap Singh. The family of Raja Harnarain Singh used to live at Vrindaban in Mathura district. Raja Harnarain Singh had two wives—Rani Swarup Kaur and Rani Hanumant Kaur. Raja Ghanshyam Singh conjectured that the adoption of the Mursan prince would not be owned and liked by both the queens of Hathras, therefore he obstructed his son at Mursan for next five years and when it became necessary to send him to Hathras, Ghanshyam Singh sent with him his trusted and loyal servants to look after the prince. Among them a barber named Jhandu was most important, who accompanied Mahendra Pratap as his sole guardian. Mahendra Pratap was brought up outside the palace, far from the harem, the ladies residence, to save him from intrigues of the palace. In the words of Raja Mahendra Pratap : *I am told that the relatives of my adoptive mother were not happy. They wanted to declare that the younger Rani was pregnant. They wanted to get a baby from somewhere and say baby was born. One illiterate elderly person, named Jhandu, who looked after me gave five Rupees to a Brahman woman, mother of family Purohit, to act as if goddess had come in her body, wildly shake her head and say that I was the God chosen person, no harm should come to me. The trick succeeded, all got afraid and I was not harmed... I was brought up mostly by men.* A Pandit and a Maulvi were engaged to teach him Hindi and Persian at home. At the age of eight he was sent to the government school at Aligarh, but soon transferred to the Mohemmaden Anglo Oriental Collegiate School, Aligarh, founded by Sir Syed Ahmad Khan, who was a friend of his father, Ghanshyam Singh. He was given two rooms in a bungalow of the boarding house of the college, where he lived practically by himself, under the guardianship of the trusted barber Jhandu surrounded by his ten servants. He was not allowed to mix up with other school-mates.

Mahendra Pratap was married to the Princess Balvir Kaur, the younger sister of Maharaja Ranbir Singh, the Sikh Raja of Jind, Punjab in 1902. At that time Mahendra Pratap was fourteen years old and the Princess was three year older than him.

He was an ordinary student, failed in the middle class and again in F.A. (Intermediate). In 1907 he finally left college, without completing final year of his graduation. During his college vacations he vastly travelled in India. Three years consecutively in 1904, 1905 and 1906 he received extra sum from Herbert Smith, the court of wards of the estate management to travel and see the country. In 1904 he went on pilgrimage tour with his brother Baldeo Singh for two months and a half and visited Puri, Rameshwaram, Kanjiviram, Kashi, Gaya etc. as well as big cities of Calcutta, Madras and Bombay. Next year he widely toured to Bengal, Assam and Burma going up to Darjeeling, travelling by train from Gauhati to Chittagong and going as far as Rangoon and Mandalay. In 1906 he visited extreme south, visiting Trivandrum and Travancore, and visiting Dwarka, Karachi, Quetta and Peshawar in extreme west. Hyderabad state, Mysore state, Bombay state and Baroda state were thoroughly visited. In 1907 he travelled to Ceylone-Colombo and Kandy. With it he occasionally visited Kashmir, Punjab, Himalayas and Rajasthan. These trips helped him to understand various geographical, social and economic aspects of the life of Indian people. From 17 August to 17 December 1907 he travelled around the world. These tours left an influence on his ideas about social reforms, indigenous functional education and unity of religions. During his travels he realized that education is the most important factor and plays the key role in nation building. He came to the conclusion that the European countries and the USA has made tremendous progress due to industrialization and realized how far India lagged behind other countries in this important matter. So to bring India at par with European countries, he established a technical college 'Prem Mahavidyalaya' in his palace at Vrindaban on 24th May 1909 and to support the college financially, he donated five villages of his estate, Wagaon, Baral, Sukhia, Akhtyarpur and Dhamera, which brought an income of Rs. 27,500 per annum. He also donated his wife's newly built residence adjacent to the college for boarding house, and Kala-Kunj and Hathras-Kunj for workshops.

To improve this institution he visited many technical schools of Europe in 1911. *I visited London, Birmingham, Leeds, Shefield, Manchester, Edinburg, Glasgow, Paris, Berlin and Zurich. I saw as many technical colleges as possible and inspected, as minutely as a layman could, the workshops attached to these institutions,* he writes. During this visit he realized, how the nation could make sufficient progress without the harmonious combination of intellectual and manual capacities. He applied all these ideas in Prem Mahavidyalaya which became the symbol of indigenous functional free education in which students would study and at the same time produce their daily necessities and thus prepare to face the challenges of life. Many dignitaries of that time including Mahatma Gandhi, Jawaharlal Nehru, Rabindranath Tagore, Madan Mohan Malviya, Dr. Sampurnanand etc. visited this institution and appreciated its functioning.

With industrial training Prem Mahavidyalaya also held classes for rural people – village level workers training. Mahendra Pratap donated 25,000 rupees to the management to carry on village schools in Mathura district. He also gave 10,000 rupees to the Magistrate of Mathura, Mr. Dampier to open a cooperative bank for the peasants of his estate.

For the awakening of rural people Mahendra Pratap appointed a number of preachers for social reforms. These preachers followed certain railway lines and stopped at every station for a day to preach nearby villagers. Others went by road to various districts, stopping at different villages. They used to send weekly reports to him. They had to get students and contributions for Prem Mahavidyalaya. To preach his ideas he started a weekly paper 'Prem' in Hindi and to publish it established a printing press in 1911. In 1914 he established a Centre of Unity of Religions and to serve the powerless at one of his houses at Dehradun started a library for books on religion and socialism.

Though Mahendra Pratap got control over his estate when he reached adulthood, but the title of Raja was neither conferred to him by the British, who had privilege to give such titles, nor he requested the British government for it, because he knew *the British were in power but they had surely usurped our family possessions.... We were only small landlords, one of the many thousands.* His subjects, the people of his estate loved him and called him Raja. So Mahendra Pratap Sinha, as he spelled his name so far, became Raja Mahendra Pratap.

On political front Raja Mahendra Pratap participated in Indian National Congress session in 1906 and 1910 held at Calcutta and Allahabad respectively. In the Allahabad session at Congress exhibition the articles made by the students of Prem Mahavidyalaya were highly appreciated. They got prizes. But during these sessions, he understood well that the independence could not be earned by the way Congress was dealing with at that time. Through his travels he gained understanding of the people, the country and the world and formed a vision to free India. He understood that love, peace and stability is necessary for the development of the society, but first of all it was necessary to get India free from the clutches of colonialists. He viewed to use force and armed rebellion to overthrow the British regime and to attain freedom for the country. He would not mind even aligning with other foreign power to achieve this goal.

The Commissioner of Agra did not permit his passport as he was aware of his attitude towards the government. So, on 20th December 1914, without passport he left his young wife weeping and two small children asleep.

He reached Switzerland with great difficulty and with the help of Virendra Nath Chattopadhyay, the elder brother of Sarojini Naidu, reached Berlin on 10th February 1915, by the fake name of Peer Mohammad. There he visited Indian War Prisoners' camp near Berlin and tried to enthuse Indian soldiers to dedicate their lives to the cause of India's freedom. He met Kaiser Wilhelm II, the ruler and Commander-in-Chief of Germany at Imperial Palace, in the Tier Garten. He reached Istambul, the capital of Turkey via Vienna-Budapest-Sofia and Constantinople, where he met Sultan Rishad, the spiritual head of the Islamic world and other dignitaries of Turkey. There from he arrived Kabul on 2 October 1915 with 28 letters, written by German Prime Minister Von Bethwen Hollweg, in which 27 were addressed to ruling Indian chiefs and one to the king of Nepal, in addition to two introductory letters of German Emperor and Sultan of Turkey to Amir Habibullah Khan of Afghanistan.

On 1st December 1915 Raja Mahendra Pratap established the first Provisional Government of India with its headquarters at Bagh-e-Baber in Kabul, Afghanistan, with himself as the President and Maulana Barkatullah Khan of Bhopal as Prime Minister. With his efforts the Afghan Government released all the revolutionaries of India from its prison. From these revolutionaries Raja Mahendra Pratap nominated Ubaidulla Sindhi of Deoband in district Saharanpur of U.P. as Home and Publications Minister, Rahmat Ali Zakaria as Communication Minister and Bashir Ahmad as War Minister. Later on he included Champak Raman Pillai as Minister of Internal Affairs in Berlin. With the help of Afghans, Raja Mahendra Pratap raised an independent army of 12,000 Afridis.

Later, this Provisional Government sent several missions, issued many proclamations to the Indian rulers and tried to come to some kind of understanding with the Czarist, Kerensky and Bolshevik Russia. It also made an appeal to warriors and heroic sons of India to rise and help the Indian revolutionaries to liberate India. Thus this environment abroad persuaded the foreign governments in favour of India. In this way Raja Mahendra Pratap carried on the struggle for complete independence at a time when leaders of national movement were demanding petty constitutional reforms from the British Rulers.

When third Afghan war between British India and Afghanistan started on 3rd May 1919, the Provisional Government issued a proclamation declaring that the Provisional Government has entered into a pact with invading forces of Afghanistan and asked the Indian people not to destroy their interest by fighting against the Afghans. The Afghans attack on the British check-posts and their cantonments all along the border and the appeal of Rajaji compelled the British to make peace-treaty with the Afghans on their conditions. This truce shattered the hopes of Indian revolutionaries to liberate India with the help of Germany and Afghanistan. After it, the Provisional Government turned to Soviet Russia for help. Rajaji met Trotsky in 1918 and led the first representative body of the Provisional Government to Moscow and met the Russian Revolution leader Lenin in July 1919. The delegation included Barkatullah, Abdur Rab, M.P.T. Acharya and Dilip Singh Gill. This meeting put a deep impact on Rajaji and throughout his life he remembered and mentioned it again and again.

Rajaji travelled around the world on Afghan passport. He interacted with the heads of the states and influential persons such as of Germany, Switzerland, Italy, Turkey, Afghanistan, Russia, USA, China and Japan. He united all the Indian revolutionary groups world over for India's independence. He set up an office at Leipzig, Germany in 1922 from where he published and distributed a large number of pamphlets and propaganda material to the great embarrassment of the British Government. He regularly wrote articles in *Pratap*, *Zamindar*, *Milap*, *Vandematram*, *Swaraj* and *Akali* newspapers in India. Till now he had turned a big menace for the British rulers. His every movement was closely watched and reported by the Home and Intelligence Department of British Government of India. After the detection of *Silk-letter, Seditious letters and literature*, addressed to Indian Rajas, bearing a German address and signed by Raja Mahendra Pratap 'in the interest of humanity' was an attempt to tell the Indian people about the dangers of the present rule and a call for the Indian rulers to stand up and work for their people in the spirit of service and dedication. The British Indian Government declared a reward on his head, attached his entire estate and declared him a fugitive. His wife died in 1925, but undeterred by materialistic impediments, undaunted by adversities forced on him by hostile forces and unshaken by setbacks, he relentlessly carried on his struggle for India's freedom.

He planned to visit far-east countries for his mission, got Japanese visa from Germany and wanted to go through France to avoid the English ports. *At the French foreign office, in Paris, a gentleman, who received me, promised to write about me to the French Embassy at Tokyo and the French Legation at Peking and he said that they would help me.*

It may be interesting to know how this official became so sympathetic towards me. He was in the beginning very suspicious and said, 'But you were with our enemies!' I happened to say : 'Why, I shall be with the Devil if he would fight the British empire.' This settled everything. And as the readers will see, he kept his promise and the French aid in China proved very valuable to me. He writes.

He did not get a US visa, so took a French Mail Boat from St. Nazaire for Mexico, and via Habana, Cuba reached Veracruz, a port of Mexico. From Mexico, he got a Japanese cargo boat for Yokohama. He landed at California port for some days where he met members of the Ghadar Party. The steamer was very slow. It took one month to cross the Pacific. At Yokohama, he was received by the representatives of Ras Behari Bose, who had good connections in Japan. With his help Mahendra Pratap established his office at the Sanno Hotel. This stay during 1922-23 in Japan helped him to learn more about the Buddhism and Japan.

From Tokyo, he reached Peking, in China. But his Chinese friends were afraid that he might be arrested by the British Government as they enjoyed judicial jurisdiction over their subjects in China. Therefore he left via Mongolia and Moscow to Kabul. In a telegram from the British Minister at Peking to the British Viceroy at Simla, dated July 4, 1923, it was stated that 'he left train at Ulgan and started for Mongolia by motor car en-route presumably to Urga and Siberia. All trace to him has now been lost, as Chinese authority does not extend into Mongolia proper.....' (NAI, Home Political Files 5/II/1923, p. 119) Another 'very secret' document from intelligence department about the Indian communists, dated 31st October 1923, shows : 'Further information has been obtained regarding the decision made at Moscow at the secret conference. Discussions were held regarding the progress of revolutionary activity in India, in the presence of several important members of the Russian Foreign office....Shortly after these discussions Mahendra Pratap reached Moscow from China, and was approached by both Chicherin and Obeidullah. Pratap undertook to use his personal influence with the Amir, and he accordingly left for Kabul....It is now reported that Mahendra Pratap has succeeded in winning the sympathies of the Amir, has organized a centre in Kabul, and has also sent Soviet funds to the Muhajirin on the frontier. In addition he has obtained permission from the Amir for Obeidullah, Dr. Nur Muhammad and Zafar Hassan to return to Kabul, where their presence would be welcomed.' (NAI, H P Files, 5/II/1923, pp. 102-3)

During his stay at Kabul, in 1924, all his activities were tapped and his next move, for going 'to some other country,' was being guessed in the British official circles. On 16th September accompanied by the Secretary of Russian Legation, Mahendra Pratap left Kabul. 'His intention, according to information in touch with him, is to visit Moscow, Berlin and thence proceed either to Angora or USA from either of which he will open communication with Swarajist Party in India.' The report says. (NAI, HP, 141/II/1924, p. 38)

He again made a whirlwind tour of Russia via the difficult Hindukush terrain where he was briefly arrested also on account of some misunderstanding and later released on the intervention of the Russian foreign office. In October 1924, Mahendra Pratap was in Russia as is evident from a secret communiqué of the British Foreign office in Moscow to its counterpart in India. This referred to a meeting of the Comintern, attended by 'Indian Revolutionaries,' held in Moscow, in which Mahendra Pratap asked for help for the Indian cause. He said the timing was right as *the Gandhi agitation had created very favourable ground in India for the revolutionary work.* In December 1924 he went to Zurich and then to Paris. He left Paris for New York on 20th December 1924.

In New York he worked in cooperation with the Hindustan Ghadar Party in the USA which sent him to Tibet to organize a rebellion against the British. The Ghadaris of California gave him thousand dollars and seven volunteers for the mission. On 28th April 1925 they left America to reach Peking via Japan. Braving all natural and man-made adversities, this group could reach the Tibetan border only on 16th October 1925. But due to sour diplomatic relations between China and Tibet, with the British as mediators, the scheme to cross Tibet could not be materialized. But anyhow with 'eight days in wilderness' in as if no man's land, marching over long stretches, between high hills along frozen lakes, covering themselves in heavy sheep-skin coats, hanging ice on moustaches, through terrible avalanches, he reached north Tibet in November and met H.H. Dalai Lama and the Prime Minister and governors at Chamdo in Eastern Tibet. Here he tried to recruit soldiers in the province to help the anti-imperialists. But the Tibetan government could not help him.

Raja Mahendra Pratap reached Nagasaki to attend the Pan-Asiatic congress on 1st August 1926. He did not have a Japanese visa so he was held up by the police. Ras Behari Bose intervened and through his influence, he was able to get off at Osaka, but again he was forced to leave for China and from there he went to Moscow, Afghanistan, Switzerland, France and thence to America. (NAI, HP/92/1927, P.3) Unfortunately Maulana Barkatullah, who accompanied him to the USA died here. Mahendra Pratap launched his anti-imperialist attack once again through talks and seminars in the USA. He declared in April 1927 that 'I am now serving humanity in my private capacity. This is the objects which has brought me to the USA and attain this end I will go to Japan.' (NAI, HP, 92/1927, p. 9)

Again in 1928 Mahendra Pratap had a quick detour of Japan, China, Russia and Germany. He formed the Indian Oppressed Peoples' Association under Sunyat Sen's influence and also published a paper *Ghadar Dhandhora* with the aim to spread the message of revolution in 1928 from Nanking, China. Mahendra Pratap was not only a patriot, but also a leader with a message of humanity and equality of races and nations, which was his idea of World Federation. In September 1929 he started publication of a monthly bulletin called *World Federation* from Berlin, but in April 1931 prohibitory orders were issued against this distinctly revolutionary and anti-British paper. In 1930 he again made a whirlwind tour of the world and visited the USA, the USSR, Germany, Afghanistan, China and Japan. It was the beginning of his tryst with the East. For the next 16 years first China and then Japan were his home. *I am not tied down to one spot. I am no more, at least for the time being that wandering nomad on the face of the earth who knew no rest.* He writes.

During all these tours, he always tried to convince citizens and government of those countries to help India in getting independence as well as to form a world brotherhood. For example on 14th October 1930, during his stay at San Francisco, when he was invited at the meeting of the Women's International League, he said, *I was asked to speak on India. I asked them to show some real activity in the cause of welfare of three hundred and twenty millions of human beings. They went to war against Germany because a few men and women were drowned in the torpedoed ships. But now the British are massacring thousands in cold blood. Should America remain quiet? No! They should at least break off diplomatic relations with the British Empire.*

I reached Peking on 31st December 1930, and the first of January (1931) found us at Peiking, staying quietly in the Pan-Asia office of Mr. Hwang Kung Su, 70 Pa Tiao Hutung. We cared little for the new year. We set to work. We remained very busy for two weeks in preparing and publishing the three different editions of the 'World Federation'. Another four days we had to spend in dispatching our heavy burden.... He writes. Mr. Hwang translated his article for Chinese edition of 'World Federation.'

It is worth mentioning that due to his revolutionary and anti-British activities, his relatives, who were pro-British and loyal to the colonial-Government, were afraid of meeting him. Such coincidence happened in Kobe, Japan where he was on short visit in 1931. His brother-in-law, Maharaja of Jind, *brought him and me from two different directions in two different steamers at one and the same time in Kobe. We landed in Japan on the morning of 14th May. I came from China, he arrived from India. When I heard the news of his visit, in the evening I sent him a little note through Mr. Sahay. I expressed my delight at his coming and told him that I would like to meet him if he had no objection. I received no written reply. Later, I sent him a registered letter asking him to help me to establish a temple at Kyoto for the unity of religions. Still heard nothing. Now my patience gave way. He was to leave Yokohama on the 30th. I must now go and see him perhaps he does not understand me......Today is the 29th. Today I must trace him and see him : such thought took me to Yokohama. I found him staying at the New Grand Hotel He was away just at that time. His secretary, however, received me. The news was discouraging. Maharaja was, perhaps not prepared to see me but the secretary could not say anything definitely. He personally expressed sympathy with my "self-sacrifice." I assured him that it was no sacrifice. Everyone is born for certain duty and he simply performs it. I am doing my job at my place.* He writes in his life story.

Mahendra Pratap again went to meet Maharaja but the secretary revealed to him that he could only meet Maharaja through the English Consul General. *It was too much for me. I told them it was absurd. I was at war with British Empire. I did not come to see the Maharaja so and so. I come to see my friend and relative Ranbir Singh. But if he is so much afraid of meeting me I care little. I left the room immediately in disgust. This is the condition of some of the ruling chiefs.* Earlier the same secretary told Mahendra Pratap that Maharaja was so overwhelmed that he would cry if he saw Mahendra Pratap, and was really desirous to meet him. *I told them to inform the Maharaja that if the princes did not behave properly as the leaders of men they shall be swept aside as in Russia and Germany.*

In 1931 he established a formal office of World Federation at Tientung Khy, near the imperial palace, Peking, China where he opened free English teaching school, delivered lectures without fee, held World Federation club meetings, and on Sundays held prayers according to the unity of religions and the Religion of Love. He met Wang China Wei, the Legal Executive Head of the Republic of All-China, and *spoke to him through interpreter, on three distinct topics-The Tibetan question, the necessity of forming Koumintang (Federation of Communist and Indian Congress Party) ; and World Federation Institute at Peking. Mr. Wang was courteous enough to see me off up to the outer door where my car was waiting,* he writes in his Life Story.

The British Government of India banned his publications in India with a notification issued on 25th April 1931 'to prohibit the bringing into British India of any copy of any publication issued by Mahendra Pratap in whatever language it may be published.' *But* he did not stop. He propagated rigorously his concept and other details of World Federation through six bi-monthlies with changed titles namely, *World Army* (January-February), *World Cooperation* (March- April), *World State* (May-June), *World Family* (July-August), *World Peace* (September-October) and *World-Religion* (November-December) published from Japan and China in 1934.

In 1933 he shifted World Federation office to Japan, and founded World Federation clubs and opened regular offices at Japan and China. But due to the British pressure he was deported from Canton by the Cantonese Dictator, a general. On 25 March 1934, he was loaded on a Chinese cargo boat and exported as goods to Hong Kong, the British territory. However, the British authorities, after enquiring him let him go to Siam (Thailand), where he continued his activities of World Federation. But on 30th June he was ordered to leave Siam also 'within 48 hours'. Because the Siamese government believed that his views were liable to create trouble between Siam and her neighbours. Due to interference of his Indian friends there he was allowed to remain there till he could get the first available steamer for Japan. But he had to stay at the police training school. In last of August he reached Japan where he engaged himself in enlisting supporters and volunteers for organizing an Asiatic Army and toured China, Japan and Mongolia several times. In 1935 he rented a house in Japan for his stay instead of staying in a hotel as on earlier occasions.

Though his experiment of the Asiatic Army could not be fulfilled due to official hindrances, but his activities concerning the work of World Federation were continued. He went on holding meetings and publishing his monthly circular. On 1st December 1937, he established a permanent 'World Federation Centre' at Kodaria Mura Kukubunji within the Tokyo Metropolis in Japan. He bought a piece of land and started building some cottages. He designed cottages as symbols of a mosque, a church, a Gurudwara and a temple. In September 1937 he moved to his cottages, *where for 10 long years from 1936 to 46 my home was in Japan,* he writes. From here he published his *World Federation* from 1933 to 1942 regularly with only a couple of exceptions. During this period he wrote many books, pamphlets, stories, dramas and other literature and held meetings from time to time at his centre.

Though he was in exile, and for fear of arrest by the British authorities, did not enter any British territory, but he was continuously in touch with the National leaders of India. During this period Mahatma Gandhi was very appreciative of his hard work abroad and wrote to him, 'I know that you are doing all that you can for the country' and took comfort in his World Federation motto that 'peace is to be attained by reconciliation and service.' (RMP Papers-Correspondence, Sr. No. 19, Letter from M.K. Gandhi, 31st October 1935). Jawaharlal Nehru informed Mahendra Pratap about proceedings of Lahore Congress where the Resolution of Purna Swaraj was passed and 26th January 1930 was declared as Independence day. He also assured him that 'the Congress is definitely and finally committed to full independence of India. This is a great gain. In the course of the year there is likely to be a big struggle for independence.' (*ibid*, Sr. No. 5, letter from Jawaharlal Nehru, dt. 4th February 1930).

So Raja Mahendra Pratap celebrated Independence Day of India on 26th January 1931 at Nanking, China. *Ten thousand hand bills were distributed throughout the city by the workers of the Eastern Oppressed People Association. The text was written by me and translated into Chinese by Mr. Sie.*

In 1935 and afterwards efforts were made by various Indian leaders to bring him back to India. Not only Mahatma Gandhi, but the members of United Provinces Legislative Assembly, like Krishna Dutt Paliwal, Lala Jagdish Prasad, Brijlal Biyani, Badri Dutt Pande, A.N. Chattopadhyaya, Shri Prakash and other well-wishers also tried their best to repatriate him to his homeland. Mahatma Gandhi contacted Prof. Jugal Kishore to help Raja Mahendra Pratap abroad and expressed hope that United Provinces Premier will do whatever is possible to call him back. Babu Sampurnanand, then Education Minister of U.P. expressed U.P. Government's eagerness in having him back soon as it will provide an opportunity to get his invaluable experience abroad. But the British authorities did not grant him permission to return India.

Raja Baldev Singh, his elder brother applied for passport to see him in Japan, but he was refused. Then he sought the permission for Raja Mahendra Pratap to return to India. It was also turned down by the Government of India on 25th March 1939. As a consequence Raja Baldev Singh expired on 27th March 1939. Under such circumstances in one of his anti-British meetings in June, 1939 in Japan, Mahendra Pratap declared : *If I am forced to remain abroad, I should surely batter the walls of the British fortress and enter the land of my birth with flying flags.*

Raja Mahendra Pratap increased the speed of his Pen War against the British colonizers through the War Number of his circular 'World Federation' in June 1939. In September, 1939, when the Second World War broke out in Europe, he became restless and tried to go to Europe, but could not. Then with Anand Mohan Sahay, in Japan, *we started a war fund with the object to have some young men at our centre here to assist in our propaganda work and to send some emissaries abroad, the object, of course, is to supplement the movement of freedom in India. We mean to move cautiously but resolutely, so that, we may remain in touch with the forward march of our Congress at home and at the same time leave nothing undone, what is possible, to bring about the political salvation of India from abroad. We hope and wish that all the Indians in the Far East, Germany, USSR, Afghanistan and US will evolve a common plan of action. But there is no time to be lost, we must act quickly.*

On 22nd June 1940 Mahendra Pratap along with his friends organized the Executive Board of India with the definite aim to free India. He was nominated its President, Ras Behari Bose its Vice-President and Anand Mohan Sahay was the Chief Secretary. The immediate aim of this Board was to make India free. After two weeks activities this Board was shifted to a room in Marunouchi Hotel at Tokyo where on 31st August 1940 Mahendra Pratap announced the regular establishment of the Executive Board of India in a very important meeting in the presence of the Guest of Honour, H.E. Mr. Shiraton, former Ambassador at Rome and then an adviser to the Imperial Foreign Office in Tokyo and forty-two other dignitaries and influential personalities of Japan. Mr. Sato spoke and dissolved former *Tohokai* to make room for the new Board. The work of World Federation was entrusted to Abe

Ratan of Ceylon and freeing himself from that responsibility, he exercised all his energy to the work of the Executive Board of India. But soon due to some differences of opinion, the fate of the Board dwindled. Ras Behari Bose and Rajaji withdrew their names to reorganize the Board with younger elements. (RMP Papers, correspondence, Sr. No. 85, Letter of RB Bose to RMP 29-12-40).

In 1941 Mahendra Pratap started his movement for the Aryan Army to spread his message of World Federation. He realized that during the whole history of British rule in India, the whole attention of Britain's military strategists had been concentrated on the north-western frontiers of India and the eastern frontier remained uncared. So he planned to attack British Indian Government from the east. In June 1941, he wrote about the German help to free India and his plan of war, *Hitler wants to corner the lion in his den and kill him there in his own lair.....I wanted to have the British Empire destroyed in India and thus pull out the teeth and nails of the lion, and making him thus quite harmless to let him live on bread and milk diet.* Meanwhile Japan had concluded its treaty with Germany and Italy. Rajaji requested Japanese to start cleaning up the Far East of all the British influence......*And we with the cooperation of Japan, Italy and Germany want to free India from outside.* But Japanese could not understand his strategy.

However, when Japan joined the Second World War on 8th December 1941, she started her own Indian organization. Prime Minister General Tojo asked Mahendra Pratap to accompany Japanese army to attack British India. Mahendra Pratap could not agree with the Japanese Plans as he knew that the Japanese had not honoured their word to make Mancho Kuo entirely free. He was stuck to his principles. He wrote: *I am glad that I remained true to my principles. It is true, I seek cooperation in every quarter. However, I insist on my own terms.* Ras Behari Bose was made leader of the Indian National Army, as he was legally a Japanese citizen and had married a Japanese girl. Though he was a hard-core revolutionary in his individual capacity, but he was incapable of leading an army or heading a mass movement of the Indian community in East Asia. The first attempt of the Indian National Army failed due to his weaknesses. Anand Mohan Sahay maintained a contact with

Subash Chandra Bose, who was then in Germany and wanted to liberate India with the help of Germany.

In June 1943, Subhash Chandra Bose reached Tokyo by a submarine. After a long discussion he accepted the offer of leading the Indian Independence Army. On 4th July 1943 Netaji was unanimously elected President of the 'Indian Independence League' at Shonan, Tokyo. Later Subhash Chandra Bose talked about and shared with INA officers the idea and inspiration he got from the work and experience of Mahendra Pratap.

On 14th September 1945 when he reached Kokubunji Railway station to go to one of his friends, a car stopped by his side. An American Senior Police Officer came out of the car, saluted him and opened the door of the car and asked him to be seated. Rajaji thought that his friend might send the car, so he set in it with pleasure. When the car reached outside the city, he asked. 'Where are you going ?' The officer said, 'Sir, you are under arrest.'

At the gate of Sugamo prison, pockets of Rajaji were searched and golden coins their-in and other belongings were confiscated. He was confined to a small cell. Most of the heads and premiers of the states, conquered by America along with General Tojo and revolutionary Toyama of Japan were put in that prison. All of them were treated as criminal-prisoners. They were engaged in cleaning floor, utensils, and clothes etc. and to do menial works, but Rajaji was kept apart from it and the jail-administration kept special attention of his comfort and a stove was burning on the door of his cell to keep it warm. Ch. Chhotu Ram, president of the Jat Mahasabha, Mahatma Gandhi and many leaders from all over the world including British leader Lord Atlie wrote to American Government to release Rajaji. Prisoners were being executed, most of them were hanged. On 12th February 1945, the day before the execution when a Christian priest came to preach him, he smilingly said, '*Father you arrived here to convert the Buddhist into Christianity, but before it you please convert these American Christians to Christianity.*' The priest said, '*Raja Mahendra Pratap, you are not going to be hanged, you will be released tomorrow, you are a true humanist.*'

On 14th February 1946 he was released from Jail. He had no money, as his money and other belongings were not returned to him. Americans were celebrating their national festival on that day, so state transport for foreigners was free, therefore he reached home in Japan with empty-pocket. The locks of house were intact and no search was done in his house.

At last the British Indian government lifted the ban and permitted him to return India. When he approached to the British embassy in Tokyo to get passport, an Englishman was sitting by the Ambassador. He said to the Ambassador, 'You are sending him to India. He is a very dangerous man.' The Ambassador replied, 'The political situation in India is so deteriorated that he cannot increase an inch in it.'

It took five months more to get Rajaji the required permission to return India, not as an Indian subject, but as a stateless person (a man without the citizenship of any country). Finally on the 21st July 1946 he left the Japanese port Kurey and reached Madras by the ship named 'City of Paris' on 9th August 1946 at 8 p.m., on Quit India day.

Boundless crowd was present to welcome their leader. Daughter of Sardar Patel, Mani Ben took him to Wardha by her car. He was taken to the Meeting of Congress Working Committee, where Pandit Nehru, Maulana Azad and Sardar Patel embrassed him. In the evening he met Mahatma Gandhi who asked him to present his Prem-Dharm hymn at Gandhiji's evening meeting.

Labour Government of Britain declared that the rein of administration of India would be delegated to any organization of India in June 1948. To get independence at once, Raja Mahendra Pratap thought of armed-rebellion in March 1947 and for it declared to raise Fauji Qaumi Sangh at a large meeting at Vrindaban and called soldiers for rebellion.

India got freedom on 15 August 1947. While other leaders were busy in lobbying for getting some post in the government, Mahendra Pratap, started travelling throughout the country. He toured a lot to know the problems and aspirations of the Indian people. Throughout his visits he preached his theory of Religion of Love. He believed the religions provoke hatred among people. I *believe, I was given birth and kept alive so far, for this task of bruiting unity among all religions through the Religion of Love.* He opposed coercion of state, as well as India's entry into British Commonwealth. He wrote to Pandit Jawaharlal Nehru, 'I say I cannot serve the state so long as it remains tied to the tail of London....'

He attended several state and central meetings and conventions of Congress Party's 'big show'. About such a meeting of 21st May 1949, he writes: *I watched from the guest's gallery the most disappointing drama of our august Congress. Leaders for whom I always had great respect, rose to defend Indian connection with Commonwealth, made in London. They even went so far to say that long established British connection could not be snapped suddenly!..... Several Congressmen rose and opposed Commonwealth but they were simply stifled by the chair. When recess came, I left in disgust.*

He wrote to Sardar Patel: *I declare war on Commonwealth.* He also opposed Indian Foreign Policy as well as the wrong system of British-made machine of administration through bureaucracy, and wrote to the leaders of its consequences. Rajaji declared his intention to contest 1952 Lok Sabha Election. Pt. Jawaharlal Nehru sent his messenger and offered him Congress ticket. Rajaji accepted the offer. Then he was asked to sign the pledge form in which it was written, 'I shall abide by the rules, regulations and decisions of the Congress party and its Parliamentary Board.' *No, I shall not sign this pledge. I shall act upon the voice of my inner soul.* He rejected the offer and contested the election as an independent candidate, though he was defeated by the official Congress candidate and Pt. Jawaharlal Nehru had to come to the election campaign twice to oppose him.

When his views on different aspects were not listened to by the Government, he declared to capture Delhi with people's force on 10th May 1954 on the anniversary of Indian War of Independence 1857. For it he toured a lot and convinced people, who attended his meetings and showed a lot of interest in his ideas. But on 10th May a few people were assembled to march with him. *I could not capture Delhi on this 10th May as I had announced. I kept all my dates. I toured through districts. People enthusiastically received me, heard me, promised me that they would surely reach Delhi on the 10th May and accompany me to the Rashtrapati Bhawan, but they did not keep their promise.*

Some important person duly arrived spoke to the people present at the meeting place. They spoke some fine words. They spoke of quality. They kindly praised me. But it was a poor show. They knew I saw. They formed into a small procession, but there was a ban on processions, therefore by jeeps and cars they had to reach Rashtrapati Bhawan, where with a delegation of four persons they tried to meet the President, but the security of the President did not allow to meet the 'old ailing President'.

In August 1956 he tried to form a Federal Front of the opposition parties to oppose the policies of Congress and to fight General Elections unitedly. He toured a lot, spoke at large meetings, met and called leaders and former rulers of the states. Many leaders joined the front. Rajaji won the 1957 election from Mathura constituency and entered the Lok Sabha. He wrote: *To present my foreign policy and to put forth my plan of happy human society I am going to Delhi. It is not in any way to say that our illustrious Prime Minister Pandit Jawaharlal Nehru is insincere or dishonest. I honestly believe him to be an honest fellow. He is however enwrapped in his own views, views which he got through his education and circumstances of life, they are harmful to our State.*

I am going to Delhi to try to convert our Prime Minister and his followers to my Views which I got through my long experience in foreign free countries and through long quiet meditation in Japan.

Throughout his term he actively participated in the proceedings of the Lok Sabha, raised problems of the masses, opposed several Government Policies, especially the foreign policy and remained a staunch critic of Jawaharlal Nehru, who often used to make a fun of his ideas. He presented many private bills, which he thought important for the well-being of the society. In 1961-62, when the relations with China were going bitter, he presented himself to the Government to use him as an envoy to China to solve the meagre disputes which would become greater in future due to the obstinate attitude of both of the governments, but Nehru refused, and 1962 saw the Indo-Chinese War.

Similarly he held Indian Foreign policy responsible for 1965 war with Pakistan. He writes: *Exactly it is ceasefire. Not more. It is neither peace nor truce, Hearts are on fire. Minds are burning. Blood is boiling. It is a temporary patch up. They do not realise that not one country in the world showed any sympathy with India. China and Indonesia openly supported Pakistan....I openly blame our government for this situation in diplomatic field. China repeatedly requested us to have round-table conference for last five years. Hon'ble late Pandit Nehru insisted that China first must agree to the proposal of Ceylon group. Hon. Mr. Shastri never seriously tried to make peace with China....*

I always offered my services to Indian Government to bring peace with China and Pakistan but they never paid any attention to my suggestions.

In 1966 he suggested to form a National Government of India comprising of the leaders of the different parties, who he thought experts in their field. He daily used to write letters and receive their reply and thus was in close contact with Indian leaders of different parties, educationists, bureaucrats, army-personnels, diplomats–people from all the sects of life, as well as his world-wide acquaintances. He many times wrote open letters to important leaders from various continents of the day—the Presidents of the USA, the USSR, Prime Ministers of Great Britain. China, Pakistan and religious leaders like Pope and Dalai Lama to solve the problems of humanity.

To form a World Government, as first step he preferred to make Aryan Federation from Iran to Assam. For it he wrote Constitution of Aryan Federation, as a part of World Federation and published it in the November 1954 issue of the 'World Federation'.

He writes: *The object of the Aryan Federation is the realization of healthy, prosperous and peaceful life by every individual in Aryan and the world, and with that object to form homogenous, practical, contiguous areas as federations. The whole Federation for the time being we concentrate on Aryan from Iran to Assam.*

In this constitution main emphasis was given on the unity of people to organize them as a joint family, irrespective of race, caste, colour, creed or sex; one party, one Government; no bifurcation of persons in opposing groups or parties.

Rajaji was against the show business and wastage of time, energy and money by the parties in this connection. When he was member of Congress party, he was invited to the session of the All India Congress Committee held at Ajmer on 27th July 1954. He wrote: *Half a million rupees might be spent on this show. These political meetings and religious gatherings of hundreds of thousands of people is a curse to our society. They tax time and energy of humanity....We must try to stop this wastage as much as possible.*

He believed in *all to work for all to make all happy*. And in this regards he found the present system of democracy very weak. He wrote that *Democracy is a bunch of some wrong ideas and misleads our people.....Our provincial governments and the central governments are wrongly constituted by wrong conceptions, by wrong dealings and by wrong means. The whole process of forming and running the governments is called democracy, governments by the people: poor people are also culled to believe that it is so. In fact it is a great hoax.*

He was asked to contest 1971 Lok Sabha election by various parties, but he denied as the election system aroused a great indifference in his views. He openly remarked that the prevailing system of election in the so-called democratic countries which gives equal vote to a prostitute and saint is responsible for this situation. Would be legislators have to seek aid of the worst evil characters and when they enter legislative assemblies, they have to satisfy those thirsty and hungry for wealth and position who supported and arranged votes for them. *It was a great waste of time, energy and money to have these elections, they create strife. Divide brother from brother. They never represent the opinion of the people. Masses are just carried away by clever and expensive propaganda......It is winning device to satisfy the people or to deceive them to believe that they build the government, so that, they may not take up arms to over throw the government.* At another place, he writes about the election system: *Not facts, but falsehood is advertised. Not truth but money wins...Why must fifty one rule forty nine? What right has ninety nine to oppress one? Our old conception of society is far superior. All should work for all to make all happy - there should be no contesting - no competition, but cooperation.* He always advocated for a high moral character in life.

All India Freedom Fighters Society held a convention in Delhi on 12th August 1972 and Rajaji presided over it. Smt. Indira Gandhi, Prime Minister of India addressed the meeting and on 15th August 1972 at Red Fort of Delhi, the President of India, V.V. Giri and the Prime Minister Indira Gandhi honoured Rajaji with 'engraved

Copper Plates' and next day at Teen Murti Bhawan, New Delhi, at the reception of freedom fighters, Mrs. Indira Gandhi came to him and politely asked him to sit on the chair and standing behind him she got photographed. He was so much moved by this incident that he favoured, praised and advised Mrs. Gandhi many times, till Smt. Indira Gandhi proclaimed an internal emergency in the country. He became dissatisfied and wrote to her about his views, strongly condemning her dictatorial decision. At that time all the leaders of opposition, as well as those people who opposed the emergency were put behind the bar, but Indira Gandhi replied all his letters and he was not touched even.

Rajaji was so much involved in launching the idea of one World Government, World Court of justice, one World army, World Federation that during his eighties he visited Afghanistan, Japan, Mauritius etc. and personally met their leaders. In 1978 at the age of 92, he wrote about his eagerness of meeting the Queen Elizabeth of England as head of Commonwealth, the king of Arabia as head of Islamic States, Pope Paul of Vatican City as head of Christians, President Brezhnev of the USSR, the Emperor Hirohito of Japan as representative of Buddhists and chairman Mao-tse Tung of China.

Mahendra Pratap was an overwhelming scribe. Important early years of his life were spent in concerning and craving for the freedom of his country, and for accomplishment of his object he strayed for thirty two years in exile in foreign countries. During this period he wrote, printed and distributed thousands of letters, articles, propaganda material and circulars. Besides this, he wrote more than twenty eight books in English, twenty in Hindi and two in Urdu. In English, he wrote : *My Life Story of 55 Years; World Federation; Aryan; Eurasian Drama; German – American Drama; Madam Mahatma Goes to Heaven; Religion of Love; Moral Front; Twelve Thoughts of Four Days; Four Salvations; A Letter to USSR; To English Speaking People; To Bengalies; Frictionless Society; Primer of the New Science of Thoughts; Bible of the Unity of Religions; First Reader; Second Reader; Third Reader; Fourth Reader; Race, Religion, Communism in the World; Human Nature; Great Problems Solved; Clean Your Mind (English man English woman)*; and, *Shadow Government*. In Hindi he wrote : *Lalaji ki Takhri* (Story); *Babuji ki Bhabhi* (Story); *Rani Kamla ke Patra* (Story); *Rajaji ka Kutta* (Story); *Chamar ka Launda* (Story); *Brajbala* (Drama); *Rajput Sansar Sanghi* (Drama); *Prem Dharm; Hamari Riyasati Azadi; Sadachar Gut; Sardar Swarg Sidhar Gaye; Sangh Uddeshya; Brajwasi Sangh; Prem Dharm ke Sadhu aur Prem Vihar*. In Urdu he wrote: *Puthwar ke Nawab* (Drama); and *Deen Mohabbat*.

Raja Mahendra Pratap was an illustrious son of India, a patriot in true sense. He was a revolutionary as well as a visionary who devoted his entire life to the service of mankind. There are many incidents world-wide, which happened to be the same as Raja Mahendra Pratap announced. For Instance, he was against the increase in pay and wrote *it would raise prices of the daily necessities, to the people government raises salaries by printing more notes, prices go up. This is vicious circle.* This we find in India that after every pay commission the prices go up, and dearness increases. About socialism in the USSR, he wrote long before the break-up: *Freedom is bound to come in all the communist countries. I only wish that it comes calmly and peacefully.* Moreover on 8th Feb. 1973 he advised the Prime Minister of India: *the division of Andhra is necessary so divide Andhra and not to say that small states are not desirable,* and now all believe that small states progress speedily and the government had to divide Andhra and Telangana.

Mahendra Pratap was a true missionary. He never cared what people think or say about him. In Parliament also Ministers and Members of Parliament many times ridiculed him. He knew this but neither he took it on heart, nor got angry. Even Jawaharlal Nehru sometimes made circastic remarks on him, but he never left politeness. He writes: *I often see my friends laughing when I speak. Today's Hindi paper Hindustan says that I am considered by my fellow members as Sanaki Raja (eccentric). My Sanakipan (eccentricity) is that when I was only twenty years old I renounced half property. This was my Sanakipan. I gave away half my property for philanthropic purposes and the schools and colleges founded then are still going on. I left my country. I left my family. I left everything and went to Germany to make India free. This was my second Sanakipan. My Third Sanakipan is that when I come back and when it was quite possible that I would have become a Minister; I would have become a Governor or an Ambassador, I did not accept any such offer. My forth Sanakipan is that I am still fighting, I am still rebelling against this wrong system of government was built up by the British for the British only to suck the blood of the country. That system of government is still going on. I am not communist but I say you who are communists, are right when you correct these people who are doing mischief in the country. I so not say that to you behave as communists, but as good men.* He further writes: *I used to get angry when people did not follow my plan. How is it, I said to myself, they do not do what I say in their interest. Sometimes I felt very disheartened. Why am I doing all this thankless task?* But he himself replies: *Now I am satisfied. There is nothing mine. I did not bring anything into the world and shall not take anything with me when die. I am here in a Plan. I should do what I can but I need not worry about the future. He who brought this human society to this stage through millions of years will take it onward through millions of years in future.*

Our anger, impatience and a bit of quarrel now and then, are too, parts of the plan, we may realise it or not.

Raja Mahendra Pratap passed away on 29th April 1979 at the age of 93 years, at All-India Institute of Medical Sciences, New Delhi.

During his life time, up to his last breathe he thought for the betterment of the society with his selfless service and benevolence, as an enlightened seer, who visualized and realized the future of mankind in the novel approach of unification of the world, directing it for well-being and happiness of all. *Let us fight evil and spread goodness in society!!*

Dr. Rajendra Kumar
Editor

I shall have My Own Army to Free India

In June 1939, three months before the outbreak of the World War II, I published War number of our circular 'The World Federation'. I saw that war was coming and I declared my war on the British three months earlier. But unfortunately, neither Germany, nor Italy could kindly call me to their side. Some how Japan too could not adopt my plan and could not utilize my services. But I continued to think loud, talk loud, through my monthly circular.

On 2 November 1941, Aryan Flag was hoisted at our World Federation office. My activities stopped when I did not agree with the plan of Japanese government, but Babu Ras Behari Bose went to Bangkok and Singapore. Shri Anand Mohan Sahay accompanied him. They surely did useful work in the interest of India. My objection was that the Japanese troops must not enter India.

On 8th December 1941, Japanese joined the World War II, and I thought the situation changed. Prime Minister General Tojo called me and asked to accompany Japanese army to attack British India. But I know that the Japanese government had not honoured her word to free Mancho Kuo, so I told General Tojo that Japanese army should not go into India. I shall have my own army to free India. General Tojo did not like it and thus our talk ended.

Later Shri Anand Mohan Sahay, the Secretary of our Executive Board told me that the Japanese authorities want Ras Behari Bose, the Vice President of the Executive Board to accompany and lead Japanese army, as they had more confidence in him. He is a Japanese citizen and had married a Japanese girl Toshoko and has two sons from her. If they wanted, what can I do. I have no objection.

I repeat, as I ever did before, that I am interested in the Independence of India, no matter to me who realizes it and how. I am always prepared to withdraw myself.

It is another story. It has nothing to do with the Government of Hind. Shri Ras Behari Bose failed and Shri Subhash Chandra Bose was invited from Germany. He came. He formed the Second Government in exile. He followed my plan. He could work on much larger scale.

One day I received a letter from the General staff of Japanese army, 'The leader of India has appeared in Japan, you should meet him and cooperate with him in the war.' This leader was Subhash Chandra Bose, but I did not like him to meet on the invitation of the Japanese Government. Afterwards some representatives of Shri Subhash Bose came to meet me. We discussed the situation. With them I sent an invitation to Shri Subhash Bose to come to my place but perhaps due to his busy schedule he could not meet me.

On 6th March 1942, in the morning representative of Japanese government came to me and handed over a letter to me asking to remain quiet at World Federation Centre, Kodaira Mura, Tokyo. And I have to keep mum. I devote my time in reading and thinking.

Now a days I write quietly many books and pamphlets, stories and dramas. I held meetings from time to time at our centre, only some rare gatherings were held in the city proper, but as a whole I was leading a life of forced inactivity. I did not have any money and Japanese government provided very little money for monthly expenditure, therefore I did not have any employee and helper. I had to do all my house jobs myself, cook food, wash utensils, clean my cloth and room etc.

Due to war there was very shortage of food stuff and price was also very high and one could not easily get butter and oil. But I used to purchase very cheap fish, which has a good quality of oil.

Twelve Thoughts of Four Days

Thursday, the 28th Dec. 1944. An inspiration came to me. I resign myself completely to this will of God.

Not what we read or heard, not even that what we may remember by heart counts, that counts which has entered deep into our spirit and ever leads it under all circumstances of pain or pleasure of danger or security and prosperity.

28-12-1944. About 4 p.m. when we are bombed. As much we have learned, that much only we can teach, we can only show you the way we know, with your own power you may further reach. But cooting and cleaverness are weaknesses, true power resides in faith. You are that much weak or powerful, as much you have faith. Faith can not be taught, nor can it be acquired by study, it is developed through meditation, and you get it if you remain steady. At moments it may slip out. You have to look out, as body stumbles now and then, so faith falls flat at doubt. But man can ever renew his faith, he needs only ever to pursue Faith.

It is midnight 28-29 Dec. 1944. I have just finished reading a bit of Koran and the New Testament after my night prayer and I remembered that in the morning of the last day I was felling troubled at the greatness of my great mission of bringing harmony among the Roman Catholics and the Protestants, the Muslims, the Hindus and the Buddhists and the followers of the earth to live as in one family of the human race, but God seemed to say within me that I must do my duty which God gave me. Now when people of the city may be asleep, now when there is also danger of air raids, we had twice on the day just passed, I was sitting alone in the lonely place of our Centre in the field away from other houses writing these lines. My human fellow beings hear my voice, allow me to explain to you these divine teachings, I just found in Koran. God saying to Rasul, they seek from thee Miracle, God makes me say, my plan is the miracle. Only through unity of religions and federation of states and production and distribution to satisfy the needs, permanent peace can be established.

29-12-1944. Say boldly that the peace maker has appeared. Say, you want peace, nothing but peace, but a peace which will endure, a true peace based on justice to one and all. You proclaim your plan of peace and move to realize it and if obstacles come in the way like stones, remove them. Local liberty but all unity in one Federated World State is the human wish of humanity now! Say.

Call upon Christians and the communists, call upon the nationalists of all the nations, hail the Hindus and the Muslims,

Buddhists and the Sikhs and the Jews, say soldiers of the World unite. And prove that you have no prejudice against any caste or creed but of-course every one must do one's job as it is fit. You cannot overload any one. A strong body, light job. Intellectuals must have jobs which are suited for them. There shall be no one jobless, except the sick, old or crippled. Such I have been made to stay so long where I have led a life of forced inactivity of over two years, now is going to help me to do my great job of world peace. I am ready to do my divine mission immediately. I am physically fit and psychologically prepared. Only honest and sincere Japanese help is needed. H.E. General Matsui kindly saw me on the 26th instant; and he was going to prove the divine means to give a meaning to my sojourn in Dai Nippon.

My friends are in the entire world, I see in it a plan of God that I, born in India, was taken to Germany during the last world war and I was received by Kaiser. And Germany helped me to free India. And God gave me the Book of the Religion of Love in the midst of war in 1916, in Afghanistan. Then in Germany in 1922 I brought out the programme of the Happiness Party or the Party of Goodness and in 1929 I began to publish the monthly circular of World Federation from Berlin, Germany. I hold, if my views could have spread in Germany there could not have been this terrible war. In 1931, I established our office of World Federation at Peiking, China. I repeat, if China and Japan would have helped me to further my plans there could not have been this devastating war in the region of Buddha. Well, what is gone is gone. Now I say, friends, hear my voice. Why must you fight further? Let us now have peace on the basis of local liberty, regional, continental and all world federation. Let us federate as we are, I mean, monarchies, republics and Soviets and by and by through the right education we shall perfect our human society. If some good hearted Japanese friends help me to proclaim my views to the world, I ask you, to see in it the divine plan unfolding itself.

31st Dec. 1944, 9.12 p.m. in my watch. Nothing doing. Read a bit. As a rule I finish my dinner much earlier, but today I have not eaten yet my evening meal. Quite unusually I felt my stomach a bit heavy and I also said to myself, as sleeping tonight intrigues with me : I am quite sure, I shall introduce in the world and specially in India and speak to strengthen the national conception, yesterday they spoke and wrote to impress our mind the religious view point, but tomorrow, I hold, we must think, talk and act to have world vision and universal enlightenment. I say, this is religion and thus alone the true interest of all the nations can best be safeguarded. Religion ever tried to show us the universe but today most of the religious people live within their shells. And by thinking, talking and acting in favour of your nation you make it worst. I wish, I could get out of this lonely place and herald to the world, saying : Stop ! Stop struggling for your petty faiths and stop fighting for petty and temporary gains. I may be ridiculed, I may be neglected, I may be just pushed aside to the wall, but I feel I must try to do my duty. (Now the sirens are announcing air-precaution.)

These conditions prevailing on earth make me more eager to deliver my message, as soon as possible. Why they keep me thus isolated in this place. If my views are not fit for Japan, let me go please somewhere, I can reach a corner of our world, where I can talk freely and loudly on my God given mission. But have I not talked for years ? Yes, why should I not talk now when God still keeps me alive, I must do my bit at this juncture. God ! I am ready, open the door !

My watch shows 11.21 p.m. So that, this day and, with it this year will soon pass. I write this one more sheet, the only sheet of this kind left. They together make full twelve sheets written in four days, from 28th to 31st December, both days inclusive. They can be printed in a form of leaflet, standing by themselves, reflecting a few thoughts as they passed with the passing time. But money and the opportunities play a great role in publishing views. I remember, a young poet once came to me fired with his enthusiasm of his warm poetry, all he wanted to have his writings printed. But to his regret, though I had money at that time, I was not interested in his views. Now the people who have today money and power are not perhaps interested in what I have to say. What an agony of fate! But I do not mind. I burned more than once my manuscripts. One collection was quite weighty which I produced in a couple of years. I burned the Bible of World Federation too not so long ago. I do not mind if these writings disappear. The all powerful creator alone has the last voice with all our production and distribution. If it pleases Him let them appear in print, if not, let them go as they came. Fragrance of a sweet flower passes without leaving a trace behind. History records that libraries went into fire in many cases. Authors were there whom we do not know today. Empires appeared and disappeared. They say that our planet also will cease to exist some day. And still some people feel a great satisfaction if they leave behind a well, a monument or some public institution as their lasting land mark. In fact, it is only the satisfaction which we realize and which we bestow on our fellow beings. I have the satisfaction of having tried to do my duty this moment and these thoughts are surely vibrating around doing their duty. They shall live in space in any case.

In Prison

In 1945 when war came to an end, I thought I would have now complete liberty to leave Japan and do as I think fit. But it was not so.

On the 14th September 1945, when I was going to Kukubunji railway station to go to one of my Japanese friend, a car stopped by my side. A senior English Police Officer came out of the car. He saluted me and opening the door of the car requested me to take seat in the car. I thought that my friend has sent this car to pick me up, so I set in it with pleasure. When the car started running out side of the city, I asked the officer, 'Where are we people going ?'

The Officer said, 'Sir you are under arrest, and we are going to Sugamo prison.'

At the gate of Sugamo Jail my pockets were searched and golden coins therein and another belongings were confiscated by the jail authorities. Then I was put in a small cell.

Most of the Japanese leaders arrested by the US forces were kept in Sugamo prison. All of them were ill-treated and were engaged in cleaning floor, utensils, clothes etc., but to my astonishment, I was exempted from this task. I do not understand why was so ?

One day Prime Minister Tojo and famous rebel Toyama were in furious arguments with each other. Dispute was so arose that Toyama hit his fist on the forearm of Tojo and cried, 'You have caused the complete destruction of Japan and ruined us.' Prison authorities separated them. But Toyama's attack on Tojo went inseperated in favour of Toyama, Americans considered him mad and excused, unless he was to be executed.

Prisoners were being executed, most of them were hanged. On 12th February 1945, the day before the execution when a Christian priest came to preach me, I smilingly said, 'Father you arrived here to convert the Buddhists into Christianity, but before it you please convert these Americans to Christianity.' The priest said, 'Raja Mahendra Pratap, you are not going to be hanged, you will be released tomorrow, you are a true humanist.'

People Demanded My Release

When the news of my arrest reached India, peoples reverence overflowed towards me and they demanded my release, as well as my entry in India. Cuttings of newspapers were sent to me later. One I quote :

President of Prem Mahavidyalaya Vrindaban, sent a letter to the Editor to be published in *The Hindustan Times*, Sunday, October 7, 1945, representing peoples' notion :

Sir,

That Raja Mahendra Pratap a more broad-minded man than whom it is difficult to come across, should have been declared by General MacArthur as a war criminal, is nothing short of a tragic irony of fate. Raja Mahendra Pratap left India in 1914 and we, in India have no direct and authentic information about his activities since then; but if any clue can be furnished by one's writings about the man looking his views than the World Federation, a periodical published by the Raja from Japan affords unmistakable evidence to show that he was a peace-loving man. His patriotism was not confined to his own country but all along he worked for the establishment of a world order, the like of which is envisaged now, after the war by the Allies.

While in India, he set an unprecedented example of broad practical and sagacious patriotism and sacrifice of a high order. When quite young he dedicated half of his property worth more than Rs. 10 lacs for the cause of the country and Prem Mahavidyalaya Association to work out the plan he had in view on education and social reforms even so early as in the year 1909 were very much identical to those that were subsequently adumbrated and brought into practice by Mahatma Gandhi himself. He introduced handicrafts along with literary education and within a few years of its working the experiment proved a great success. He has respected all religions alike and worshipped the Vedas, the Bible, the Koran and the Granth Sahib with equal revelation. In the manner of social reforms, he made no distinction between men and men on the basis of caste of birth. To him a Harijan was as good a man as a member of any other caste and we have in our midst eye-witnesses who have seen him dining at the same table with the Harijans. It cannot be expected that a man of that calibre should have given any assistance voluntarily in the prosecution of the war against the British or Americans. It is therefore the duty of the British Government as well as the people of India to see that the antecedents of this patriot are properly placed before the American authorities.

Yours, etc.

(Illegible)
President Prem Maha Vidyalaya
Vrindaban (U.P.)

On 14th February 1946 I was released from Jail. I had no money as my money and other belongings were not returned to me. Americans were celebrating their national festival on that day, so transport for foreigners was free, I reached home in Japan with-empty-pocket. The locks of house were intact and no search was done in my house.

I received many messages that my countrymen are eagerly waiting for me at India. President of Prem Mahavidyalaya wrote :

My dear Raja Sahib,

We are all very much delighted to learn that the American Authorities in Japan have released you. Immediately after the receipt of the news in India of your having been arrested as a War Criminal, there arose amongst the people, who know you well, indignation as in their views it was the ideals you held. It was impossible that you had taken any part in the last war. I wrote to the press re-iterating the above news and am herewith sending a cutting from *The Hindustan Times.*

Your letter to Mahatma who has been good enough to release a copy of it to me, confirms the above and we are now certain that it will not be long before you will find yourself once more in the midst of your countrymen.

I may mention that we do not consider you to have been released finally unless you are able to leave Japan and are really in India once more. I had the honour of meeting the Mahatma in Wardha on 13-2-46 with the sole object of arranging with the Government of India through him for obtaining facilities of your entry in the country. Mahatmaji as usual has assured me that he will write to the Governor General and I am now informed that he had already done so.

I am also sending herewith a cutting from the papers in respect of certain questions and answers in the Central Assembly concerning yourself. I have further approached the Secretary in-charge of External affairs, Government of India to elicit the information if the Government of India are prepared to arrange for your travel and entry in this country at an early date. I have promised on behalf of your friends to pay all the travelling expenses if they agree to do so.

I can well imagine the difficulties that you may be confronting these days in Japan specially financial. I have requested the Chief Commissioner, St. John Red Cross Society, Simla to agree to arrange for the dispatch and deliver to you a sum of rupees one thousand and in case he so agrees, the money will soon be dispatched. I have also requested Mahatma Gandhi to send the money that we may be able to place at his disposal for the purpose.

I am,
Yours very sincerely
D.N. Bhargava
M.A., LL.B., Advocate
President

Entry into India

Government unwilling to Make inquiries about me. My friends sent me a cutting of *The Hindustan Times*, Thursday, February 14, 1946 :

The Indian revolutionary, Raja Mahendra Pratap, was the subject matter of a question in the Central Assembly on Wednesday.

Answering a question by Pandit Shri Krishna Dutta Paliwal (Congress), the External Affairs Secretary, Mr. Weightman, said that the Government had no information about the Raja other then the Press reports that he was arrested by the US Army of Occupation in Japan and subsequently released.

The Government 'are under no obligation afford him entry into India,' 'said Mr. Weightman answering another question, 'since he had renounced his British Indian nationality.'

Prof. N. G. Ranga (Congress) asked the External Affairs Secretary through a supplementary question if the Government would make inquries about Raja Mahendra Pratap as 'the people of India are anxious for his welfare'.

Mr. Weightman suggested that the Raja's family 'had better make inquries about him.' Prof. Ranga immediately got up and said that the Raja had 'left India more then 30 years ago and it is doubtful if he had any relation left.' He claimed that the people of the country could therefore 'be considered as good as his blood relations.'

Several Congress members rose up at this stage with inquiries whether 'there was a definite ban on his entry into the country.' No answer was given as the President Mr. G. V. Mavlankar, called for the next question.

At last the British Indian government lifted the ban and permitted me to return India. When I approached the British embassy in Tokyo to get passport, an Englishman set by the Ambassador. He said, 'You are sending him to India. He is a very dangerous man.' The Ambassador replied, 'The political situation in India is so deteriorated that he cannot increase an inch in it.'

Though it took five months more to get the required permission to return India, not as an Indian subject, but as a stateless person (a man without the citizenship of any country), but finally on the 21st July 1946 I left the Japanese port Kurey and reached Madras on 9th August 1946, on Quit India day.

I reached India. I reached Madras on 1st August 1946 at 8 p.m. by 'City of Paris' ship. I had no luggage except the dress I wore and few books which I brought with me for my journey.

A large gathering was assembled at port. They were waving flags of Congress and banners in their hands and shouting slogans in enthusiasm. Friends garlanded me. At last I was capable of touching my motherland. I was excited after 32 years I could see my people.

I was brought to the residence of Shrimati Annu Swaminathan. I felt homely there. In the evening I spoke in a public meeting on Hindu Muslim Unity.

On 11 August daughter of Sardar Vallabh Bhai Patel and some leaders of Congress came to me to take to Vardha Ashram of Mahatma Gandhi. Kumari Mani Ben was driving the car all the way. We had a long talk during this long journey. At Wardha first I was taken to the office of Congress party where Members of Congress Working Committee greeted me. We discussed the condition of the country. On 13 August I met Mahatma Gandhi and Pt. Jawaharlal Nehru, our Rashtrapati, the President of Congress Committee. Pt. Nehru embraced me and said, 'We will be benefitted with your experiences.'

Next day, on 15th August morning I reached Mathura by Madras Delhi express. At station I saw a large crowd. People were in rage shouting slogans and shouts of victory. They were singing and dancing. I was loaded with flowers. I was excited.

People were touching my feet. A big stage was made on platform. I was taken there. Again I was garlanded. I was asked to bless the gathering.

I spoke, 'This is the city of Shri Krishnaji. Cows were honoured here. Shri Krishnaji and his friends reached Gujarat, grazing the cows. That is why Gau-Charat became Gujarat. You will find everywhere the signs of Brajwasi. Now we have to live in harmony with Muslims, Christians and to eliminate the causes that come between the unity of Hindus and Muslims. Our Shri Krishanji was not weak. His brilliance and splendor was not less than any initiator of religion. All religions accept this. We should go ahead on his teachings.

'Foreigners came here due to our sins. We have to free country from their yoke, God is helping us. We have to search new paths, and to go forward.'

At 3 o'clock a big procession was arranged. I was sat on a chariot drawn by four horses. The whole city was decorated with ornamented arched gateways.

Day was cloudy and rain was coming some times, but the crowd was increasing. I stood in the chariot and greeting people with folding hands. On each square people were garlanding me. At 6 the procession reached Dampier Park where 25-30 thousand people were gathered to greet me. I spoke at length here.

India got freedom on 15 August 1947. I toured a lot to know the problems and aspirations of the Indian people. I opposed coercion of state, as well as India entry into British Commonwealth. I wrote to Pandit Jawaharlal Nehru, 'I say I cannot serve the state so long as it remains tied to the tail of London....' Throughout my visits I preached his theory of Religion of Love. I believe, I was given birth and kept alive so far, for this task of bruiting unity among all religion through the Religion of Love.

Jew Karl Marx

He had all the intellectual gifts of the Hebrew race. He was one of those gifted lawyers who could prove night in a bright day. But he used his great wisdom to destroy National organizations of Germany and Russia.

He created a new history of the origin of the human society. He based all progress on class war. Leaders of Russia and Germany who became slaves of the thoughts of Karl Marx killed their own countrymen.

As a Jew he took full revenge on those Russians and Germans who held the Jews down, treated them as menial men.

He knew Christians were made to hate Jews by their priests. He could arouse the followers of Jesus to pull down the Christian priests.

I was pro-Jew, as I was pro-Brahman. I admired their racial genius. I was instinctively helped by the Jews in Russia. A Jew commissar took me in a special train from Taskent to Petrograd in early March 1918.

Trotsky welcomed me. He sent a young Jew secretary with me to Berlin, where I arrived on the 21st of March 1918.

A Jew helped me at Budapest. A Jew at Moscow joined my Religion of Love. Another Jew Mr. Sukermanov who was an in-charge of Central Asia and India in foreign office or Narkomendel at Moscow always helped me up to 1930, after that I was never in Russia.

I myself saw the power of the thoughts of Karl Marx. Young Russians considered it treason to have Russian nationalism. They fervently denounced Church. Inside the Church I saw a procession of the priests, church was full, outside the church a film was shown, showing priests as asses.

A reaction took place. Russian mind brought Stalin to the top, Stalin who was anti-Jews. He drove out Trotsky and degraded many Jew leaders.

'Workers unite' has certainly a great catching power. Men of ordinary intellect can easily become leaders of workers. Demand to raise pay is very attractive. People gather round men who demand more pay.

They do not care to know increase in pay raises prices of the daily necessities. To please the people government raises salaries by printing more notes, prices go up. This is vicious circle.

Merchants of China had some talents. Karl Marx got them killed. I believe, I have to bring the message of peace and unity in the Buddhist land of China, home land of Kong Futsu.

It is the greatest bravery to admit one's blunder. Mahatma Gandhi gladly admitted his own mistakes. Himalayan blunder. Even Leader Mao said that he admitted his faults.

I must confess that I miserably failed in influencing the army. When I was at Cabul as the president of the Provisional Government of India in 1916 I tried to bring about a revolt in the Indian army. Not ripple was created. I wanted to see a storm in the country.

When I returned India in 1946, I said, well perhaps the army did not hear my voice from Afghanistan, I was too far off, but now I was in the country, now the army would listen to me.

On the 30th of May 1947, I reported to the Hon'ble Pandit Jawaharlal Nehru ji that I had found Fauji Kaumi Sangh, Federation of the army castes or the union of the martial races. He said that it was good.

I asked a Jat Major whether it was possible to react here what Comrade Lenin could do in Russia. I told him the story how Kaiser's Germany helped us three, Comrade Lenin, Sir Roger Casement and myself to proceed to our respective lands to start revolutions. Sir Roger Casement was captured and hanged in

Ireland by the British. I failed. Lenin could influence the army. Army revolted and Lenin became the Premier. The Jat Major said that they had learned to salute, formerly they saluted the hat, now they salute the cap ! I failed. Our leaders succeeded in coming to terms with the British and in getting this independence, within the British Commonwealth, and in getting control of divided India.

My Plan

When I was in Sugamo prison in Japan, I was five months behind the bars without trial. And because I was entirely innocent of World War II, I was released at the end. I asked those who came to do justice to give me some decent compensation for robbing me of my freedom but of course they who considered themselves conquerors had no time to listen to a poor sufferer. 'The galloping horse stops not to beg the pardon of a trampelled over frog' was perhaps the philosophy of General MacArthur ?

The other day as I was looking into some pieces of papers written by me in prison I came across a plan which I submitted to the Jail authorities for the consideration of higherups. I give it below without additions or alterations. It needs consideration.

7th October 1945, Sunday War Criminal Camp, submitted to camp authorities on the 8th Oct. 1945.

Christ was crucified. Thank God, I am still alive to write these lines as service of humanity.

It was a mistake to bring me here to the 'War Criminal' camp of prison. But if this mistake can bring out something highly useful for humanity, it can be of great value as Crucifixion was. God works to correct human mistakes.

I saw some sad faces of soldiers, longing for their homes and I felt for them, went with them in thought to their dear ones and I saw something was needed to correct the wrong, common wrong to me and them !

And I came to the conclusion, in them and through them World ideal of world home, of world justice, Universal love could be founded and established strong, right here, right now !!!

I ask You to form World Party !

I prepared rules and regulation for world party during my prison days :

Ten Aims : 1. To stop at all cost another War. 2. To help organized labour to get equal share in management of industries, mines, big business and means of communication. 3. To promote the growth of educational institutions where students produce their necessities as they study and when students attain marriageable age they should be free to marry and settle at their school buildings, fields and factories. 4. To strengthen by all means United Nations of the World. 5. To try best to get as many as possible World Party members duly elected into Congress and Senate. 6. To make common cause with the like thinking men and groups in the United States and the world. 7. To restrain youths from wild life, soiree of slavery. 8. To promote healthy joy and means of healthy enjoyment, 9. To combine here and now and to help each other in life here and when return home. 10. Not to allow the enemies of humanity to pull persons by ears in the name of class, creed or color.

Rules : 1. Any and every one who appreciates and approves Ten Aims and pledges to work to realize these objects of World Party can become a member. 2. When two or more members live together in the same place they will combine and try to work in harmony. 3. To promote the cause of the Party, every member will contribute some money, weekly or monthly, as mutually agreed by members of any locality. 4. There will be no permanent chairman or president but each group will have a secretary or president or secretaries according to the strength of groups. 5. Secretaries will keep account and record of members and arrange meetings. 6. As the conditions of each group may differ, every group should be allowed to make its own rules to better unite and to better promote the cause of the Party. 7. Groups by holding common meetings, through travelling and correspondence, will establish and keep fresh most friendly relations and harmony of thought and action. 8. Close watch shall be mutually kept to make each member adhere faithfully to the aims of the party. 9. Once a member is always a member (no one can expel a fellow man), unless one leaves the

Party voluntarily. 10. People, somehow differing in some details of life, can have their separate groups. 11. No difference should be permitted from basic principles. By common action members and groups should be kept within the right frontiers of the Party. 12. We start with Soldiers and extend the party to the soldiers of all the countries but we do not exclude any fellow man who may kindly cared to join the Party. 13. We remain loyal to the laws of the land wherever we happen to be. 14. We observe the discipline of the army or the armies to which we belong. 15. In meetings however members meet as friends and forget ranks. 16. Service to the needy will be taught. 17. Sense of humanity will be evolved. 18. We unite to so change society, now and in future that no man-made misery remains. 19. In case of natural calamities Members shall help humanity. 20. Ultimate aim is One Federated All World State. 21. It should be tried that all the lands develop such parties. 22. World Party in all the world is needed for our first aim–No War ! 23. All decisions in one group must be reached by unanimous vote. 24. If some, one member, or members, hold up a decision approved by others, once, twice, thrice, it is then time to separate. 25. Any number of groups can exist but each group must have unanimity. 26. Human mind shall not be tied down. 27. All means shall be tried for human growth in mind and in body. 28. All means shall be tried to promote social health through exchange of thought and common action. 29. Rules will be added as needed. 30. Every improvement shall ever be tried.

This was the plan, written in prison, and presented to American army in Japan, in October 1945.

I wrote to Congress President Babu Rajendra Prasad in November 1947 about my plan and asked him to discuss with other leaders of the Party. I sent letter to Raja Rajgopalachariji also but I could not get response from any side. I thought the new government is engaged in various problems, so I kept silence.

Congress President The Hon'ble Babu Rajendra Prasad replied me in December (1947) :

My dear Raja Sahib,

This is to Thank you for your telegram. I have still not been relieved from my office of the Government although I sent my resignation to the Prime Minister the day following my election as president by the All India Congress Committee. At my request Acharya (J.B.) Kripalani is continuing in office of the Congress. You May write to him whatever you want to bring before the Working Committee of the Congress.

But if you want me to take an interest in it you will please also send a copy of your scheme so that I may study it.

With kindest regards,

Yours sincerely
(Signed) Rajendra Prasad

After receiving the above mentioned letter I visited Acharya Kripalani Sahib and had a long talk with him. He happened to say that 'you have not sacrificed less than Jawahar Lal, call a meeting of the Delhi citizens and take votes and see whom the public supports.'

Mahatma Gandhi wrote me a little before his death in Hindi that I better (again) approach the Congress President. I have preserved those lines of our beloved Mahatma, they are the last words to me.

I am sorry to say that webs of secretaries is so thick round our leaders that it is hard to meet our coworkers in the cause of our country. They too, it seems, have taken to certain official ways and remain preserved in their ice boxes. With all respect to our Ruler, our Congress President, I must say here openly that once his secretary could not get for me some time to meet him. Poor secretary may not be entirely at fault. The whole system, as inherited from the British, is wrong.

I stand for the liberation of our country completely and to bring about freedom of our President. Should he himself advise me not to molest him. I cannot sit quiet so long as I can talk and write freely. Let the British-made traps, through the British agents in the country, entrap me if they can and if our freedom loving brethren are too weak to take the right step I must continue to herald loud that this is not complete Liberty and the division of the country is done in a way that we shall ever fight till we destroy ourselves. We must stand for our Aryan–Iran to Assam and for our complete independence. Aryan will be secured in World Federation.

Short Tours : I am writing these lines on the 24th of March 1948. This month, or during these twenty four days, I did very little travelling. I had to remain at our Headquarters, Vrindaban, preparing for our Annual Function and the Aryan Day, on the 21st instant.

On the 5th of March I had to proceed to Mursan to take part in the marriage of my nephew. My jeep broke down. Next day first in a car then in a bus, I went with my friends to Pali in Bulandshahr district. I had to ride an elephant in gold-silver throne with the bridegroom. Procession of elephants and horses and motor cars was taken out and taken in to the large residence of the bride. I shall not pause to describe how a band greeted us or how grand feasts were given or what beautiful presents were presented to the groom nor can I start to give you the list of many important guests, I am telling you my story. I could deliver a lecture to a large influential audience and thus carry on my mission amid the show and rejoicings. It was my purpose in joining the marriage party.

Returning to Vrindaban on the 9th, I left for Dholpur State on the 10th instant. At night on the 11th I could hold long talk with H. H. Maharana Sahib, now Rajpramukh of Matsya Raj. I believe in doing my duty and I did it by presenting my views.

Aryan Day . (Sunday, 21st March), As it was announced, in the forenoon a meeting was held at Prem Nagar. Prayers from different religions were chanted. Acharya Jugal Kishore, the General Secretary of our Indian Congress, presided. I read the report. He delivered the convocation address.

In the afternoon, high school held sports. We attended our meeting of the executive committee of the Trust. I presided over. Acharya Jugal Kishore kindly attended.

At night, my drama 'Rajput' was played. Our students showed great ability. Some of them can become professional actors. Whole night we kept watch. Singing, lecturing and praying made the night pass quickly. We enjoyed, we learned, we taught and we helped our minds to grow spiritually ! Sweets were distributed and tea was served through Students Co-operative Society.

Dr. Vishwapal, one of the proprietors of the wellknown Sukh Sancharak Co., of Mathura visiting our College on the Aryan Day promised to pay one thousand rupees to help us in more ways than one. His business experience can prove very valuable, without doubt.

Raja Bahadur Kushalpal Singh of Kotla paid us visit on this memorable day and expressed his desire to become our Life Trustee by paying the minimum fee. Rao Sahib of Gabbana also sent word on Aryan Day that he would be our Life Trustee.

Shri Badshah Mian Shahji of Gwalior also came for Aryan night. He is held in high esteem by the Muslims as well as Hindus. He is the Muslim high priest of the Hindu Darbar of Scindhia. We were naturally very glad to receive his visit.

Here I must also thank all other visitors, friends and coworkers who made our Aryan Day and the Annual Function of our college and school successful. Pandit Sitaram Shukla came all the way from Dehradun by jeep, lecturing on the way.

Premier Pandit Nehru : H. E. Premier Pandit Jawahar Lal Nehru has kindly written me the following letter : 'My dear Raja Mahendra Pratap. Thank you for your letter of the 5th March. I am sorry you have got the impression that I avoid you. This is completely wrong. I am afraid I cannot attend your annual function, I am overwhelmed with work.'

To tell the truth I was sincerely happy to receive that assurance from our premier that he did not avoid me. But for that clear statement his not coming to our function would have been taken as another proof of avoiding me. I must say in so many words that somehow I was never invited to any official or unofficial function of our Central government or of our All India Congress Working Committee. Once Maulana Abul Kalam Azad, that veteran statesman and one of the greatest leaders of our country himself tried that my views were at least heard by the Congress High Command but be regretfully found that 'they' were all opposed to my views. One thing is common between Maulana Sahib and me that we both opposed the British government during the First World War. Unfortunately the same thing is not common between me and any other member of the working committee of our Indian Congress.

My Story : Whenever I am at my headquarters, Brindaban, or now as it is spelt Vrindaban, my routine work is very simple. As our high school starts I pray and speak a bit for a few minutes at the students' gathering. I attend to my correspondence. I receive visitors. I look into and answer questions sent up to me by the school, college and World Federation office. Now and then I may drive up to our College, four miles distance and meet our college students. But I often go out on short tours.

I left Vrindaban on the 26th of March. I took morning train at Mathura for Delhi. I stayed for a few hours at the house of Mr. Agarwal, one old boy of our institution. In the afternoon I took train for Hardwar where I arrived in the early morning, next day.

On the 27th March I presided over the Convocation Meeting of the Girls College and walked round the famous place of pilgrimage at Hardwar. Same night I left for Delhi. Next morning, the secretary of the Jat Maha Sabha took me from Delhi Junction to Sonipat. There at the crowded meeting of the Jats I spoke twice. They told me that over ten thousand persons were present. Defence Minister Sardar Baldeo Singh also spoke at this meeting.

That night I spent at Dholpur State House, New Delhi where I was a guest of the Maharaja Sahib of Charkhari and Thakur Gaya Prasad Sahib.

On the 29th March I returned to Vrindaban. On the 3rd April I left for Mursan. Passing a night there, at the Kamra Bagh, taking morning tea with Raja Bahadur, lunching with the Manager, Central Bank, Aligarh, visiting Raja Bahadur at Gabbana, I arrived in the afternoon of the 4th April at Pisawa. Kr. Krishan Bihari Singh accompanied me. We were the guests of Rao Sheodhian Singh Bahadur. Thakur Sahib and Kunwar Sahiban gathered to hear me in a family circle.

Next day Kunwar Devendrapal Singh, a congress worker, called a public meeting for me. I gave a long talk at night.

Two nights I passed at Aligarh as a guest of Thakur Jhamman Singh. I met Nawab Ismail Sahib and Prof. Habib and received several visitors.

On the 13th April I spoke at Mathura Gurdwara. In the afternoon I went with Acharya Jugal Kishore and Prof. Krishan Chand to campaign for Hakim Brajlal. On the 15th I once again spoke for Hakim Brajlal. On the 15th I once again spoke at two different places on behalf of the congress candidates for the District Board. Minister Pt. Paliwal Sahib also spoke at one meeting.

In the afternoon, I left for Sangrur. Early next day I arrived there. It was a family reunion. Princesses had come to meet their brother, the new Maharaj. My daughter was also there. It was indeed sad that my brother-in-law, the old Maharaj had passed away but I was glad that the young Maharaj, Maharaj Kumar and the family took me as one of them. I was equally glad to meet Maharaj Kumar of Tikari.

On the 17th April I could speak at length at a large public meeting of the Akalies who kindly suported my movement of Aryan. It was a pleasure to meet thus the public of the Jind State.

Passing a night at Delhi Junction I arrived at Vrindaban on the 19th April.

On the 21st April I left for Aligarh. I stayed at the old Boys Lodge of the Muslim University. Hony. Secretary had called a meeting of the working committee, I attended it as a member.

Next day I took breakfast with Nawab Ismail, the Vice Chancellor and lunched with S. Abdul Majid Khwaja Sahib, and talked on my plan. At night I addressed the University Union and invited the students to found their own groups to push forward our programme. I was very glad to notice some fine sparkling faces approving my scheme of Aryan—Iran to Assam.

Next day I paid a visit to Prof. Habib. In the afternoon I took tea with the select committee of the Union and spoke on our Technical College at Vrindaban. In the evening I attended the farewell meeting of the outgoing students and heard speeches and oratory. Late at night I spoke on my life to a few members of the Sultaneah Historical Society.

On the 24 of April I returned Vrindaban. Thus, this is the account of full one month, from the 24th of March to the 24th April 1948.

My Diary : I passed days quietly at Rajpur, between Dehradun and Mussoorie. I did not go out any where from the large compound of my house, our summer home. Only twice I rolled down at the back of the residence to the river below to take bath in the mountain canal of sparkling water. It was a treat. But I did not idle away time. I wrote a pamphlet, World Federation circular and lot of letters to friends in India and abroad.

On the 29th of June I left Rajpur, took train at Dehradun and arrived next day in the afternoon back at Vrindaban via Delhi.

On the 1st of July I had to attend to the election of a trustee out of our Old Boys. On the 2nd July I went to Mathura to attend a meeting which was however postponed. I met some local officials.

On the 3rd July I left for Lucknow via Agra. On the 4th of July I attended the Provincial Congress election meeting. I wanted to sit far in the crowd but some friends led me to the platform. I sat there with the leaders of the land. U.P. Premier was there, ministers were in full strength, an Ex-President of the Congress sat in his usual jolly mood, General Secretary of the Congress sat by my side, Provincial Secretary was busy but the President did most of the work that afternoon.

I was given a little time to express my views. I said that I did not know this business of election. I saw that the British ruled the land by their rod. And I thought that if we could develop a stronger nod we should be able to take back our country. It was the meaning of my joining the Germans and the Turks and of my going to Kabul during the First World War.

Audience was not in the mood of hearing this story of the rod. I reminded them that they were under the influence of the British poison. They should cure themselves and make India completely independent.

As it was evident that the trained British slaves were restless and British agents were howling I could not properly finish my talk. The President asked me to give up my thankless task. I went and sat by the side of the President.

Next day I left Lucknow for Sangrur via Delhi. I here thank my host at Lucknow Janab Mujtaba Hussain and my nephew Sardar Narendra Singh who made my sojourn very pleasant and comfortable.

In about twenty four hours I arrived at the capital of Jind State. It was a pleasure to meet once again his Highness and his family. Next day I attended public garden party held in honour of the coronation of the young ruler. In the evening of the 8th July was held State Banquet. Here I made acquaintance of H.H. Nawab of Maler Kotla. As between him and myself was only Maharani we could talk a bit.

I proposed the 'health of India' at the function. I reviewed the history of our country and expressed the hope that there was bright future for our land and I asked the friends, present in the hall, to Join me in that hope and wish ! Band played.

On the 9th July I left Sangrur. Travelling via Delhi I arrived back at Vrindaban on the 10th July. I must thank His Highness Maharaja Rajbir Singh of Jind, my nephew, for the hospitality at his capital.

Letter : H.H Maharaja Sahib of Alwar kindly writes :

My dear Raja Sahib,

I have received your letter of the 23rd June, 1948 and read the June issue of your 'World Federation'. The views expressed by you in this issue are very interesting and I admire the zeal and perseverance with which you propagate them. I am returning to Alwar on the 8th instant.

With kind regards,

Yours sincerely,
Tejsingh (from Mt. Abu)

Thus writes a crowned head about our mission. He has his large following far beyond the frontiers of his State. He was duly elected unanimously as the President of All India Rajput Mahasabha. He is thus the recognized head of the Rajput warriors of all India. And the Rajputs are not only Hindus but also Musalmans. Rajput Hindus and Muslims, Jat Hindus, Muslims and Sikhs, Pathans and Marathas build up the mighty Aryan army. The famous Gorkhas are mostly Rajputs. We are very glad that Maharaja Sahib of Alwar appreciated our June 'World Federation'.

His Highness Maharaja Patiala acknowledging the receipt of the latest issue of 'World Federation' and 'Aryan'. I have been able to snatch a few minutes to glance through, despite the terribly heavy call on my time. I dare say, 'You have struck the right chord by what you have said; it is naked piece of truth that you have put in black and white.'

Friends take note of the fact that our princes can think right, decide right and are acting right. The British mischief coupled with misrule did not allow opportunities to the crowned heads to do their share in building our country. Now rulers such as Patiala, Gwalior, Alwar aand Bhopal are showing to the world what princely India can do, given the right opportunities.

A friend has written me from Dholpur that the sagacious Maharana is hampered in his service of humanity. Interference must end.

My Wires : I wired to Excellency Governor General New Delhi and sent the copies of the wire to Moulana Abul Kalam Azad Sahib, Editor *Hindustan Times*, Editor *Indian News Chronicle* and Honourable Representative of Hyderabad at New Delhi :

> Our Premier said government (is) against coercion of States, how then economic pressure (is) pressed against Hyderabad. Masses (are) suffering privations. If we (are) not ashamed of recognizing English King above us why can we not recognize Hyderabad King as our cooperator. Let not foreigners meddle. We shall settle our affairs ourselves and build united Aryans–Iran to Assam–completely independent within World Federation.
>
> I shall better also mention that I had wired to His Majesty King Hyderabad :Highly admire your Majesty's independent spirit. Let British go. We shall ourselves settle all our questions of building Aryan–Iran to Assam.
>
> I also wired to Syed Kasim Razvi Sahib, Majlis Ittahadul Musalmin, Hyderabad : 'Highly appreciate your appreciation of Excellency Raja Gopalachari. We as Old

Boys of Aligarh should join hands for Aryan Unity (and) Independence.'

In this connection I also wrote to Premier Pandit Jawahar Lal Nehru Sahib. I say I cannot serve the State so long as it remains tied to the tail of London but I am prepared to assist the cause of peace in the interest of humanity. I need only air-lift to Hyderabad, Cabul, Teheran and Kathmandu. Talking to gether on the principle of Aryan unity and liberty we can settle all our problems.

Diary : On the 29th of July 1948 I left my retreat, Pratap Kothi, Rajpur and took train at Dehradun. It was only about two hours run, I alighted at Hardwar where two emissaries of Gurukul University were waiting for me. We went to the Gurukul Kangri. The Governor of the University Dr. Indra (Vidyavachaspati) caught me up on the road and received me at the inner compound. He had gone in his car to the station to meet me but missed me by a few minutes. Meeting after a long time we talked of things old and new.

The same night I met college students and gave a talk of full one hour and later talked answering questions. About midnight I went to bed. Next day at 10 a.m., and again at 3 p.m., I lectured twice and replied at length to their questions. The subjects on these three occasions were of course different. In the night I spoke on politics, on international and Indian problems, in the morning I preached unity of religions and the Religion of Love and in the afternoon I related the story of my travels abroad. Thus within twenty four hours at the Gurukul Kangri, I spent five hours in lecturing and in explanation, explaining the points which the audience thought needed more elucidation. After the dinner with the college students I left by the night train. I had reserved the berth, I slept comfortably, at about 9 a.m. next morning, reached Delhi. Same afternoon, I came back to Vrindaban.

Rani Remarries

My daugher-in-law, widow of my deceased son, Rani Prem Baldeo married here at our Love Centre to Captain Raghunath Singh of the Indian army. Marriage was performed by me according to the Religion of Love of the unity of religions.

Since my son suddenly died last year it was a problem full of worry, how to shape the future of my daughter-in-law ? At my suggestion she engaged herself in conducting a girl school but the family question remained to be tackled. Whem I heard, therefore, that she had found for herself a mate in the captain I gave her quick consent.

On Monday, the 2nd August, 1948 marriage ceremony was duly performed in the presence of large local gentry. First the Captain duly accepted the Religion of Love and next they were united by me. Of course, in our religion, conversion is not absolutely necessary but as Captain Raghunath Singh of Indian Army expressed his desire to enter the fold of the religion of Love he was duly taken up in our brotherhood.

On the 11th August I attended the anniversary of Goswami Tulsi Das, that Light House of the medieval Hindi literature. The elite of Vrindaban was there. I also spoke a few words in harmony with the tune played on the occasion. Famous speaker Pandit Bindu ji harped as he liked with a view to instil the spirit of reform. Pandit Danbihari Lal Sharma and Goswami Indu ji are to be congratulated for getting up this fine meeting.

Our Vrindaban was highly decorated like a lovely bride and the swinging festival of "Jhulan" was in full swing from the 7th of August to the 19th. I did not however went round to see the show. Pilgrims and the enjoyment seekers come this time in very large numbers.

On the 18th of August I went by my Jeep to village Chonki Shabpur about forty seven miles from Vrindaban. Rain and muddy road made it a hard Job to reach the destination, but I arrived at the meeting place all right. People there took me round on an elephant, in a procession with a few smart volunteers in their military air marching in front. At this meeting of the Congress I spoke long at the need of the hour as I presided at their annual function.

In the afternoon I left by jeep to the Hathras estate village of Hussaini. When on account of a deep breach in the road jeep could not move further I left it and walked to the village and stayed with late Chowdhri and enjoyed his hospitality. Jeep was later brought by the aid of the village folk. I spoke to the peasants who cared to visit me. I asked them to change their old ways and to fit themselves in new picture of life.

My Diary :What for do I write this personal story, a man uninterested in my work is likely to ask ? But I have friends. A friend from Canada once wrote me that he enjoyed most my diary as it appears in our circular.

In the afternoon of the 12th November 1948, I got into the Bombay Mail train at Mathura. I got a berth for myself, and I settled down with the easy feeling of getting a nap. A police man got in and addressing me told me the sad tale of the provincial police force. He said that they were getting only thirty rupees per month with seven or eight rupees as allowances. It means that in American money they get only about eleven dollars per month, while in the United States some workers earn eleven dollars per day ! I promised him to bring his case to the notice of the public and the government. I strongly suggest that as in army policemen should receive food and clothing plus quarters for their families with sufficient scale of pay.

At about 2 a.m. I had to change train. In the early morning I reached Sangrur, the capital of Jind State, now a part of the union of Panjab States. That day and half of the night passed joyfully in the company of His Highness and the family. Ceremonies of marriage of the brother of the Ruler were going on. Singing and beat of drums intercepted our conversations. People were bent on fun. It was the happy occasion. Illumination and banquet enlivened the evening.

Next day we got into a large aeroplane at Patiala air-field and started off. We got lunch at Bhopal. H. H. Nawab Sahib had sent his private secretary to welcome the party. In the afternoon we reached Poona and got off the plane. Dining at a hotel we slept in the Special train. In the morning it started and we reached Kolhapur at about 5 p.m. Right royally we were received by the Maharaja of Sawantwadi, a Marattha prince. Our Maharaj Kumar, Raja Jagatbir Singh, was being married with his sister. In a long procession we proceeded to the Royal Palace, by the lake beautifully situated.

Ceremonies and stuffing the stomach followed each other. Marriage was performed twice on the 16th of November, first performance was according to Sikh religion and next Hindu Pandits sanctified the union of the couple. Same night we left and got into Dakota at Poona next morning. At Bhopal, Prime Minister gave us a big reception on behalf of the State and the Ruler. Delicious lunch was given in a ceremonial fashion. At Patiala in the afternoon an uncle and brother of H.H. Maharajadhiraj gave the marriage party afternoon tea. 18th was passed quietly at Sangrur. At dinner that evening I was asked to propose the health of the newly married couple. That was the only opportunity I got to speak something. I referred to the union as the union of the Jats and Maratthas. Maharaj Kumar has also a stran of Rajput blood from his mother side. I could also bring in my talk our friendly neighbours–the Afghans. And I spoke of our Aryan–Iran to Assam.

In the morning of the 19th I left without seeing any body. I had thanked the Maharaja and the family late last night. In the afternoon I reached Delhi. The Minister of Communication, Hon. Janab Kidwai sent his car and private secretary to the station. I went to see him and had dinner with Hon'ble Saksena Sahib, another minister of Central Government.

Who am I ? Who am I, you can ask, to promise this to India and that to humanity ? I am a man, my friends, who honestly believe that I have found a cure for present ills in society. I advertise my cure.

If all kinds of advertisements can appear in print. I have also my right to exhibit my wares. You can say that my language is faulty, my assertions smell of egotism and I am good for nothing. I know, millions of Muslims condemn Krishna and Buddha as heretics, Hindus do not believe Koran as the Holy Book but these facts cannot effect either Hinduism of Islam or Buddhism.

I write for my friends. Thousands already get satisfaction and consolation through my views. Here, I show a way of universal unity. With many high sounding words people still teach hatred and prejudice. Many people simply try to divide cults, groups and parties. I try to explain that every individual and group can prove useful to humanity if one tries one's vest in one's place, in the common interest of humanity.

I build, as if, one great machine of all mankind and make all the groups and individuals its so many wheels or parts.

Sheer ignorance of the laws of the universe creates friction. The great Builder who has built the universe is constantly trying to keep it in as good condition as possible. All the ideas, emanating from the forces conducting the universe, are to help the process of life. Our ignorance, due to our limitations, make us commit mistakes. We are, however, righted in course of time.

I herald my belief that the time has come when States must be federated, religions should unite and an economic system of joint family has to be evolved making one human family of all the human race.

I say, as child grows into man, our human race has reached the age of puberty in our times. I seek those who can believe this fact. We, coming together, will surely develop unity in the present chaotic world. I believe, this is the aim of my life and therefore I say and do what I do and say.

My Diary : On the 1st of December, being my 63rd birth day, our College and School celebrated that day in their own way. A meeting was held at Prem Nagar. I spoke to the college students. Sweets were served. In the evening the school boys put up a dramatic show. I said a few words from the stage. For one full week games, meetings and functions continued. At the end prizes were distributed by my daughter, Kumari Bhakti Devi.

On the 6th of December I proceeded to Mursan. High School staff and boys gave me a grand reception. I spoke for over an hour on my five points programme. In the evening, a Love Center was established at the Kamra Bagh, Mursan. This is the third Temple of Love duly opened for public in India.

On the 9th I left for Gwalior. Janab Shri Sahib and Raja of Magrora received me at the railway station. I went, however, with Dr. L.C. Jain and was his guest for two days. In the evening I went to Raja Pahargarh and spoke in his family circle.

Next day I visited Jat Boarding House and spoke to students. In the afternoon was performed the marriage of the daughter of Dr. Jain. The whole of the State Cabinet came. I sat with the Prime Minister and took that opportunity to explain to him my plan of Aryan.

On the 11th I addressed the students of the Victoria College. My audience roared with laughter at times. It showed that they were following intelligently my speech. I returned to Vrindaban in the evening.

On the 12th I left for Bareilly. On the 13th I visited some friends with Capt. Chauhan. In the afternoon I spoke at the tea party where over forty military officers were present besides Congressmen and gentry. Major Rampat reechoed my spirit. He asked his brother officers to throw off the old ways and take to new life as Pandit Jawaharlal Nehru too asked the people to do !

On the 14th I addressed the students of Bareilly College. In the afternoon, I spoke at a Congressmen tea party. At night I took train, returning to Vrindaban. On the 15th December, I plunged into preparations for a long trip.

On the 16th December, I left in my jeep car, accompanied by two friends and coworkers as the car developed some trouble, we got very late. Half an hour before midnight we reached our destination. We became the guests of Mme. Proprietress of New Hotel, Jaipur. She made us quite at home.

Next day I attended the meeting of the Subject Committee of Indian National Congress. I was led to the platform and I sat with the leaders of the country. The premier of Jaipur kindly gave me special tickets.

On the 18th was full open session. I was given this day a formal lunch by Thakur Sahib of Bissau, who also took me in his car to the Congress. It was grand. I sat with the chosen few but there was a huge crowd on the raised platform and the vast space in front. Speeches were delivered by the president and some of the ministers.

On the 19th I again attended the Congress but I came away early to avoid the melee at the end, when people would rush to meet the leaders, as they did last night.

On the 20th I left, thanking profusely my hostess and her daughter and grand children. I accompanied Rao Sahib of Masuda in his car. In less than three hours we drove to Ajmer. I stayed with him at his house. Several kind visitors called on me. Mr. W.D. Begg, Thakur Shiv Pratap Singh and some members of the Railway Union tried to get up a public meeting for me but due to RSS trouble and the official ban on meetings nothing could be done. I called on Swami Bhawani Dayal of foreign fame who was sick and we visited friends.

On the 22nd I left Ajmer. Some kind friends saw me off. In the evening I reached Ahmedabad. Friends came to receive me. I stayed at the house of Chandrakant Motilal Seth Sahib. On the 23rd I paid a visit to Hon. Mavalankar, the Speaker of the House, who also took me out to show me the proposed Gujarat University.

I spoke at the Ram Charit Manas Conference. I was delighted at the reception I received here. I was under the impression that the orthodox Hindus did not like me but my suspicion was falsified. I am very thankful to the authorities of the Ram Charit Manas Society and I am specially thankful to Goswami Bindu Ji, famous speaker.

My host brought me to the station and I left for Bombay. In the morning of the 24th, I reached there. Friends came to meet me. I stayed with Mr. H. H. Ismail, my friend, who was always helpful in Japan. I spoke at a Sindhi Gurdwara. I was very happy to meet Sadhu Vaswani, saint of Sindh. He embraced me and repeatedly said that he did not want to leave me. I addressed his congregation. H. E. the Governor of Bombay invited me to lunch. And at the lunch of my host I met my old friend Janab Bahaduri, Consul-general of Iran, and Madras personalities.

On the 27th I left Bombay and reached Poona. City Congress president and secretaries met me at the station and brought me to Dave Hotel.

On the 28th I spoke at the Women's College of the Grand old man Dr. D. K. Karve. I was given rousing reception at the 'Kesari'. I spoke there and at Lok Shakti. I visited Ayurvedic institution. City president gave me lunch. In the afternoon I addressed the Congress workers. Later I spoke at the great public meeting. In the evening I was taken to a social drama preaching against alcohol drinking.

I left on the 29th. Friends saw me off at Poona and friends received me at Bombay. My old friends Seth P. Parsram gave a lunch party. Seth Kotak, a millionaire, took me in his car to the Socialist leader and his meeting at College where I was the chief speaker. Same night I left Bombay. Next day at midnight I reached Gwalior. I stayed with Shri Sahib, Badshah Mian. On the 31st December I received visit from Raja Pahargarh and Dr. Verma and I visited Sardar Angre Sahib. At 2 p.m. our train left and in the evening I was back at Vrindaban. Thus ended this trip and this year!

My Diary : The first seven days of the month of January were spent at Vrindaban. I received many visitors of places far and near. Seth Khetani, my old friend, came all the way from Bombay. On Sunday the 2nd January 1949, first we held private discussions, next we held our executive committee meeting and in the evening we held service of the Religion of Love when six new students joined our Faith. I spoke to our students at the daily prayer. On the 5th the Reception Committee of World Religions' Congress held largely attended meeting. We elected office bearers and the working committee. On the 7th I went out to our College and spoke to our students at Prem Nagar.

On the 8th January began my long tour of twenty one days. First I went to Bulandshahr where I was a guest of Capt. Khazan Singh, veteran military man. Next day Col. Nepal Singh took me in his car to Jat College at Lakhaoti. Capt. Bhagwan Singh, the district magistrate, kindly accompanied us. I spoke to the students twice, in the morning and in the afternoon. One student, Mr. Mahendra Singh gave very elaborate tea party. Principal of the college, Mr. A. Dayal Chand, a Christian gentleman, played the part of a very kind host. Raja Sahib of Sahanpur and Kunwar Sahib of Pali came to see me.

On the 10th I reached Etawah at about 5 p.m. via Bulandshahr and Khurja. Kunwar Panchbahadur Singh came to the station and took me to the tea party which he and his friends had arranged. Officers of the town were in large number. Soon after, in the adjacent hall, I addressed a meeting which was presided over by the magistrate and the Chairman of the Municipality. At midnight I left and in about half an hour reached Bharthana. Teachers and professors of the college gave me a warm welcome at that late hour of the night.

On the 11th, I was taken in a procession, with band playing, to the college where I presided at a very large meeting. I spoke at length. I am always speaking on my five points programme: 1. India should come out of the commonwealth, 2. We shall develop Aryan–Iran to Assam and Himalaya to Ceylon, as a district of the province of Asia, in one Federated World State, 3. We will bring home rule to every village and town, 4. We shall make the workers full half partners in the factories, mines, railway, post, telegraph and shipping, 5. We shall give all the expenses of all the students. All the schools and colleges will have factories, gardens and fields. Students will study and produce as will. And when they will finish the study they will not be driven out. They will own in common all the school property. Thus each school of yesterday will grow into one joint family. Elders will be respected, children will be properly looked after and healthy and strong, work from six to eight hours with most modern machines. Qualities of humanity will be developed and respected: Beauty, strength, intellect, morality and enlightenment. We call that enlightenment which can see all the universe as one unit and realize that the universal laws govern every thing and all life. We are here to help the process of the creation and not to destroy it.

Friends of Bharthana, Principal Pandit Pathak, Prof. Yadav, Prof. Saksena and my host were all very kind. Rupees hundred twenty seven were also presented to me. Out of that sum eleven rupees were given to me by the Harijan society. Again at midnight I left. Friends saw me off at the railway station.

I reached Lucknow in the early morning. I stayed with my nephew Sardar Shamsher Singh Sahib at 9, Butler Road. Chowdhari Mujtaba Hussain was there. My sister kindly came to meet me. Raja Bahadur Mursan was also staying there.

As the students were on strike no large meeting could be arranged. But at two tea party meetings I addressed. One at Janab Hyder Hussain Barrister-at-law and other at Babu Ram Bharose, famous advocate. It was a pleasure to meet Shrimati Shradha Mata, a lady preacher of religion. She gave me dinner. I also met the Minister, Hon. Hafiz Ibrahim Sahib. Minister Hon. Nisar Ahmad was present at the tea party of Janab Hyder Hussain. We were once school fellows. I must also thank my host and his brother Sardar Narendra Singh for the hospitality and for taking me round in their cars.

On the 15th January I arrived at Banaras. I was taken to the palatial house of Babu Kishori Raman Sahib. I took tea there and soon left by the Banaras State car to Ramnagar. I was two nights there. I stayed with the State Minister of Education, Thakur Bansnarayan Singh Sahib. On the 16th a large public meeting was held. I spoke. And I was also received by H.H. Maharaja Sahib.

On the 17th at Benaras, I lectured to the Mehta College students and staff. I was greatly pleased with the rousing reception which I got here. I spoke at Netaji Samiti. In the afternoon I addressed the students of the Hindu University. Pandit Gobind Kant Malviya, the Vice-Chancellor presided. I thank here my host Babu Kishori Raman and his brother.

On the day that I left Banaras I visited Dr. Bhagwandas, another grand old man and a philosopher, and I addressed the students of the Kashi Vidyapeeth. In the evening of the 18th I reached Patna. Friends came to meet me. I stayed at the house of Dr. Syed Mahmood, the Hon. Minister but he was himself absent. His son and secretary made me feel at home. Here too were strikes of the students in full swing. No large public meeting could be got up. I addressed the students in full swing. No large public meeting could be got up. I addressed the students of Xaviers College who were not on strike. Rev. Moran, the principal, showed me round and gave tea. Gurudwara Harimandir Sahib kindly arranged a meeting at the temple. I spoke. I was very pleased with the pleasing atmosphere. Sikhs, as usual, warmly received me and my views.

I called on famous, old time leader and writer, Babu Sachidanand Sinha. Mr. Sahay, my old friend, and Mrs. Sahay, gave me fine lunch. Babu Jagatnarayan arranged a small meeting at his place. Sjt. Jugindra Babu and Verma Sahib often came and in my presence organized Asiatic Youth Federation. I am very thankful to all my friends at Patna and specially to Dr. Mahmood's household and Mr. Amritnath Verma.

I left Patna on the 21st and arrived on the 22nd early morning at Howrah-Calcutta. Friends received me and took me to a fine garden house where I stayed. I went and visited Janab Suharwardi, former premier of Pakistan. I paid a visit also to the Nepalese Consul General.

On the 23rd I was very busy. At 8 a.m. I presided at Tollygunge, at 9.30 a.m. I rushed back to Salkia and presided at a Congress function. Once again at Tollygunge I presided at another meeting at 1 p.m. At 4 p.m. I spoke at Shradhanand Park. I visited Political Sufferers' Association and Mr. S. Lahiri. In the evening I was given dinner by Mr. Sen Gupta who also presented three hundred rupees on behalf of the Tollygunge Netaji birthday celebration committee which had specially invited me to Calcutta.

On the 24th I lectured to the Bajauria Industrial School. The Tollygunge Municipality presented me an address in a silver casket. In the afternoon I spoke at the Yogashram, Dhakuna. And took train at Howrah.

I must express my thankfulness to my hosts Ch. Indrajeet Kumar Singh and family. They made me feel comfortable as well as their car took me round for three days. Family of Sir Chhajuram gave princely dinner in their magnificient mansion. Mr. B.C. Bose, Mr. A. Lahiri. Mr. Sinha and all others, including the workers of my hosts deserve my thanks for the goodwill shown to me and my cause.

It was a long journey. It took me thirty four hours to reach Bhopal. In the early morning of the 26th January I arrived there. Superintendent Sahib of the guest house took me in the State car to the Guest House. It happened Pandit Sunderlal also arrived. I attended his meeting. On the 27th I took lunch with H.H. the Ruler Nawab Sahib. On the 28th I had a personal interview with His Highness. The premier and some Congress workers had visited me. I came here receiving an express wire from Nawab Sahib in response to my telegraphic message. I wanted to settle the trouble which arose between the two sections of the State Congress to the satisfaction of all concerned. But as Mr. Menon of the State Ministry had arrived earlier and he had held talk with the Ruler it was thought that I need not try my surgical operation on revolutionary lines. Well and good. I decided to leave Bhopal on the morning of the 29th and this I did. But before my departure a secretary of His Highness handed me one thousand rupees as personal gift. I call it a royal gift. I thank the Ruler whole heartedly for this consideration.

I arrived Vrindaban on the 29th, at about 7 p.m. My wire did not arrive, sent from Bhopal on the 28th, and therefore my car did not come to the station.

On the 30th January, Sunday, I delivered my sermon to the Congregation of the Religion of Love. Four new persons, including one professor, joined our brotherhood. On the 31st, at the time of the opening prayer meeting of our school, I spoke long to our students, describing my tour. This day I also opened the Prem Vidyarthi Sangh.

Revolutionary Platform I preach

1. We Shall preach unity of all religions. 2. We shall practice unity of religions by visiting temples, mosques, churches, Gurdwaras and synagogues or such other places of worship. 3. We need not try to force others to do as we do. We cannot force a boy of a primary school to study the course of the university. 4. We shall not hate those who will disagree with us. We cannot hate children who cannot understand us. 5. We shall try to find those ideas in all the religions which separate men from men and instill hatred. 6. We shall propagate all such ideas which establish justice and develop love in society. 7. We stand for the principle that religions, political and economic co-operation are needed to make human life well balanced and harmonious. 8. We believe that socialism and communism are natural growth of the modern age. 9. We also believe that among people believing in any religion or in the efficiency of the socalled capitalism, there are many fine specimens of humanity. 10. Our task is to find a common platform for all what is best in the human race. 11. Around the platform of the spiritual World Revolution all good Catholics, Christians, Buddhists, Hindus, Sikhs, Muslims, Jews, Shinto, Confucians and the like will be gathered. And we shall gather too all the honest communists, socialists, nationalists or fascists. 12. We shall link up ourselves with all those who stand in some way or other for unity of religions, federation of States and a joint family of all mankind. 13. We shall discourage all that discussion which creates more disunity of discord. 14. We shall develop the habit of seeing good in others and of overlooking weaknesses. 15. We shall teach goodness, which acquired by systematic practicing goodness, as body is built by doing exercise. 16. We shall recommend reorganization of our human society on the basis of local liberty but all unity in one Federated World State. 17. Our world should have one world

capital, world cabinet, world parliament, world army, world court of justice, world religious board, world economic centre and world cultural head-office. 18. World capital will be at Honolulu. Australia, New Zealand and the islands there about will be included in world capital district. Asia, Europe, Africa, North America and South America will be five continental provinces. Continents will be divided into three, four of five districts. 19. Organization will be perfected to that degree that no one will be left out. Villages and towns will be perfect village families and town families. 20. All will work for all, according to their ability and capability, believing that the well being of all is the best well being of every individual. 21. We shall recognize human qualities of beauty, strength, intellect, morality and enlightenment and shall try to improve them. 22. We shall proclaim : Merge or separate but federate from a village to the world capital. 23. Human currents will be allowed to flow but when people flow out they should mix with those among whom they settle. 24. You can build separate colonies but you must federate with your neighbours. 25. Production and distribution will be on the principle that no one in our entire world remains destitute. 26. On principle every village and town will have home rules of self-government. 27. Every factory, mine or any one system of communication, production and public work will be self-governing. 28. We shall build such schools all over the world where all the students receive free all their needs from their States. 29. All the schools will have factories, fields, gardens and dairies. Students will study and produce their daily necessities. 30. Students will permanently settle on their school property and own it all in common. 31. We shall enlarge our humber by preaching, propaganda and persuasion. 32. We shall work openly and squarely. 33. But knowing that all governments are maintained by force the principle has to be accepted that they can also be set aside by force. 34. We shall expose that humbug of non-violence which helps violence to rule. 35. We want to see entirely non-violent world but to reach that stage we shall have to fight violence. 36. Hinduism, Hebrew and Islam have definitely recommended war to destroy evil in society. 37. Agents of violence glibly ask, but who will be the judge to decide which is evil, we say, we are the judges! 38. We shall suffer, if we must suffer, at the hand of evil for our principles. 39. We shall continue to move on, fight on, so long as one united world is not established. 40. We shall protect with all our might one federated World State, when it is finally established.

Religion of Love : At Cabul, Afghaniatan, in April 1916, on the birth day of Raja Rama, I began to write the book of the Religion of Love. In November, on Diwali, great festival of illumination, at Mazari-Sharief, in Northern Afghanistan, I finished that book. In 1919 it was published in Germany, both in English and German. In 1923 and later in 1912 the book was thrice published in Japan, in the Japanese language, by two different persons. In 1931, It appeared once again in English from Peking, China. Since 1946 it has appeared in Hindi, English and Urdu in this land of Aryan.

We believe that mankind has now reached the age of puberty. Buddha was the late incarnation and Mohammed, the last prophet. Krishna was the greatest incarnation in the ancient time. Christ stands in the middle on the Cross between two series of incarnations and prophets. Now that schooling of humanity is finished, we need no prophets of incarnations as teachers of mankind. I am simply a worker of Universal unity. I am a servant of mankind.

I believe, I was given birth and kept alive so far for this task of bringing unity among all religions. Mahatma Gandhi has prepared my way as John the Baptist prepared the way of Jesus Christ.

The Book of the Religion of Love was personally presented to comrade Lenin in 1919 by me. He called it Tolstoyism. It is the only book of its kind which can be acceptable to the godless communists. It is the book of this age.

Vrindaban, Boddha Gaya, Jerusalem and Mecca are four great places of pilgrimage. You remain free to go the different places of worship and pray as your neighhours do. It instills the spirit of tolerance.

It says it places the roof of love on the four pillars of Hinduism, Buddhism, Christianity and Islam. It mentions four ancient religions Zorastrian, Hebrew, Confucius and Shinto. It speaks of four modern Faiths of Sikhism, Bahai, Brahmo and Theosophy. It also pays due regard to all other creeds, with out distinction.

It creates a band of volunteers to work for the unity of Religion.

News and Views :

The Sikhs : It is a sad fact that our Sikh brethren are greatly agitated. I believe that if the Jat Sikhs come forward to join hands with Jat Hindus and Jat Musalmans, the socalled problem of the Sikhs will disappear in a day ! Jats will be able to build their Jatasthan–from Indus to Ganges–as a part of our federated Aryan. They will thus help themselves and help our country.

The Communists : It is another most disturbing question of the day. Many, a few hundred, communists are supposed to have been arrested. Why? What for? Is this being done at the suggestion of London? Are not the British dogs more active and creating a situation on a plan that the Indian Public opinion turns against Soviet Russia?

Peace in China : It is a very good news that they are talking peace in the celestial land. But up to the moment that peace is signed there is possibility of renewed war. Martial Chiang who got American help to wage war against Japan is still alive. He is still, perhaps, setting terms with United States.

Mr. Churchill : He is also not dead. He is busy with his schemes. The plan of socalled United Europe is simply directed against the USSR He wants war for his imperial plans.

My Diary : Arrived from by long tour of Lucknow, Benaras, Patna, Calcutta and Bhopal on the 29th of January. On the night of the 2nd February I left for Rohtak. Up to 3 in the morning I was pacing the platform and dropping in a chair for a nap. At last I got Punjab Mail which was ten hours late. It was a job to get into a first class compartment, the door was locked. I entered it from a window. Then, I got asleep in full dress. In a bit over three hours I reached Delhi Junction. The train was going to Rohtak but I alighted. It was prearranged that I would come by another train and I should proceed to Rohtak by car.

Friends took me in their car from Delhi to Rohtak. I presided over the great grand meeting held on the birth day of the late Sir Chaudhry Chhoturam. Eight to nine thousand persons were present. People said that the audience was of over twenty thousand. I spoke at length. The same night I returned. In the morning of the 4th went to Mursan and had lunch with Raja Bahadur.

At Vrindaban my routine of work is monotonous. The change is only in the faces of the visitors. I open the school with a prayer and a talk. I write letters. I receive visitors. On Saturdays I speak to the students in their weekly meeting and on Sundays I deliver a Sermon in the weekly service of the Religion of Love. I go seldom to our College, four miles away, to meet the students there.

On the night of the 7th February I left for Bareilly. In the early morning of the 8th I arrived there. Captain Chauhan and Captain R.S. Singh met me at the station and took me to Capt. Singh's residence where I stayed for full six nights.

I have just crammed up dates and the names of the places. But the story of each date is very fascinating. Receptions by the village folks were enthusiastic and ingenuous. At Ballia I was given tea parties, one after the other. At Bidhawali, after a short procession and a long lecture a big tea party and a banquet were given. Officials of the city were also present. It was such a big affair that I could only reach Bareilly at 3-30 a.m. Kiyara could not be visited in the big government's propaganda car which took me to several villages, I had to ride an elephant and returned by an oxen native cart. Rajputs, Kurmies and Ahlowalias made themselves conspicuous by their lunches, dinners and the tea parties. Pandit Deena Nath and Captain Chauhan gave banquets. Mrs. Sharma gave tea. I also joined the dinner of Mr. Gupta. Our Captain Singh filled in the gaps, I was staying with him.

At Meerut I stayed with Lala Ram Richhpal Singh and had dinner with Chaudhary Yad Ram advocate. I addressed the meeting of the Bar Association. Pleaders, Barristers, Advocates and a Judge were present. I was glad to see that they appreciated my views.

On the 16th February I visited Baral Fair and gave a talk to the Baral students and the village folk who came to the Fair. Later in the afternoon College students of Khurja gave me reception and heard my speech with love and patience. I was promised by several students that they would carry on my Mission at Khurja with devotion. Two Mr. Sharmas and one Mr. Gupta took the trouble to see me off at the distant junction.

On the 17th morning I arrived back at Vrindaban and on the 18th February I left by jeep car for the village of Bisara in the district of Aligarh. With great difficulty I reached after 10 p.m. my destination. Next morning we left for Nibbera in Bulandshahr district. I went all this long distance over some bad roads too, just to perform the marriage of Thakur Rajpal Singh according to the Religion of Love. History was made. All around the world went round that some thing new had come ! A new Religion, a new salvation, a new system of life had appeared !

On the 20th February I spoke to the people of the village and of the surrounding villages who came to hear me. On the 21st I left. At Aligarh I visited Janab Abdul Majeed Khwaja Sahib, Barrister, my old class fellow. Dr. Syed Mahmud was also there. It was a pleasure to meet my Minister host of Patna. I had tea with them. I also dropped on the way at my friend Thakur Jhamman Singh. And I returned.

On the 25th Feb. there was only one local function at Sevashram. I went to it. On the 27th Feb. our weekly service beat all previous records. Gathering was largest so far and eleven new young men joined our fold of the Religion of Love.

It was a pleasure, I should relate, to receive the visits of Swami Satya Deva ji and Swami Satya Bhakt. 'Satya' is common to their names but they are poles apart. They kindly came and spoke to our students. Janab Maulana Khadim came to fetch me for a meeting at Delhi but to my great regret I could not proceed. The notice was too short. Ch. Dharmvir Singh, our co-worker at Muzaffarnagar, dropped in. It is a pleasure to see how earnestly he is carrying on our Mission there mostly single handed. I should not leave out to mention that real brother-in-law of the late Mahatma Gandhi came too to meet me. He was all polite. He has invited me to stay with him at Bombay when I should be visiting that port city.

Correspondence : After years, heard from His Majesty H.M. King Amanullah Khan. I am very glad to hear that he is hale and hearty and still living peacefully at Rome. The great storm of the Second World War did not uproot our Royal friend and patron from his new abode in the foreign land.

His Majesty writes in English :

Rome, 28th January 49.

My dearest friend,

I think, it is really a long time you have heard from us. It is not my babit to write often and so you must not think that I have forgotten You. With this letter of mine I should love to show you my best friendship and all my love.

Yours sincerely
(Signed) Amanullah

The letter has too his signature in Arabic characters.

As soon as I got the letter I answered. Within fifteen days I got another air-mail letter of King Amanullah Khan. This letter was written in French. He explained that there was none in the house, at the time, to write in English. He complained that his financial position did not allow him to visit India and attend our World Religions' Congress. I wrote him back immediately on the 22nd of February, saying, I had not money enough to defray his tour expenses but if His Majesty could once come to India there would be no dearth of money. His prestige is still very high among the Hindus and Muslims alike. And I am sure the present Afghan government of Afghanistan will rejoice if King Amanullah Khan accepts and works for my plan of Aryan. We shall make the governments of Afghanistan, Iran and Nepal still stronger and firmer in their places. Wealth of India will help them to modernize their lands quickly. And we shall all remain in one federation of Aryan.

Aryan will be federated with other districts of Asia and Asia will be a province of the Federated World State.

My Diary : On the 3rd I left for Ajmer. A wire from H. H. Maharaja Umed Singh set me flying in that direction. Late in the evening I arrived there and became his guest. I thank His Highness for his hospitality. But it happened that I could not attend the meeting to which I was called. Maharaja thought it fit not to go and not to allow me either to proceed thither. Two factions were at logger head.

I left for Ratlam. Travelling for about fifteen hours I arrived there before 2 p.m., on the 5th March. Same afternoon I inaugurated the grand meeting of the martial races. H. H. Maharaja of Sailana presided over and H. H. Maharaja of Ratlam attended. There was a great gathering of many Rajput chieftains. Meetings followed in the night and early next morning. In the afternoon there was another open public meeting. I addressed it for over one hour. I was a guest of Thakur Sahib of Pancher. Great organizer of the function was Thakur Ramdayal Singh. Same night I came to the railway station and had a nap in the princely waiting room. At about 5 a.m., I got into the mail train and reached back Mathura in about twelve hours.

On the 19th I had to take part in College Trustees meeting and the meeting of its executive committee. A meeting of the reception committee of our Congress was also held.

Changing train at Delhi I arrived in the afternoon at Jagadhri station. On the platform I was profusely garlanded. And I was taken to the car which was specially sent from Delhi by the Provincial Congress President for my use throughout the tour.

I stayed at the house of Seth Garg ji. I spoke at Sanatan Dharma and Arya Samaj. I addressed the workers of the local Congress. I went out to the Muslim refugees camp and expressed sympathy with sufferers there. I told them in a speech what they should do now. My plan of Aryan was their only salvation. I paid a visit to Sardar Sahib of Buria who was lying ill. He in fact saved these Muslims from the fury of Hindu mob by giving them shelter in his castle. The reception given at the Paper Mill was simply grand. Banquet followed. And I left Jagadhri by Congress car.

In the afternoon of the 25th I came to Ambala. I visited local Congress President who was also ill. I addressed the large meeting of the students gathered together to celebrate the memory of Sardar Bhagat Singh who threw a bomb in the legislative chamber in 1929 and who was later hanged. The meeting was held at the Gandhi Memorial College. I was greatly pleased by the reception the students gave me. My speech was widely reported in the press. I stayed at the residence of Sardar Sahib of Manauli. On the 26th I expressed my views to the local Congress workers in a meeting and after lunch I left Ambala and same afternoon I arrived at Ludhiana.

I was taken to the house of L. Balwantrai, where I stayed. Congress workers and students came and heard my views. In the evening I spoke at length in a meeting of Congress workers and friends. Next day, a bit early, I left.

On the 27th March I stayed at the residence of Mr. Bhalla. He is the chief manager and a partner of the Enamel factory, Jullundhur. I addressed a youths' meeting and the meeting of the Provincial Congress workers. General Secretary, Dr. Lehna Singh, came down from cool Simla heights to hear my talk, he left same night. I enjoyed at night the dinner given by Major Rao Krishnpal Singh Sahib at his military residence. Next day I addressed the students of the D. A. V. College. I was greatly impressed by their enthusiasm. British have done havoc with our national mind yet the young blood is comparatively free and is ready to take up my plans.

Fine car driven by a smart driver, brought me quick to Hoshiarpur. A sister of Sardar Bhagat Singh, the martyr, met me. Lunch was served at the residence of the Congress General Secretary. Soon we were driven to the nearby town of Hariana. A large public meeting was held. I addressed. Returning Hoshiarpur I spoke to the Congress workers. In the evening I gave a long talk at the public meeting. The District Magistrate was wise enough to realize that my talks, inspite of their roasy thorns, served best the cause of peace. He allowed for me public meetings inspite of restrictions imposed through out the province. Next day I spoke at the D. A. V. College. Pandit Raliram, the principal, supported my five points programme and explained that my plea for free education, paying all the expenses of the students by the State was fully supported by Aryan ancient culture.

By car, via Jullundhur, I came to Amritsar. Paid respects at the famous Golden Temple and stayed with Sardar Jodh Singh, Principal of Khalsa College. Next day I addressed the College students. It is becoming clear that hot blood of India can best appreciate my views. My speech was warmly received.

Now I started on a long stretch of road. Direct road to Ferozepur was closed by the unnatural division of Pakistan. Driving via Jullundhur, taking lunch at Ludhiana and taking tea at Moga we arrived at Ferozepur at about 6.30 p.m. on the 30th

March. President of the Congress of the city arranged a meeting of the workers. I spoke at length. Banquet was given. Next day I addressed the students of the R. S. D. College. Students seemed to be electrified. The whole atmosphere was pleasing.

31st of March 1949. I driving fast towards Moga. Reaching that town and taking lunch with the local Congress President, I spoke at the D. M. College. Students, as usual, enthusiastically received my talk.

It was a pleasure to pay a visit to Jagraon, village of the late famous leader Lala Lajpatrai. I met here his brother and a son-in-law. I spoke to the local Congress workers. As I got late, cancelling some engagements, I arrived at Ahmadgarh with my friends. A big reception was given. I was asked to speak in the local Mosque and then I addressed a large meeting. I spoke till the station came and got into a first class compartment, where to my surprise I met an old friend of Sangrur. Car was left, driver was thanked, accompanying friends said good-bye. I stop this account here.

I Wrote Open Letter to Hon'ble President Truman

Sir,

I dare to approach you thus through this open letter. I beg to represent that your government is still not learning by the happenings in China. Those hot heads who compelled the Chinese people to adopt the present course are still going strong in your country. They are misleading you to adopt strong policy against the 'communists' and speak loudly of communist menace. It is all wrong and highly explosive talk. This is not the way to establish peace in our struggling society.

For God's sake, leave our Aryan alone. We can best settle our problems with Red Russia and Yellow China. British imperial intrigues are trying to create the same situation in our land as in Burma, Java, Indo-China and China. Please take in England and Canada as States of your union. And declare hands off Europe, Asia and Africa.

You have lot to do in North and South Americas. There are still vast spaces lying vacant in those regions. You have to populate them. You can get millions of Germans and Italians to mix up with Anglo-Saxons and Latins to strengthen your new world.

Your scientists should devote more energy to find out ways and means to blow out race hatred. New faith is necessary to create new, outlook on life. Our World Federation is presenting new ideas and is evolving new strong belief of the unity of our human race.

Just think a bit, please. When United Nations Organization has been built up why must British commonwealth remain, hampering the growth of World unity? It is not a regional institution. It grew blindly, unsystematically. It is entirely out of date.

I also beg to suggest that United Nations should be given their own home. I propose that Hawaii islands are allotted to them for their capital. The pacific islands of the south together with Australia and Newzealand should form part of the World Capital District.

United Nations should be evolved into Federated World State. Backward countries now dependencies of England, France or Belgium should receive guidance from UNO. This is the way, sir, bring peace to our earth.

Sir, I sent you two private letters. Now I write you this open communication. I beg to remind you that as early as 1931, when our circular was published at Peiking, China, I proposed that a Co-Co-Co-Party be formed. Meaning thereby that Comintern, Congress of India and Comintang of China form an alliance. To my regret, no progress was made along my suggestion. Now things as they are, it is urgently needed that Soviet Russia, China and Aryan–Iran to Assam–make common cause in their own interest and for the sake of the peace of the world, which is threatend by war mongers. I am prepared to work for this union if you approve of my plan.

Let there be formed in USSR, China and India groups working openly and squarely for this cooperation. There should be nothing secret with us. We should declare openly that we would not take part in any underground activity. In India if the government will not support us we would blame it for foreign influence. It is the best way to work in this country.

I can assure you that Red Russia commands here in my land great respect. That respect is being undermined by subtle propaganda of the British agents. For every strike, opposition of the over burdened peasants and any supposed sabotage your country is blamed, because Red Russia is supposed to assist the Communist Party of India. Some such tricks were utilized to defame Kaiser's Germany. I speak of these things by my own experience of two world wars.

I beg you that you, on your part, declare openly that you support my this idea of close cooperation smong Red Russia, China and India. You need not say Aryan for the time being. With your open declaration I shall gather together students, peasants, workers and the military castes of martial races for the unity of our three countries.

I have my little following of sincere workers. We are working for local liberty, Aryan unity in one Federated World State.

My Diary : On the 16th of May I left by car. What a harassing journey it was. Heat was oppressive. Furnace like gusts of wind appeared to be blowing in the face. Car got over heated at times. In the afternoon we reached Delhi. We passed on. But now car refused to move. Getting it restarted, continued going, again there was some trouble and at last at 2 a. m. stopped by the road side and slept as we could to take some rest. Getting up early at 5, we were soon on the road. Car went fine. But now to our surprise petrol was all used up and car came to a sudden stop. A man had to be sent to the town of Roorkee, five miles distance, to fetch some gas. I took bath in the cool canal, in the mean time. As the man returned we were soon off. Now car simply flew head along. Soon after we had to stop, finding tyres burning hot. It was cool and nice as we began to go up the hill. At 2 p.m. on the 17th May we arrived at our Summer House, named Pratap Kothi by me, situated at the road for Mussorie mountain. This is Rajpur. Three thousand feet above sea level. Hills are green, a hill stream flows below through the dale. Our house commands fine view, it is picturesque at the back. I settled down quietly.

I called at some friends, received visits from several more. Maharaja Tikari kindly called and I and my daughter visited him. Princess Bhuban of Nepal kindly came. We had left our circular at her home, with a note that we had called.

I went to Pandit Mahavir Tyagi, famous leader. He was at the time making arrangements for great public meetings for topmost leaders. He was at the microphone. By the way he introduced me to the people around. I took up the thread and began to speak. I said. I was a rebel of the former government and I am greeting rebel once again. I denounce this Commonwealth connection of our government. Microphone went wrong. When it was once again in order, I continued. Soviet Russia had helped Afghanistan, Iran and Turkey and I saw, how in 1923 Soviets made China free of extraterritorial bondage. Microphone again stopped functioning. I stopped speaking, knowing full well that it was mischief of the British agents. Someone whispered it to me too that is purposely done.

On the 20th May I saw the procession of our Congress President. It was a big show Meeting in the evening was attended by thousands. I got a chair and sat for a while but I did not stop to hear the speeches. It was getting too late for me.

On the 21st of May I watched from the guests gallery the most disappointing drama of our august Congress. Leaders, for whom I always had great respect, rose to defend Indian connection with Commonwealth, made in London. They even went so far to say that long established British connection could not he snapped suddenly! They defended Pandit Jawaharlal Nehru, saying that he acted just according to the instructions of the Congress. We were quite free and independent, they repeated. I murmured 'quite false.' Several congressmen rose and opposed commonwealth but they were simply stifled by the chair. When recess came I left in disgust.

Today is the 29th of May. The month is coming to end. I may visit Dehradun tomorrow but I have no plan to fly somewhere during the next two days. So that, it is the end of the story of this month.

In this connection I should more properly introduce Ch. Mukhtar Singh who arranged my four day tour to and around Sir Chhotu Ram Kisan Girls School, Mavi, Yaqootpur, District Meerut. He is the manager of the girls school and ardent worker for women's education. He assures me that he would like to work hence forth for my mission. I welcome his cooperation.

Purse not many but still some paper rupees notes dropped into my coffer. I got fifty rupees at Nagla Musa and twenty six more rupees were received from individual sympathizers. One thing in this connection is worth noting that the Muslims of Nagla paid more than half of the village purse, expressing admiration for my Pro-Muslim stand. The Jats, as Jats, also showed great regard and sympathy with my plan.

I apologize to my friends who kindly invited me during the month of May and I could not go. A friend thought that I had agreed to visit Deoband on the 15th of May. He had made great preparation for my reception. I believed that Thakur Yash Pal Singh M. A. will kindly inform me later after arranging with the Muslim College. Misunderstanding made me miss my opportunity of service. I am sorry. I could not also go to a marriage of a friend who wanted me to perform his marriage according to the Religion of Love. I am equally sorry for not being able to go to Muzaffarpur, Kanpur and Ajmer.

Correspondence : The Hon'ble Sardar Patel. I wrote him, I am a rebel. To prove my rebellion I sent him our May circular, where-in I declare war on Commonwealth. But I said that the difference of opinion could not make me lose all regard for our old Congress leaders. Having regard for his health I offered him the use of more than half of my large house at Rajpur. The climate of this place is far superior to Deharadun where he is staying at the Circuit House. He kindly sent me a polite answer addressing me as 'Dear Friend' and thanking me for 'very kind invitation to me to stay with you...' He tells me that he might go to Mussorie if that suits him. 'If not, I think I had better stick to Dehardun. With kind regards, yours sincerely, Vallabhbhai Patel.' You see, I value this communication from our Deputy Prime Minister and a great popular leader of our country. It does not say much. It entirely ignores my declaration of war on the Commonwealth. I may be expelled from the Congress party for my opposition to the declared policy of our Congress and the Indian government. And yet this well tried leader has a soft corner for my devotion to the land of my birth and for humanity. I am very thankful.

My June Story : First of June, 1949 saw me at my large, comfortable summer house at Rajpur. I was thinking, however, was it right to live so high up above the common man down in the hot plains, thousand or two thousand feet down below? But I myself was far. Far below those higher ups, living three of four thousand feet above in those cool hills of Mussoorie, Nainital or Simla. I had hardly a fraction of their wealth. And I was not living just to enjoy. I was writing and touring to serve our human society. At least so I thought and so I think.

On the 4th June I left by Bus and catching train, changing twice, arrived in the early morning at Kalka. Now a fellow passenger, in the first class, finding my identity, did not allow me to buy tickets for me and my servant to Simla. He bought. Such are some of my kind unknown friends in the country.

At Simla I stayed for eight days as a guest of Sardar Sohan Singh Sahib of Rawalpindi. He lost several million rupees worth of property in Pakistan due to London made partition of India. Along with my host I went to take dinner with H. E. The Governor of Punjab, Pandit Trivedi ji. There I met a Central Government Minister, the Hon. Mr. Divaker and Sardar Teja Singh, Chief Justice of Patiala. I talked Revolution. My host said, he could not agree with my opinions but they were very interesting. Mr. Divaker conceded that I must have some ideas to live by.

Sardar Sobha Singh, a millionaire of Delhi was also staying here as a guest of my host. His younger brother is one of the ministers of Punjab. He came to dine with us. I got an opportunity to explain my programme. Presidents of the Congress committees of Simla and Ambala kindly called on me. Meetings were settled.

I spoke to the staff of the S.D. College. I preached at Arya Samaj and I lectured at a grand public meeting. Simla Congress celebrated the birth day of the Killer of that General who murdered over thousand in my plan of world order. I was heartily applauded when I said that we would have federated Aryan–Iran to Assam.

I must here thank my host and the charming hostess and their family for making me quite at home during my sojourn at lovely Simla.

On the 14th June I was back at Rajpur. I was writing a book and attending to my correspondence. I called on that famous writer, Sardar St. Nihal Singh. I visited Swami Shahanshah. I received my visitors. Days passed quick. On the 23rd June, I, my daughter and my grandson, went to Mussoorie. We stayed for four days at the Savoy Hotel. I had explicitly arranged with the kind proprietor, Captain Kirparam, that he would charge me this time, we would be his paying guests. Hotel is very comfortable, commanding fine views. You have here modern comforts including running hot water. You can have a nice room, three meals, two teas for only five US dollars per day.

Mr. S.P. Gidwani proved very helpful. He would come to me, take me out and introduce me to his numerous friends. I met Indore Princess, a prince of Patiala, Hon. Minister Ambedkar, Raja of Khairagarh, Seth Sahib, Babu Kishoriraman of Banaras, who also gave a tea party, our relation H. H. Rani of Kalsia and family of Kunwar Sahib of Peerpur, who invited us to see a show at the hotel, and many others, including some Congress workers of repute, but no meeting could be arranged. I attended the school function of Manobharti.

I may mention that in July I am going to Bombay and Madras. In August I shall be visiting Bengal and some places on the way. In September I am scheduled to visit Rajasthan and Bijnor.

I must also express my hearty gratitude to my daughter Rajkumari Bhakti for all her cooperation in our work. It is true, she is not trained like the energetic daughter of the Hon. Sardar Patel but she gives her support to our cause. She is desirous of visiting foreign countries. She is about forty years, still unmarried. She lives at Pratap Kothi, Rajpur, U.P., India.

Story of July : On the first of July I was at Deoband. In the afternoon workers of the local sugar mill gathered to hear me and my host Thakur Yashpal Singh. Next day in the morning, sweepers gave me reception and I spoke at their meaning. It was touching, these poor workers and sweepers presented me purses of rupees fifty one each. I must also thank Lala ji, our one Old Boy who kept me at his house as his guest.

Car gave me lot of trouble. In the afternoon we reached Muzaffarnagar. Our coworker Ch. Dharamvir Singh gave us tea at his 'Yuvak' office. He insisted that I stay there that night. He arranged a big public meeting. I addressed it. Doctor gave us dinner. I slept at our 'Love Center,' Church of Religion of Love. In the early morning of the 3rd July, we left. Car ran fine. I reached in time Vrindaban for our Vidyalaya meeting. In the evening, I delivered a sermon at our Vrindaban Love Center.

On the 11th July I left by train for Bombay. Next forenoon I reached my destination. I was glad to have the company in the train of the Labour Commissioner Babu Jaleshwar Prasad of the Central

Government with whom I discussed labour problems. At Bombay a couple of friends came to receive me. I stayed three days with my friend Janab Ismail, at 1, Club Road, Byculla. He kindly introduced me to his many friends at the Radio Club. I met Janab Agha Bahaduri, Irani Consul and paid a visit to Afghanistan Consul Sahib.

Mr. Lachhman Singh took me to his multi-millionaire friends. Four days more I stayed with Seth Parasram, Sunrise Bldg., Third Pasta Lane, Colaba. I lectured at four colleges–Islamia, Khalsa, Bhartiya Vidya Bhawan and Nair Medical College. I also spoke at Buddha Vihar and at a meeting of Sindhi merchants. Mme. Nair gave lunch at her residence. She is the wife of the gentleman who gave nearly two million of rupees in charity to found Nair Hospital and College.

I must thank my hosts Janab Ismail and Seth Parasram for making me quite at home during my sojourn. Mr. Lachhman Singh took, too, lot of trouble for me.

I could not proceed to Madras as I had planned. To my great regret I heard that all the five friends whom I expected to meet were absent, one of them was about to leave !

As I got a little time at Delhi, I paid a hurried visit to Afghanistan Embassy and met H. E. the Ambassador. On the 26th July I was back at our Head Quarters.

On the 27th July, I fasted, right in the Islamic way, and on the 28th I joined the Id-Namaz, at our Love Center, conducted by Hafiz Mohammed Akbar Khan Sahib. Hindus and Muslims prayed to the only God, God of all the religions, shoulder to shoulder. Why this cannot be done through out our world? It shall be done.

On the 29th July, Hon. Babu Sampurnanand, Minister of Education, of the U. P. Government paid a visit to our Prem Mahavidyalaya. Our students warmly welcomed him. He was once a teacher at our school. He spoke of his old days here. I spoke on my new plan of Education. We took tea together. I accompanied him to another function of H. H. Bon Swami.

My Story of August : In the evening of the third August I left Mathura. The train got four hours late. At 2 a.m. we reached Faridabad. Villagers were there to receive me with native band

and gas lanterns. A chariot took me in procession. People going in front and following the vehicle.

Next day I addressed the High School students. Later I spoke in a mass meeting of the peasants of the villages around. Government is acquiring their land to settle the displaced persons from Pakistan. 'What nonsense' I said, 'to make permanently settled homeless to settle the refugees'. This should not be. I was delighted to hear that some of those very persons whom authorities wanted to settle here spoke against the official plan. They asked me to convey their wishes to Premier Pandit Nehru. I refused to undertake the mission. I taught them that they should rely on themselves.

On the 6th of August was held a unique function. I say unique because a unique personality, Babu Lachhman Prasad Sufi, joined the brotherhood of the Religion of Love. He is the editor and proprietor of 'Mastana Jogi.' a very popular magazine. He told me in 1914 that if I was to found a new religion he would be my first disciple. His holy wish has been fulfilled by God !

On the 9th August I left on my long tour of the East. In the morning of the 10th I reached Allahabad. Several College students received me. They arranged for me a very heavy programme for the day. I spoke at the Radha Raman College and S. K. P. College. I addressed the students at the University Union. I expressed my views at a Rakshak Sangh meeting, held at the residence of Shri Narendra Singh. In the evening I delivered a long speech at the large Public Meeting. Rai Amarnath Agarwal M. L. C. gave me a fine dinner. In one day I could do as much work as I did in one week at Bombay. Mr. Virendra Nath Verma and his co-workers deserve special thanks for all this busy programme at Allahabad.

On the 11th I reached Benaras. I stayed at Raman Niwas. I spoke at the Netaji Samiti and opened their Reading Room. I addressed the students of the Hindu University in a hall of a hostel.

On the 12th I stayed for four of five hours at Patna and spoke to a representative meeting at the office of the Asiatic Insurance.

On the 13th I arrived at Howrah and the same night continued my journey, reaching at midnight the town of Midnapur. On the 14th I raised the Revolutionary flag. I spoke at the Political

Sufferers' Association. Next day, on the 15th of August, I raised Gandhi flag and spoke a few words at the great public meeting and delivered a long speech. It was grand affair.

On the 16th I returned to Howrah and stayed with Salkia Transport. On the 17th H. H. Kumar Rishi took me to Krishna Nagar. Municipality gave me address. There was a large open meeting. I spoke at length.

Passing night at Shivanand Ashram, I went to Nawadweep, most holy town of Bengal. Here too municipality gave me address. I replied and thanked. I visited six temples and spoke to the College students. In the afternoon Ashram gave a tea party.

On the 19th we returned Calcutta. I addressed the employees association and lectured to an audience at Dhakuria. On the 20th H. H. Kumar Rishi gave me an address at a tea party.

On the 21st August I spoke at a large public meeting at the Shradhanand Park Calcutta. The Meeting was called by Mr. B.C. Bose and Sjt. Hemendra Prasad Ghose, a famous journalist, presided.

On the 23rd I came to Bardwan. A rousing welcome was extended to me. I addressed a very large public meeting. A cousin of Maharaja, Sjt. Khanna Sahib, was my host.

On the 24th afternoon I arrived at Lucknow. I stayed as usual at 9 Butler Road. Chowdhari Sahib made me at home. On the 25th I could meet some friends who came to tea at my residence. On the 26th I spoke to the students of Lucknow University Union. Every where I received most hearty welcome by the students. Young blood is warm !

My September Story : On the 3rd and the 4th of September I spoke twice at the Jagirdars' meeting. It was a big affair. Six to seven thousand land-lords and peasants took part at the historical Barehdari of Lucknow. I told them some bitter truths and showed them the way of salvation.

From the 11th to 20th September I was touring in Rajasthan. Raja Bahadur of Bhinai, who is also the chairman of the District Board of Ajmer made my visit to Baghera, Kekri, Bhinai, Bijainagar, Masuda and back to Ajmer via Biawar. Meetings were held, rich dinners were given and my Mission was widely advertised. At Baghera, Thakur Sahib of the place get up a big gathering with tom toms. At Kekri, Municipal Chairman took special interest to make our meeting successful. The main square of the town was all full up and people occupied surrounding roofs. Bhinai meeting was more like a Darbar. The officials of the Thikana were present in their official dress.

At Bijainagar there was some opposition. Some people got into their heads that my hosts, being big pots, were trying to preserve thus their feudal glory. Masuda Rao Sahib was not there but his Diwan put up a big show. We were also right royally entertained.

On the 15th of September, late at night I left for Udaipur. Thakur Sultan Singh accompanied me. Next morning at Udaipur, we were warmly welcomed. We were taken round to see different schools and institutions. Boating in the famous lake and a visit to an island palace were very pleasant indeed. I found the view more beautiful than what I had read about it in the books.

On the 17th September I spoke at eight different places. The College meeting was most thrilling among school meetings but the public meeting surpassed it by sheer weight. Ten thousand persons were supposed to be there! In any case, six to seven thousand people formed the audience.

H. H. Maharana Sahib was also pleased to grant me an interview. He is at present Maharaj-Pramukh of all-Rajasthan. Nepal Royal family is a branch of the Udaipur House.

On the 18th I visited Doongarpur and saw the ruler Maharawal Sahib. The journey proved very tiresome and troublesome. A bridge was washed away. Car could not pass it, in a truck and a military car we finished the trip. Puncture further delayed when returning.

On the 20th morning I reached Bharatpur, travelling twenty four hours and twice changing trains. Only about six hours I stopped here. I could meet several local leaders. In the afternoon I returned Vrindaban.

On the 22nd I once again left. On the 23rd morning, in just about one hour, I could address a small meeting at Allahabad. Students kindly arranged it. At noon I reached Mirzapur. In the afternoon I was taken out in a procession with the student leaders. Later I addressed the huge gathering. The Hon. Janab Rafi Ahmad, Kidwai Sahib, a minister of Delhi government, inaugurated but I was the chief speaker. I was pleased to see that the audience was fully responding to my views.

On the 24th I spoke on my life for only half an hour. The speaker of the evening was Babu Gobind Sahai, a parliamentary secretary of the U. P. government. He spoke for two hours. But a section of the audience, RSS workers disturbed his talk and for half an hour there was confusion.

Taking train on 26th I came direct to my Summer home at Rajpur in the Himalayas. It took me again twenty four hours by train to reach my destination. Month came to end here.

Correspondence : Swami Sivananda of Ananda Kutir, Rishikesh, kindly writes to me:

'*Salutations and prostrations...*

The One order works through us all... God in one... Truth in one... Unity is the door that leads to this truth. And that unity should be established in every human heart... And, there is the example of your own life–a life devoted unceasingly to bring about this unity... May God bless you with health, long life.'

Many thanks for this overwhelming kindness, moral support and spiritual cooperation.

Honorable Babu Sri Prakasa Sahib, the Governor of the province of Assam wrote to me:

My dear Raja Sahib,

I am most grateful to you for your affectionate felicitations and good wishes on my having escaped... The pilot lost his way... Beyond an initial shaking, not much harm was done.... I am sorry they have done nothing yet for your property. I admire you greatly for your enthusiasm in continuing your good work.

I am very thankful for thus kindly answering my communication. His Excellency feels sorry that my government did not restore my property back to me!

My Story of October : It is neither long nor exciting. On the 5th of October 1949 I returned Vrindaban from Rajpur and I plunged into my routine work of my headquarters.

On the 7th I visited Mursan. It was the birth day of my cousin Kunwar Swami Hari Krishna Singh. On the 12th I left Vrindaban by bus. At Agra our Court of Wards manager received me and gave me a lunch. In the afternoon Captain N. S. Chauhan gave a tea party. I could meet here several officers and congress workers. It was a pleasure to visit Seth Achal Singh at his home.

Next morning I changed train at Lucknow and arrived at Gonda. In the afternoon I reached Balrampur by a car. It was a surprise to see the illuminated gates and the big pandal of the great gathering. I stayed at the Maharaja guest house.

On the 14th October I spoke for half an hour at the Religious meeting where numerous priests, pastors and holy personalities were present. Maharaja left the meeting as soon as I concluded my talk. Goswami Bindu Ji was very kind to me personally. Many kind friends called on me.

On the 15th I arrived at Lucknow and stayed with my nephew at 9 Butler Road. He and Chowdhari Sahib made as usual, my stay very comfortable. On the 16th I attended the meeting of landlords. But they did not ask me to speak. At night at Kanpur I had a quarrel with a fellow passenger. He had usurped my seat. But when he found my identity he profusely apologized. He thought, I was a musalman. My beard often makes one think so. Such experiences prove to what extent prejudice has gone deep into the Hindu mind against Islam!

On the 24th October I left once again. In the early morning I got off the train at Bhatinda. At about 10 a.m. I reached Abohar. Many friends welcomed me. In the evening there was a large public meeting.

It was a four day intensive tour programme. My friends provided a jeep, at times two jeeps were there. I lectured at Jhumainwali, Fazilka, Khui Khera, Rup Nagar, Panchkoshi, Kular and Sangaria. Village folk showed great enthusiasm. At Fazilka which is a nice little town gathering was quite large. They showered flowers at places and presented purses. At Sangaria,

Swami Keshavanand Ji has built up a museum which can proudly adorn a large European city. I have never seen such a collection in any high school any where and here at Sangaria it is just a Jat high school. They have recently dropped the name 'Jat' following the new official policy. I must thank here Ch. Tegram who kindly invited me and made the fine arrangements of my tour. He is the editor of weekly 'Deepak'.

On the 29th October I arrived at Delhi. Many kind friends took the trouble to receive me at the railway station. I put up with R. S. Lachhman Prasad Sufi Sahib. He publishes famous magazine Mastana Jogi. In the afternoon I spoke at Gandhi Ground. At night Mr. Advani gave a dinner party to introduce me to some of his friends.

On the 30th I received visitors and I visited some friends. A friend gave afternoon tea. On the 31st I arrived back Vrindaban. Here ended the month.

Correspondence : I have received many letters, some important letter, as usual, during this month. But this time I consider it necessary to publish my two letters which, I wrote, because I never got their answer.

To Premier Pandit Nehru

Dated 5th August 1949,

Hon'ble Friend Pandit Jawaharlal ji Nehru, I am shameless enough to approach you once again when I did not receive any answer to my last communications under your signature. The last letter that you signed is dated 7th March 1948. And I have not had an interview with you since 29th May 1947. On the 1st Feb. 1948 I just met you at your residence for a minute.

I enclose our August Hindi Sansar Sangh. You read please atleast my meeting at Calcutta and Lucknow where-in I speak about you. Please do not get annoyed at the words, go to the spirit, reading the last four lines of 'Lucknow'.

Today I am troubling you once more about my plan of Aryan. Now is the time to realize it and settle the question of Kashmir permanently. Now when Afghanistan and Pakistan are having quarrel we should immediately shake hands with Afghanistan and help it to absorb Pathanistan and Baluchistan. In turn Afghanistan, Iran, Nepal and Ceylon will join our Aryan Federation.

If the fanatic Hindus or fanatic Muslims will have a hand in the matter they will ruin our country. I am therefore prepared to command that Rajput, Jat army which shaking hands with Afghanistan will realize Aryan unity.

I honestly believe that it is God given to ask for me and for humanity, there can be nothing better than to do this job right now.

If you and our high command care to hear me speak on this subject for one full hour I shall gladly run to Delhi. On the 9th August I am going on a tour of Bengal. I shall return to Vrindaban on the 27th inst.

Yours sincerely (Sd.)

Note : Copy sent to Afghanistan Ambassador.

To Sardar Patel

Hon. Friend Sardar Vallabhbhai Patel Sahib,

I am obliged to trouble you. I think, blunders are made and the command is slipping away from the Congress. You openly supported 'Services' which are not yours in the true spirit. They have to he purged. If the report is correct you blundered to say publicly that the British made it a condition that the future of the services should be assured! By this declaration you unfortunately made the services more loyal to the British!! Word or no word, workers of freedom will have to purge, including leadership, if things get worse !

With all respect to your age and for all what you did for our common country I honestly believe that you should kindly take advice of honest revolutionaries. There is now every possibility of the extention of the Chinese conditions into India. I am prepared to build a strong military force which will truly help us under worst situation. Give me one hour, full one hour, on the 24th or the 29th instant, please. I just want to explain my view point and plans.

Yours sincerely (Sd.).

I am leaving tomorrow on a tour. I hope to be back on Deevali.

This letter was dated 11th October 1949 and sent to New Delhi from Vrindaban.

Congress President : He is uncrowned State President. So writes the Pandit B. Pattabhi Sitaramayya, President of All India Congress:

Dear Raja Saheb,

Many thanks for your kind letter. I do not know why you are so unkind as to say that ' I do not now readily recognize my friends.'

I always recognize them and remember them.

I have received your paper 'World Federation' and have gone through it with interest and profit.

I hope you are keeping good health.

Yours sincerely
(Signed) B. Pattabhi Sitaramayya

I am delighted to receive this certificate. Yes, I call it certificate and more. It is a solemn declaration of our Honourable President that our World Federation is interesting and profitable. Some British dogs howl and call me 'communist.' British net work of their clever and cunning spies is still widespread in our country. Some foolish or simple friends reecho the enemy allegations. But I care little for the enemy mischief. I continue to work hard for our federated Aryan in Federated World State.

Divine Life Society : Rev. Swami Sivanand ji, Founder of the Society, with its headquarters at Rishikesh in the Himalayas, writes :

Beloved Atman (soul),

Salutations and adorations... I am glad that there is to be another session of the World Religions' Congress next year. I have sent my humble contribution. I am sure, God will crown your efforts in this regard with sanguine success. Religion ought to be the basis of society. God should be the foundation of society. Only then will there be peace, prosperity and happiness... The task is no easy one, but (let me quote your own words) 'God can open a door in a wall...' Let us have this faith... That is the only road to success. May God bless you ! Thy own Self.

(Sd.) Sivananda

I thankfully received twenty five rupees and a set of his latest publications. These are my friends, men like him encourage me and keep me at the helm of my God given Mission. This earth has to be turned into Heaven. All kinds of man made miseries must disappear. A joint family of all the human race has to be created. We will produce to satisfy all the needs of all mankind.

On the 9th December, I left in the afternoon. I stopped at Mursan. My nephew, Raja Bahadur Kishori Raman Singh had come with his relations and retinue to receive me at the station. On an elephant I went with him to the fort. He gave me very rich feast. After a sojourn of four hours I left by the night train. Next morning I arrived at Farrukhabad. Congress leader Babu Kalicharan Tandon, Mr. Roy, Manager, Central Bank, Pandit Seetaram Shukla of Basti with their friends received me and garlanded me. Congress volunteers saluted me and led me to the waiting car. I was taken to the house of Seth Gopinath Parmanand Bagla, here I stayed. Taking tea I proceeded to the Congress subject committee. I took a seat on the dias. Ministers and the leaders were here. Our premier Pandit G.B. Pant came and sat down just before me. We talked. I told him that peasants of Meerut were bitter against him. They resented official restriction on the movement of native sugar. Prices had gone down hundred per cent and the village folk had lost heavily. The same day Congress passed a resolution and later the restrictions were removed.

I also brought to the notice of the president that the Kashi Raj gave free education, there were no fees charged of any kind, what about them now, after the merger. Babu Sampurnanand, Minister of Education, assured me that proper care will be taken. In the afternoon, I attended the open session. I went up the high platform. I found only one place vacant by the side of Pandit Jawaharlal Nehru. I took seat beside him. I said :'You seem to have forgotton me, Pandit ji?' He said :'How could I forget you.' (not in English but in Hindustani we spoke) I told him, how Sardar Daleep Singh, a president of the Ghadar Party of California was kept in prison as a communist by the Punjab Government, I had moved in the matter but I had not received any official news. He just nodded. People said that over forty thousand persons were there at the meeting.

Next day on the 11th December in the afternoon, I could speak at the open session of our Congress. I said that 'grow more food' was no solution to our lack of food. We should open up empty East Africa to our hundred million population. British Commonwealth is the only hindrance. United Nations will be failing in their duty if they do not find channels for their growing population of Germany, Italy, Japan, China and India.

My friends detained me one day more. Next day a number of leading citizens of Farrukhabad visited me and heard my plan of work in detail. In the evening I opened the Gandhi Night School and gave a talk, later spoke at the Islamia Arabic school. Friends saw me off at the station. I thank them and my hosts. I arrived at Vrindaban on the 13th December.

On the 14th December I spoke to our college students and left for Rajpur, where I arrived early next morning. My daughter, driving herself, took me to Dehradun in her car. We visited our friends, including of course, H. H. Rani Sahiba of Kalsia.

On the 17th my daughter drove me to Narsan. Here a High School is run in my name. They were holding their annual function. I presided and spoke at length at today's meeting. On the 18th I spoke once again and left for Muzaffarpur in Bihar, via Lucknow. Thakur Phoolsingh, Congress General Secretary of U. P. happened to be in the same bogie, we talked long on the present situation. At Lucknow I took lunch with Sardar Shamsher Singh and Chowdhari Mujtaba Hussain and met my sister.

In the morning of the 20th I reached Muzaffarpur. Students gave me very warm welcome. Shouts of 'Victory' resounded through the air. I was taken to a beautiful garden of a Marwari Seth, Mr. Kapur gave lunch and dinner. Meeting was grand though an opposing students party tried to disturb it. Police turned them out. The hall was overcrowded and people were standing out, hearing me through loudspeakers. As soon as I finished half of the audience left. I was sorry. I was simply inaugurating the meeting. It continued but more people went away. Next day I did not speak but I attended the meeting. I should also mention that I put a wreath at the memorial of Babu Khudiram Bose.

On the 22nd I left very early. Crossing the Ganga by a steamer I reached Patna. I stayed with Mr. Amritnath Verma and visited my friend Hon'ble Dr. Syed Mahmud. I spoke to a few friends who came to meet me. This news was published in the Indian Nation. On the 23rd I reached Gaya. I stayed with Maharaja Sahib of Tikari. Congress president of Gaya visited me. I paid respect at Bauddha Gaya. And I left, arriving back at Vrindaban on the 25th December. We celebrated Christmas and sweets were distributed. Center was illuminated.

On the 28th I spoke at a Jat conference at Gwalior. They gave me a room in the best hotel but I passed night in the train. I thank Jat leaders.

Correspondence : Hon'ble Minister, Rafi Ahmad Kidwai writes :

My dear Raja Mahendra Pratap,

I have received your letter... I will look into the matter. Sometimes back the dispatch of post to communist occupied area was stopped. I will see if we can dispatch it now. I am sending your Urdu letter to Jawaharlal Ji for such action as he thinks advisable.

Your sincerely
Rafi Ahmad Kidwai

He is the Minister for Communications. He is kind enough to attend to every little detail connected with his department. He is energetic and far seeing. We admire him.

Pandit Binodanand Jha, Minister of Local-self Government and Medical, Bihar, wrote from Patna : 'I have been invited by the District Congress Committee, Gaya, to attend a conference... which is going to be addressed by your goodself... it will not be possible for me to attend the conference. The Dist. Congress Committee being informed of my inability to attend the conference, has asked me to request you to agree to the conference being held either on the 21st of 22nd January 50. I do not know how far the changed dates will suit you but shall be grateful if you favour the President Dist. Congress Committee, Gaya with your reaction to the proposed change and send me a copy of the same. With respects...' I have been asked to inaugurate the conference. I am thankful. God willing I shall reach in time.

Year 1950

The first day of the first month of this new year saw me rolling down South. I left my Bombay Mail. I met Thakur Madan Singh and later Janab Shri Sahib, Muslim Guru of Gwalior, in the train. Late at night I alighted at Itarsi. In the early morning I took another train. At noon on the 2nd January 1950 I arrived at Jubbalpur. Many friends were there on the platform to receive me. I was profusely garlanded and taken by a grand car to the official rest house.

At night there was held a very large meeting. I presided and I spoke at length. Maulana Abul Wafa Sahib delivered a long speech. The function was in honour of the birth day of Prophet Mohammed.

I was detained next day. On the 3rd a public meeting was held only to hear me. And I again presided and spoke at the Seerat meeting of the Jamiat Ulema. It was nearing midnight. I had to tell the audience that a bit of selfishness too made me shorten my talk as I was leaving very early morning. I slept hardly four hours that night. My hosts took the trouble to see me off.

H. H. Nawab Sahib of Bhopal had sent his car to the station. I was taken to the palace. But H. H. was staying at a lake side villa over twenty miles from Bhopal. On the 5th of January I went by car and took lunch with H. H. and Her Highness at their beautiful resort. Beautiful lake, wooded hills and well laid out garden around fine villas and official quarters made a picture of a fairy tale.

On the 6th January I spoke to the professors of the Government College, Bhopal. And I left. In the morning of the 7th I arrived back Vrindaban and as our school opened I conducted the prayer.

On the 19th January I left Vrindaban. Next day at Banaras I was glad to meet Mr. Seth, President of U. P. Students Congress. He came to see me with his secretary. In the evening, I arrived Gaya. Congress president and secretary with Jamiat friends came to receive me.

On the 21st Jan., I was taken with Bihar Minister, Pandit Jha to Sherghati, where I inaugurated the political conference. I was the main speaker, I took more time than any one else. Hon. Minister presented his official views. In the evening Jamiat Ulema arranged for me a public meeting at Gaya. I spoke here for one hour and twenty minutes. Next day very early I left. Friends kindly saw me off.

It was a long journey from East to West. I found some friends in the train. I changed trains at Delhi and in about twenty seven hours I arrived Rohtak. I stayed with Ch. Shri Chand. I was asked to preside at the huge meeting held to commemorate the birth day of Sir Chhoturam. I delivered my harangue. Same evening I left and next morning on the 24th I returned Vrindaban.

On the 31st January I again left. Midnight of this last day of the first month saw me changing trains at Rewari. Beyond Delhi, on the way to Hisaar in Punjab. Such is my life, a rolling stone which gathers no moss, vet rolls on the stream of time, playing its role!

My February Story : This month is mostly passed in two different tours. The first tour lasted for sixteen days. I was on tour from the 31st January to the 16th February 1950. I was all these days in Punjab. The second tour was of only seven days, from the 20th to the 27th of this month. So that, I was only for six days at my headquarters during the second month of this year.

First of February saw me at Hissar. I was a guest of Rao Surajmal and Sardar Mahinder Singh Thind joined us. My private secretary Kunwar Panch Bahadur Singh B.A. accompanied me. My Nepali Gorkha servant Mr. Kaji Bahabur was also with me as usual. Soon after breakfast we started. We went by car to the village of Gangan-Kheri. We spoke. The gathering was large. Second day we went to Bapaura. This was a village of Rajputs. They gave us lunch. We spoke. On the third I addressed the staff and the students of the Jat High School, Hissar. My views were attentively listened.

On the 4th I went to Bhiwani. I raised the flag and said a few words. I lectured before the staff and students of the Vaish College. Enthusiasm prevailed. Questions were put and I answered. Later I could express my views for a few minutes at the Labour Conference. A Punjab State Minister also spoke. I caught bus, reached Rohtak, borrowed a car and arrived at Sonepat and took train. It was passed midnight when we arrived at Karnal. We were the guests of Ch. Dharam Singh, advocate.

On the 5th Feb., I went with our host and Sardar Thind to Jeysinghpura. We addressed the huge meeting there. Friends presented over fifteen hundred rupees which I passed on to the party which has arranged this tour. At night one Mr. Agarwal, a graduate of our college, gave us dinner.

Next day we left very early by train. At Ambala we hired car and went to Shahzadpur. A huge meeting was held. I spoke at length. At night we returned to Karnal.

On the 7th we went by car to Kaeth. We addressed there a large meeting. I, as usual, presided. We spoke. Friends presented over twelve hundred rupees which I handed to the conveners.

On the 8th we went to Patiala. Raja Narpal Singh and friends received us. No meeting could be held as the meetings had to be entirely stopped, due to some local tention. I expressed my views to the reporters at our Press Conference. Sardar Gurbachan Singh took us to Nabha, gave us fine dinner and got us into train. It was raining hard.

On the 9th, changing train at Ludhiana we reached Talwandi. By bus went to Zira. By horse cart we arrived at our destination. It was bitter cold. Fog was hanging low, visibility was narrow. Far from habitation, under a canopy, we held meeting. Sardar Hazara Singh gave us feast.

On the 10th morning we reached Jallandhar. We were tired. having been in train all night. But we did not take rest. We hired a car and went to Adampur. We delivered our harangues. A local doctor gave us tea.

On the 11th I addressed the students of the Jallandhar Khalsa College. We went to Urmur and spoke to the large gathering there. At night Capt. Bhandari gave a feast.

On the 12th we went to Amritsar and proceeded to Gurdwara Budha Baba. I presided and spoke. The pilgrims made the crowd. Next morning we went to Pathankot by train. There we hired a car and went up into Himalayas. We took rest at Palampur beyond Kangra.

On the 14th we addressed a large meeting at Maranda. And stayed this night with Ch. Randayal Singh. He gave a dinner party. Next day I spoke to the staff and students of the Khalsa College, Amritsar. It is the greatest institution of the Sikhs. Principal Sardar Jodh Singh is my old friend.

On the 16th I returned to Vrindaban. We were received by the enthusiast public of Manhar village. They gave us lunch and heard with pleasure our views. We went on to Amba. Here was at the time some kind of festival and a public market was held. We spoke. We stayed there for the night. Next day we proceeded to Sukhpura. It was a lonely well built house. But the gathering was pretty large and people were very enthuslastic about the Rajput cause. Hospitality was unexpectedly rich.

On the 25th Feb. we spoke at the meeting of Kherala. Rao Sahib of the place received us. Dinner was given at Rajakator, home of Thakur Ramdayal Singh. Next Morning we returned to Gwalior. I stayed for the day at the Rajput Boarding House. I spoke at the College, at Gian Mandir and at the public meeting.

I returned to Vrindaban on the 27th and spoke at two meetings, one was the meeting of the cooperatives and the other was that of Swami Chakrapani Ji.

March Story : The story of tours during this month is short. But the story of our Congress session is very long. For lack of space I shall have to relate it briefly.

On the 2nd March I left. On the 3rd March I was taken out in a big procession at Samalkha, in Karnal district. Twenty two oxen were used to pull my cart. Two ex-M. L. A., or former members of Panjab Parliament and Sardar Thind was there too. Indian band was playing, flowers were raining and volunteers were marching in front. A large crowd followed.

I was asked to preside over and deliver my presidential address. The meeting was grand. I spoke long on the need of overhauling Congress and on reforming our society.

Next day Raja Narpal Singh of Patiala presided over. I just sat for a little while and took leave. It was past midnight when I could lay my head on my pillow, in my bed room, at Vrindaban, travelling via Delhi and Mathura.

On the 10th March I left Vrindaban. At New Delhi I stayed with Commodore Narendra. His sister-in-law or the daughter of my late brother-in-law, Maharaja Ranbir Singh was to be married here next day. There were many guests that evening. Next day on the 11th March simple marriage ceremony was performed according to Sikh rites. In the evening I took the light railway and reached Sona-Arjunpur in early morning. Here today on the 12th March I presided at a large meeting and spoke at length. Next day, Rao Krishnpal Singh presided but I again delivered a long speech. I reached back Vrindaban in the afternoon of the 14th March.

So far as my tours are concerned the only other outing was made on the 27th March. I was out for two nights. I went by car to our villages. Here we own eight large and four small villages. Our estate in under government management. They just give us allowances. They have recently given us one thousand acres of land for farming. This I mean to give for a colony of coworkers. I, my daughter and my two grand children, still little kids, performed formally the ceremony of starting Prem Vihar.

My April Story : On the 2nd April I left by car for Saantruk, a village on Bharatpur frontier. I was called by a hermits' organization but I spoke on politics to the village folk of the warrior caste. One of them confidentially told me that two hundred fifty youths were ready to lay down their lives at my bidding. With this material one can surely expect a sure victory.

On the 4th I left by car to Karoli State. I was called by the greatly agitated and disturbed peasantry. A serious incident had occurred. Twenty four government servants including a local magistrate and a police officer were killed. I went to investigate on behalf of the harassed people. They were crying, they were bowing low to the ground, they related their stories of torture. It was already late in the afternoon. I went with my friends to the village where all that happened, taking leave of the people on the main road. Government officials were courteous and gave me straight answers to my straight questions. The people of twelve villages had run away for safety rearing revenge. They lost thus most of their property. Arrests were being made and confessions were taken.

I sent wires to the Rajasthan Premier and Sardar Patel and Congress and Parliament presidents. I said, people had suffered much, strongly suggest general amnesty.

On the 5th of April left for Jind. My daughter left for Rajpur. On the 6th I addressed a large gathering at Jat High School. Premier of Patiala Union presided over, Captain Ranjit Singh, a Minister of Panjab, and Rao Suraj Mal Bahadur M.L.A. also spoke. School got about ten thousand rupees in donations. In the afternoon a tea party was arranged. Here too I said a few words. The same night I left after dinner.

It was my third night when I could not sleep till. Returned from Karoli tour at 2 a.m. and held prayer meeting of our school boys at 7 a.m., I arrived at Jind after midnight and went to bed at 1.30 a.m. and in the morning I had to receive visitors. This night I had to change twice, once at Jakhal at about 1 a.m. and then next at 5 a.m. at Hissar.

At Dadri I took lunch and my friends took me to Birhi School. I spoke to the boys. On my return trip. I had to ride a camel as the car got out of order. I visited at night Dalmia Cement Factory.

Fourth night I passed sitting or writing letters at Rewari railway station. There was no train.

On the 8th April at about 11 a.m. I got into the through beige. I was alone in my first class compartment. I slept well this day. Next day I reached Jodhpur. Kunwar Rup Singh drove me to Colonel Mohan Singh's residence. Three local Rajput leaders came at lunch. We held long talks.

On the 10th April I was received by H. H. Maharaja Sahib of Jodhpur at his palace. He was quite out spoken and expressed his concern at the troubles spreading in the country. He said, he was ready to do his share as a citizen. He also said that in the interest of Rajasthan Jat and Rajput unity was urgently needed.

I must say here a word for the palace. It is very high, on a high hill. It has beautiful stone work and beautiful Indian art paintings. In the afternoon I spoke to the Rajput Sabha. In the evening I lectured to the students of Rajput High School. The same night I left.

On the 11th, in the morning, I reached Bikaner. A large crowd had come to the station to welcome me. The former Minister, Chowdhari Khialiram had kindly arranged this reception with the help of his numerous friends. Students gathered to hear me. Mr. Mathur arranged a press conference. I paid a visit to H. H. Mahant ji. In the evening I addressed a public meeting. The enthusiasm of the people was electrifying the atmosphere. The same night, after dinner with Advocate Achariya, I left.

At noon on the 12th I arrived at Bhatinda. Friends had come to receive me. Congress workers visited me and gave a tea party. Another tea party was also given by Sardar Gurdev Singh Ramana.

Same evening I was taken to Dam Dama Sahib by a jeep. Raja Narpal Singh of Patiala had already arrived. The famous Sikh leader Master Tara Singh visited me and we talked together for over two hours. In the afternoon I addressed a public meeting. I also of course visited the temple and went round the thak.

In the evening I returned to Bhatinda and took train. On the 14th noon I arrived back Mathura. Staying only seven hours at Vrindaban I left for Datia.

On the 15th I addressed a public meeting at Datia. Then I was taken to Jhansi. On the 17th I visited Kumbrar, paid a visit to the famous poet Mr. Maithli Sharan Gupta and addressed a public meeting at Jhansi. On the 18th I returned to Vrindaban. On the 20th I addressed our College boys and visited Mursan.

On the 22nd I reached once again Jodhpur. This afternoon I could meet several Maharajas and the premier of Rajasthan. I was also introduced to Mr. Menon of the State ministry. It was the marriage of the princess of Jodhpur with the Prince of Baroda. As I was talking with Maharaja of Patiala, a young man came and greeted me. He told me that I had met him. Where ? At his office at Gwalior. Now I discovered that he was the Ruler of Gwalior State! He gave such a surprise that I have been talking about it to many friends. I could meet H. H. Nawab Sahib of Bhopal and express my views on the present confused situation.

On the 10th May we celebrated the Revolution Day. It was on this day that the so-called "sepoy mutiny" broke out against the British in 1857. Actually it was a revolt against the British Occupation. I reviewed our history. The same afternoon I left. I could hardly sleep that night. In the morning I reached Rajpur, where is our summer home.

On the 12th May, we went to Mussoorie to attend the Christian marriage ceremony of Mr. Misrilal Bhatnagar, held there at a Church. Tea party followed, here I spoke on the place of religion in life. Next day we remained at Mussoorie. My daughter wants to buy a house at this hill station. I accompanied her to see several vacant houses for sale. Prices have gone down.

On the 14th we retuned Rajpur. I am living here quietly. Now and then my daughter takes me to Dehradun in her car, driving herself excellently. We go to meet our several relations living there in their villas. We visit some friends. H. H. Maharani Kalsia, H. H. Mother queen of Patiala, H. H. Maharani Jind, Rani of Sahanpur, Prince Mhd. Musa of Afghanistan, Maharani Tikari, are all living here round about. Some times we receive our friends too. Most of my time is passed in writing.

My June Story : First of June saw me at my summer home of Rajpur. Today this morning of the 29th June meets me in her car, so that all this touring was during these places and not exactly for my Mission work, though I tried to utilize my visits to friends for a bit of propaganda when possible. On the 4th at the Savoy Hotel, Mussoorie. Often during this month my daughter was taking me down to Dehradun. Sunday evening, we held our weekly prayer meeting. But only our household members attended. It was a little fine congregation and I delivered my Sermon. I explained religion at length.

The daily routine work at Rajpur was reading news-papers and attending to my correspondence. My private secretary, Kunwar Panch Bahadur Singh B. A., wrote for me some letters as dictated by me.

Friends visited me. It was a surprise to receive the visit of Acharya Jugal Kishore Sahib, a prominent Congress leader, on the morning of the 10th of June. At the same time came in H. H. young Raja of Kalsia with Doctor. Introducing the doctor to Acharya ji, I told him that Acharya ji blessed my rebellion against the present policy of our congress and the government. Acharya ji atonce remarked, 'Yes, but it must be nonviolent.' But the government is never nonviolent. It keeps the loaded gun all the time and fires it at random against the unarmed workers and students !

The same evening, on the 10th of June began my ten days tour. At the railway station I met another surprise. The Speaker of our Parliament, Pandit Mavalankar Sahib was there, travelling by the same train to Delhi. He asked me to sit a while with him. We talked about the present situation. We all want reform. The present state of affairs can not pull on long.

Travelling that whole night and the next whole day, I arrived at about 9 p.m. at Ratlam. Once it was the capital of the State of that name. Today it is only a district town of Madhya Bharat. My friends received and took me to the Guest House. I was comfortably lodged. Early in the morning of the 12th June I was taken to the meeting of the workers of the Rajput Sewa Sangh. Here I spoke for one hour and forty five minutes. I was also answering their some questions. In the afternoon I had to speak once again for the same length of time.

After those two long talks I was under the impression that the workers had enough from me but no, they asked me once more to speak for them on the morning of the 13th June. This evening they arranged a public meeting in the centre of the town. Several thousand persons must have heard me. The loud speaker was carrying my voice all round.

At about 2 p.m. on the 14th June I left Ratlam. Friends came, garlanded me, brought fruits and presented a purse. If our Rajput brethren, our fighters, back up my movement, it would not be long when we should be in control of Delhi, in the interest of our entire nation and humanity.

Travelling back, passing Mathura and Delhi once again, I went to Nabha in Panjab. It took me twenty six hours on this journey. I put up with Sardar Shivdeo Singh Sahib. Next day we went to Dhanaula to speak at a meeting. It was very hot but it was our duty and we did it. Rao Surajmal and Sardar Mahinder Singh Thind went too. The same night I took train and arrived Vrindaban, at noon on the 17th June.

On the 18th June I attended our College meeting at Prem Nagar. The Magistrate of Mathura, as a government representative, also attended our meeting. Our college is now a government aided institution. In the evening we held a prayer meeting at our Vrindaban Center of the Religion of Love. After that I left for Rajpur.

I am thankful to all the workers of the Rajput Sewa Sangh. I thank here also the supporters of the Zamindara League of Panjab. They made arrangements for my talk at Dhanaula in PEPSU.

Correspondence : H.M. King Amanullah Khan wrote to me. I am very glad to receive once again a direct communication from His Majesty, the former king of Afghanistan, now residing at Rome, Italy. His address is 14-16 via Orazio. He writes in Persian, (translation) :

Dear friend Janab Raja Sahib,

Your letter of the 23rd May is received. I am very glad to hear that you are hail and hearty. Really, much time passed since I wrote to you last. I got your circular. I thank you for it. All of us are keeping good health, thank God. I wish you and your family good health and pray to God for your success.

(Signature) Amanullah

He is the third monarch of Afghanistan who lost his throne for pro-Russian and anti-British stand, in the true interest of the independence of Afghanistan. On one hand he received hearty welcome from the British government in India and in London and secretly the British agents spent millions to create chaos in his country. All kinds of underground means were employed to make people rise in rebellion against him. I am an eye witness of the tragedy. I also suffered due to his sufferings. And still I am suffering and still I am fighting but I hope that now complete success is not far off !!

H.E. Prince Mhd. Shah Wali Khan, the Ambassador of Afghanistan in London, England. His letter is dated 12th June. It came quick by air. He kindly writes in Persian (translation) :

Very dear precious friend, Janab Raja Sahib,...

I express my thankfulness for kind sentiment that you have for me and my dear country. Believe me, I do not simply wish well of my country but of all humanity. And I wish that my country will work together with the lands of the East. If the Eastern Peoples will join their hands together there will remain no difficulty which they will not be able to solve. I have always been for the unity of the East and for the happiness of all mankind.' Then His Excellency goes on to quote the famous couplet of poet Saadi of Shiraz, Persia, that all men are just parts of one body and if one part or one man suffers the rest of the body feels pain ! In the end he says :'I appreciate your valuable thoughts and I again thank you for your fine sentiment which you have for my country, Afghanistan.

Your friend

Shahwali (Signed)

I am surely proud of my such friends for ever. One can rely on them under all circumstances. He is real uncle of H. M. King Zahir Shah, the Ruler.

H.E. Afghan Ambassador at Moscow, Sardar Sultan Ahmad Khan Sahib, kindly writes in English :

My dear and very honourable Friend,

I have received your esteemed letter dated 18th May, 1950, and No. 4 and No. 5 of your publication 'World Federation' for which I thank you.

I am sending you enclosed a check of the Bank for Foreign Trade of USSR No. 052625, dated 13th June, 1950, on the sum of $ 20 (twenty American dollars), for your subscription.

Yours very sincerely
(Signed) S. Ahamad

It is far more valuable than the money mentioned in the cheque. Kindness and hearty good wishes which it carries are very precious indeed. They come from the capital of our mighty neighbour, Red Russia and they are sent by the Royal Representative of Muslim Afghanistan. Armed with such powerful cooperation we can settle all our accounts with the British trained brethren in the two divided parts of India and realize Aryan-Iran to Assam.

My July Story : First July found me at the Savoy Hotel Mussoorie. My daughter was with me. We occupied two comfortable rooms at this fashionable hotel of the beautiful hill station. The day, however, ended with a disappointment, I was under the impression that when Pandit Pandey ji, founder of the famous Manobharti school, was arranging for me a meeting that afternoon at the Prince Hotel, it would be a grand affair but it turned out a very sham thing. No proper advertisement was made. The man who announced the meeting in Hindi mispronounced the name of the Prince Hotel. Many people were eager to hear me but they ran here and there and could not find the place. Only about a dozen persons could hear my views that afternoon.

On the 2nd July we left Mussoorie and drove straight to Dehradun. Here this day, the Bharti Club organized a very fine meeting of the intellectuals. H. H. Mahant Sahib, the head of the famous Darbar Sahib or Sikh Temple, presided. I spoke for about an hour. My views were very well received indeed. A rich tea party followed. The whole month I remained here. On the 29th July I hope to leave on a tour, going as far as Patna and visiting Banaras and some other places.

Correspondence : Pandit G. V. Mavalankar, the Honourable Speaker writes :

Dear Raja Sahib,

I got your paper with your statement about lawyers and others. I regret I am unable to accept the wholesale attack on the class. I myself once belonged to this class, and there are many others in our public life. Though there are many lawyers who act with a purely mercenary motive and do not care for equity and morality, it does not follow, therefore, that the whole class deserves the condemnation. It depends essentially on the man. Training and practice of law fits us better for social service, if one practices the same keeping in mind, as the uppermost arm for the good of society. I am afraid you may not agree with me; but this is what I believe.

The real point is that our entire social level has gone down, so far as morals and fellow-feeling are concerned, it is of no use. Therefore, picking out any particular class as an unmixed evil we must see as to how best we can raise the level and the only remedy that I think open to each one is to conduct himself with a high standard of morals, justice and equity, irrespective of what others do. We must act with faith and strength. I need not add more.

With regards,

Yours sincerely
(Signed) G. V. Mavalankar

I have copied here the full letter. I have great regard for the Honorable friend. But it is not the question of his personality or my regard for him. I condemn that system which does not base justice on truth and facts but on the ability of the lawyers to argue a case. Laws have become so numerous and confusing that only the best brains are able to remember them and win. And they charge exorbitant sums, making it impossible for poor people to get the services of the best lawyers. It is not Justice. This machinery of doing injustice must be smashed and our lawyers should be employed in some productive service.

My tour of July-August : I left, my berth came reserved from Delhi. I got comfortable accommodation at Hathras junction. Travelling that whole night and the next whole day I arrived at Patna at about 6.30 p.m. My friends came to receive and took me to the official residence of Babu Gokarn Nath Sinha, Director of Public Instructions, where I stayed.

It was all arranged. Babu Brinda Prasad Sinha took me to a library and club of the Clerks and officials of the Provincial Secretariat. I spoke on my five points programme. My audience was very intelligent and they followed my line of thought very attentively. Some questions were asked which I answered at length.

Next day a Kayasth family gave me lunch at Saidpura, Khagaul. In the afternoon I addressed the students of the Industrial School for Harijans and the Theosophists at the Theosophical Society.

On the 1st of August 1950 was held a semi official meeting of the Patna University. My host, the acting Vice Chancellor presided over. The large spacious hall was thickly crowded. I explained my plan and asked the students to contribute their share in making it successful. It pleased me to see that my talk was well received.

Later I proceeded to Gandhi Sarovar Library and delivered a general lecture. Nawab Syed Mohammad Mahdi M. L. C. presided over.

Next day, I spoke in the morning at an engineer's club and left Patna at noon. In the afternoon I arrived at Benaras. Friends saw me off and friends received. I was taken by car to Seva Upvan on the river Ganga. Here is a palatial house of my old friend, late Babu Shiva Prasad Gupta. My host Babu Bhupendra Kumar made me comfortable. We took dinner together and talked of old things.

In the afternoon on the 3rd of August I visited students head-quarters and spoke at a public meeting in the Town Hall ground. Professor Radheshiam Sharma, the rebel leader of the Assembly also gave a talk. Next day I took breakfast with the leader of the Socialist Party, Babu Jai Prakash Narain and exchanged views with him. Then I rushed to the Arya Orphanage and received address and spoke at length on the duty of the youths. A group photograph was here taken. In the afternoon heavy rain stopped our public meeting at the Hindu University. I addressed the students of Udai Pratap College. It can not be properly described, Rajput enthusiasm was bubbling out. I gave more time to the caste consciousness in the country. And I said, we need not be afraid of it. We need only utilize every caste for common good. Fighting material can best keep peace.

On the 6th I arrived at Lucknow and stayed with Sardar Shamsher Singh, as usual. Chowdhari Mujtaba Hussain lives here too. There was no programme of propaganda. On the morning of the 9th August I arrived at Etawah. Kunwar Panch Bahadur Singh and his friends received me. I spoke at the Islamia College. I stayed with Kunwar Sahib.

On the 10th I was taken out, fifteen miles or more, in a jeep to the village of Ram Sunder. Here I spoke at the local school. Reception was very hearty. Father-in-law of our Kunwar Sahib gave lunch and presented a purse. Thence we hurried to the site of Pratap Nagar. Here was a nice gathering of the village folk. I spoke and put up the engraved stone of Pratap Nagar by the road side. Later we proceeded to the village of Dharwar. Young Pandit Paliwal gave us here royal tea. Heavy rain marooned us for a time. Riding a horse, with many people following on foot, we came to the metalled road where the car of Sethani Shanti Devi M. L. C. was waiting for me. At half past eleven at night we reached Jaswant Nagar. Rich dinner was served. Upto half past twelve, midnight, I was preaching in a drawing room company.

In the well built and well furnished guest house of Sethani Sahiba I went to bed. Early next morning my hostess came and gave us tea. And I caught train before seven in the morning. Congress leader Seth Achal Singh was in the train. We talked. Captain Chauhan kindly came to the Agra Station. I took lunch with him. By a direct bus I arrived back at Vrindaban in the evening of the 11th August.

From the 18th of August to the 28th of that month I stayed at Vrindaban attending to my routine work. I prepared our

September number. I finished the Hindi paper of the 1st of September. I wrote or dictated lot of letters. I received visitors. And I also attended to our School and College problems. Now a boy will run up to me, now a couple of students would represent their case, why don't they go to their headmaster, you better first go to your principal, well, you need not pay any fees. Now I would sign the cheques as the Governor.

On the 30th August I went to the village of Majhoi on horse back. I ordered that the house there must be fully repaired. I explained my plan to the village folk. 'You join our Religion for Love and cultivate the land jointly. You immediately own one thousand acres of our land. After defraying all your expenses you would need, give one fourth of the net income to me and our family. One fourth will be paid as bonus and the half will be spent in improving the colony.' They did not like the idea of collective farming. They were prepared to give cash if I would let them have separately ten, twenty or thirty acres. As I was returning from Majhoi on the 31st of August rich Rajput Thakur of Shahzadpur stopped me and insisted that I must be his guest that night. He gave a feast. We talked long on my plan.

On the 1st of September I lunched at Ujhani and dined at Jatwari. In both these places I spoke long on our Prem Vihar. On the 2nd of September I returned by car to Vrindaban.

On the 7th September I went to Bisawar. Our car got out of order. By bus we reached the bus stop near to our destination. I was nearly two hours late but the students, staff and gentry were all waiting for me. I lectured at length. Great enthusiasm prevailed in the audience.

I hurried, driving in a horse cart I arrived at Sadabad. Here too they were waiting for last two hours. I spoke to the students and the citizens of the town. Nawab gave me elaborate tea. Our car arrived. We left. Visited an Ashram on the way. Now petrol was all finished. It was brought from Mathura. Past midnight I reached Vrindaban. Our friend and coworker Chowdhury Vijay Singh has to be thanked for arranging these two meetings.

On the 15th of September I left. At Delhi I got into a through carriage. In the morning I arrived Hissar. On the 16th and the 17th I spoke long at two different meetings. One was of the Jat Sabha, the other was of the Zamindara League. Several thousand persons were present. Sardar Mahinder Singh Thind and Rao Surajmal have to be thanked for giving me this opportunity to preach.

On the 18th September, evening, travelling by train to Delhi, by bus to Dehradun and there taking taxi, I arrived at our house at Rajpur. I am staying here with my daughter.

Mrs. Hogan of Los Angeles came to tea on the 20th instant, and today came the famous Mr. M. N. Roy and Mrs. Roy and had tea with us. We receive visitors, we visit friends, my daughter takes me in her car, I write letters and I am now finishing this account before 11 at night.

My Story : You like it. I relate it day to day, month to month, it continues. You saw me last at Rajpur, writing quietly at my Summer home. And I announced that 'tomorrow is Eid.'

On the 23rd September 1950, Eid came. I had asked Hafiz Mhd. Akbar Khan Pathan to come all the way from Vrindaban to Rajpur for Eid. He came and he became the Imam of the Eid prayer at our Love Center of Rajpur. I stood behind him. We prayed. Babu Misri Lal Bhatnagar joined us. Later came several friends. God is Great. He is helping me to create a new atmosphere of religious unity in our country.

In the evening of the 25th I left Dehradun. My daughter saw me off. I passed the night in the train. At 6.15 a. m. on the 26th Sept., I arrived at Delhi Junction. Private Secretary of H. E. Minister of Commerce Babu Sri Prakasa greeted me and took me in the Minister's car to his residence. My friend was there. We talked and took tea together. Hon'ble Minister Janab Kidwai also dropped in for a minute.

I went to see H. E. Sardar Najibullah Khan Sahib, Ambassador of Afghanistan. And my friend, Babu Anand Mohan Sahay came from the Government House to see me. He is going to West Indies as Indian Commissioner. I am not glad that he accepted this job. It is, as if, going to Andamans with a crown ! In any case, I wish him happy life.

I returned Vrindaban and plunged into my routine work. Lot to do and to prepare for my 'Digvijai'.

On the 29th Sept., with band playing, I went through the streets of Vrindaban in a long procession. School and College students with a few friends went before me and after me. Youths were shouting slogans : 'Victory to Aryan ! Victory to World Federation! Victory to the Unity of Religions! Success must come to the system of joint family !' We came to Gandhi Park and I addressed the gathering. Photograph was taken. I with my friends visited four temples. In the evening I delivered a sermon at our Center. History was made.

On the 30th September, in the very early morning I left by car. At New Delhi I took lunch with H. E. Sardar Najibullah Khan and Lady Khan Sahiba. Their two young sons were also present. I visited my friend Mr. Gidwani and left for Rohtak. Late at night I reached the house of Ch. Hari Ram Sahib, Advocate.

My Story of October : On the 1st of October 1950 I presided at the big meeting of Bharat Tek. It was the meeting to bring together all the parties. It was along my line of thinking. I was very glad to see that it was so well attended. More than two thousand persons sat there in front of us but if we count hundreds more who were coming and going, a thousand more surely got some benefit from the convention. I spoke long. The famous speaker Goswami Ganeshdatta spoke too at length. Ch. Hariram Sahib has to be congratulated on the success of the meeting. Chowdhari Sahib told me that I was his 'High Command.' If he resolutely keeps to this declaration, I believe, we can together mould Delhi along our line. I should also thank him for his liberal hospitality.

On the 2nd October Ch. Hariram Sahib arranged and Ch. Baldeo Singh Sahib went to gather and we held a successful meeting at Bohar in the evening. In the morning, I should also mention, I lectured to the widows, displaced women of Western Panjab, at the Widows Home at Rohtak. Thus opened our 'Digvijai' campaign on the birth day of Mahatma Gandhi. Next day I spoke thrice, at three different meetings, held at Jat High School, Government College and Vaisya College. Principals of all the three institutions gave me their valuable cooperation. I spoke long at three meetings and invited students and staff to enlist themselves in our registers. It was a sight to see, how Jat students flocked with enthusiasm and enlisted in our several Federations: Students Federation, Religion of Love, Aryan Federation, World Federation, Martial Races Federation etc. Students of other castes or races as well gave their names willingly. I stayed with Ch. Sri Chand Sahib.

On the 4th October, in the morning, I addressed the students of the Jat College Rohtak. Great enthusiasm prevailed. Students were greatly interested in my talk. I must here mention that Principal Sanyal, a historical revolutionary, kindly gave me many names, good names, so much so, asked the students to worship me. But I teach worship of the only One God, none but he deserves all that worship which we can offer. Students in a large number enlisted themselves in our federations.

At a village differently written and pronounced, Karawar of Kulhar people hurriedly called a meeting for me, heard me and presented me a purse. Bohar also had given me two purses of Rs. 25 and Rs. 31, this village presented Rs. 51, we thank them.

Principal Hari Singh M. A. of our High School is accompanying me. Ch. Dharam Singh is cooperating. We stayed at Sampla. I lectured in the evening at Ismaila. Band played. Kind words were showered.

Next day in the morning I spoke long at the High School of Bhaprauda. In the evening a large meeting was held at the public hall–Choupal–of the village. Euthusiasm prevailed. Band and the singers, coupled with the gramophone records singing through the loud speaker, were filling the air with music. I spoke at length as usual on my plan.

On the 6th a way side village, Asanda halted us, presented eleven rupees. Bhaprauda had given a purse of fifty one. We thank these brethren for their generosity and good will. I returned to Rohtak. I stayed with Rao Bahadur Lal Chand. With him I went to his village of Bhalot. A crowded meeting was held. I addressed. Rupees one hundred and one were presented to me for my work. I should here also thank Rao Bahadur for his hospitality.

On the 7th we reached Gochhi, a village famous for military atmosphere. In the home of a captain we stayed. Rooms were well furnished and food was Nawabi. I spoke here in the afternoon. In the evening I spoke at Digal. Streets were all full and people were filling roofs. Silence ruled. They all heard me with rapture. On the 8th we went to Beri. Here we were guests of a big merchant, Mr. Ramgopal Atmaram. In the evening I addressed the huge gathering of the town. On the 9th October I addressed a meeting at Matanher in the morning. I spoke a few words to the people at Ladan. At Subana a very great reception was given. Right royally I was taken round in a procession. I addressed the large audience. At night I spoke for the fourth time this day at Dhakla.

I should also mention that Subana public gave me rupees one hundred and one and the garlands of notes were presented to me at Gochhi and Digal.

On the 10th proved the toughest journey. Car went wrong, road was worst and once it was a job to pull out our car from a canal. We reached Badli over four hours late. Still the crowd was there. Band announced my arrival. More people came. Ch. Hari Singh introduced me and I spoke. Right royal lunch was served at 5.30 p.m. It was 9.30 p.m. when we arrived at Delhi. Time of the meeting was finished. We were guests of Professor Swarup Singh.

Next day on the 11th we went to Bulandshahr. Captain Bhagwan Singh, District Magistrate and his wife treated me with coffee. Ch. Richhpal Singh Sahib proved very helpful. Kr. Kalyan Singh joined me. We stayed at Pali this night as the guest of Kr. Jagraj Singh. A meeting was held and I told the people my plan. Names were written in our registers.

On the 12th I addressed the students of the Jat High School of Lakhaoti. College was in recess. Over seven hundred students are in the school. They heard me with faces sparkling with joy.

At noon I spoke to the village folk and students of Dhamera and Sardarnagar. They took me out too in a procession with a band. Great enthusiasm was in evidence. This evening I addressed the fourth meeting of the day at Baral. This village has over four thousand population. It is one of those five villages which I gave in trust to Prem Mahavidyalaya, the Technical College, which I founded in 1909, and which is still going strong.

I stayed at Baral another day. I addressed the village students, over four hundred and held another meeting to elect a new village committee. It continued till about midnight.

On the 14th, 15th, 16th I stayed at Rarkatpur as the guest of my old friend, Kunwar Kalyan Singh ji. On all these days I spoke at different villages around. Lukrara, Khirpur, Kuchesar and Banhpur heard me and so heard the people of Barkatpur. Rao Sahib of Kuchesar, Rao Jagdish Pal Singh gave a rich lunch and Banhpur friends gave a banquet. On the 17th I stayed at the town of Gulaothi as the guest of Rao Harpal Singh and spoke at the market.

On the 18th I addressed the town meeting of Bulandshahr. People appreciated my talk. It was a pleasure to feel their response. I stayed this night with Khan Bahadur Rahmat Khan who gave a luxurious dinner. Many persons present entered their names in our register. Friends promised to send more names later.

On the 19th I returned by car via Aligarh, visiting on way Gabbhana and Mursan. On the 20th we celebrated Dashera at Love Centre, Vrindaban. On the 22nd I presided at a big Rajput Meeting at Serbas, going twelve hours by train. Rajput brethren gave me good reception and gave me a purse of Rs. 51. I returned on the 23rd October.

War Must be Stopped

Rebel !! I was a rebel. I am a rebel. I rebelled against oppression. I rebel against suppression. I ask you to rebel against coercion ! Ask, what the United States would get out of Korea ? Why all this massacre of the Americans as well as of the hundreds of thousands of poor Koreans ?

Americans are supposed to have some sense. But why then this senseless war ? America has lost all the good-will which it could win through philanthropic institutions. Some Americans atleast have shown most heartless cruelty. Besides all those proved brutalities of certain American soldiers, the worst butchery is all that bombing, dropping of tens of thousands of tons of bombs. None can possibly deny that through these bombings thousands of innocent women, children and the aged mercilessly perished. How can any one safeguard poor people. Innocently walking along some target.

If you have any heart, if you are at all with a grain of sense, if you can understand the complications of this Korean war, I ask you to rebel against those who order you to fight in Korea, China or the East generally.

Thinking men of the world, women with soft hearts, men of religion and statesmen, our brethren, the world federationists of all the lands, stir up, hold protest meetings, shout at the top of your voice to bring this war in Korea to end immediately. Every moment which passes makes the situation worse. Hurry, friends hurry. War must be stopped.

Condemn Hindustan Times :It is very serious. How it happened? Why the Hindustan Time gave this news in a big page wide headline that Pandit Jawaharlal Nehru had declared that India would not recognize the boy king of Nepal ? Our Premier had to deny the statement. Government should bring a case against the publishers of the Times. This paper is considered a responsible paper but for this crime people might think that our government, as whole, is carrying on a double faced policy vis-à-vis Nepal, our powerful neighbour, infact, blood of our blood, our Himalayan-self, part of Aryan!

Another Crime : It is criminal to indulge in such propaganda of America and England. The same Hindustan Times wrote a leading article :'Whither China' ? on the 28th of November, 1950, in its Delhi edition. The worst agent of the Anglo-American imperialism could not write a worse article from our standpoint. Who are you? What are you ? China did nothing wrong. China is doing the right thing. She has a correct aim. The British trained slaves in our country can not think and act as free men do. It is the trouble with our brethren who are more Englih than blue-blooded Englishmen. We support China, the celestial land.

October Diary : On the 27th October, in the morning I left Vrindaban by train. I took the frontier mail at Mathura and I was off. To my great annoyance I learned from the railway staff at Sawai Madhopur that my servant, Gorkha Shri Padam Bahadur, was left at Mathura. He was pushed out by the police, so the story ran, from a coupe reserved for the guards of the train !

Train went on merrily and I passed the whole day looking at the passing country side of fields, pastures, hills and streams and I also read newspapers. I took meals, tea and also held conversation with fellow passengers, who as it often happens, finding my identity began to take special interest in my views and opinions.

At 9.30 p.m. I reached Ratlam. I changed train, got into metre gauge carriage. At about 2.30 a.m. reached Indore. At this odd hour score of Rajput brave warriors had assembled to welcome me. Garlands were put round my neck. And they shouting "Jai" i.e., victory, led me to the waiting car. I was taken to the Ratlam House.

On the 28th in the morning I attended the Rajput working committee meeting and I spoke. In the afternoon was held the big annual function of the Rajput Seva Sangh at the Gandhi Hall. It was overflowing and men around were hearing through the loudspeakers. The Chief of Neemkhera declared the function opened with an impressive speech and I was made the president of the meeting. Kunwar Ramdayal Singh and Maharavat Sahib of Sukhera spoke and I deliverd extempore my presidential address. I was glad to see that my views were applauded by the audience.

Next day on the 29th came many visitors. I was talking with them for hours. In the afternoon a press-conference was held and I gave my message to the press. Later I visited the labour club run by Bhai Ramsingh. It is indeed a great institution providing recreation to the mill workers. In the evening was held the huge meeting of the Indore city. I was the main speaker. Thousands of people sitting in the square, standing in the streets and in windows and on roofs heard me silently for an hour. My talk was punched by cheers.

On the 30th I was taken to Dhargaon. The meeting was more like a Darbar and I was, as if, put on the throne. Colleagues spoke and I gave a long talk. Jagirdar of the place gave us tea and dinner.

On the 31st I visited several institutions in the city. At three different places I spoke: at the Arya Samaj, a girls school and at the labour library of the Rajkumar mill.

November Story : On the 1st November 1950 we went to Ujjain. The meeting was held in the heart of the town. A couple of thousand people heard us, but it was not half or one fourth of the Indore public meeting. Next day holding a meeting at Sanver we returned Indore. On the 3rd we visited Bagli and held an open door meeting in the front of the local palace. In the evening I addressed the students of the Jain Boarding House of Indore.

On the 4th Nov. we visited Rau and took tea with an old teacher of our Prem Mahavidyalaya. Later we went to Dewas. In the evening a very crowded meeting was held. Very different institutions welcomed me, orthodox Hindus, Muslims and labour and students garlanded me. Kr. Mullu Singh and Kr. Ramdayal Singh spoke as usualers and as usual I presided and gave a long talk. At about midnight we returned Indore.

On the 5th Nov. we took leave of Indore. This evening the meeting was held at Dhar and we stayed at Ganga Nagar, the residence of the Chief of Neemkhera. Next day we had to go quite far on hills and through dales. Meeting was held at Jhabua. It was about eleven at night when we returned Ganganagar.

On the 7th we held two meetings, at Piploda and Sukhera. We were here the guests of Maharawat Daulat Singh, quite royally we were entertained.

On the 8th we had to travel over one hundred and sixty miles, going as usual by car. The meeting was held at Neemuch. Procession was taken out. I was made to sit in an open car, heavily garlanded. Chief of Neemkhera, Maharawat Sahib, Thakur sahiban, all walking in front, crowd following, Rajput flag flying, slogans shouting, we reached the place of the meeting. Mine was the chief speech but my colleagues, as usual, spoke. It was declared today that they meant to follow my programme ! At about midnight I was brought to Ratlam by my friends. They brought my and my servant's tickets and presented me two purses.

In the early morning of the 9th November I got into the Frontier Mail and returned Mathura, reaching about 4 p.m. In the evening I was settled at my suite of rooms at Vrindaban. I must here thank all the Rajput friends, including Col. Rana Keshri Singh, Kunwar Sahib Khuman Singh of Karadia and friends whose names have already appeared in this account. From the 9th to the 19th November I was at Vrindaban, writing letters, receiving visitors and attending to my daily routine.

Digvijai Continues : In the early morning of the 19th I left by car. Raja Bahadur of Mursan, my nephew, gave us fine breakfast. Ch. Ram Singh gave us lunch. At Gothna I delivered my speech and stayed for the night as the guest of my cousin Swami Kunwar Hari Krishna Singh. They presented a purse.

On the 20th I stayed with Janab Abdul Majid Khwaja and spoke at the Malviya Library. Next day I attended the special convocation meeting held at our Muslim University, to confer the doctor's degree on the Governor of the province. It was a big pageant. I felt sorry for H. H. the Nawab of Rampur, ruler without a state, and for the Governor without authority, playing here in a thankless show for the benefit of the audience.

Just after, rich lunch of Khwaja Sahib, I proceeded to Khurja where I stayed with the Seth Sahib of Mahesh Ghee. At our meeting, held at Gandhiganj, I delivered my message of 'Digvijai'.

22, 23, 24 at Ganga Snan mela I stayed at our camp, on the bank of Ganga at Garhmukteshwar. I must mention that our camp was erected by my old friend Kunwar Kalyan Singh at his own cost. Let us thank him.

Our meetings here were not well attended. But I was invited to a large gathering of the peasants where I spoke at length. Another interesting thing was that the R.S.S. supposed to be our opponents gave me a simple banquet in their camp. I preached my 'Digvijai'.

A staunch follower of H. H. Karpatri, Pandit Sailani, whose camp was by the side of our camp, became very friendly and he accompanied me to Delhi. The way was all blocked with the returning piligrims. It took us seven hours to cover sixty five miles. I got however a comfortable room at the Constitution House of the government hotel, room reserved through Acharya Jugal Kishore ji and Thakur T. N. Singh Sahib, M. P. I stayed three nights at Delhi. I could not hold any public meeting as it was necessary to take special permission of the local magistrate and it was Sunday on the 26th Nov., offices were closed. It became clearer to me that it was indeed necessary to capture Delhi ! And it must be done as early as possible.

I called on Swami Karpatriji. To my astonishment he said that his and mine object was the same and that he wished me success.

Meeting at Ahrwan, in the Gurgaon district on the 29th Nov. was a grand fair. I presided and lectured. A resolution was unanimously passed that the Government should 'invite Raja Mahendra Pratap to enlist an army of six million men.' I am very thankful to the Peanuts' League for giving me this opportunity to preach my word.

My Diary of 1951

Let me call it my diary. Our Indian Congress wants us to write our diaries. Well, here it is !

On the 26th January 1951 our school and college students celebrated the Republic Day. I hoisted the flag on the old building at Vrindaban. I spoke to the students saying that we are glad for the stage reached but we can not stop here. We must proceed further and further !

On the 30th January Subedar Tekchand ji took me to Rohtak. Principal Hari Singh ji accompanied us. At midnight we arrived there and stayed with Rao Bahadur Lalchand.

On the 31st I, with friends, attended the 'Sarva Khap' huge gathering. But I was not asked to speak. The president wanted me to give just my 'blessings.' But I did not agree with their programme. People began to go away. When only a couple of thousand were left I could express my views quite independently. The same night I returned. It was past three in the morning when I could lay my hand to rest in my bed room at Vrindaban.Though I went to bed after 3 a.m. yet I got up early and opened the school as usual with a prayer and a speech and a bit longer speech as I was leaving for Calcutta. I left in the afternoon, took a night train from Mathura, passed that night at the Hathras Junction waiting room.

On the 2nd February I caught the Calcutta Mail at about 11 a.m. and reached next day at Howrah just after 10 a.m. Kunwar Inderjeet Singh had come with two motor cars. Representatives of H. H. Swami Kumar Rishi were there and my old friend Mr. Deb Nath Das had come to meet me. Visiting Salkia Transport office I proceeded to Rishi Ashram fifteen miles off. Now there were furnished rooms in the country cottage. Swamiji welcomed me and made me at home. But the function for which I was invited had been put off !

On the 6th I moved to the garden house of Salkia Transport at Lilooa. This day, on the way, it was my great pleasure to meet the famous revolutionary Babu Barindra Ghosh, younger brother of Yogiraj Arbindo Ghosh of Pondicherry. He immediately phoned to friends to arrange a public reception for me.

On the 9th afternoon reception was given to me at the large hall of University Institute. Mr. Debnath Das presided. Several famous revolutionaries were there including of course Babu Barindra.

I visited Dr. Bhupendra Nath Datta, once president of the Berlin Committee. He is the younger brother of the famous Swami Vivekananda. Now he is too ill and too weak to move freely. It was also a pleasure to meet Pt. Asutosh Lahiri and Mr. K. B. Sinha and his Japanese wife. Mr. Mukerji, the Chairman of Howrah Municipality, Mr. Sushil Banerji, a parliamentary secretary and Mr. Atta kindly called at my residence, so came too the District Congress President and the Congress Treasurer and some other friends.

I left Howrah on the 11th Feb. at 7.25 p.m. and arrived back Vrindaban on the 12th at about 9.30 p.m.

My March Story : First of March saw me very busy with my routine work. On the 3rd, in the morning I left. I caught Bombay mail at Mathura. Travelling whole day I arrived about ten in the night at Bhopal. Rajput brethren gave me a rousing reception, garlanding me profusely. A representative of H. H. Nawab Sahib had also come. He informed me that I was to be the guest of His Highness. I took leave of the Rajput Sewa Sangh and proceeded to the Royal Guest House. I need hardly say that here I was very comfortably housed and fed.

On the 4th in the morning, I called at the Sangh meeting place. In the afternoon I presided at their meeting. I spoke at length.

On the 5th I was taken to the Chiklod fairy place, by a beautiful lake, and had lunch with their highnesses. After the rich feast I got ample opportunity to herald my views. His Highness thought that the Muslims were in a plight and the only hope was Congress's declared policy. I of course had to plead that my programme alone could save the country. I am a Congress man, minus party trickery. I stand for hundred per cent good of hundred per cent population.

In the evening I was taken in a procession through the streets of the town. Latter I presided at the public meeting of the Rajput Sewa Sangh. Several speakers spoke. It was nine thirty when I started my presidential address. I was glad that my programme was enthusiastically received.

On the 6th morning I had breakfast with the Police General and lunch with his assistant. Both are Jats and in a way my relations. In the afternoon police general called on me. Later I was taken to the government farm. Mr. Dube, the chief officer, showed us round and gave a reception. I thanked him and his coworkers. In the evening we took train. At midnight we arrived at Ujjain. I passed the night at the railway station's waiting room.

On the 7th Maharawat Sukhera took us in his jeep car to Agra. Here I was taken out in a proession and I was asked to preside at the huge open-door meeting. Darbar Neemkhera hoisted the flag, Maharawat Sukhera inaugurated and Kr. Ramdayal Singh explained the object of the Rajput Association. I heralded my plans and asked the audience to support me.

On the 8th morning I spoke a few words at their workers meeting. Rao Sajjan Singh presented me a purse of one hundred and one rupees. I rushed to Ujjain, got into the waiting train and took the express at Nagda.

It was four in the morning of the 9th that I reached Mathura. Returning to Vrindaban after six days I attended immediately to my heavy mail. And at ten, I prayed with the school children and told them the story of my tour.

On the 18th March was held the convocations of our Engineering College. Wellknown Congress leader Pandit Gokulbhai Bhatt presided and the Minister of the Central government Mr. A. P. Jain delivered the convocation address. In my annual report I criticized the government for not paying sufficient attention to our old institution of forty two years. The function was well attended. Officials and the nobility of the city came in force. Tea party followed.

On the 20th, as advertised, three meetings were held, of all the profession, of all the parties and of all the castes.

On the 21st in the morning and in the afternoon, Religions' Congress was held. Maulana Abdul Jabbar Kheri Ph. D. presided in the morning. And H. H. Swami Raghunathdas ji presided in the afternoon. At night our college students played a drama. From 1 a.m. to sunrise martial races met in conference.

On the 22nd we held meetings of the Moral Front and World Federation. This year attendance was poor on the whole. On account of Holi festival people had to remain at home. But the fact that our Aryan New Year coincided with Holi should be considered very auspicious. In fact Holi is the true Aryan New Year but due to the moon calendar it now changes dates.

On the 24th I left Vrindaban. Travelling whole night, I arrived Patiala in the morning. Here it was raining. Three months' hard preparations of the Zamindar Leaguers were cruely undone by the bad weather. At night I joined their discussions in a closed room.

On the 26th I had an interview with H. H. Maharaja Rajpramukh. In the afternoon I addressed the public meeting of the League. Same evening I left, again travelling by night, I returned Vrindaban on the 27th March.

My Story of April : On Sunday the 1st April 1951 I held our weekly religious meeting at Love Center. On the 2nd I left by car in early morning. At Hodal a big function was held at the High school. Several thousand persons gathered. I presided and delivered my long address. Ch. Shamsher Singh was the chief worker, he gave us dinner, as well.

On the 3rd I went to Bisawar College and spoke to the students. I went on to Sadabad. The town President joined our Moral Front. On my way back my car developed some trouble, it stopped. Just here is situated Sarvoday Ashram, run by Babu Jainti Prasad, a local congress leader. He too arrived just at that moment. He took me to the Ashram, where his father is living like a Sadhu. It is well kept. Fruits and vegetables are growing and flourishing. Without any more trouble car brought me back to Vrindaban. This evening a special meeting was held at our Center. I delivered the sermon. Five new persons joined our Religion of Love, five rupees sweet was distributed.

On the 4th, in the afternoon, a meeting of Moral Front was held at the Congress office. Mathura. Hakeem Brajlal and Magistrate Babu Ram Yadav (retired) were present. It was decided that we all try to enlist as many members of the Front as we possibly can.

On the 9th I went by Bus to Agra. I lectured at the Indian doctors meeting. On the 12th April I together with my daughter and a grandchild left for Rajpur. Taking a taxi at Sahranpur arrived at our Summer home in very early morning.

Today is 30th April. It is now nearly 2 p.m. I have been writing this account. Sudden illness of Acharya Narendra Dev deprived me of a discussion with him this morning. May be, he gets better and we meet. This night at 10.30 I am leaving for Agra.

New Party In India

For this country it is the greatest news of this month. A new party is formed at Patna to fight the coming general elections. Most of the leaders of this new party are old Congress members. And they do not say that the Gandhian policy is now anworkable. They assert that they are better Gandhite and that the present Government have forsaken the Gandhi-principles ! Head of this party appears to be Acharya Kripalani. Mr. P.C. Ghose of Bengal, Mr. Prakasham of Madras, both former premiers have joined the party, so runs the press report. In fact it is a big manouvre on the part of the different struggling groups and individuals, including Pandit Jawaharlal Nehru. It is an open secret that Rajarshi Tandon, President of the Congress and Pandit Premier Nehru do not see eye to eye. Tandon ji is more Hindu and Mr. Kidwai is in opposition. Nehru ji favours Shri Kidwai. Acharya Kripalani thinks Sindhi, as Ghose babu is more Bengali in his mind. They dare not say as they feel. They come out with new plans to win their points. I say, let us stop his wire pulling. Call an apple, an apple ! People think in castes, provinces and in religions. Let us make a plan that we satisfy all their deep rooted desires. Our plan presents such an alternative. Congress and Congress alone will function but it will be of all the people, based on religion and morality !!

Mr. Mussoorie : I was shocked to read that at the Savoy Hotel a function was being held and that women were to select the most handsome man and give him the title of Mr. Musssoorie. I wrote a letter to the proprietor of the hotel, Captain Kirparam and expressed my disgust. He wrote me: 'My dear Raja Ji, Thanks for your remembrance. We shall talk about it when we meet, it is so late now. I shall be delighted if you have your tea with me tomorrow, Saturday, Rotarian Tea, at 4 p.m. as my esteemed guest .....if Maharani Kalsia can honor us by joining you, we shall be so happy...' Later I learned that it was much worse in the 'British-days' Parties continued from evening till 5 a. m.!!

Rotarian Tea : On the 23rd June, Maharani Kalsia, my daughter and myself, went to the Rotarian tea as the guest of Captain Kirparam. It was a big affair. Hall was crowded. Speeches were being delivered. Captain Sahib arranged some chairs in the front row and we sat quiet, hearing the out pouring. Tea followed. We met many friends. Now a farce was held. It was a mock meeting of U. N. O. Kashmir was discussed. Many serious people in life were indulging in the political fun. We got tired and came away.

Princess Kamla Devi of Baroda invited me and my daughter to lunch on the 25th June, at the Savoy Hotel. She is a fine lady with modern out-look. She agreed with me that many youths squader money received from their fathers, such youths should not inherit money.

Pilgrimage, Braj Tour Digvijai : 16th Sept. I am doing something at present which I never did before. I am going round this holy land of Braj entirely on foot. I started from Vrindaban on the 16th of September 1951. After returning to India, all these five year I never took bath in the river Jamuna or Ganga. Today very early in the morning, I took bath in Jamuna and after taking light breakfast crossed the river by boat and started hiking with my companions.

Three miles brought us to Mat. Our friends welcomed us. Thakur Chhidda Singh ji, full blooded Rajput, gave us rich lunch. Pathan Khan Ghulam Safdar arranged a meeting. I explained my programme.

Principal Hari Singh and World Federation staff returned to Vrindaban. Accompanied by Ch. Vijai Singh and Kr. Dalbir Singh and companions we walked to the village of Bari, attached to Jabra. Here a large crowd was waiting for me for three hours. I started to harangue at once. Thakur Dharam Vir Singh Jat gave us dinner.

On 17 Sept. the morning we marched to rich breakfast. He also accompanied us. At Chowkra we were entertained by Th. Ram Chand. I addressed here a meeting.

We continued hiking to Raya. I spoke to the school students. I was guest of Lala Agarwal. He gave us rich dinner. These rich meals had already spoiled my stomach, today I felt still worse.

18 Sept. This morning I visited Kunwar, he is eighty two years old, still keeping good health and busy in translating Upanishada into English. His Gita translation is already famous. We walked on, passed several villages, spoke a few words at each. At a village many people joined our Moral Front. At noon, a kindly Chowdhari insisted that we must take lunch, it was getting late. His equally kindly wife soon prepared light healthy meal. We took it, thanked the family and went on.

It was 4 in the afternoon that we reached Mursan, my birth place. We entered the fort by a back door, went up to the old palace of my father. My nephew, Raja Bahadur Kishori Raman Singh gave us tea. I addressed a small meeting at the weekly market. Raja Bahadur naturally gave royal dinner.

19 Sept., after rich breakfast we left. Raja Bahadur wanted to send an elephant with us but I declined the king's offer. We went hiking as here before.

We passed several villages as yesterday. And again we held meetings in them. Kareel village gave us royal reception. Band was playing. National flag was flying. Crowd was large. I spoke long. We reached Bihoin in the evening. People were waiting for me for five hours. Many of course had gone home. Still a fine small meeting was held. I was guest of Kr. Narendra Singh. He is my distant nephew.

On 20 Sept. after breakfast we proceeded to Sonkh-khera. I addressed a large gathering for over one hour, some village people had also come.

I was taken to village Arjun and the head of the village gave us lunch. We continued our walking tour. Only at one village we preached a bit and came to Baldeo. We stayed at the High School. Principal gave us dinner. We visited the Temple of Baldeo and addressed a meeting in the town. Audience was greatly pleased and I rejoiced seeing their pleasure.

21 Sept. I walked to Brahmonand Ghat. I was astonished to see here a very fine charitable institution built by some rich merchant of Bombay. Here is a large garden, a Sanskrit School, a hospital and rooms for hermits. They all get free food. All visitors are served free meals too !

We went on to Mahaban. Here are surely some interesting ruins, they deserve prompt attention at the hands of our government. Further on, we visited a Sadhus' place, Ramanreti. We came to Gokul. We stayed at the school. Pandit Heeralal, president of the local Congress, called and made arrangements for my lecture meeting in the town. Temple gave us very rich feast. Later I addressed the meeting. Young men were full of enthusiasm.

22 Sept. I visited the main Temple. Pandit Heeralal accompanied me to the Mathura side of river Jamuna. I stayed at Jamuna Hotel of Rao Krishnpal Singh Sahib.

23 Sept. I attended our District Congress office. I spoke to friends and coworkers. I cast my vote. I was called to see the son of Kr. Onkar Singh but he died before my arrival. I went to Vrindaban. I presided over our Executive Committee, which was called for today. At night I delivered sermon at Love Centre. Nine new persons joined our Religion of Love. Sweets were distributed.

24-25 Sept. Two days I stayed at Vrindaban. As usual, I opened the school with a prayer and a talk, finished Hindi Circular and attended to my correspondence and the school work.

26 Sept. I came by car to Mathura and started the pilgrimage, walking on foot. Six tenth-class students are also accompanying me from Vrindaban. We took our lunch and addressed a meeting. We visited Jamuna Ashram of Thakur Kirori Singh. An idol of Mahatma Gandhi is placed here, as well.

We stayed this night at Khushipura. We were guests of Ch. Baldeo Singh. In the night I spoke to people who gathered to hear me.

27 Sept. We got rich lunch at Aring. Harijan leader of the locality Mr. Dalchand's community was considered as untouchable till yesterday but now our Congress has been able to break the chains of suppression. He is today a respectable citizen of this village. I spoke at the meeting held at the school.

We came to Giriraj. We visited temple and spoke at the public meeting, called to hear me. Local school teachers and students were specially kind. They gave me room to stay in and heralded my coming to the town.

28 Sept. In the morning I visited the main buildings of Bharatpur Raj. Reaching Radhakund I addressed the students of the local school and held a small meeting where I explained my programme. We walked to the village of Palson. Here was held the biggest meeting of my walking tour. Brahmans showed me their greatest love and regard.

29 Sept. We left very early. We stayed for beautiful temples, and left in the afternoon. We came to Nandgaon. We visited the main temple. At night another large meeting was held. Here Jats predominate.

30 Sept. We left early and came to the village of Jab. People gathered and I addressed them. We walked on to Kosi. Our students left back for Vrindaban. And I came to Delhi by train. I have come here to attend Chinese Embassy's National Day on the 1st October.

I shall go back to Kosi and resume my hiking for five more days. I must say that during this trip I found very anti-Congress sentiment. At a place, where I mentioned the name of Pandit Nehru with a fine remark, people took objection and said 'Is Nehru deaf? Why he hears not our complaints ?...'

My October Story : 1st October found me at the Constitution House, New Delhi. I got good breakfast and palled the whole day in writing October Circular and some letters. At half past six in the evening I took taxi and went round to see some friends. A little after the appointed time, I reached the Chinese Embassy to join their celebration. Tiny electric lamps were peeping all round through green foliage. Quite a big crowd was loitering in the spacious garden. Drinks and refreshments were served. I met many friends. Mr. Hu, a secretary of the Embassy, tried to make me feel at home. Later on fire-work brightened the sky and the movie brought Peking to the lawn. I took leave. Our police arrangement in getting the ears quickly was splendid. I came to the New Delhi

Railway station. After 10 at night I got into the train and after midnight arrived back at Kosi where my companions and some students were waiting for me.

2nd October. We started on our walking tour of Holy Braj. We are continuing it, you know. People of Rajaki Garhi welcomed us and gave us lunch. I was telling on my programme, as well as I was trying to bring about better feelings between two fighting groups. Near here a man was murdered by his own relation. For that one death thirteen persons were under trial ! We went on to Majhoi.

Majhoi. It is the head office of our Prem Vihar. Here we have a well built house over looking the river Jamuna. It commands a beautiful view. In the night, people of the village Majhoi gathered to hear me. I explained my plan. We celebrated Mahatma Gandhi's birth day by taking an extra dish of rice pudding !

3rd, We established Love Center the building and I appointed a sweeper to act as priest. I gave him some land to support his family. Dr. Mathura Prasad of Shergarh presented an address, and we left. At the village of Shahzadpur Thakurs gave us lot of hot milk and showed their village school. I spoke a few words. At Ujhani Ch. Prahlad Havaldar gave us lunch. In the afternoon, I addressed a public meeting at shergarh. Sub Inspector of police gave us tea. We stayed here for the night. Next for night I travelled the interior of Mathura.

On 17th. My daughter, in her car, saw me off, beyond the town of Dehradun. I stopped at the High School at Narsan, named after me. I delivered a lecture to the students. At Muzaffarnagar, at the office of 'Lalkar' weekly, Ch. Dharamvir Singh gave us tea. Another round of tea was served at Meerut by my friend Advocate Yadram Sahib. We talked on the burning topics of the day at both these towns. I left children and two servants at the house of Rao Umrao Singh and I came to the Constitution House. But lo ! It was all full due to the Congress session. I had to put up in the room of a Nepali Rana, Rana Kunjar Shamsher Jung Bahadur. Miss E. Bruner, a well known Hungarian painter, was very helpful to get for me a bed from the room of the Hon. Minister Sidhwa Sahib.

18th Oct. I got a special ticket. I went to the meeting of the Subject Committee. I sat near Rajarshi Tandon and Sheikh

Abdullah. We talked on my plan for Kashmir. U. P. Premier came, asked me: 'How do you do Raja Sahib.' I thanked him. Pandit Jawahar Lal came. I said to him: 'I hope, you have not forgotten me? 'He answered: 'How can I forget you? You are attacking me bitterly. You wrote, as if, Jawaharlal died but Congress does not allow Jawaharlal to die. Now we would fight some where.' I laughingly remarked: 'Let us continue this fun.' (free translation of the Hindustani conversation).

In the evening I attended open session of the Congress. I walked up the raised platform and took a back seat. Pandit Rajgopalacharya betokened to me and I went and I sat with him and Maulana Abul Kalam Azad. We were laughing and talking.

19th. I with Rana Sahib went and visited Maulana Abdull Jubbar Kheri of Turkish fame and Rao Lachhman Prasad Sufi, wellknown for his magazine, 'Mastana Jogi'. In the evening, I again attended the Congress. I met many friends on the platform and had talks with them.

20th October. Acharya Jugal Kishore ji came to my room. Rev. Shri Sahib came to lunch with me. Pt. Sitaram Shukla ji visited. I thanked Rana Sahib and left. It was 4 p.m. Half past 7 in the evening I returned Vrindaban.

From 21 to full week I visited Mathura twice.

At night, we reached Vrindaban being Diwali we celebrated this great festival, at our Love Center. I prayed according to the Religion of Love.

31st October. I with some friends went to Bharatpur by car. We held a long talk with Raja Girraj Saran Singh, widely known as Raja Bachchu Singh. And peasant leaders Thakur Deshraj and Kr. Ratan Singh. I am trying for universal unity, for common welfare.

Letters : Rev.Otto Maria Saenger, Clergy, Dettighofen ob Tiengen, Oberrhein, Germany, writes :

My dear friend Raja Mahendra Pratap,...

We must continue to make known the causes of world disease without condemning other confessions of racial prejudices. I found you are right, the U. N. is utilized for other aims... Moral and religious principles are often pronounced by war and hate mongers to veil their aims–poor and exploited nations. I will write of your work in India in my next circular letter... You make appeal to German friends to come out to India in a missionary spirit to teach German language and cultivate friendship. I spoke to my good wife of it and she means we could perhaps come, as we have no children... I am 65 year and my wife 55 years. We can live without comfort... The souls of men must be turned in all nations and prepared for a real brotherhood...' You are welcome. Get some how here and you will find friends. You can settle in our school or college or at my Prem Vihar !!

Rev. Upo Ka, Director-in-Chief, International Buddhist Mission, Thaton, Burma, writes :

'There is only one Buddha. No one knows what he is and what he taught by merely going through the holy scriptures. The best thing is to meditate on Him and His teachings... May your efforts to complete the unfinished work of Lord Nirvana Buddha be completely fulfilled... Thank you very much. If my teachings, which are according to this age, would prevail Man should see the Truth in all the religions.'

Rev. Yonosude Nakano, Founder of the new religion of Ananai, Shimizu City, Japan. He was formerly working with the founder of another new religion, Rev. Deguchi. Now he has founded his own religion. In Japan and in the United States of America this is a common phenomenon. Religions are born at very short interval and die out as quickly as they appear. Some of them persist. Rev. Nakano seems to have been able to gather a big following. He writes to me :

'Well, I am very interested in your thinking and predict concerning the New Messiah...' He adds: 'New Saviour has on the earth (with) three virtues: First, Bestowed with Divine Wisdom... to do the unification of all mankind... Second, Endowed with genious–Power of explanation... Third, Tender-mind that of a father...' He asks my opinion. As I heralded that Mahatma Gandhi prepared my way, some friends think that I mean that I am the Christ. I have given to the world the Book of the Religion of Love, it is the religious book of this age, but I say that the last incarnation was Lord Nirvana Buddha and the last prophet was Rasul Mohammad and Jesus stands there in their middle, on the Cross, without stretched hands, joining both. And up there far behind we see Lord Shri Krishna. Recently we have had teachers, such as Guru Nanak or Hazrat Bahaullah. Now in this age we should have unity of religions, economic system of a joint family, throughout all mankind, and federated.

My November Story : 4th Nov. I went by jeep to Delhi. It took me four hours including the time spent on lunch on the way. Hon. Minister, Mr. Sidhwa got me a room at the Constitution House, a semi government hotel, New Delhi. At 6 p.m. I attended the opening ceremony of the Chinese exhibition. Later I joined the reception at the Chinese embassy. I met at these occasions several old friends and made some new acquaintances. I may mention: Hon. Dr. Katju, Dr. Kichlu, Pt. Sunderlal, Premier Pt. Shukla of Nagpur. Of course I had the pleasure of meeting H. E. Chinese ambassador, H. E. Soviet ambassador and H. E. Dr. Najeebullah Khan, Afghan ambassador. I went to Delhi only for these two functions, at the invitation of the Chinese embassy.

5th Nov. I went and saw Pt. Sunderlal and Babu Devdas Gandhi, son of our late Mahatma. Pt. Sunderlal wished me success against Acharya Jugal Kishore in the elections and authorized me to mention it in our circular. I met many friends at Palwal on way back and had tea with them. By 7 p.m. I was back at Vrindaban.

6th Nov. I went to Mursan by car. I addressed a few words to a few people at the cattle market. I visited Kamra Bagh and saw my Swami brother and relatives. Proceeding to the village of Aira Khera spoke at the meeting called to hear me. At Raya, visited the Chairman of the town and had tea with him. Due to party politics this fine and learned man remains neglected. This evil I am determined to remove.

11th Nov. Today I had to be very busy. I presided over three meetings at our College, at Prem Nagar. Then we received their Excellencies Mr. Modi, the U.P. Governor and Mme. Modi. Address was given to him and he replied in very encouraging words. Then followed our tea party. The Commissioner and the District Magistrate together with the Superintendent of Police were also present. Nobility to the town joined us. Many friends followed to Vrindaban and we remained in conference till late at night.

12th Nov. This was typical programme of my work of universal unity : I went to Fatiha and met Thakur Ramchand, the recognized leader of his community. I visited H. E. the Governor at the appointed time. He was on tour and was staying at Mathura, his capital, you know, is at Lucknow. Lady Modi was going out. She saluted me in right Indian style and left. His Excellency talked about the old events of my life: How I met Kaiser and the like. I found time to call on Rao Krishnapal Singh, president of U. P. Jan Sangh. And then I addressed the sweepers at their meeting.

13th Nov. Ch. Babu Ram Yadav brought Mr. Patel of K.M.P. party. We talked. I presented my plan of work. I went to Tarauli and spoke to the people. I spoke at Choumuha as well. At night I addressed the sweepers' meeting at Vrindaban. I am deeply interested in elevating these suppressed brethren. Thus the full month I spent my whole time in meetings the people.

Corespondence : Raja Bachu Singh. It is his pet name. But he is known all over India by this name. His real name is Raja Girraj Saran Singh. He is the youngest brother of His Highness Maharaja Sahib of Bharatpur. He heralded that he was to contest for a seat in the parliament. He presented his nomination paper. All of a sudden we read a news in the *Hindustan Times*, Delhi, that his paper was rejected. I was naturally very sorry to read that news. I wrote him a letter of sympathy. Now he writes :

'My paper was rejected was malicious and untrue propaganda... I am really very deeply touched by your interest in me. I hope and pray that I may be able to serve the people or the nation to the best of my ability.

Yours sincerely
G. S. Singh of Bharatpur

I wish him complete success in his campaign to get into Parliament.

Bharatpur Raj. It is of course no more. It disappeared together with hundreds of other States of Indian India. Indian national opinion is supposed to rejoice at this great change. But I am afraid that as great injustice is done to Rajput, Jat and Pathan Maratha clans, these warrior races are highly dissatisfied. Soviet Russia did not displease her such clans. She created Uzbek, Turkmen and such States and during the last world war got their full cooperation. I believe that our government's both foreign and home policy is completely wrong. They are disintegrating our nation and weakening it in the world. Bharatpur Raj fought against the British and defeated them, history records it. Later overpowered it established treaty relations with them. Our Raja Bachu Singh is a scion of that Family.

From U.P. Congress : I got the following express telegram from U.P. Congress office Lucknow :

> 'Raja Mahendra Pratap Singh,Vrindaban, Executive Council asks, you withdraw from contest immediately stop Inform us and election officer your withdraw telegraphically by eighth December Algurai Shastri.'

> I wired back :

> 'Pandit Algurai Shastri Provincial Congress, Lucknow. Honestly convinced, Executive council misled by corrupt persons stop I believe, I am working for universal unity and for purification of society. All opposed to me are degenerated persons or misguided fools. Mahendra Pratap.'

Now it is a holy war against all the evil, prevailing in the Congress party. Evil has usurped power. It has formed a kind of robber band. It wants to destroy the very foundation of our country. I hope, my friends, wherever they are in the Congress Party or outside it, will support me and cooperate with me. Evil must be dethroned.

I appeal to those mental slaves, as well, who are led like cattle by the evil, to free themselves from the clutches of the Satan and gather round my Mission. We want to establish Dharam Raj in our land which is the meeting of Hindu Ganga and Muslim Jamuna. Our land is the birth place of Lord Buddha and Christianity flowed in and Sikh Gurus preached here the Hindu-Muslim unity. Our land has a duty at this juncture. Mahatma Gandhi prepared my way. I presented to Comrade Lenin my book of the Religion of Love. We shall teach Universal religion to Moscow, London and Washington. I hope to establish peace on earth through World

Federation, with the economic system of joint family of all humanity.

Views on News

Our Elections : Elections in India are in full swing. They are no longer schemes or conjectures. In certain districts they are to start. In Himachal they are already finished. By the next few days in distant lands, the elections would have been added to the facts of history. You would know the results by cables much earlier than the news conveyed by my circular. The evil side of these elections is now glaring in the face. Not facts but falsehood is advertised. Not truth but money wins. Still resolution persists and it is hoped that in the long run the right cause would have its victory. Thank God, without my serious endeavour, on a large scale, people are recognizing my services which they call 'great sacrifices.' I have yet to see whether this spirit of my fellow countrymen sends me to the parliament or the false propaganda of the opponents, backed with wealth, succeeds in suppressing me? Any way, I shall continue to point out the evils of this democratic system. Why must fifty one rule forty nine? What right have ninety nine to oppress one? Our old conception of society is far superior: All should work for all to make all happy. There should be no contesting–no competition but cooperation !!

United Nations : It is following the path of late league of Nations. They sit up in council and talk, debate and waste precious time. Hot words create storm. Is it right? The scenes created in the council chambers are the result of the wrong training and schooling going on in the different States. You waste time in discussing while the trouble breeds and grows on which you exchange words in useless discussions. Better not talk nonsense, better spread in all the world, throughout the States, teachings which will help federation of nations, unity of religions and the economic system of a joint family of our human race.

I say, I assert that my plan of World Federation will bring peace in the fighting camps. Do not prepare your States for war. Only get permission of all the States to preach my plan. I can assure you that my plan, when properly understood, will be acceptable both by the USA and the USSR All the world has to be federated. The shims of political or religious conquest or the dreams of forcing your opponents to your way of life should vanish. We should direct all our energy to make Man happy within our spheres. Religions should make Man a better man. Let us fight evil and spread goodness in society!!

Stop Murders : In Indo-China, in Malaya, in Korea and on the Suez canal they are murdering men on a large scale. These murders should be stopped. What right have the foreigners to impose their brutal rule or what spiritual of moral right have the British, Americans or the French to take selfish control in distant lands? UNO is becoming a laughing stock like the League of Nations in face of these murders, aggression and robbery. History will give verdict against these 'statesmen' who are blindly following the path of destruction. They will be condemned as murderers !

My Story of December : 1st of December was my birth day. People began to come from early morning and continued to garland me, one by one. Strange to say, Prof. Krishna Chand, Chairman of Vrindaban Municipality, who is opposing me in the elections for parliament, also came ! He later joined us in the breakfast party at the Love Center. Here I told the audience that Professor said openly in a Congress meeting that he wanted to send me to the parliament because I was the only person who could oppose Pandit Jawaharlal Nehru, why now he was opposing me in the elections?

I proceeded to Prem Nagar. Our college students had put up a show, arranged a meeting and gave a big lunch party. Acharya Jugal Kishore, Hakeem Brajlal, Dr. Shri Nath and Prof. Krishna Chand came and joined our lunch. I had to tell them straight that as I was not given a Congress ticket and as I was contesting as an independent candidate I would be obliged to oppose bitterly Congress candidates.

In the afternoon prizes were distributed at the school function. I spoke. Elite of Vrindaban was present. In the evening Raja Bahadur Mursan came and Mr. Kamlesh Bhartiya gave dinner.

December 1951, the month I toured my constituency. Today ends this month and this year. I took a bit of rest in the morning as I caught cold. In the afternoon I went to Verni and spoke at a well attended meeting. I visited my election office at Mathura and met some friends. I went to bed after midnight.

I am Defeated

On the 13th February the result of election was practical clear. I was defeated by the official Congress candidate. People said: 'Is it right? Is if the reward electorate gave for honesty and sacrifice?' I believe, spiritually I have won. It is another proof that honesty hardly wins in such elections. Money, influence and official pressure decide the issue. The Prime Minister, Pandit Jawahar Lal Nehru himself came to oppose me. He came to Mathura on the 20th January and on the 22nd Jan. just two days after, Mathura City and Tehseel went to polling! He made fun of me. He ridiculed my plan of Aryan. He spoke against my suggestion of building six million army. City went against me. Villages voted for me. But I got defeated any how.

Economic break down : I spent all the money I got from the Court of Wards i.e. from our estate under the government management. I got ten thousand rupees for the elections. Some of my friends presented purses. My daughter shared some expenses. But I had to spend all, all what I had. I still have to pay some bills. I had to relieve seven members of my staff. I am very sorry to part company with them but there was no alternative. They are all capable hands. They will get good jobs. I wish them success in life.

World Federation : The capital of Asia will be at Srinagar in Kashmir. Europe will have its capital at Geneva. African capital at Addis Ababa, North American capital at Los Angeles, and South America will have its capital at La Paz.

Kashmir, Switzerland, Ethiopia, California and Bolivia will be called capital districts and will have autonomous governments.

Asia will be divided into the following three purely Asiatic districts : 1. Aryan, Iran to Asam; 2. Golden Land, Tibet to Japan;

and 3. Golden Aryan, Burma to Philippines. USSR will be common to Asia and Europe and Arab will be common to Asia and Africa as already mentioned.

Aryan	Capital	Karachi
Golden Land	Capital	Tsingtao
Golden Aryan	Capital	Bangkok
USSR	Capital	Tashkent
Arab	Capital	Medina

Europe will be divided into three purely European districts : 1. Nordic includes Germany, Austria. Norway, Sweden, Denmark and Holland.

Note : England will have option either to join the Nordic District or join the North American Federation.

2. Latin includes France, Italy, Spain and Portugal.

3. Oriental extends from Finland to Greece.

The fourth district of USSR will be represented in European government as well as that of Asia.

Latin	Capital	Monaco
Nordic	Capital	Copenhagen
Oriental	Capital	Budapest

Africa will be divided into three purely African districts : 1. Transvaal which will mean all South Africa. 2. Liberia, meaning all West Africa, including a part of Central Africa. 3. Ali which will include all East Africa with a part of Central Africa.

Arab will be common to Africa and Asia.

Liberia	Capital	Monrovia
Transvaal	Capital	Pretoria
Ali	Capital	Zanzibar

Note : I have also a suggestion to make Tunisia the National homeland of the Jews. It will function as an autonomous locality of Ali.

North America will be divided into three districts of 1. Canada, 2. United States, and 3. Mexico, Including West Indies and central America.

Canada	Capital	Vancouver
United States	Capital	Washington
Mexico	Capital	Mexico

South America will be divided into three districts : 1. Brazil, 2. Argentina plus Chile, and 3. Peru. Adjoining states federating with the neighbours.

Argentina, Brazil and Peru will have their capitals as at present.

Australia, New Zealand and Fiji islands, neighboring islands with Hawaii islands will form Capital District.

The capital of the world will be at Honolulu.

Hawaii islands will be called the Heaven.

My Story : It is rather dull this time. I am at my summer home, Pratap House, Rajpur, U.P. since the 8th of May, to be accurate, I arrived here at 8 p.m. on that date. My daughter and two grand children accompanied me. We travelled by jeep car from Vrindaban to this place. My driver drove too fast and therefore we were longer on the road ! Is it not funny ? Twice we had puncture and at the foot of the Shiwalik range our car refused entirely to move forward. Excessive heat burnt the coil. Full three hours we were detained here. A kindly sikh driver of a passing truck lent us his spare coil and we could continue our journey to the hills.

On 27th April I went to the village of Takha, in former Bharatpur Raj, where the family of my maternal uncles lives. It was a surprise visit. Once when they had made special preparations to give me a royal reception I could not keep my appointment. My car failed on the way. A passing car gave me a lift and I returned Vrindaban. At a moment's notice, my arrival was heralded and a crowd gathered. I lectured on my Mission. An uncle presented a purse. We hurried back. Today being Sunday, we must hold our prayer meeting. We arrived in time. Meeting was held. Boys were baptized, admitted into the Religion of Love !

On the 30th of April, correct to the fixed schedule, we arrived at the village of Darbe, accompanied by Ch. Virendra Singh, Advocate, and my daughter. A very high seat was prepared for me. I sat on it. Boys sang songs of welcome. Kunwar Dalbir Singh spoke a few words welcoming me. I delivered a long harangue. Ch. Virendra Singh also made speech. The village presented me a purse of two hundred and thirty one rupees. Taking rich tea at the residence of Kr. Dalbir Singh we returned home.

On the 11th, 18th and 25th of May, Sundays, we held meetings of the Religion of Love. Lala Krishna Gopal, the editor of 'Pawan' of Muzaffarnagar and a Sikh took oath of our religion. Sikhs, Muslim and Hindus attended our prayers. On the 25th I also fasted according to Islam, the 1st Ramzan.

Usually, I get up at about 6 or 6.30 in the morning. Washing, exercise, bathing and the prayer take about two hours. By 8 or 8.15 I am in the dining room. My breakfast is a piece of bread and tea. My daughter and two grand children take meals with me.

After reading the newspapers and the mail, I start writing. After 1 p.m. I take my lunch of three courses. These days we have lot of mangoes, leechies finished a week ago. Now I write letters. By 4.30 p.m. mail is dispatched.

Afternoon tea is served before 5 p.m. I take a walk in our spacious garden. Occasionally we go to Dehradun by our jeep. Dinner is served at 8.30 p.m. After prayer, I start writing. Today is the 9th June. It is 10.25 p.m. I am writing these lines. At 11.30, I go to bed.

During the last twenty six days, I fasted on three Thursdays, and the last day of Ramzan. On the 14th June I prayed at Idgah in Muslim congregation. This is my contribution to Islam.

I often go to Dehradun. I visit my friends. They also drop in people who have no cars as it is a dificult to come up to Rajpur. Two friends came and stayed with me for over a week. Shri Prashant, a journalist and an author, stayed here from Sunday the 28th June to Saturday the 4th July. He asked me many questions about my revolutionary activities. He is writing a book.

Diwan Shamdas Gidwani is the elder brother of Shri Choithram Gidwani, the great Sindhi leader of all India fame. He stayed with me from the 7th July to the 16th July. It was a pleasure to have his company. He introduced me to his several friends.

My trip to Musoorie was also due to the suggestion of Diwan Gidwani. He arranged with Babu Mahabir Prasad that I speak at the weekly Theosophy-meeting on the 24th June. On the 23rd June I went to Mussoorie and stayed at the Charlville Hotel. Diwan Sahib was also staying there. Diplomats from Delhi and their families come and stay at this Hotel. I met H. E. The Ethiopean Representative and the Counsellor of the German Embassy.

I gave two speeches at a religious congregation of Swami Hari Om in the big house of Sardar Ranjit Singh. On the 24th June, in the afternoon, I went to tea with Maharani of Kalsia, my sister-in-law, and later I spoke at the Theosophical Lodge which is conducted in a room of the Central Hotel. Audience was very poor. There are only about twelve members of the society and some guests come.

Wrong Foreign Policy : Our Delhi Government is blundering. Delhi high officials do not know what they are doing. The British made machine of administration is not obeying the guidance of the congress hands. They who think that they suffered due to the new set up of cabinets and legislative assemblies are trying to deceive the new rulers of the country. Voices such as mine are not allowed to be heard. My resolve to capture Delhi on the 10th of May 1951 was my way to bring the misled leaders to their senses.

With my long experience of China from 1923 to 1941, I can surely assert that the present Delhi government is going the way of Kuo Mintang. Our Pandit Nehru is committing the mistakes of Marshal Chiang. Red revolution is developing round the corner !!

And–And–Pandit Jawaharlal Nehru is unnecessarily annoying the United States of America, the most powerful States of the present age. I can not dare to abuse of give names either to USA or USSR, I say, our country should be strong. Military strength and contentment of the people within the boundaries make a country safe from within and from without. Delhi is unfortunately not doing that.

Wrong Governments : They are responsible for the present wrong conditions prevailing in society. The so-called democracy, a bunch of some wrong ideas, is misleading our people. Pandit Nehru does not care to think, why he thinks, what he thinks ? He thinks, because his thinking was developed under the direct influence of the English education. And in that education was the secret hand of the English desire to keep the British Empire intact. Pandit Nehru in spite of this harangues of independence and neutrality is keeping India within the British commonwealth, and is sticking to the British plan of Pakistan. He is led by the ideas instilled into his head by the British.

It is also wrong with our people. Over two hundred year of the British rule in the country has made our people British pupils by training. If I had not lived long in foreign countries, in Japan, Afghanistan and China, if I had not visited eleven times Moscow and Berlin and six times United States, I would have thought and talked as most of my countrymen, including Pandit Nehru, do.

Our Provincial Governments and the Central Government are wrongly constituted by wrong conceptions, by wrong dealings and by wrong means. The whole process of forming and running the governments is called democracy, 'government by the people.' Poor people are also lulled to believe that it is so. Infact, it is a great hoax.

My Tour to Capture Delhi

I announced in December that I would be touring in January.

I have already toured the districts of Muzaffarnagar, Meerut, Bulandshahr, Aligarh, Mathura, Bharatpur and Gurgaon. On the 14th of March, this month, I spoke at a very large meeting at Delhi. All over, I preached the World and declared that we would capture Delhi on the 10th of May, this year! At three different places, centre of the Religion of Love were also established. Thousands have promised that they would support me in my plan and programme.

I was very glad to see that some Congress men and government officials also intelligently appreciated that I would be able to save the country from the chaos of red revolution and the invasion of Pakistan.

Our Aryan New Year was observed here at Rajpur on the 20th-21st-22nd March.

I am leaving again on the 2nd April. Via Hardwar and Saharanpur I am proceeding to Chandigarh. Via Patiala and Karnal I shall enter the district of Rohtak about the 14th of April. I shall enter Delhi district on the 4th of May. On 10th of May I shall reach Delhi. Some changes in the tour had to be made as I was called to Mathura side. And further changes are made as I am going to the capital of Punjab. Dates may still have to be altered according to the wishes of my co-workers

My Story : On the 2nd April 1954 I left. I started late. I arrived late at Rishikesh. I just called on the Shivanand Ashram. I did not enter it. I sent greetings to Rev. Swamiji. A young Swami came out and touched my feet. I was surprised. It was the first time that a Swami paid such homage to me. At Hardwar I visited the 'Hindu' office and called at Shakti Ashram and Gurukul. It was agreed that I once again visit Hardwar on the 12th April and preside over a meeting on the 13th.

14th April. Jeeping back one hundred and sixty miles arrived at Sonepat. Stayed with Ch. Chandrabhan Advocate. Visited a village, eight miles, here was a marriage. I spoke to the guests. Established Love Centre at the residence of Shri Virendra Harijan. Rohtak district has a ban on meetings. I just got some people together at private houses and explained to them my programme, at the villages of Rohat, Jharaut, Sisana, Kansala and Pakasma. I stayed at night at Rohtak with Ch. Sri Chand ji M. L. A. I had a long talk with Pandit Sri Ram, ex-Congress leader, ex-minister.

16th April. Visited Bhor and Bhalot. Had lunch with Zamindar Ram Swarup. At Bhor I could meet many people who listened to me with great interest. In the evening came from Rohtak to Rukhi. Many People gathered to hear my message, the plan to capture Delhi, on the 10th of May.

17th April. I met a few persons at Bhainswal. Dr. Ram Mehar who is accompanying me from Sonepat can easily get people gathered. At Rabra a crowd heard me. This is a village where police recently blundered and trespassed and committed atrocities. I appealed to the people to fraternize with the police. In the evening we reached Shahpur in Karnal district. Here we held open meeting. Gathering was fairly large.

18th April in the morning reached Bijawa. Held meeting. Had lunch at Kaith. Many people came to hear me. In the evening I came to Butana School. I was a guest of principal Ch. Bhaja Ram.

19th April. I addressed the students on my educational programme. Stayed a bit at Ghillor. Spoke to people. Met Rao Lal Chand at Rohtak. Stayed at night at Bahu Akbarpur. Many people came and heard me with keen interest.

20th April. At Kharkhara had lunch and spoke to people who visited me. Proceeded to Mahem and stayed with Captain Bharat Singh. Right royally he gave us feast. He is a specimen of old chivalry.

21st April. In the morning I spoke to a group of people at Mahem. Had lunch at Chandrapal Bhaini. Spoke to people. Came to Balhamba. Here I visited the Monastery, spoke to monks. At night I spoke on religion to a large crowd.

22nd April. Visiting Rohtak came to Maina. Stayed with a local supporter. At night fairly large gathering heard me. Three boys sang.

23rd April. Visiting Rohtak at noon came to Karontha. Had lunch with a former Bharatpur I. G. family. Spoke to a few people. Again visited Rohtak and had tea with Ch. Sri Chand Ji. At night came to Deeghal and stayed with Captain Dalpat Singh. He plainly said that he served the British loyally and now he was loyal to the present government. He is the chairman of the District Board for many years.

24th April. At Gochhi met Ch. Jainti Ram, another specimen of the old school. At Beri Seth Atmaram gave rich lunch. Subedar Tekchand was helpful. All night stayed with Ch. Mahboob Singh, fine young man of modern ideas. Here a fairly large gathering heard me, but of course in a private house, no public meeting was possible.

25th April. I visited the villages of Shalipur, Malikpur, Majra and Dubaldhan, here I had lunch. At all these four places people gathered to hear me. Visiting Rohtak came to Kanehli and stayed for the night with Ch. Sunder Singh. Here a large private meeting was held.

26th April. Visiting Rohtak came to Kherawar. A large crowd heard me at night. I stayed here in a temple.

27th April. Had lunch and a private meeting at Kheri Sadh. Visited Rohtak. Came to Ismaila and spoke to people. I stayed with Ch. Surat Singh.

28th April. Stayed a couple of hours and met some friends at the house of Ch. Mehar Singh at Sampla. I addressed the students of Bhaproda School. Had lunch. Had talk. Visited Garhi, the birth placed of Sir Chhotu Ram. Met many friends. At night stayed at Chhara. In the house of Rai Sahib a large crowd heard me.

29th April. I visited Matan and at a road side place, had lunch at Kharar. People heard me at the three places. Captain's wife was over courteous. She gave fine lunch and tea. Stayed at night at Madoth. Risaldar Sahib was very helpful. People came and heard me.

30th April. Visited Rohtak. Had lunch with Ch. Sri Chand. Ch. Sultan Singh, a red leader, accompanied me to Asauda. There was a marriage. I spoke to the guests. Late at night another group heard me.

1st May. In the morning I spoke to the guests of a marriage party at Asauda. Had lunch at Bahadurgah. Visiting a village, passing Najafgarh, stayed at Chhawla. It is in Delhi State. A large open meeting was held. Here there was no ban on meetings.

2nd May. Met some people at Mitrau, meeting was held at Dhasa. Visited Badli, did not stay, stayed at Jahangirpur. Here people enthusiastically received me. Spoke at night in a private meeting. It is in Rohtak district.Via Jhajjhar came to Rohtak. Took leave of Ch. Sri Chand. Came at night to Saidpur. It was very late.

4th May. Had breakfast at Jatola. Fairly large meeting was held. Came to Halalpur. Explained my programme to some Panchayat members. At Jhinjhili had lunch and a private meeting. Visited Acharya's Ashram, a fine hospital, had tea. Came to Auchandi, Ch. Bamal arranged a large meeting. I spoke at length. It is again Delhi State. A purse of Rs. 51 was presented.

Now open meetings are held. I spoke at Nagla Thakran. D.A.V. School of Bawana gave me a good opportunity to propagate my views. Principal endorsed my programme. I spoke to a marriage party at Bazidpur. Stayed at Narela for the night. Here a small meeting was held late at night, after a marriage feast.

6th May. Visited Nayabans, Khera Khurd, Khera Kalan, Swami Vedanand Ashram, Jat School, stayed at Alipur at night. Here storm gave some trouble but good meeting was held. Meetings were also held at Nayabans and at Khera Khurd where we had lunch.

7th May. Visited Sahibpur, Puth Khurd and Sultanpur, where I had lunch, Kanjhawala, Ghewra, and Tikri Kalan. Here again a marriage gave me a good opportunity to reach people of many villages. I spoke at all these places to many people. At night I stayed at Pahladpur. Storm again obstructed my work but kindly a large meeting was held. I was a guest of Captain Kunwar Singh.

8th May. This morning I came to Delhi City to meet friends and to see the arrangements for the 10th May. Our headquarters was at Rao Umrao Singh's Dharmshala. In the afternoon we visited Palam and stayed at Bijwasan. Th. Sansar Singh accompanied me. At both the places large meetings were held. We spoke at length.

9th May. Came to Delhi. Had second breakfast with Dr. Bhattacharya, Chief Medical Officer of New Delhi, who visited our headquarters. Went to Maharauli, on way saw Qutab Minar. Spoke to the village folk. Passed night at Delhi.

The story of the 10th May I had written before. I and many companions got dinner at Rao Umrao Singh's residence. At 8 p.m. left by jeep for Rajpur.

Travelling the whole night we arrived at 6 a.m. on the 11th May back at our Rajpur home. It was a hurried retreat.

My Story : I received several important visitors. Kunwar Asghar Ali Sahib, Rais of Loi, Muzaffarnagar, paid a visit on the 12th May. Rani Sahiba of Khairigarh, General Lakshmi Shamsher Jung Bahadur Rana of Nepal, Colonel Shamsher Singh, H. H. Rani Sahiba of Kalsia and the Kalsia family, former Diwan Sahib of Kalsia, Raja Charat Singh and Rani Sahiba of Sahanpur, brother Swami Achint Chintanswami Anand of Delhi, Princess Kookoo. Wife of famous Air Commodore Narendra and other kindly dropped in. My daughter Kumari Bhakti Devi had to entertain our guests.

On the 20th and the 27th May, both Thursday, I held Muslim fast, Roza. I did not eat in the day time and ate at night according to the dictates of Islam. This month is the month of Ramzan, the month of Muslim fast.

28th May. At 5.30 pm. Princess Kookoo, widow of famous air commodore Narendra brought car and took me and my daughter to Mahatma Kirpal Singh. The only son of the late Dr. Tagore was also present. After tea we went to a hall at Dehradun. Mahatmaji asked me to speak. I spoke on my Moral Front. I was glad to see that the audience intelligently followed my arguments. Mahatma ji delivered his sermon for over one hour.

I Admit Defeat

I could not capture Delhi on this 10th of May as I had announced. I kept all my dates. I toured through districts. People enthusiastically received me, heard me, promised me that they would surely reach Delhi on the 10th May and accompany me to the Rashtrapati Bhawan, but they did not keep their promise. Some important person duly arrived and spoke to the people present at the meeting place. They spoke some fine words. They spoke of quality. They kindly praised me. But it was a poor show. They knew. I saw.

Schedule was kept. We formed into a procession. Flags flew high on poles. People walded. I walked. Maharao Krishnpal Singh walked by my side. Captain Khan Iqbal Mohemmad Khan and Swami Abhekant remained with me. Slogans were inspiring. 'We have power.' They often repeated 'Victory to Aryan Peshwa'. 'We shall build Aryan–Iran to Assam.'

We walked through crowded streets. At Ajmeri Gate we got into jeep, taxies, tongas and a truck. We reached the President's Palace. Here the police officer of the police van, which was accompanying us, asked me very politely that we should proceed no further. Here was a ban on processions and on meetings. Only four persons could enter the palace. I chose Thakur Sansar Singh, Founder of Shakti Sandesh, Kunwar Kaim Singh Chauhan and Captain Iqbal Khan to accompany me.

We had to wait long at a lawn. A Secretary came and very politely told me that Mr. Chatterji could receive me. We went in. Soldiers at the gate saluted me. We were ushered into a cool room. The officer shook hands. I addressed the officer as colonel. Smiling he said that he was already a general, since three years. Noticing that he had some difficulty in speaking Hindustani I started talking in English. I explained that I was conducting a campaign for last several months and now I wanted to see the President and put before him my programme. He told me that the President was asleep, he did not receive my letter, he would have been pleased to see me if I had written him before hand and fixed time. I said, I admit my defeat. I could not bring the crowd as I had wished. I could have obliged the President to receive me. I have a revolutionary plan. Thakur Sansar Singh, speaking in Hindustani put in that I had not come to ask for an interview but to place the plan before the President. General Chatterji made it clear that it was not possible. The president is a poor old ailing man.

We took leave and returned to our friends outside the palace. I spoke to my friends and followers. Let us disperse, return home quietly. We should admit our weakness and build further strong movement. This government cannot last long. The only question is who and who are to replace them. If we do not succeed in making this government healthy and strong, communists must succeed.

My story : I have not much to report. From 28 May 1854 I am living quietly at my Rajpur home. I do not call it now my summer retreat, I live here permanently.

Bhakra Dam Opened

It is the greatest news of India during the period. It has created wildest commotion in Pakistan. Sense of universal well being is lacking on both sides. Pakistan Press is said to have demanded war on this account and on account of unsetteled problem of Kashmir ! Thousands may die now and thousands my die in future, it does not concern these hot heads led by wrong ideas and agitated by nervous blood.

The remedy in not the blind press on both the sides. It is in fact responsible for attacks and counter-attacks. With cool and head open eyes we should work for the creation of Aryan, it is the only remedy. We shall then see to it that all the resources of Aryan benefit all the peoples of this land.

Supposing war comes on account of the canal system, will not then the green fields of this territory be destroyed due to army movements and will not hundreds of thousands of people be killed! What is the use of building of the banks which are cut by a rushing stream? We should first destroy the causes of destruction.

The same thing is true all over the world. They are building huge buildings in Russia and America which are sure to be destroyed, together with their occupants, if people allow themselves to be led by wrong ideas. I want immediate purification of mind.

Congress Session at Ajmer :

All India Congress Committee is meeting at Ajmer on the 27th July. I am writing these lines on the 20th of July 1954. It will be a great function, thirty or forty thousand persons might gather there. Half a million rupees might be spent on this show. These political meetings and religious gatherings of hundreds of thousands of people is a curse to our society. They tax time and energy of humanity. I know that all over the world such functions are held and lot of time and energy are wasted in the name of party or religion. We must try to stop this wastage as much as possible.

There is another evil side to this Congress meeting. People gather in the name of the Congress asposed to all other parties. Pandit Jawaharlal Nehru, as the president of the Congress, might ask all the people of this country to unite but his Congress as a struggling body, opposed to other parties, dominating the Government, is creating disruption. Slaves who served the British for gold or copper can continue to serve the Congress for pittance but how can a free man agree to serve a party of its Government which rules as the ruler and keeps all others as subjects? It is not the people's Government, It is party's administration to exploit the people outside of the party! Down with it !!

Impeachment of Pt. Nehru on account of the following charges :

1. He agreed to the division of the country.
2. He agreed to keep India within British Commonwealth.
3. He deceived the people at home and abroad by saying that the country was entirely neutral when it remains within the British empire under a new name.
4. He is responsible for this new system of political slavery: India under the British, China under the Russian, Japan under the USA and the like.
5. He is responsible for miserable condition of Indians in Ceylon and South Africa.
6. He is responsible for Pakistan's treaty with USA.
7. He did nothing to stop carnage in Malaya and East Africa.
8. He displeased the Hindus by his pro-Pakistan policy.
9. He is displeasing Muslims by doing nothing to stop anti-Muslim feeling which is rising in the country.
10. He did not do anything to save Tibet.
11. He is responsible for the present unsettled situation in Nepal.

12. He should have made alliance with Afghanistan and Iran to realize Aryan and thus end Pakistan danger.
13. His foreign policy is extremely faulty, India has no friends abroad, friends who could help India in time of need.
14. Money of India has been squandered on show of Embassies, Legations and Consulates.
15. Time and energy is wasted in Congress meetings, opening, foundation laying and darbar functions.
16. Money is wasted in dinners and tea parties.
17. Morality is not introduced in administration.
18. Immoral cinemas, prostitution and gambling are not banned.
19. Intoxication is not prohibited all over the country.
20. World Federation with unity of religions and the economic system of a joint family has not been accepted as the creed of the Government.

**There are more points but these are sufficient to impeach the Prime Minister.*

My three friends died. When I had just started our Campaign to capture Delhi came the sad news that my friend, who had blessed our campaign, H. E. General Bijaya Shamsher Jung Bahadur Rana, Ambassador of Royal Nepal, died in a bath tub with an electric shock. When I entered Rohtak, the great recruiting ground of the Indian army in April last, I was shocked to hear that my friend Dr. Satyapal, the speaker of Punjab Assembly, suddenly passed away. It was reported his heart failed. Only thirteen days previous to his death he gave me fine reception at the capital of Punjab. On Monday the 19th July 1954, died my very good friend Dr. Bhattacharya, the health officer of New Delhi. On the 9th May, a day before the date fixed to capture Delhi, he gave me royal breakfast, at his residence, at New Delhi. Bengali spirit of the family appreciated my revolutionary programme. According to newspapers, he was stabbed on Saturday by one his ex-subordinates! Rushed to a hospital where he died. I am horrified by the news. I wired my hearty sympathy to his family. All three died under suspicious circumstances. I wanted to visit the late doctor in August in connection with unity of Bengal but it was not to be!

My Story of July : Miss Kahn and Mr. Alter came and invited me to their newly opened Christian Centre. My daughter and my grand child went and saw the films of Jerusalem on Monday the 5th July. A Professor of Princeton University, USA lectured, explaining Biblical sites.

My grand son and grand daughter have left for their schools. Shri Amar Pratap has gone to Vrindaban to study at the Institution I founded in 1909. Shri Sarla Pratap has gone to Banasthali Girls Vidyapith, a famous institution, founded by Pandit Heeralal Shastri, former Premier of Rajasthan and once one of the most influential leaders of the Congress.

It is now rainy season. It is raining as I am writing these lines. The monsoon has been two weeks late this year. But in some places it has been very severe. It struck Bombay with violence.

25th July Sunday. At 10 a.m. spoke at Shahanshah congregation. At 11 a.m. held prayer at Dharma. Raja Charat Singh, Sardar Qudus Khan Kaji and Shri Garg were there. We brought in our jeep Sardar St. Nihal Singh, the famous writer and his American wife and Mr. S.P. Gidwani. Shri Ulfat, Mrs. Pandey also joined us. My daughter gave them a lunch party. In the evening we held our regular Sunday service. Many people came. I delivered the sermon.

I end the story of July here I was attending to my routine work : writing circulars and letters, meeting friends and visiting Dehradun. It rains these days but it often happens that it rains hard at Rajpur and it does not rain at Dehra Dun, only six miles away.

My Story of August : 1st August 1954. Sunday. This morning arrived Mr. Hitaka from Japan via Calcutta and Delhi. He is staying with me. As usual we held prayer at Dharma, Dehradun at 11 a.m. One new visitor was Sardar Baisakha Singh, retired contractor of Delhi, one of the richest men of the capital. Neither we asked him nor did he present any offering to our Club or the Centre. In the evening at 8.30 we held Sunday Service at Rajpur. I spoke on unity of religions and on the need of this teaching in our country.

5-8-54. Diwan Gidwani came. We had lunch together. My daughter had arranged a tea party at Dharma, World Federation club. Newspapers' reporters, local editors and correspondents were invited to meet Mr. Hitaka and to hear my programme of the Aryan Federation. The meeting was lively. Mr. Hitaka declared that he would devote his life for World Federation and Religion of Love. Rani Sahiba Sahanpur gave us dinner, packed in a neat box. My daughter and Raja Charat Singh saw us off. I and Mr. Hitaka left by the night train.

6-8-54. In the early morning we arrived at Delhi. Mr. Hitaka went to the Japanese Embassy. I took a room at the Constitution House. In the afternoon I had tea with H. E. the Afghan Ambassador. To my great delight he was the same person who entertained me at Rome in 1930. Princess Cuckoo took me to Rev. Sant Kirpal Singh. He gave us heavy tea.

7-8-54. At about 9-30 a. m. I arrived Mathura. Mr. Hitaka accompanied me. Maharao Krishnpal Singh and Ch. Birendra Singh met us at the Station. Maharao Sahib brought me in his car to Vrindaban. In the afternoon we went again to Mathura to attend the tea party given by Ch. Birendra Singh. We talked on different topics. I delivered a speech on our movement.

8-8-54. Sunday. Captain Ram Swarup Singh took me to Mathura. At 1.30 p.m. we arrived at the Gandhi Park. Here the meeting was held. I formally inaugurated the Aryan Federation as a party to fight all elections in all Aryan. Taking tea with Maharao we returned to Vrindaban. In the evening we held the Prayer meeting at our large Love Centre, the first Centre opened in India in 1946. I spoke on the history of the Religion of Love.

10-8-54. Today was Id. I wanted that Muslims would come and hold Id Namaz at our Centre as once Hafiz Md. Akbar Khan was doing. I received visitors at our Centre but no one arrived for the prayer. Later two Muslims came and informed me, 'they got afraid.'

14-8-54. Today was Brahman festival (Raksha Bandhan). Three Pandits came and tied Rakhi on my right hand. Brahmans change their sacred thread on this day.

15-8-54. Sunday. Before the Indian flag I spoke to the School students on the significance of this day. I repeated however that the full freedom was yet to come when we would be out of the British Commonwealth and Aryan would be realized.

18-8-54. At 2-30 p.m. I left by car. At Mursan we had tea with Raja Bahadur. He accompanied me. We had another tea at Sasni with my cousin Swami. Raja Bahadur brought me to Aligarh opened his house for me. He returned to Mursan by the same car.

19-8-54. I visited Th. Jhamman Singh, Th. Todar Singh and my old class fellow Abdul Majid Khawaja. I attended to our estate business.

20-8-54. By bus I came to Meerut, changing bus I arrived at Dehradun at about 7 p.m. It was all along fine drive.

21-8-54. Today is the birth day of Lord Krishna. I fasted. At midnight we celebrated the birth of the Lord with our town people.

Corespondence : Premier of our province Hon'ble Pandit Govind Ballabh Pant kindly wrote :

My dear Raja Mahendra Pratap,

I was glad to receive your letter of 9th. It is always a pleasure to hear from you. It is long since I last saw you. If some such opportunity offers itself, I shall of course be delighted to meet you. The Trust has, I understand, been running both the institutions to which you have referred in your letter so far. How far it will be proper of advisable to split the two I cannot say. The Trust has been making a substantial contribution towards the cost of maintenance of the College and unless it continues to receive this assistance, its work and progress will both be hampered. Hope this finds you well.

Yours sincerely
G. B. Pant

I am very thankful for this kind response but the fact remains that the Trust that I created has not at present sufficient income to run both the School and the College. When I created the trust the net income was twenty seven thousand and five hundred rupees. It rose later to over thirty four thousand, still later it came down to 24 thousand but now due to the new land policy of the government only sixteen thousand rupees will be received by the trustees. I once again dare to suggest that U. P. or Central government should run the Technical College and the Trust should run the school.

My Story : 2nd October was Mahatma Gandhi's birth day. We had a homely feast at home.

8th October. The casual meeting with Maharana of Dholpur assumes importance because His Highnes passed away on the 22nd October. His words : 'We are going' were significant. I asked him where ? He said, Hardwar, Rishikesh. I asked him, was he happy at heart ? He said, 'How can I be Happy under the present circumstances !' Here I pray for his soul.

14th. Shri Someyendra Nath Tagore and his Gujarati wife came down from Mussoorie. We had tea together. Shrimati went to a friend. Mr. Tagore stayed with me. I met him first at Moscow. He told me, it was in 1927. It was a pleasure to exchange views with him. I requested him to co-operate with me in my plan of reunion of Bengal within Aryan.

Travelling by bus and train I arrived at Aligarh on the 16th October evening and stayed with Thakur Jhamman Singh, advocate.

From 8 to 11 a.m. next day we had Old Boys meeting at the Muslim University, occasionally I expressed my opinion on different topics. I invited brethren to visit our Dehradun World Federation Club. At noon in the big hall Sir Syed Day was observed, lectures were delivered. At 1 p.m. rich lunch was served by the Old Boys Association. Later I visited my old class fellow Khwaja Abdul Majid Sahib, lying in bed with a bone fracture. I was very sorry to see him in this sad condition. At 5 p.m. rich tea was served in the Old Boys Lodge. At this occasion I delivered a harangue, pointing out the dark side of Pakistan and presenting my remedy of Aryan. At about 7 p.m. started Students Union meeting and later dinner was served to over 4 thousand students and guests management was excellent, food was delicious, gathering was jolly.

In the morning of the 21st I was back at Dehradun. My jeep brought me to Rajpur. I plunged into my routine work. Kunwar Asghar Ali, our Nawab dropped in with his retinue and stayed with me one night. On Sunday I held usual prayer meetings. I am busy with circulars, visitors and correspondence. I have finalized the constitution of Aryan Federation.

Constitution of Aryan Federation

As a part of World Federation.

Article I

Object. The object of the Aryan Federation is the realization of healthy, prosperous and peaceful life by every individual in Aryan and the world, and with that object to form homogenous, practical, contiguous areas as federations. The whole Federation for the time being we concentrate on Aryan from Iran to Assam. With the above object we establish the following fundamental rules :

1. One party. one Government. No bifurcation of persons in opposing groups or parties. Every one shall try to achieve absolute good.
2. Every one to follow his own faith or religion with love and consideration towards his fellow men. All religions to strive for unity. All castes, tribes and nations to be interwoven for common good and Religion of Love and joint family, where elders shall be respected, children will be brought up with care and able bodied men will work with the motto 'all to work for all to make all happy'. There will be no untouchability, and an equal opportunity of status for all irrespective of race, caste, colour, creed or sex.
3. Emphasis shall be laid on moral character – sadachar. Gambling, drinking, prostitution, bribery, oppression and immorality of all kinds shall be suppressed.
4. Every village and town shall have complete home rule, i.e. it will be organized as a joint family with its schools, hospitals, police, courts and administration in every possible way, self sufficient with full control of its agriculture and industries, levying taxes according to their requirements.

5. Villages and towns shall be interwoven into districts, provinces and federated states. Every unit paying one tenth of its income to the districts, districts paying one tenth to the provinces and province paying one tenth to the States with the object of coordination and project of common good. The State will be in charge of only defence, communications, exchange and foreign policy. In a nutshell there shall be local liberty but all unity in federation.
6. There shall be no one without work and no one without the daily bread and lodging. All will work according to their ability and get according to their needs. The difference between the lowest and the highest will gradually be narrowed and universal prosperity shall be evolved. Teachers, doctors, vakils, judges, administrators and the able and learned will work for the good of the people and shall not be allowed to amass fabulous wealth with selfish greed.
7. Every village and town shall have a council of elders and honest men and village and town shall function as a joint family. They shall build their own schools, with fields, gardens, factories and dairy farms.
8. Soldiers shall produce through farms and factories all their needs in the cantonments and will be allowed to live with their families.
9. Workers in big establishments, factories and mines will be made partners and will get half the share of profits, the other half forming a reserve after paying at most 6 percent dividend on the capital.
10. Wars will be abolished. Disputes shall be settled by negotiations and arbitration by elders or chosen representatives.

Article II

The Aryan Federation will hold Annual and special sessions of the Federation and it shall have:

i. Aryan Federation Assembly.

ii. The Working Committee.

iii. Pradesh Federation Committee.

iv. District Federation Committee. Every city to have City Federation Committee.

v. Tehsil Federation Committee.

vi. A group of villages to have group federation committee.

Article III

The present tehsils, districts and provinces to be reorganized for the federation and the head quarters shall be constituted at their present positions.

Article IV

i. Any person of the age of 18 and over who accepts Article I, on making a written declaration to abide by the fundamental rules, shall on payment of an annual subscriptin of annas four only shall become a member of the Aryan Federation for the place where he resides.

ii. The year of membership shall be from 1st Jan. to 31st December of the same year.

Article V

The term of every federation committee, its office bearers, executive committee and members shall coincide with the corresponding elections of the Government.

Article VI

a. Permanent registers of members would be maintained by the group tehsil, district and Pradesh federations. And the Pradesh federations shall supply a list of their members to the Aryan federation.

b. Full name, address, age, occupation and caste and date of enrolment of every member shall be entered in the registers.

c. Membership shall cease by death, resignation, and non payment of the annual fee.

Article VII

All the members shall be entitled to vote. The elections for tehsil, district, Pradesh and Aryan federation shall be made from amongst the members. Castes can organize caste Sanghs and send representatives.

Article VIII

a. The date for the election shall be fixed by the Aryan Federation working committee.

b. Every Pradesh shall be entitled to return delegates to the federation in the proportion of one to every 10 lacs of population.

c. Aryan Peshwa Raja Mahendra Pratap shall be the patron member of the Aryan Federation for life with the power to veto any proposal and add or anull any rule. A President may be elected out of the delegates by a majority vote.

d. Members of Parliament, Assemblies and Councils who have filled the written declaration shall be associate members of the Aryan Federation and can take part in the discussions with a right of vote.

Article IX

a. Every Tehsil, District and Pradesh committee shall be constituted in the same manner by sending one representative for 500, 10,000 and 1 lac population each respectively. Each representative for Tehsil committee will pay Rs 1/-, District committee Rs 2/-, Pradesh committee Rs. 4/- and Aryan Federation committee Rs. 5/- as subscription. This subscription shall be utilized for the upkeep to the committee concerned.

b. Subject to the general supervision and control of the Aryan Federation working committee, every Pradesh committee shall be in charge of the affairs of the committee in its own Pradesh.

c. Shall submit its annual report of the work done and audited balance sheet.

d. Pay to Aryan Federation working committee its share of member fees, say 1/10th of the total collections from the members.

Article X

a. Aryan Federation working committee shall arrange to implement the programmes of word laid down by the Federation Assembly and shall have the power to deal with matters and situations that may arise during its term of office.

b. Form its plan of work with the approval of the patron and president.

c. 50 or 1/5th of the total delegates of Aryan Federation shall form the quorum for the Assembly meeting.

Article XI

Election disputes of the Tehsil, District, Pradesh and Federation shall be decided by the Tehsil, District, Pradesh and Federation committee by negotiations or arbitration by the elders or the chosen representatives of the committees concerned.

Article XII

Annual session of the Aryan Federation Assembly shall be held by the Aryan Federation working committee. Special sessions may also be called as and when necessary.

The working committee shall have the accounts of Aryan Federation audited and take such action in the interest of the Federation as it may deem fit provided the action so taken shall be submitted to the Federation Assembly for ratification.

There shall be a treasurer to be in charge of the funds, subscription, donation etc, who shall keep proper accounts of all investment, income and expenditure, There shall be one General Secretary and two joint secretaries who shall be in charge of the office of A. F. The General Secretary shall be responsible for the preparation and publication of the report of the proceedings of the Federation.

Article XIII

The flag of Aryan Federation shall consist of a yellow wheel of eight spokes in green back ground.

Article XIV

The constitution of the A. F. can be amended, altered or added by a full session of the Federation by a 2/3rd majority of the members present and voting after advance notice of the proposed change has been sent to each member one month before the date of such meeting but the special powers of Aryan Peshwa cannot be cancelled in any case.

My Story : 27th to 31st October. I was very busy in writing our Hindi, Urdu and English Circulars. Visitors also came. On Sunday we held prayer at Dharma, Dehradun and Pratap Kothi, Rajpur. Police got vacated half the house from a tenant who had not paid rent for a long time. We have four houses at Dehradun and one at Rajpur.

My Story of January 1955

I presided and lectured at a function of the Shahanshah Ashram School on Tuesday the 11th Jan. On two Sundays, the 9th Jan. and the 16th Jan. I prayed at Dharma at noon and at Pratap Kothi, Rajpur, in the evening. On these occasions I speak on the unity of religions. Different ideas filled into brains under different circumstances have been setting people against people. This fact should be realized and it should be understood that the needs of the different groups produced different ideas. Travelling that whole day-night and another day-night, via Delhi and Baroda I arrived at Borivli, near Bombay at 7 a.m. on the 23rd January. About a dozen friends were waiting for me since 4.30 a.m. as the train was to arrive at 5 a. m. It was two hours late. Friends garlanded me and showered flowers as I alighted.

On the 26th Jan., the Republic day I was kept busy from morning till late night. In the early morning I hoisted the National flag at a small school. At noon I presided and spoke at a Jan Sangh meeting. The whole afternoon was passed at a large gathering of several schools. Here they gave show, sang and danced. I had to stay till very end because I was asked to distribute prizes. At night took dinner with Swamiji and Mr. Sharma who put up this big function at Borivli.

27th Jan. Mr. Yagnik brought me in his car to Bombay and we returned. At night I came by train to Bombay and stayed at the Astoria Hotel.

28th. Seth Kotak and Janab Abu Fateh Ali and his brother came. I took lunch with Maharaj Kumar of Limbdi and family. Mrs. Ali took me out to Bandra in her car and I took dinner with her and Janab Fateh Ali. Several other friends came and we talked long. It was midnight when I went to bed at my hotel.

29th. Janab Ismail took me to Japanese and Afghan Consul Generals. I took lunch with Maharani Kalsia, my sister-in-law. Several friends visited me. Hakim Ikram and Ch. Lachhman Singh remained with me till the train moved out of the station.

30th Afternoon I arrived at Mathura. Visiting Ch. Birender Singh I came to Vrindaban. In the evening we prayed at the Love Centre. I conducted the prayer.

My February Story :Sunday, the 6th Feb. at Aligarh, I had heavy breakfast at the residence of Thakur Shivdan Singh M.L.A. Several friends were present Th. Jhamman Singh, advocate, Th. Netrapal Singh Chauhan M.L.A., Pt. Sharma were present. The Government pleader and a couple of others were there besides the host. I lectured on my programe quite informally, holding conversation. I was glad that my views were admired. May God give them strength to follow them. In evening I lectured formally and held prayer in one of the houses but now out of the Congress. Several B.A., M.A. students were present. I formally established a Love Center in this building. The time is not far distant when such Centers will circle the globe.

7th Feb. I left Aligarh by Bus. In four hours I reached Meerut. Swami Abhekant was waiting for me. He took me to his Gurukul, a school, at the town of Hastinapur. It was the first day of their function, they had put it for today to suit me. They presented an address. I delivered my sermon from the presidential seat. I need not repeat. I spoke on my patented educational system. I stayed here for the night. The people here believe in primitive style, thatched huts with open doors. Songs continued till late at night. It was very cold.

8th Feb. In the morning photos were taken. Primitive style did not object to this modern progress. Mr. Mehta gave breakfast. People complained bitterly that government settled them there but there was no business, no industry. This newly built city at the old historic site was going into ruin. Government wasted over ten million rupees on this pet scheme! 'High officials are getting high salaries, they are giving fine reports to government of the great progress but the people are running away having spent the loans received from the government !'

I came back to Meerut, came to Dehradun by bus and by taxi, arrived back at my house at 6 p.m. Thus ended this tour of eighteen days.

From the 9th Feb. to the 28th Feb., these twenty days I am quietly living at Rajpur. I have been very busy. I had to write and publish Hindi, Urdu and English Circulars. Hindi edition dated the 1st March, has just arrived from the press. On Sundays, 13th 20th and 27th of this March month, I prayed at noon at Dharma, Dehradun and in the evening at Pratap Kothi, Rajpur. On these occasions I always spoke on unity of religions. A former State Minister of Bikaner Mr. Khialiram came to visit me and stayed with me three days. Th. Harishchandra, a member of Municipality called a meeting here at my house to consider ways how to improve our town. It was decided that a public meeting should be held to take up and discuss the needs of Rajpur. Three suggestions were unanimously approved. The railway line should extend from Dehradun to Rajpur, distance of eight miles; government should be floated to acquire ruins and build modern cottages. Beautiful scenery and the fine climate all the year round should attract thousands of old people to pass their last days here in comfort. It is never here too hot as in the plains of India and it does not snow. Three thousand feet higher up is the queen of hill station, Musoorie. You can walk up there in three hours.

My Story : 1st April 1955. Visited Shahanshah Ashram. Met Miss Kahn. Went to Devi Temple. Held Prayer of Ramnomi, the birth day of the Religion of Love. Sardar Gurbachan Singh came to see me.

On 1.5.55 arrived at Delhi. Stayed at Constitution House. Received friends. Met friends.

2.5. Went with friends to see old cars. Took Tea with Rai Om Prakash Gupta, Tea party at Raizadeh Sahib, Pandit Sunder Lal who recently visited Russia and China was present.

3.5. Bought an old car and left by this car in the evening. After midnight at 2.30 a.m. arrived at my Rajpur home. Saw mail, heard report and went to bed at 3.30 a.m.

26.5. Pandit Hardev ji Astrologer of Solan came. He was interested to know the time of my birth. I went with companions to Sahasra Dhara. There are caves and sulphur spring.

Sunday 5 June. I went a bit earlier today to Dharma, Dehradun. Mr. Gupta and his friends, Mr. Rahi and others came. We talked together and prayed as usual. A bit earlier, held evening prayer at Pratap Kothi, Rajpur. At night I again went to Dehradun. There was a Muslim congregation at Doon School. Mr. Martin, the Principal, was also present. Molvie Al Mamoon presided. I spoke for twenty minutes. Returning I had to write my Circular. I went to bed after 1 a.m.

10.6. Sardar Abdul Qudus Khan Haji of Afghanistan brought valuable fruits and had lunch with me. Ch. Mahender Singh and Ch. Surat Singh had a tea with me. I went and paid a visit to ailing Janab Mujtaba Hussain Sahib, advocate and government pleader at a Hospital. I call him 'My Third Mujtba Hussain' One at Kabul, second at Lucknow and third this gentleman.

13th to 17th, June I was at Mussoorie. Here was cool and at night cold. Walking on the Mall one meets many friends. It was a pleasure to meet Ch. Hyder Hussain M. P., Mr. Gidwani, Sardar Gurbachan Singh and Kr. Mehdi Sahib. I and Maulana Al Mamoon had tea with Chowdhri Sahib. Once I took tea with Maharani Kalsia. Twice I went on invitation to Sanatan Dharm Temple where I had a talk with Swami Bhagwan and his friends. Jodhpur volunteers gave right military salute. I also attended a Theosophical meeting. I stayed at Walnut Grove Hotel.

18.6. An Englishman, Mr. Carter, former secretary of State in Tehri, has come to stay at our Cottage for a few days.

22.6. to 25.6. I visited Amritsar. Akali leaders kindly gave me good reception. I visited the Golden Temple and Akal Takht I attended the grand protest meeting. It is held daily in the afternoon. I spoke a few words. I saw the scene of Satyagraha. Batches of four came forward, shouted 'Long live Punjabi (speaking) Province, Hail Independent India,' and leaped into the waiting police van. When it was full it was taken away, another police van took its place. I came away at 9.30 p.m. on the 23rd June but the process of arrests continued till half past ten.

Akalies were jittery hospitable and also gave me full train fare. Sardar Hukam Singh M. P. and Sardar Hari Krishna Singh were there to bid me good-bye, on the 24th. Sardar Dhillon gave me lunch.

29.6. At tea, in the afternoon when both M. P.s came, I agreed to pay rupees thirteen thousand government bonds to Shri Hari who was trying to auction our house for his decree against my son who took a big loan from Hari. 30th turned to Rajpur.

Pt. Nehru and I

I sent an open letter to Pt. Nehru ji : You want to carry on the administration. You are satisfied with your position. You consider yourself very wise and fortunate. You look round and find millions of your admirers. Government servants support you. Congress is behind you. Thousands come to hear your speeches. You talk and talk and believe that you are a great orator.

I believe that you are a great failure. You are not what you wanted to be. Your policy is not carried out. You are led. You are not the leader in the true sense. This is the same government machine which suppressed the Congress till you made the agreement with the British and you agreed to act as an agent of the British Commonwealth. You began to herald of independence and of neutral stand to satisfy the people at home and to deceive the foreign States. But you deceived yourself most.

You speak of socialist pattern to please the British labour and to win over some of those Congressmen who separated from the Congress on the issue of socialism. The administration is running much the same. You do not pay any attention to the corruption rampant under your very nose in every department of the government. You dare to defend corruption. You are afraid of this huge racket. You feel, you are at their mercy who really rule the country. You lack the guts to suppress corruption.

I stand for Moral State. It is my strength and it is my weakness. Strength is of the great principle. Weakness is that corrupt rabble is opposed to me. But I know that the great principles win in the long run. We have to show great determination, strength of character and we should face and endure suffering in the path of our goal. Whatever Congress party achieved is the result of the work that it put in for the cause. I believe that now Congress party is working for the party and not for the country. And you are supporting the party.

You get angry if some one dares to point out to you that all is not well in the Congress, country and administration. You are happy and fully satisfied with your position. I do not seek your chair.

I want that our country comes out of the British Commonwealth. We build Aryan, Iran to Assam, as a district of the province of Asia of Federated World State. We give immediate Home Rule to every town and village. Workers are made full half partners of mines, factories and railways. Every School and College should have factory, fields and dairy farm. Students should produce their own necessities. They should own in common all the school property.

You do not listen. Struggles in Punjab and Rajasthan are signs of unrest in the country. Your army, as it is, is built up chiefly of Rajputs and Jats. I told you often that I can satisfy them through my Fauji Komi Sangh, union of the castes of the army. If they are not quickly satisfied you may have to face serious rebellion. You are kept in dark by the corrupt official class. As I often said, our country will suffer if extreme Reds of Hindu Fascists will create revolution. Mine is the only way of peaceful reorganization of the administration. I am prepared to help you if you agree to transform our society into a joint family !

I can do it. How can I be your enemy ? Believe me. I do not seek a job to make myself rich or to get fame. I believe in religion. I see the universe as ever changing phenomenon. Our tiny earth is a drop in ocean. I simply do my duty in my place. I feel, it is my duty to save the country from chaos. For the entire world there are today only two alternatives which you also declared : 1. Destruction, or 2. Long lease of security. You are trying to play the role of mediator. Mr. Menon runs to and fro. But you and Mr. Menon are utilized by Powers which count. I would like to build our own huge powerful bloc with Germany, Japan, Latin America and small States.

Army is to be overhauled. You can not do it. You are in the grip of your own secretaries. You are incapable to break the traditions. You simply can not do. Your convictions hold you in their webs. I wish to assist you in what you have failed so far. I said and I repeat that the traditions behind the Army officers and behind the soldiers should be wiped out. We build an army to be useful to our country and humanity. There should be fields and factories in all the cantonments. Our soldiers will produce necessities. You fear to bring in such a great change.

Do not get angry. Three persons recently approached me that I should not write against you. I should become your friend. I was never your enemy. I thought it better to put before you and your admirers this open discussion. If you can accept any one item of my program, we can cooperate on it. If you accept my Religion of Love I can myself initiate you in it by coming to your residence. If you help me to build World Federation Centre at Delhi I shall work for it with you. But if you feel I am entirely opposed to your way of thinking, please admonish your admirers who approached me.

Congress and My Plan

I was in the Congress. Indian National Congress, which worked for the entire country, to liberate the country and to make all the people happy.

Now Congress is a party which gives jobs for those who join the party. It may speak of the people, it may build some dams but when booty is divided the lion's share goes to the 'Congressmen.' I am opposed to this anti-national stand of the Congress party. I want to bring home rule at once to every village and town.

Organise castes, professions or religions in every village and town. The natural heads of these groups should build village and town governments. There will not remain a single fighting faction.

Municipalities and the District Boards will build provincial governments and the Provincial governments will build all India or all Aryan Central Government.

All the religious Institutions will be utilized to make Man moral. I say, morality can considerably reduce the expenses incurred on police, courts and hospitals. Make Man, I say do not burden him with unnecessary laws which create more corruption.

My Story : I was nearly dead in the morning of 29th July at Vrindaban. I was delivering a sermon to our school students after the prayer of the Religion of Love. I began to perspire. I felt weak. I sat down. I continued. I could not carry on. I said, I was feeling ill. I rose, I walked across the courtyard. I could not go up the steps. I sat and asked for cold water. Two school teachers were holding me, supporting me. In a split of a moment world disappeared for me. Cold water revived me. I got up. I felt extremely tired. I took bath. I was well enough to take some tea.

That afternoon two provincial ministers and a deputy minister were coming to our college. I went. I attended the meeting. The Hon. Babu Chandra Bhanu Gupta, Minister of Industries in U. P. highly praised me. He said, he would help the institution that my dream could be realised !

Next morning I had tea with the Hon. Minister at the residence of Hakim Brajlal ji Verman M.L.C. He told me personally that he would like to see that some industries are started at our school, so that both the school and the college flourish.

What a great contrast, here the State Minister was polite and wanted to oblige me but the district judge of Mathura got angry because I presented him a letter, addressed to him by one Mr. Hari. There was no case. The letter made the position clear. And how could I withhold the letter when I got it for the Judge.

One little incident tells volumes. On the 18th July it happened that I had only four rupees in my pocket. There was no bank balance left at my bank account at Dehradun. To get money from our estate would take several days. Just then came a man who bought five trees from one of our Dehradun houses and gave me four hundred rupees cash. The ways of God are mysterious. Men often do not realize the plan of the Creator and get worried but in our utter failure sometime hidden our great success. But for that sudden sickness on the 29th July I could not have got the opportunity to attend the Namaz at the Muslim University. God, God let Thy will be done! Men in their wisdom give me many advices: I should have complete rest. But I feel very happy as I finish these lines at quarter to twelve, just before midnight !

My Open Letter :To The President of the Congress :

Hon. Friend,

With all respect to your position I want to ask you, what really you are, the Boss of the Congress or a peon of the State? Are you dependent on the Prime Minister or he is dependent on you? It seems, you run to him, you receive his instructions and you simply carry on his wishes ! This is not the function of the Congress. It never was. I do not speak as a member of Half India Congress party. I speak as a man who joined All India National Congress in 1906. The present Congress party is creating friction, breaking up the nation and keeping the country within the British Empire. The word 'symbol' for the queen and the name 'commonwealth' for the empire are only meant to deceive the people and to give to the leaders some self-satisfaction. I stand for complete independence and for Aryan, Iran to Assam, a district of the province of Asia of World Federation or Federated World State.

I wrote you twice drawing your attention to our present internal problems. I assert that my solution is the best for Punjab and Rajputana. Congress could not stop the partition of the country and now the disruptive forces are developing on the newly created border and further down deep in the country.

As a religious teacher, or as I assert, as the Teacher of the age, I denounce drinking, immoral dancing, gambling, dirty shows and the time worn economic system but here in this letter I am confining myself only to one point : The cute condition in Punjab ! You do not seem to know its causes and therefore you do not know the remedy. I know and in the interest of our country and humanity I want to tell you, High Command and the Government Officials how, to cure the disease.

You do not pay any attention and your secretaries only send official answers. The matter is very urgent. I write this open letter that the public might also know that I tried my best to bring to your notice my remedy.

Is it not a fact that the Sikhs and the Hindus in Punjab are seriously struggling? All what you say or all what the officials do deepen the gulf. The Nationalist Sikhs or pro-Congress Sikhs do not bridge the gulf. Hindu Mahasabha is widening it.

The only remedy is that you and the honest workers of unity found immediately Khatri, Jat, Arora and Ahluwalia and such other caste associations. In these castes there are Hindus as well as Sikhs. The gulf in the name of the Sikh and Hindu will disappear.

Our Prime Minister, Hon. Pandit Nehru has many brilliant qualities but his hatred to the very name of caste does not allow him to see the expediency of this plan.

I shall be happy if Pandit Nehru ji can be converted to my Religion of Love or World Federation but if he would continue to impose English pattern on our society I shall earnestly request of the future of our country and people. I beg you to listen to me, discuss and understand my plan.

Goa massacre :I must confess my ignorance of this Satyagrah business. I was and I am for open warfare if fight we must. These brethren have committed suicide. Suicide is crime. And those rulers of Goa have committed man slaughter. It is most bastardly act, beastly behavior! I repeat that when we want peace, world order and justice for all it is not the right way. I am to intervene. I am ready to proceed to Lisbon and bring about peaceful settlement. I believe, we can arrange a new treaty with Portugal which will be of great benefit for both of our countries. Things as they are, our brethren are not uniting Goa to India but then are presenting it to the British Commonwealth.

Foolish Pakistanis :All are not fools. There are saints, scientists and great philosophers too living in that part of our Aryan which is called Pakistan. But they are great fools who have been misled to believe that the opposition to Afghanistan is a religious duty or National service ! Oh ! Ye fools ! How can you believe that yours is a Islamic State when it is still a part of the British Commonwealth? And when the ruler of that empire is the Defender of the Christian Faith? Believe not humbug, act not foolishly. Pull down your leaders who are deceiving you. I was greatly annoyed hearing a Persian discourse from Radio Pakistan. It was most mischievous. It openly dared to condemn Afghan rulers and instigated the peoples of Afghanistan to rise against their government. U.N.O., in fact, all the same peoples of this earth should not tolerate such acts leading to murders and wars. I shall not be astonished if some

Afghans of blue blood getting wild, hearing such discourse, murder some Pakistani officials, or war breaks out between Afghanistan and Pakistan ! We should take early notice of such aggressive propaganda and try our best to stop it immediately.

My Story : I am now practically my old-self once again. I have recovered 95 percent. I am taking medicines for heart toning and I work. I have restarted light exercise.

On the 3rd August I remained in bed but I dictated to my secretary both Hindi and English articles. I may tell you here that as a rule I always write myself. I take delight in writing. I seldom use typewriter.

On the 4th August, inspite of illness, I went to the Court and handed over before the Judge Bonds to the value of rupees thirteen thousand in paying off the decree against my late son. I had to get out one tooth by a dentist.

From the 9th I started to sit on chair. Shri Krishna, the pharmacist visited me on the 10th. Three Chaudharies of Muzaffarnagar came. Mr. Khanna with Mr. Singh and Mr. Carter were here for a little while. I went to Dehradun and brought Hindi and Urdu circulars. I visited Raja and Rani Sahanpur.

On the 11th I observed the fast of the birth day of Shri Krishna. At midnight today I held prayer meeting.

Shradha Mata came and took leave. She would leave tomorrow early morning by her car.

16th. A bank agent with a court officer came and attached my house for a petty decree of two thousand rupees. Our house in worth over one hundred and fifty thousand rupees.

17th. I took Raja Charat Singh with me and visited the bank manager and told him that I would give bonds as I gave to Mr. Hari for the bank decree. Today there was a general strike and processions were roaming the streets denouncing Goa massacre.

Correspondence : The Hon. Babu Sampurnanand ji, the Chief Minister of U. P. has been pleased to write me thus :

My dear Raja Sahib,

As desired by you, I went through the first two pages of the issue of your paper for August, as well as your open letter to the

Congress President. There was nothing new or surprising in these writings. The old Raja Mahendra Pratap whom we used to know and respect fifty years ago is no more. The body is there but an alien mind, which can only think in terms of Jat and Rajput, has taken possession of it. Your Aryan or whatever you call it is a dream which prevents you from seeing the realities of life. The country is going forward but you have deliberately shut your eyes to the march of time. One may not agree with all that Nehru says but today his voice is the voice of India. You are deceiving yourself and are perhaps yourself being deceived by some flatterers, if you really believe that there is discontent all round specially in the Army, and that you are in a position to set things right. I have been brutally frank in this letter but I thought this was the best service I can render to you as an old friend and well wisher.

Yours sincerely
Sampurnanand

I thank our Chief Minister that he took the trouble to serve me as a friend and well wisher. Thank God. I have not been brutal. And I am 'deceived', I did not deceive any body.

I replied :

Hon. Babu Sampurnand ji,

I see the march of time and I believe that to turn the tide I have been given birth. I mean to stop this trend to atheism and to make the world once again religious.

Aryan is only a district of the Province of Asia of World Federation. I have to realize this dream of the sages, prophets and incarnations to bring heaven on earth.

Alien means foreign. Rulers of today at Delhi have foreign mind. They think in terms of elections, democracy and parliamentarianism. To think in terms of Jats and Rajputs, Brahman, Bania, Kayasth, Chamar or Chandal is the thinking of the native Indian mind.

Fifty years before I was a student. In 1906 I joined the Congress when I was in the 3rd year. In 1909 I gave five villages and my big houses to the school and technical college which I founded at Vrindaban. In 1912 you kindly came to help me to serve as a teacher at our institution. In 1914 I let India to free the country with the help of Germany, Turkey and Afghanistan. In 1915 I founded the first provisional Government of India at Kabul. I was its President. I remained over thirty one years in foreign countries because I was declared traitor by the British. Still you respected me. In 1937-38, when you were the Minister of Education for the first time, you wrote me to Japan that you would like to introduce in U. P. my system of education of my institution. I still have your that letter. When I returned in 1946 your boss Pandit Nehru embraced me. Mahatma Gandhi so much liked the prayer of my Religion of Love that he asked me to hold prayer at his prayer meeting. I was in the Congress. I addressed hundreds of the Congress meetings.

I thank you once again for kindly sending me a response to my communication, with a view to serve me.

Yours
Mahendra Pratap

My Story : During these days only three items are worth mentioning. Swami Krishnanand ji Brahmchari of Calutta came. We arranged for him a tea party at the World Federation Club and a lecture at the Panchayati Temple, Dehradun. I conducted the prayer of the Religion of Love on Sundays. And I visited Moradabad to speak on the annual function of the World Federation Club.

Swamiji stayed at the Ashram of Swami Shradhanand ji. I visited the Ashram and had a long talk with ninety three years old Swami ji. I was very glad to see that the old Swamiji entirely supported my views of establishing Religious government at Delhi, a religious government which will be equally claimed to be their own by Hindus, Muslims, Sikhs, Christians and Buddhists ! It will be truly religious Government based on morality. Swami Krishnanand ji condemned cinemas which he said were spoiling our youth.

On all three Sundays 28th August and 4th and 11th September I held Service at Dharma, at noon and at Pratap Kothi, Rajpur, in the evening. Now more people attend our prayers.

Correspondence :I am very thankful that Hon'ble Prime Minister of Pakistan. Chaudhari Mohemmad Ali, cared to send an answer to my communication. He did not say whether he is the same gentleman whom I met at lunch at Karachi in 1947. But the fact that he wrote me. In spite of my very strong attack on Pakistan policy towards Afghanistan, speaks highly of his broad mindedness. He says :

Aryan Peshwa, Mahendra Pratap Raja, My dear Pratap,

Thanks for your kind message of congratulations on my assumption of office as Prime Minister. I have not yet seen your book 'Ittihadi Duniya.' I shall be interested to read it when it is received.

With kind regards,

Yours sincerely
Mohamad Ali

His addressing me by my name reveals his intimacy which he feels for me. I still addressed him with his titles, saying that I hesitate to respond in the same spirit, fearing that my attack on Pakistan policy which he would read in my circulars might annoy him. I sent him that it is not a book but a tiny journal. If Pakistan can agree to my plan of Aryan with local liberty but all unity in federation, I should like to visit Karachi at an early date. Now that Pakistan and Afghanistan have reestablished diplomatic relations my main fight is over. I want to explain that my plan of Aryan, Arab and Turan will benefit the Muslim world and humanity.

Hon'ble Babu C. B. Gupta, U. P. Minister of Planning, Health, Industries and Supplies, writes only a couple of lines but they have great significance as they are in response to my circular World Federation of September. He says :

My dear Raja Sahib,

I am in receipt of a copy of your paper, 'World Federation' and thank you for the same. Hope this finds you in the best of health.

Yours sincerely
C. B. Gupta

Our Chief Minister is a Doctor, philosopher, religious person, with a tinge of fanaticism, but Babu C. B. Gupta ji is a practical man, yielding here, compromising there, to carry through the work of the State. Some times he may be too kind to his friends but that makes him a very successful minister. I appreciate his good will for me.

I am very glad that Karachi has made peace with Kabul but I am very sorry to hear today the 19th September that Khan Abdul Ghaffar Khan is arrested.

I repeat that let the authorities of Karachi, Lahore and Dacca accept my plan of Aryan then we can do great service for the Islamic nations and humanity. United Punjab, united Bengal and united Pathans will live happy and will prosper within Aryan. Kashmir will be the Capital district of Asia and Sindh will be the Capital district of Aryan. Arab will extend from Oman to Moroco and Turan from Turkey to the Bering Strait. H. E. Janab Wahaba, ambassador of Hadjaz in London and many Turks of Central Asia appreciated this plan. Some prominent Afghans and Iranians approved of Aryan.

World Congress for World Federation

My Story : I left on the 12th October 1955 by the evening train which goes direct to Calcutta. I had my berth reserved. There was only one other passenger in the coupe.

In the morning we passed Lucknow. About noon we left Ayodhya back. In the afternoon the famous Kashi came and went. We crossed Ganges. Gaya was reached at about 9 p.m. Another night was passed. In the early morning of the 14th October we arrived Howrah.

Many friends and a batch of volunteers had come to receive me. I was profusely garlanded. Some volunteers said : 'The World' Others added: 'is one!' I was brought to a waiting big Buick car. I was taken to the large beautiful garden house of the Salkia Transport Co. I took lunch at their office premises.

At 5 p.m. the Meeting of the World Congress for World Federation began in a spacious hall of the Great Eastern Hotel, one of the two most fashionable hotels of Calcutta. I spoke at the meeting.

On Saturday, the 15th October, I presided at the two sessions of the World Congress. At the two sittings I spoke at length. I explained my programme.

This day I also visited two younger brothers of two great men, Mr. B. K. Ghose, brother of the late saint Aurbindo, and Mr. Bhupendra Nath Dutta, brother of the late Swami Vivekananda. Both of them have a reputation of their own. Mr. Ghose was in the Andaman, condemned by the British for his political activities. Mr. Dutta was the last president of the Indian Committee of Berlin. He lives in the same house where Swami Vivekananda was born. Great figures of the Indian freedom movement live neglected by the present Indian Govt. which is walking in the foot steps of the British overlords. Petting their pets, frowning at their bitter enemies.

Mr. Debnath Das came to see me at the last session of the World Congress. He was once put in prison as a communist. I spoke publicly in his favour. But now he has found an entrance to the official palace. He is a planning officer, having his office in the government house.

On the 18th I went to Haur. Here I got very rousing reception. Three kinds of bands were playing, As I walked along, village people came touched my feet or bowed to the ground. I asked them not to do it but they would not listen. By boats we arrived at the village of Jardoi. Here a big meeting was held. I spoke for fifty minutes. People were very interested in all what I said.

On the 19th I returned Howrah. On the 20th Hindu Mahasabha of Bengal gave me reception. And I spoke at length to the friends present.

I left Howrah the same night. Next whole day I was in the train. At Allahabad I changed to the boggie which goes direct to Meerut. At 9.15 a.m. on the 22nd October I reached Meerut. At 11 a.m. got bus for Dehradun. The Calcutta trip over shadowed all the rest of story of this period. But I must mention in a few words my visit to Kalsi and Sahiya on the 23rd-24th September and a visit to Mussoorie on the 7th-8th October. Pandit Thapliyal took me to Kalsi. Here in the Arya Samaj hall I delivered a lecture to the Kalsi people. It was raining. Still we went to Sahiya by car. We could not go up the mountain as it was planned. We were guest of Thakur Chohar Singh. I spoke on my plan to a few persons who came to Dharmshala next day. And we returned, taking tea at Kalsi and visiting the famous rock edict of Emperor Asoka.

On the 24th October I left by car for Aligarh. We arrived 11.20 p.m. nearly midnight, at our destination.

From the 4th Nov. to the 10th Nov. I was at Rajpur, often visiting Dehradun, six miles off. Rana Kunj Shamsher Jung Bahadur and Thakur Chandan Singh, Thakur Sansar Singh, Sardar Abdul Qudus Khan Afghan and several friends came. But the most important event was the lunch of H. M. the King of Nepal given by Raja Sahib of Poonch. Col. Ajaib Singh brought invitations for me and my daughter and we went. There I had the opportunity to have a little talk with His Majesty. I told him how I got the title of His Majesty for the Maharajadhiraj of Nepal from the Kaiser of Germany in 1915, after that the British recognized that title. His Majesty was pleased to tell me that I could come to Nepal after the first week of December when he would be back home.

It was another great delight to meet some generals of our army. I had a long talk with them. Retired General Nathu Singh was there too. Thanking H. H. Raja of Poonch we returned Rajpur.

11th Nov. Car gave a bit of trouble. I left Dehradun at 11 a.m. and arrived at Aligarh at 8.15 p.m. I went straight to Khwaja Sahib. There arrived the Hon. Minister Dr. Syed Mahmud, Minister in our Foreign Office. We took dinner together and talked long on my programme. A little before midnight I took leave. Next Day, early, before the time of lunch, I and Thakur Todar Singh arrived at the residence of Khwaja Sahib. There was great bustle. Many great leaders had arrived. The Hon. Pandit Jawahar Lal Nehru was coming to lunch. Over three hundred guests were invited by Khwaja Sahib. I was specially invited by my friend to meet the Prime Minister. I met many friends but the meeting with Pandit Nehru was confined to twice hand shaking.

The Hon. Pt. Nehru P.M. : Some People who do not know facts think that I either neglect our Prime Minister or avoid him. It is not true. My class mate at Aligarh and class fellow of Pt. Nehru in England called me from Rajpur to join the lunch party which he gave to Pt. Nehru. I came all the way, two hundred miles, but besides two times hands shaking I got no opportunity to talk to the Prime Minister. Bidding him good-bye I told him that I would come to Delhi to meet him. I wired to my old friend Dr. Syed Mahamud, Minister in Foreign Office that he might arrange an interview with Pandit Nehru on the 17th Nov. His secretary. Mr. Naim, wrote me an express letter saying: 'Panditji will be heavily preoccupied during this month, it is not possible to arrange an interview for you in such a short time.'

On the 7th January 1956, in the afternoon, I held a public meeting at a lecture hall at Dehradun. I spoke on my plan of Aryan Federation, as a party to fight elections. My daughter was chosen as the president of the Gundog League's Field Trials, Dehradun. She went to H.H. Poonch House where H. H. Shahpura also came. Sardar Ajaib Singh came to our house at Rajpur, in this connection several times. I did not attend the Dog Show or their Field Trials. I am not interested in hunting, shooting.

On the 13th January arrived Dr. Rahmat Ali, Head of the French Department at the Punjab University, Lahore. He is my old friend, he was the Minister of Communication and Propaganda in our Provisional Government of India, founded on the 1st December 1915, at Kabul. You know, I was its president. Dr. Rahmat appealed to me to drop off my propaganda for Pakhtoonistan. It helps none. He pleaded. I thanked him for his advise but I had to tell him that it is a matter of principle. He should excuse me. He left on the 14th Jan. He was with me for only eighteen hours. He was to fly from Delhi to Lahore on the 15th Jan.

Pakhtoonistan :We read with horror the news of serious clash on the frontier as reported by the 'News From Afghanistan, 'New Delhi. 25 Pakistani Militia soldiers have been killed, on the side of the mujahids were eight wounded and killed. Sisters crying, women widowed, for what? Can they not all live happy tilling their own lands? Powers, struggling for world control make people fight from Korea to Germany, from Indo-China, Malaya, Pakhtoonistan to Palestine ! I say, let us combine, to bring about ceasefire on all fronts, on the principle of local liberty but all unity in regional federation of World Federation. Pakhtoonistan is a well defined locality. It must have its local liberty but it will of course be knitted in to Aryan Federation along with Iran, Afghanistan, Sindh, Bluchistan, Punjab and all local units up to Ceylon, Assam and Nepal.

On the 18th May I left Mussoorie and came down to Rajpur. On the 19th I left by car for Delhi but as I had started late I passed the night at Muhiuddinpur with my relation Kunwar Bhoopal Singh.

My friend Babu S. M. Ghose M. P. at New Delhi insisted that I stay at his residence. It was home like. Bengali fish lunch and dinner were served. It was very hot, I did not go out. In the evening I attended Maharana Pratap celebration. A Central Minister Thakur Satya Narain Singh Sahib presided. The Defense Minster Pandit Katju inaugurated and I spoke at the meeting. I said, I was doing what the Maharana did, I was fighting the present day Akbar, Pandit Nehru, of course not with sword but with pen.

Federal Front :I am forming Federal Front in India to fight the General Elections. I mean to co-operate with all the parties which care to defeat the Congress party and change the government.

Some of my best friends are very busy, here and there in the country, to develop the United Front of all the opposition parties. Our Federal Front is not different from the United Front. I have chosen the name of Federal Front for two reasons:

1. Ours is World Federation movement, as such, Federal Front is more liberal programme. I can not expect, at the present stage, that the parties merge or give up their identity, therefore what we can expect more I see with federation of these parties.

2. Let us unite to change the present system. This has been loaded on us by the overlords, the British. It is what all the conquerors do. Muslim conquerors converted a large population of this country to their Faith and ruled for centuries with the help of these converts. Earlier Aryans had done the same in this land. Aryan conquerors brought Vedic religion and converted the people to their culture and civilization. Now Russians, using communism, rule or guide the Chinese, Hungarians, Rumanians, Poles and Bulgarians.

I am not opposed to the English people. They played their part very honourably in the development of our human family, they surely brought light to many dark corners of our world. But I assert that the time of this democracy, made in England, is gone. This Jewish invention of communism has also contributed some thing valuable in cleaning the degenerated society in many lands but it is no longer needed in the present aggressive form. We need a great harmonising plan to federate all the races, all the cultures and all the religions.

It is wrong that a party rules and the others are ruled. I do not want that we rule and the present day Congressmen are ruled. I have to contest the elections because there is no other way to change the system. I would have been very glad if I could have received the cooperation of the revolutionaries and the army. I tried to force the rulers to accept my plan of life of local liberty but all unity in federation. I wanted to transform every village and town into a joint family. I had declared that we would capture Delhi on the 10th of May 1954. I toured. I preached. I addressed thousands of our countrymen around Delhi. I had planned to bring ten thousand followers and friends to Delhi on that date and force the President to accept my programme.

I said, I was not against our honourable Prime Minister or the most venerable President, I simply wanted to save the country from the danger of a red revolution or of war started by Pakistan. I was not hindered the government machinery. I reached Delhi but the followers did not arrive. One single lieutenant of our army assured me, however, that the army was sympathetic to my move.

Be as it may, I could not capture Delhi, nor Delhi captured me !

Pandit Jawaharlal himself felt perhaps guilty in his conscience that had he not opposed me bitterly in the last election and had I been in the Parliament I could not have taken this revolutionary step. He tolerated my movement.

Now I am trying his own method, his own religion of democracy, to change the prevailing system in India, England and Russia. I am waging war to end war.

I hope to introduce morality in politics. I wish to develop moral individual, moral family and moral State. I mean to utilize all the best ideas of all the religions, philosophies and parties to make life happy.

This is my mission, divine mission. You may or may not believe, you may be very proud of your tiny wisdom which was not produced by your wisdom, but I know, I was given birth, I am kept alive, my wisdom was also developed by the same laws which are running the universe. To me it is very clear that I am brought into being to do my job of removing all friction from society, to make all religions right evil and to develop Federated World State, based on morality.

How can they bring peace who believe that without opposition there can be no democracy ! There should be no opposition any where. All should work for all to make all happy.

I shall have thorough organisation of all humanity. Not one will be allowed to remain out side of human family. All will receive their daily necessities. And all will work, in one way or other, in the interest of society, honestly believing that in the welfare of all is one's best welfare.

My Conception of Society

There will be no courts in the present form where cases are dragged for years, where money wins and often justice is not done. The city and village States will decide their cases then and there.

There will be no jails. There will be moral hospitals. Through moral teachings and medical means we shall make criminals useful citizens. Murderers and chronic cases of syphilis or leprosy will be emasculated.

We shall insist on some kind of soul exercise or prayer for every individual. We shall see to it that every family remains pure and follows family rules, obedience to elders. We shall have a Corps of moral workers, monks or sadhus to preach morality and to discover wrong behaviour in society. Guilty persons will be put in moral hospitals under proper doctors.

To check excessive breeding we shall encourage people to become monks or nuns, if they feel so inclined.

Religion, if properly taught, can do wonders. Religion, through out human history, made saints of dirty persons. All the religions aim at soul cleanliness. Religions provide food and medicine to the soul. It is, however, foolish to quarrel about this or that religion. There are different systems of medicine so there are different systems of religion. We do not insist that all must take medicine from our doctor likewise we must not insist that others must follow our prophet, incarnation or religious teacher. Teaching and rigid organisation will do the miracle of converting this immoral society into pious human family.

There should not remain any friction creating party. Immorality produces wrong ideas which give rise to struggle. Ignorance makes people fight. Every conceivable fraction of our society should be organized with the clear view point that every part must work in the interest of the whole.

Castes, tribes or professions should be organized and their leaders should form village or town governments. Every town and village shall function as a joint family. All will work and all will receive their daily necessities. Qualities will receive better food, dress and lodging, but qualities will work for common welfare.

We shall utilise all the available knowledge and resources to make life comfortable and happy on this planet and help Man to fly to other worlds of our solar system. Lack of world vision, lack of universal knowledge, old prejudices, wrong feelings are hampering us in evolving human family. My divine Mission will bring about unity of religions, economy of joint family and Federated World State.

My Story :1st and 2nd August 1956 were passed in making arrangements for departure. On the 3rd I left for Meerut by bus. I had hoped to find my car in good condition and reach Delhi same evening but it was not to be! I found Thakur Hukam Singh, once prime minister of Bharatpur, at home. But my car was not there. He had sent it to the garage of the Inspector General of police, in the neighbourhood. I proceeded thither. To my great annoyance the car would not start. I. G. was not there. He is I. G. of M. B. at Gwalior. I did not go to Thakur Sahib to complain about the bad condition of the car. I stayed for the night at the residence of Ch. Yadramji Advocate.

On the 4th August I went to Delhi in the car of the advocate. I tried to see some friends but none of them was in. In the evening I went to the Sanitary Institute. I addressed the students. The Principal Mr. Verma took me to the Standard Restaurant. It is a gay and expensive place. Here we took dinner with the members of the Executive Committee and attended to business. I signed the documents as the chairman. I did not like that the committee spent over sixty rupees for dinner of six persons. It was surely waste of money. And the place where people were dancing was not suitable for business.

I returned Meerut on the 5th. I had to give my car for overhauling. I came to Mathura by train, took a horse cart and reached Vrindaban at about 3 a.m. on the 6th.

13th September. I ran to Ballabhgarh. I spoke at the meeting held in memory of Raja Nahar Singh who was hanged by the British in 1857. In the afternoon I went to the opposition room in parliament. Mr. H. V. Kamath had invited me to express my views to the opposition members. I spoke at length. I paid a flying visit to Yogashram. I left at night by train. Changing train at 2 a. m. I reached Sangrur at 4 a. m. Here I witnessed the huge procession of the farmers who are against the fixing of limit of the farms to thirty acres. In the protest meeting I spoke on injustice of the government. Raja Maheshinder Singh, Maharajkumar Brijender Singh and many other owners of big farms were there. Sardar Gurdial Singh brought me in his jeep to Patiala. Here I got a reserved berth in special bogie.

15. 9. Morning brought me to Delhi. I took tea with Sardar Bahadur Baisakha Singh were I had left my car. I visited Babu Ram Narayan Singh and left Delhi. At 2 p.m. I was back at Vrindaban.

From 26th September to the first of October I was on tour of Aligarh and Lucknow. At Lucknow I attended the united Front Conference. I spoke twice on two days. Pandit S. K. D. Paliwal presided. Ch. Mujtaba Hussain gave right royal tea. I could meet some of my old friends and make new acquaintances.

From 17th to the 25th October I went on another tour. On the 18th thousands of people took me out in a procession to the village of Shoron in Muzaffarnagar district. The head of the Afghan family at Shahpur gave a big party. On 19th I spoke twice at the huge gathering of Sarva Khap Panchayat. I inaugurated it and I explained my plan of World Federation on the pattern of the Sarva Khap.

On the 24th October I came to Delhi. Sardar Surjit Singh Majithia of the Central Government had kindly reserved a room for me at the Kotah House. On the 25th I visited Sardar Sahib and Dr. Syed Mahmud, the Foreign minister my school fellow. I presided at the Executive Committee of the Sanitary Institute in the evening. Dr. Verma, the Director, is the soul of the institute. Several doctors were present.

The Hon. President : I wrote to Dr. Rajendra Prasad, Rashtrapati, that what he said about the robbers at Gwalior I had been saying for last many years. It was a pity that their manhood with priceless bravery was wasted. I would like to utilise them in the army or to bring these people into the main stream of the society. I also expressed my pleasure at the fact that after years of hammering government accepted my suggestion of having our New Year Day on 21st or 22nd March. Government has declared that the next 22nd March will be the first day of the New Year ! I simply received the acknowledgement from his secretary. It is something. Something is better than nothing. I thank the Hon. President and his office.

Late Shri Ambedkar :

Dr. Ambedkar passed away. It is a great blow to the cause of the most suppressed and oppressed section of the Indian nation. Lala Lajpat Rai, Mahatma Gandhi and the Congress in general did some service to this cause. I also by taking food with a sweeper in 1912 helped the untouchables. On my return to India in 1946, I appointed a priest in our Love Centre from this class. But Dr. Ambedkar, being one of them, fought as a General of the scheduled castes. He got so enraged by the attitude of the high castes that in October last he together with two hundred thousand of his followers embraced Buddhism. His followers might sense mischief as he died suddenly, he died in sleep, finishing preface to his book on Buddhism going to bed ! I met him at Mussoorie at his request. He was then minister at the Centre. We talked about Religion of Love. I wish his soul perfect peace, with all living or dead. I am holding prayer meeting for him.

News & Views

P.M. & Mr. President : This is the greatest news of the month of December. Our Prime Minister and USA President met and talked long. There were great receptions, praises were showered on Pandit Jawaharlal Nehru. It was stated that the differences between India and USA were removed. But, as if, in the same breath, news came that USA will not stop her military aid to Pakistan. She will give more aeroplanes of the most modern type. Our people might have been bewildered at these 'contradicting' news. On their wounded feelings some salt was applied by the British conservatives by asking questions about Kashmir and suggesting that India was wrong in the matter.

I must say that our countrymen are blundering, as the people of all other countries make the same mistakes in the like situations. They forget that having brought the greatest empire of Britain under its wings, USA is out for world control. Soviet Russia, with its new weapon of Communism, and having subdued the greatest nation of China, is the only obstacle in the way of USA.

India is still within the British Commonwealth. With all great talks of our great leaders. India is utilized by Anglo-Americans in their war against Soviet Russia. Cleverest cajolery is used to keep the slaves in good humour.

My Story : 29.11.56. In celebration of my birth day on the 1st December a week long sports are going on in our School and College. I was invited to Vrindaban cricket match. Two elevens were introduced to me. I shook hands with the players and spoke a few words. I said, I would like to have cooperation in place of competition. Recreations will also take new forms, but as things are, we must enjoy the present system till we can replace it.

1st December 1956. At 9 a.m. friends came and garlanded me. At the Centre I prayed. Tea was served by the school staff. I hurried to our Prem Engineering College at Prem Nagar, four miles from our school. Here lunch was served by the college staff. I addressed the students and distributed the prizes to the winners at the sports. Staff member and some students representing their Union spoke congratulating me. The present and former principals wished me long life ! Together with the honorary Secretary I returned to our school. Here a large gathering was awaiting me. After drama and lot of fun friends spoke congratulating me and wishing me long life. I delivered a long speech and distributed prizes to the students of several schools who took part in the sports at Vrindaban. Kunwar Panch Bahadur Singh, my former private secretary and now a government official, Chowdhri Bharat Bhusan of Batavli and others came to take part in my birth day function. I thank all my friends.

On 11.12.56, Pandit Shri Krishn Datta Paliwal ji came from Agra. We had lunch together. At 2 p.m. our public meeting started at the Gandhi park. I spoke and spoke for one hour and a half. It was all to set up "effective opposition" in legislatures.

13.12. At an invitation of the Jatavs (Chamars), the oppressed section of our society, I went to the Village Premnagar Nagla of Mant. They had prepared for me a warm welcome. They spoke of their difficulties. A richman, by hook and crook, bribing, tot them dispossessed of their lands, ruined their crops and is making their life miserable! I heartily sympathised with them. Jatav M.P.s, Jatav M.L.A.s and even Jatav Ministers enjoy high life and care little for these oppressed brethren.

On 15.12.56, I took Punjab Mail train from Mathura. I was received at Jhansi by several friends of the United Front. In the evening there was a grand meeting in the beautifully lighted large pandal. Over two thousand people were there. I was voted to the chair. After the welcome by the secretary of the Reception Committee I delivered a long speech. There were smiles and clapping of hands. Mr. Verma and Pt. Pannalal together with youths made the meeting a great success. I took leave and took train. At 3.15 a. m. I reached Mathura. My car was waiting. I came to Vrindaban.

25.12. Thakur Nepal Singh gave a tea party to launch my election campaign in the city of Mathura. Chosen people had come. I spoke at great length. Next days accompanied by Ch. Birender Singh I went to village Bharan. We spoke on election and enlisted volunteers. At Pachawar was held very large meeting. Musicians sang songs. I showed the necessity of changing the system of government.

It is now exactly 10.30 p.m., Friday, the 28th December 1956. I close this account here. I must explain that some dates have been omitted because there was nothing special to write on those days. I was busy as ever on those dates with my routine work, receiving visitors, writing letters or circulars. On all Sundays, during this time I could hold prayer meetings which were all well attended.

On 29th Dec. I left in the afternoon by the Frontier Mail. Via Delhi I arrived at midnight at Muzaffarnagar. My niece was waiting for me. I stayed at Moulaheri House.

30.12. Chowdhari Ranbir Singh arrived. He took me in his car to the college at Narsan, named after me. They were holding annual function. Volunteers gave salute and done march past. I presided and spoke long at the meetings. The gathering was large of several thousand and the famous singer Prithvi Singh Bedharak was supporting me with songs. When I was discussing my society, and told that there will be no courted in the present form to drag the cases for years, Bedharak pushed his harmonium *Ho jayen mukadame band, babu chaat bechenge, aur unke muharrir bagh mein laukat bechenge*...and when, I told that when through moral teaching the criminal minds, we shall ehiminate. The principal was very obliging. But for naming the institution after me, for inviting me for this occasion and for the great progress of the College the sole credit goes to Ch. Sher Singh and his vast circle of friends. The village presented me a purse of one hundred and one rupees. After tea I returned Moulaheri House. Kr. Chandravir brought me to the station. I left by train, reaching Delhi at midnight.

31.12. In the early morning got ready and took the Punjab Mail for Mathura. Just after 10 a.m. arriving Mathura I rushed by car to a village Barhon on the other side of the river Jamuna. A retired military officer received me. I spoke at the meeting called to hear me. Crossing the river hurried to the far off village of Sehi, I got late, still the people garthered again and I addressed them on the elections. I thanked God. My health stood well too, though I had days and nights journey and this busy day!

1st of Jan. 1957. Another great meeting was held at the village of Jabra. The well known singer and writer of songs Swami Shivram sang song in my praise, he even declard me an *Avtar*. I preached Religion of Love and spoke on the unity of religions. Our last *Avtar* is Lord Buddha and our last prophet is Rasul Mohamed. The village presented a purse of rupees one hundred and one.

Next full fortnight I visited villages and addressed people to vote for me in coming election.

20.1. Today I acted as a priest and got a couple married according to the religion of Love at Love Centre. It was intercaste marriage. A Jat boy was groom and a Kaisth girl was bride. Hall was full. Sweets were served. The groom presented eleven rupees. I rushed to the village of Dehgaon. I addressed the large meeting. We went to Lalpur, here another meeting was held. I spoke. Seventy five rupees were presented at these two places. Swami Shivram sang and thundered in favour of my election. Ch Nepal Singh also spoke. Our second car had trouble. It was left.

22.1. Friends came. I addressed two meetings today at Paigaon and Chhata. The first meeting was very crowded. Swami Shivram's songs rang the air. Next day I went to Hussaini and spoke long on religion and elections. Hence I proceeded to Shergarh and held meeting. The audience was intelligent. They asked me to come again.

24.1. Today at Kosi Khurd was a great public discussion as to who was to oppose the Congress candidate? Rajputs and Jats fraternized and selected one Thakur Krishnapal ji. Maharao Krishnpal Singh and Chowdhri Baburam Yadav went and returned with me. I assisted the deliberation with my opinion. I insisted on honesty.

25.1. This noon my nomination paper was duly filed. Ch. Birender Singh and Babu Kamlesh proposed me. Now I am a regular candidate for parliament.

He Made Me Win

He who gave me life, He who keeps me alive, He who gave me the idea to contest the election, made me win. It is the news of these days. I got successful in the elections. I am now a Member of the Parliament with the voice of the people.

During the last elections I did not want to contest. My friends forced me to fight the election against my wish. This time I was myself eager to enter the Parliament. I felt and feel that our foreign policy is extremely faulty. And as things are, we can only correct the policy through our parliament.

To present my foreign policy and to put forth my plan of happy human society I am going to Delhi. It is not in any way to say that our illustrious Prime Minister Pandit Jawaharlal Nehru is insincere or dishonest. I honestly believe him to be an honest fellow. He is however enwrapped in his own views, views which he got through his education and circumstances of life, they are harmful to our State.

I am going to Delhi to try to convert our Prime Minister and his followers to my Views which I got through my long experience in foreign free countries and through long quiet meditation in Japan. I also strongly believe in God or that universal Power which keeps the universe going. He helped me to develop these views in the interest of the suffering humanity.

Not only our country but all our world needs regeneration, reconstruction and a world order of world unity.

Our Prime Minister speaks a great deal of Panchshila. He gets emotionally excited over Kashmir, he sympathizes with this or that country but he does not realize that all the ills of all the world will be cured if we can establish world government. And it is what our World Federation has been trying to achieve since 1929.

We do not want to rule this earth. I show a way to end all kinds of friction. They will fight and destroy themselves and murder humanity if we are not successful in bringing world order immediately.

During the last fortnight I did not go out of my district. I toured and toured my constituency practically every day. Three cars were used to take me and my coworkers and supporters. Only on three occasions I stayed out in villages, otherwise I always returned Vrindaban. It happened that several nights I went to bed after midnight. Once I could sleep after 2 a. m. It was indeed hard work.

The bright side was that the people gave me warm receptions. Here and there they presented purses. Shahpur village presented five hundred rupees. Next comes Jat village which helped me with three hundred and eight rupees. Rajput Thakur Puran Singh and Jat Chowdhri Bhullan Singh collected these donations for me.

Maharao Krishnpal Singh, retired Major of Indian army gave his valuable time and energy and spent his money too to make me successful. Soldiers of the army and police were very sympathetic towards me. Government servants voted for me. This was something strange and unbelievable when I always spoke of changing this system of government.

Chowdhri Nehpal Singh Advocate was my election agent and Chowdhri Shivdhian Singh M.A., LL. B. was my election manager. They did wonderful work. Hundreds of others voluntarily helped me in the campaign.

I am heartily thankful to all my voters and workers who secure for me a seat in the Parliament.

It was a great scene, a scene from the Arabian Night, when thousands took me out in a procession through the streets of Mathura. Shopkeepers were presenting their goodwill in different forms. I was garlanded, flowers, sweets and money were showered. Once I was bodily lifted and carried to the Stock Market and given warm reception. They had heavily gambled over my victory. All parties, rich and poor, communists and religious groups joined in doing me loving homage. I was greeting them left and right with folded hands.

The scene was repeated at Vrindaban. Beautiful gates were erected across the streets. Congress too joined in this welcome. Vrindaban friends had spent their own money in my propaganda work and now they rejoiced seeing their own success. Jait duplicated the process of procession.

Gurukul, Institute of Arya Samaj, gave me a great reception on the 16th March, yesterday. The governor of the institute has also been elected to the parliament. He welcomed me and the students and the staff recited poems congratulating me. Speeches were delivered enlogising me. I heartily thank them.

We Independents : We, who do not belong to any party, have a great responsibility at this juncture. After the Congress members in the Parliament we form the largest one unit. We must stand together and try to better our position by converting the socalled party members, including the Congressmen, to our creed of free conscience, honesty above party and sincere service to the people.

I can not believe that these apes of the London democracy have lost their souls, are entirely slaves to their party bosses and refuse to hear to reason and common sense.

We should put up a united front against this party system which kills conscience of the individual and stabs the country in the back in the interest of Party. With Faith in God the Creator, who created the world in the universe and evolved man on its planet, let us work to develop happy human family in our country.

We should try to remove all friction from society. Fools may not understand, dull headed might take some time and the selfish, getting profit through the party system, would oppose us for the present. All opposition will melt away like snow under the May sun. We should not be in hurry. We know, we did not give birth to ourselves. We are kept alive by the Laws of Nature. Our wisdom was not developed by our wisdom. We are doing our jobs in the plan of Life–this creation !

Fools know not why they believe as they believe and act as they do. Microbes of thoughts, during the complete slavery of the country and education in England or under the influence of over lords, were developed. It is a social disease, racial infection.

We shall have to act with great patience. They are our brethren. They have great irritability of the eccentric type. If you call a fool, a fool, he gets annoyed.

At present they are soaring high as the successful candidates. Congress members speak of their great party. They might have joined the party only yesterday but they speak of making India free. They are poor four Anna bits. We shall give them time that they regain the balance of mind.

We shall continue to say that all those ideas which make us fight are hard and all those ideas which make us unite are good.

We make an humble beginning. We start making our own group. We keep open our doors for all parliament members.

And what we do in the Parliament, our independent brethren should start doing in every State Assembly. We shall have a power which will guide the destiny of our people.

News & Views

Defeat of Congress : There is a great deal of talk these days that Congress suffered great loss during these elections. Congress leaders are advancing different reasons for their defeat. Many ministers failed to win. Pandit Nehru says that the Congressmen took to pompous living. Ministers paraded the country with lot of the police guards. He advises simple life. If he sets himself some example of simplicity, Congressmen would follow his advice. He lives in a magnificent house, heavily guarded by police, he flies in air, drives in expensive cars, how can his advice bear fruit.

Congress still commands huge majority in the Parliament and in State Assemblies. They can still pull the state with their minority. They can destroy the country if they foolishly so decide. Coming up of opposition, however, shows which way the wind is blowing. Opposition gained great strength.

My programme is to convert the Congressmen themselves in the Parliament and in State Assemblies. The situation for our country is getting dangerous. The present leadership is responsible for the present plight.

Communist State : Kerala turned red. Out of thirteen states one is lost to the Union. Who is to be blamed? The present leadership ! I am not anticommunism. I consider it a set of ideas born of the suffering Jews. Now Russians are using these ideas in their war against the Anglo-Saxons for world supremacy. Kerala getting red becomes a battle field of the two fighting camps. This kind of elections, campaigning against one another, creates friction in society. I am sure the intellectual Congressmen will soon discover that they were duped by these agents of London, the pupils of the English culture. Oath or no oath, discipline or rebellion, it is in the interest of the country that these warring parties must be liquidated and harmony must be established in the land.

My Story : 18th March 1957. Today many people visited me. Heavy mail arrived, going through it, it came noon. Muslim Pathan Mistri who repaired my cars came and offered me a loan. I thankfully refused it. At the residence of Mr. Rahman at Mathura a tea party was given to me this afternoon. Visiting Bibi Sardarni I returned to Vrindaban.

19.3.57. People came in large numbers. At Bansibat I visited the religious leader, Acharya Kishoredas ji, over eighty years old. He gave me his blessings. At night Pandit Radha Govind ji gave me a rich banquet. Some notables of the town were present. Poems were recited enlogizing my work, service to the land. I was astonished to find such love and regard among my fellow citizens.

20.3. Today was the Meeting of all professions and castes. It got late. It began at 1 p.m. I spoke on universal unity, all to work for all to make all happy. Raja Bahadur Mursan who became M.L.A. defeating the Congress organized this meeting.

World Federation Day : On 21st March, to celebrate World Federation Day, famous leader Thakur Todar Singh arrived. Raja Bahadur delivered his speech as the chairman of the reception committee. I spoke on the Unity of religions. The secretary Pandit Danbeharilal Sharma read the messages of goodwill received. Several friends spoke. Swami Raghwacharya of Bareilly, the president of the meeting, delivered his address. He spoke highly about my Religion of Love. He said that politics without religion can not succeed. Seth Chandrakant ji of Ahmedabad attended the meeting.

This evening Swami Shivram and Pandit Shiv Shanker and party sang songs with music. Weather was stormy still gathering was good. At midnight we made bone-fire. The whole night night-watch was kept. Chowdhri Dharam Singh and Thakur Todar Singh spoke very long. I explained the necessity of the Fauji Kaumi Sangh–Military castes Union. Tea was served twice. As sun came out we ended this meeting. Then we dispersed. I went to bed.

22.3. Major Dr. Chauhan arrived. World Federation rally was held. I spoke on the necessity of world order. A resolution was proposed by Pandit Haridatta Sharma that to give shape to my plan of local self government in villages and towns, to make them joint families, centre of world federation should be established all over the country. It was unanimously passed.

9.4.57. Today I observed Ram Naumi and the day of the Religion of Love. Friends gathered and we prayed at noon. Raja Bahadur Mursan and Thakur Jhamman Singh came. In the afternoon Old Boys Association of the Muslim University gave me reception at the residence of Khwaja Sahib. Nawab Sahib Chhatari and members of the Association together with the Hony. Secretary were present. They congratulated me at my election to the Parliament. A golden garland was put arround my neck. I spoke on my programme. Mr. Tonki took me to a restaurant. Here I met some leaders of the students of the University.

19.4. I hoisted the Aryan Flag at the Jat Mahasabha, Birla Mandir. I received my advisers at Vrindaban. From 3 p.m. I presided over Jat Maha Sabha. Ch. Birender Singh, advocate welcomed the guests. I spoke for full one hour. Delegates had come from Rohtak, Delhi, Jodhpur, Aligarh and many other places. Next day at 9 a.m. I arrived at Birla Mandir. It was a subject committee meeting. Resolutions were formulated. At 3 p.m. I presided at the open session. Resolutions were passed. Jat Maha Sabha accepted my programme of Fauji Kaumi Sangh, Aryan Federation, World Federation and Religion of Love. My advisers held a meeting at Vrindaban.

22.4. I was very busy. I visited friends at the Mission Hospital. At about half past eight in the evening I arrived at Delhi by car. I stayed at the Constitution House. It was a pleasure to meet some old friends. Next day, early morning I attended the meeting called to remember Martyrs at Raj Ghat. Pt. Sunderlal presided. General Shah Nawaz was present. I spoke for a few minutes and took leave. Mr. Kamath, the well known leader, took me to Parliament, introduced me to several officials. Oath Ceremony was held. The Speaker of Lok Sabha congratulated all members. I visited friends. It was a small tea party at 6, Windsor Place. I expressed my views. Next morning I started early. Visiting friends on the way I took light lunch at Moulaheri House, Muzaffarnagar. Kunwar and Bibi were there. At the College, named after me at Narsan, I met the Manager and the Principal. My daughter came in her car and met me at Chhutmalpur. Mr., Mrs. Prassad and two Bibi were with her. This place is twenty eight miles form Dehradun. I went with my daughter in her car. In the evening we arrived Rajpur.

My Budget Speech at Parliament

Here I quote what I expressed on Budget :

I must make it clear that I do not think you are doing me any favour in allowing me to speak. I am serving my people.

When I speak, I speak only with one motive, to serve my people whom I am representing here.

I went to say here a great deal because I think the very conception of taxing the people is basically wrong. I beg to say that the whole machinery should be run in the interests of the people and for the people.

If there is a cry, and if some people are shouting, that these taxes are very heavy, that itself shows that the people are not satisfied. If it is not a conspiracy to depose our Pandit Jawaharlal Nehru and to make him so to say the target of the people, and to make the people believe that this Government is run by Shri Jawaharlal Nehru only to tax the people, I think this bill should be withdrawn, I mean that this Budget should be withdrawn.

The basic idea should be that the time and the energy of the people should be well utilized. We should see that the time and energy of the whole nation is not wasted. I can say that many of our sadhus are wasting their time and energy.... Of course, not the sadhus like Reverend Sivanand ji, or Baba Mehar or some such great men. But most of the sadhus are wasting their time and energy.

The students only eat and do not produce anything. The soldiers also only eat and eat and do not produce anything. I have a suggestion to make in this connection. I do not merely criticize, but I always present a remedy.

I say that our sadhus should be utilized as policemen. We do not need policemen. But we need sadhus to make people moral;

and if the people are moral, I think there will not be so much necessity of our idling sadhus, of course, choosing from them only the best elements.

As regards the students, I say that in every school there should be a factory, a farm, a garden and a dairy farm. The students should study for only three hours, and for five hours, they should work in the factory, farm, garden and dairy farm, so that they will be producing their daily necessities. There will be no need them of any fees, and the parents will only have to breed children and send them to our schools; they would not have to worry at all as to how to bring up their children.

As regards the soldiers also, I have the same suggestion to make. For three hours, the soldiers should learn military science, and for five hours, they should work in a cantonment factory, a garden and dairy farm and in the fields. Thus, the soldiers also will be producing, and they will not be a burden on the nation. We can have ten million soldiers in this way, country, from Kashmir up to Cape Comorin.

I say that the very conception of having the present system should be overhauled, and should be reorganized. I should also say that on account of the great blunders of our Government along the political lines, we are suffering from the idea or the danger that there might be war. And because there is the danger that there might be war, we sanction any expenses that you demand for our military. But I think it is a great mistake to create this sort of situation.

I have always been hammering at the idea that the only remedy for all the ills of the World is World Federation, a federated World Government, with one capital, namely the World Capital, at Honolulu and with a World army and with a world court of justice, and having all the continental provinces as self governing, Asia being self-governing, Europe being self-governing, and so on. I have detailed plans, and the capital of Asia will be at Srinagar in Kashmir.

I beg to say that if we would only work out with concentration on this idea of one world, one world order, world peace, World Federation, World-Federated States, we shall solve all the problems.

Next day in Parliament : The other day, I happened to say something very bad. I myself admit it. I said :

When our great speaker Shri V. K. Krishna Menon was speaking, I said that it was a criminal talk. That was something very bad, and a great charge. What I meant was this: instead of talking of atom bombs and atom age, why not say that there should be world federation? It is very clear that if you play with ink, your hands will become black. If you will play with sand, your hands will become dirty. But if you play with scent, your hands will get scented. So, I say that instead of playing with atom bombs and with the idea of war danger always, let us play with the idea of world peace and world Federation.

I say, as my Hon. Friend, Shri Dange, Communist leader, was saying, that these taxes fall over the common man. Hon. Congress leader, Shri Ranga my friend too created here a cold War between the Congress and Communists. I want peace in this Chamber. We do not want War.

So I say that we should have taxes in a way the common man does not feel the burden of the taxes. Here I agree, but I do not say that I agree with Communism. I agree with sensible people who have this idea. I say that there should be only one tax, a single tax, and that should be on land, on house property and on bank balances. There should be no other tax; there should be no licences and no other harassment. All should be free to do as they please. Only we shall have a check to see that they do not do wasteful things, immoral things and unsocial things. There only we will check the people. So I say that this system of taxing is wrong.

In our society, there are only two things-production and distribution. We should produce as much as we can and we should justly distribute it. We should not blindly distribute. Today shopkeepers are doing the work of distribution. They think that a particular thing is dear in a particular place and if they move that thing there, it will bring them profit. In this way, they are distributing the production.

Now, there are two things: either the Government should control all for all so that we all become Government servants and we all are sure of our monthly salaries, bread and butter which we need, it should be in such a way that by Government's management not even a beggar remains out-side the Government organization, or there should be freedom to produce and distribute.

One thing about these great plans of the Government to make bunds, dams. I do not mean damned things, I mean these dams, it is better to ask the merchants to do that work. Then we will not have to spend so much money and tax the people. Suppose there is the Bhakra dam to be built. We are building it. We know how much money it is going to cost. Now, instead of raising taxes and spending them on that dam and then taxing the people for the water and electricity, why not allow the merchants to do that? They will raise the money and then they will take the water tax, and then we will tax the merchants. A very simple thing.

So instead of taxing the people, we help the people to build great factories, great dams and great industrial plants and then we tax these merchants. This is very simple. In the end, I beg to say that the parties are very much misusing our time and energy. Even in this House, we see the tussle, and this is waste of time and energy. Here there were speeches I beg pardon of my Hon. Friends not so much for the common man as to show that one's Party is very just, very right and doing very good things, so that the leader can step into the administration.

I say if Pandit Jawaharlal Nehru is Prime Minister or Shri Dange is Prime Minister or even if Mahendra Pratap is Prime Minister, it would not change anything; so long as the Government machinery remains the same, I shall also be a puppet like Pandit Jawaharlal Nehru in the hands of the Secretariat.

Mr. Deputy Speaker : Order, order. After becoming Prime Minister, he should conclude.

My Story : On 15th June I got ready very early. I left by bus from Delhi. At noon reached Muzaffarnagar. Ch. Ram Singh and friends received me. By car we came to Shahpur. Here was a very large gathering. It was called peasants meeting but it was a communist move. I spoke I said that one my Congress friend wrote to me that I should not come here, as I was not a Communist but why should

I not, I said, when I want all to work for all to make all happy. I am a preacher of religion. At night I reached Delhi by train.

16th midnight I took train for Mathura. I passed a few hours at Vrindaban. It was extremely hot. At about midnight I reached Gwalior. Many friends had come to receive me. I went with Shri Sahib Badshah Mian and stayed with him. Midnight passed talking with my host and Raja Sahib Magrora.

In the evening of 18th I spoke at the large gathering of Hindu Mahasabha held in honour of Rani of Jhansi. One hundred years ago she was killed here on this date fighting against the British. I spoke on the necessity of removing all friction from society. I said that people say I had captured Delhi as I had entered the Parliament but I say that I had just entered the fortress, I still had to fight the rulers of the castle. At midnight I left, reaching Delhi in the morning.

Correspondence : H. E. Afghan Ambassador, Afghanistan Embassy, New Delhi, kindly writes :

Dear Raja Sahib,

Thank you very much for your kind letter of the 16th instant. Allow me first of all to congratulate you on your being elected as a Member of the Lok Sabha, which I feel, you very rightly deserved. I take this opportunity to express my cordial sentiments about your struggle for the independence of your country and also for the feelings you have in your heart to honour the freedom of other countries and particularly in respect of Afghanistan. And I am sure that as a Member of this august body you will always be rendering the same selfless service to your country as you have been rendering hitherto. Raja Sahib, I do very distinctly remember our meeting long ago in Kabul and Mazar Sharif and later in Germany and Russia and I can assure you that the passing of years has not in the least affected our friendship. I am looking forward to meet you again and leave it entirely at your convenience to see when we could meet. As my personal friend and as a friend of Afghanistan you are always welcome; our doors are always wide open to receive you at any time convenient to you.

Yours sincerely
M. Omer
Ambassador of Afghanistan

What a kind letter! It sent me floating in the old lovely air of Kabul. Memories revived and I began to feel that our young folk is not doing justice to Afghanistan. Our Government did not recognize the great help our neighbour gave to our freedom movement. I repeatedly tried to bring the importance of Afghanistan to the fore but the present rulers of Delhi did not pay due attention to my views, based on long sojourn in Afghanistan. The same is true about Germany and Japan.

Speech on Railway Budget in Parliament

I quote what I spoke on Railway Budget :

Hon'ble Lady in Chair, I wish to bring a few points before the House. There have been very fine speeches and many good suggestions have been made. I do not think I can give a better account, but I have to bring to the notice of the House the complaints and grievances which I have received. At Mathura Junction coolies had to strike and go on hunger strike. I went there. By the grace of God I could settle the matter. But the causes of the hunger strike are still there. The coolies are not satisfied because a certain man by name Shri Munna who was removed from service for a small mistake has not been reinstated. This is another instance of the continuance of the bureaucratic mentality, or the *Burra Sahib* approach which still persists in our Government departments. I am sure the Hon. Minister will look in to this matter.

I have received a complaint from Moradabad. People who have served the Railway Department for a long time and have retired are not given pension while people who have only recently taken up work are given pensions and all facilities. This is a matter which concerns men who have served you well and should be looked into seriously.

My people from Vrindaban, the holy place of Vaishnav religion, have asked me that I should insist and persist and repeatedly bring forth the necessity of constructing a railway bridge. Because of lack of a railway bridge whenever there is a flood the waters enter the town of Vrindaban and certain portions of Mathura town and cause a great ideal of damage. If a railway bridge is constructed at Vrindaban there will be no floods in Vrindaban and Mathura. The suggestion is that the railway line which comes from Mathura to Vrindaban is a meter gauge line, it should be extended to Aligarh. When there will be a bridge and the line will pass through a well populated area and also bring good income to the exchequer. Another suggestion is that, that line may be connected with the station of Jalesar. I just bring this suggestion before the Hon. Railway Minister.

I honestly believe that the Railway Department is much better managed than any other Department of Government. I am very much satisfied with the conveniences they give. I have always found the railway servants very obliging. At any rate they always attend to me, I do not know about others.

There have been some complaints that nowadays the trains are late. My train was also late. I left Dehradun for Bombay on the 6th by the Express. The train got late but I was glad that the train was late. While the scheduled arrival time of the train was 6.15 it arrived at about 8 a.m. So I could wash myself and I was very thankful that the train was late. But it is unfortunately a fact that nowadays trains are late. When I returned from Bombay, the Punjab Mail also got late by an hour. I hope the Railway Department will look into it.

Another point which I wish to bring to the notice of the Railway Minister is that when I was going to Bombay three persons fell from the train. One man was standing on the footboard and nobody knew of it till the train reached a station. The train had to be backed for some distance. That was very considerate of the Railways. But the man fell because the compartment was overcrowded and he had to stand outside. I might say that this is a universal fact that trains are very crowded all over our country.

I may also bring to the notice of the House a little matter. It sometimes happens that some people get ill in certain areas because the air of that area or the climate does not suit them. The Railway authorities should take this fact into consideration and if some people get sick and want to be transferred, facilities should be given to them because every individual who serves the Railways is doing some service and if he gets ill, it means that the Railways suffer and the country also suffers. So, I beg the Railway

Administration to be very considerate in such eases where persons get sick.

When I was coming from Bombay I do not know how they came to know that I was in the train–a man from Kalyan, serving as an assistant driver came and told me that a few days ago, a man was suspended, perhaps he might be dismissed simply because he dared to refer to rules. He had already worked for 12 hours as a driver and when they asked him to work for one more hour he said : 'Look in to the rules; I have worked for 12 hours and you cannot ask me to serve longer than that.' The officer got angry and said : 'You disobey me; therefore, I suspend you.' This is again an instance of the bureaucratic way, the *Burra Sahib* idea. I hope the Railway Department which is so well managed will also take into consideration such little matters.

I am bringing another point to the notice of the House. The vendors in different railways are really suffering. They are forced to give bribes. I found that at Mathura junction and Dehradun junction. A vendor came to me and said: 'We have to pay Rs. 20 or Rs. 30 per day.' If it is a fact–I do not say it is a fact–you investigate into the matter and find out if it is a fact, then it is very serious. A man who takes a contract from you for only Rs. 500 or Rs. 600 per month gets an income of Rs. 4,000 per month. I think many ex-landlords will be very envious of this man getting Rs. 4,000 a month, Rs. 50,000 a year. This has to be investigated. I think it is a general complaint. From Ludhiana also I received a similar complaint. I find that you have a certain remedy for this but you are not extending it to all places. I heard that you have been very kind to establish some sort of co-operative at Ghaziabad. This can be introduced at other palces also like Dehradun and Mathura. Why should there be any contractor? If vendors are themselves prepared to organize into a co-operative, it is very good. The Government speaks of socialism; I speak of morality and religion and not of socialism. In any case, the object is the same. We go through morality and religion and you go through the new names of Socialism and other things. All the people must be made to work for all the people to make all people happy.

I think I have spoken enough. They are economizing in money and I economise in time. Thank you very much.

My Story : I am now at Delhi. Since the evening of the 12th July 1957, I am practically marroned in the capital. The Parliament keeps me tied to Delhi.

I left Rajpur, Dehradun, on the 6th July. I arrived Bombay on the 8th morning. Friends came and garlanded me and took me to the residence of Rana Chandra Pal Singh. I stayed at Astoria Hotel, Church Gate.

On the 9th I was at Poona for just twelve hours, from midday to midnight. I addressed the students of St. Meera High School. It is the movement of devotion and holy work of Saint T. L. Vaswani. I know no words of gratitude to express my feelings rightly for the reception which Reverend Sadhu gave me. He was all kind.The Governor of Bombay kindly asked me to tea at Poona. My old friend Seth B. Naraindas took me to his Poona residence.

Hindu Mahasabha arranged a meeting at the Tilak Temple. It was a pleasure to meet the grandson of Lokmanya Tilak at the Kesri Office. The evening prayer meeting of mostly Sindhi community was grand. Saint T. L. Vaswani introduced me in some very sweet words. I spoke on Universal Unity.

At Bombay on the 10th July, I spoke at an Id meeting of Asian Brotherhood. My friend Mr. Ismail gave me lunch and introduced me to the people. Rana Chandra Pal Singh and friends gave dinner.

Phone came and I ran to the Life Insurance office. Mr. Shapur N. Randeria handed me a cheque for rupees one thousand two hundred and fifty. Mr. K. F. Nariman got me this entirely unexpected gift. At his suggestions I paid some premiums some forty years back. I forgot all about it but the account was there and I got that amount.

Here at Delhi it is all very regulated life. Visitors come mornings, evenings and I go daily to Parliament. I hardly find time to answer all my correspondence. The lack of accommodation does not allow me to keep here my secretary. My Newspaper office remains at Vrindaban. My estate office is at Aligarh. My daughter lives at Rajpur, Dehardun.

In the Parliament I must just hear others speaking. At my age it does not look nice to get up like school children and say 'May I know Sir.........' They ask questions. I want to give some new ideas, this they do not like.

Governor of Bihar

It is what I saw on Sunday the 28th July 1957, at Aligarh Railway Station. The Governor was travelling in the airconditioned wagon. I was to board it for Delhi. Every first class accommodation was occupied by the Governor's staff. Policemen were guarding the Governor's wagon. Pandit Jawaharlal Nehru said in the Parliament that now no guards will be used by the Ministers and Governors. Is it not making a fool of Pandit Nehru or proving him a liar ! Against the Hon. Prime Minister's solemn declaration, this Governor was provided tens of policemen at every stop of the train. Sheer waste of time and energy of the police force. I had some trouble with the police but the police officers came to me and asked my pardon. I pardoned them.

Correspondence : President of India. Babu Rajendra Prasad ji, Rashtrapati, kindly wrote :

My dear Raja Saheb,

I received your letter dated the 26th June, 1957. In reply to your letter I can only say that the meeting of Sarva Dharma Sammelan was not convened by me. As a matter of fact it was arranged by others and I had nothing to do with its organisation and only addressed a few words at the end of the second day's sitting. So please do not feel offended. I had gone to Patna in connection with Shri Anugraha Babu's serious illness. I have returned only this morning, hence this delay. Hope you are doing well.

Yours sincerely
Rajendra Prasad

I am very thankful for the kind letter. I had written him that I was always inviting him to our yearly meeting of All Religions' Congress but some how he forgot me when Religions Conference was held at the Rashrapati Bhawan.

The Hon'ble Home minister, Pandit Govind Ballabh Pant ji kindly writes :

My dear Raja Mahendra Pratap,

I have just received your letter of the 15th July. I am glad to know that you had occasion to meet Sri Prakasa at Poona recently.

The untimely death of his son has left a permanent scar on him. It is but natural as his son was young, well-behaved, affectionate and loyal to his father. Thanks for the issue of "Sansar Singh" enclosed with your letter.

Yours sincerely
G. B. Pant

Grief and pleasure are with body. I do not mind it this body weeps or laughs. Religion, however, helps us to rise higher and beyond this atmosphere of storms and we fly tranquil in serene space ! Just as medicines are needed to remove some ills of this body, religion is a necessity for our souls. I recommended Religion of Love to Babu Sri Prakasa Sahib, the Governor of Bombay, when I found him sad and sorry for the loss of his son.

My Story : Up to the 13th of this month the Parliament was in sesson, I was chained to Delhi in the vicinity. I toured once, went to Lucknow.

This night I am writing these lines in my Himalayan home at Rajpur. I arrived in the evening of Sunday, the 22nd instant.

My intensive tour of Rohtak district for four days, 2nd to 5th of September requires special mention. Punjab Congress General Secretary Chowdhri Ranbir Singh and Chowdhri Partap Singh Daulta, Communist M. P. accompanied me. Punjab government gave us a jeep and a car. Police was also helpful. It was officially supported propaganda tour. I went to bring peace. We went round the district. We lectured at sixteen different places. It was raining all these four days but it did not deter to hear us. At Rohtak the meeting of the heads of the villages of the entire district was presided over by a deputy minister, Thakur Pratap Singh, and the District Magistrate was there. I spoke on my plan of establishing permanent peace.

On the 8th September I was at Lucknow, the capital of our province. Here I was the guest of Raja Jitender Singh of Chandpur. I spoke at the meeting of Martial Races Union. I met many friends conneted with the movement.

On the 13th September the President of the Punjab Congress and General Secretary took me and Mr. Partap Singh Daulta M. P.

to the grand meeting at Sonepat. It was raining again this day. The crowd sat and stood, not minding the wet weather. The Chief Minister greeted me, left his chair, asked me to sit on it and he himself sat down. I was surprised at this overwhelming courtesy and goodwill. I gave a talk for a few minutes. Then we had lunch with ministers and the local leaders.

This morning of 14th September 1957 at New Delhi I had breakfast with the Hon. Minister Mr. K. C. Reddy. Messrs Gopalan, Ranbir Singh and Daulta took me to him to discuss the question of the acquisition of land by government.

It was a great affair. Nearly two thousand peasants gathered at Connaught Place, New Delhi. I led them to the residence of the Hon. Prime Minister Pandit Jawaharlal Nehru. It was on the 30th August 1957. Their land has been acquired by the government to extend the city. 'The Statesman' of the 31st August reported thus : 'Mr. Nehru addressing the farmers at his house assured them that their grievances would be looked into by him. Replying to Raja Mahendra Pratap M. P. who had earlier addressed the Prime Minister on behalf of the farmers, Mr. Nehru said he would always like to give full consideration to farmers if their land was purchased from them. Raja Mahendra Pratap pointed out to the Prime Minister that colonizers were selling the land at exhorbitant prices while there purchase price was very nominal. Raja Mahendra Pratap said that any expansion of Delhi should be towards the hills.'

Several daily newspapers gave the account in their own words and printed photos of the procession and of Pandit Nehru when I spoke to him.

I had a ten minutes interview with the Prime Minister a couple of days before this demonstration. I had informed him that I would be leading the peasants to his residence. Many of them were ex-service men, retired soldiers, their brethren were on active service. They deserved full sympathetic consideration.

On the 16th September I left by car. I was at Vrindaban for three nights. I inspect the flooded areas. I attended an election tea party at the residence of Maharao Krishnapal Singh at Mathura. Friends will contest Municipal elections.

My Story : All these days I have been on holiday. There was no meeting of our Parliament. I was, however, busy as ever. I prepared my Hindi and English circulars. I attended to my correspondence. I received visits. In my Himalayan home too, friends drop in.

On Sunday the 29th September 1957 I held prayers, at Dharma, at noon, and at Rajpur in the evening. Next day I left for Delhi and attended the brilliant National Day function at the Chinese Embassy on the 1st of October. Electric bulbs were shining. Decoration was elaborate. The Ambassador received the guests. It was a pleasure to meet many friends.

On the 14th I left with my daughter for Patiala in her car. We reached the destination at about 7.30 p.m. Rajmata, mother of Maharaja Patiala had kindly prepared rooms for us but we stayed with the Rani of Raja Maheshinder Singh ji. She made us quite at home, fine place, fine food. I phoned to Rao Surajmal at Chandigarh. He promised to come next day.

On the 15th Oct. I attended the big gathering of cooperative bank workers. I spoke for a few minutes. I had tea with the minister and a large number of guests. At night we had dinner with them.

On the 16th we had lunch with Sardar Satwant Singh and came to Karnal. Ch. Bhim Singh Dist. Magistrate greatly disappointed me. He refused to arrange meetings for me. He thought it was against service rules. He could not think that my preaching would bring peace as it did in Rohtak district. We left and came back to Dehradun. Acute struggle is still going on in Karnal. Some one told me yesterday that the officials themselves want this struggle to continue. Be as it may. I want peace, permanent peace removing all kinds of friction.

On the 7th Nov. evening I and my daughter attended Soviet Russian annual function. There was a huge crowd. Some said that the guests were over two thousand. Electric bulbs were profusely used in decoration.

My daughter left on the 10th Nov. From 11th Nov. started our Parliament. My routine is that I attend the Parliament at noon and remain at home, writing circulars, or letters, in the afternoon.

My Recognition Bill is Not Allowed

I could not speak at the Parliament during all these days. It was officially published in the proceedings of Parliament that I would present my Recognition Bill on the 22nd November but I was opposed by two Ministers. The Bill was not allowed to be introduced. I had proposed in the Bill to grant five hundred rupees per month to Vir Savarkar, Mr. Barindra Kumar Ghose, younger brother of Saint Arbindo, and Dr. Bhupendra Nath Dutta, younger brother of Swami Vivekananda. It was a case when 'defeat proves victory.' The entire opposition walked out of the House when the result of the voting was announced: Forty eight votes for me and seventy five for government. Next day all the dailies in all the country carried the news, many on front page, with big head lines.

1st December 1957 : It is my birth day. It is also the date when The Provisional Government was founded at Kabul in 1915.

Today in the early morning Mr. Seth and Mr. Verma arrived, garlanded me and congratulated me. They are celebrating my birth day in their school. At noon I received telephone call from Vrindaban asking me to come immediately. It was said that public of Vrindavan had arranged a meeting. Mr. Khankhoje, the famous revolutionary came to see me, I took his leave and left by car. At 6 p.m. I arrived at Vrindaban. I held prayer at the Love Center. I addressed the public meeting. I had dinner at the residence of Mr. Mukerji, It is 10.45 p.m.

Barindra Kumar Ghose ji, younger brother of Saint Aurbindo, writes from 93-3-1-1, Hari Ghose Street, Calcutta-6 :

My dear Mahendra Pratap ji,

Please do not take the failure of your honest attempt so much to heart. It is not worth it. The present rulers of our country are creatures of circumstances. Imprint of centuries of domination of foreign rulers impede their movement. The Congress rule is a necessary interim stage. Real independence will grow out of these mistakes. You are a man of love, selfless love of man. Then why worry over this small thing? The whole epic play, with all good and evil, is the manifestation of One Supreme truth that is God. He is the apparent good and evil. In reality, he transcends all, unsoiled like the blue dome over head. Your *tapasya* (penances) of love and self dedication will bring the desired change very soon. Bless our misguided brothers. Your Soul touch will work miracles and True Mother India will rise in the full glory out of these ashes. My love and good wishes. Note my new address. I am here for the last three months. Please send World Federation your paper here.

Yours Sincerely

Barindra Kumar Ghose

As I wrote earlier, I tried to get a bill passed by our parliament that he, Dr. Bhupendra Nath Dutta and Vir Savarkar get each five hundred rupees pension per month. But two ministers did not let the discussion on the Bill. I informed Mr. Barindra Kumar about it. He kindly sent the above reply. His brother's relics were brought yesterday to Delhi. Today's papers have brought out photographs of their arrival. Today they are to be enshrined. And the living brother who suffered in Andaman and in prison for years, in neglected, this in the queer behaviour of our society and official bureaucracy.

Dr. Bhupendra Nath Dutta, younger brother of famous Swami Vivekananda, writes from 3 Gourmohan Mukherjee Street, Calcutta-6 :

My dear Pratap ji,

I am in receipt of your letter dated 25th Nov. 57 but as I am bed ridden I could not answer you in proper time. I have noted the contents of your letter and I am thankful for your effort. I have said my say previously that many are suffering extremely and the Provincial Govts. do not pay any heed to them. I have given their names already to you. If necessary I will again give their names and information in detail. But what is the use ! Thanking you for the effort and hoping that you are well, I remain.

Yours truly

B. N. Dutta

His five words 'but what is the use' speak volumes. Thus feel thousands who worked hard for years to liberate the land, and they show the condition of our society and of our government. Sufferers Unite ! We can change the government !!

Vir V.D. Savarkar Ji, Savarkar Sadan, Shivaji park, Bombay, kindly writes :

Dear Raja ji,

Your kind letter dated 25th Nov. 1957 was duly received. Apart from the personal mention of my name included in the bill you wanted to introduce in the Lok Sabha, I as a common citizen feel it my duty to congratulate you on behalf of the class of Indian Revolutionaries as such on your patriotic efforts to call up on the nation through its parliament to express its sense of recognition of services to the country which the revolutionaries had rendered in our struggle for the achievement of Indian independence during the last hundred years. You must have been aware of the fact that for the last five years or so my health has been steadily declining and consequently I had to retire from all public activities and tours, that is the reason which disables me from any active support to your public and patriotic activities which you often expect from me, there is no help for it. Though almost confined to bed I read now and then your newspaper which you had been kindly sending to me. By and by I may draw your attention to the fact that almost all the leading Marathi papers have been writing in favour of your 'Recognition Bill' and expressing gratitude to you. There was a public meeting held at Poona under the auspices of the Hindu Maha Sabha in your support in the matter of the Bill and grateful compliments were paid by speakers for your patriotic activities throughout your revolutionary career. Generally I have stopped even public correspondence as it taxes my broken health but I could not but write this letter to you as I have come to cherish the pleasant memories of your short company and personal chit-chat at our accidental meeting in Delhi in last May. Wishing you long life and good health.

Yours sincerely
V. D. Savarkar

Shame ! Shame ! Shame ! Shouted the opposition when a couple of Ministers did not even allow the discussion of my Bill which was to recognise the services of Vir Savarkar, Shri Barindra Kumar Ghose and Dr. Bhupendra Nath Dutta.

Government found it too heavy expenditure to give five hundred rupees per month to these three leaders, as I had suggested in my Bill.

All the dailies of the 23rd November brought out this news, Indian Express gave a fuller report. I want patriots all over the country to raise their voices against this unpatriotic and ungrateful move of a couple of Ministers and their supporters.

I expect even honest Congressmen to protest against this action of the socalled Congressmen. It is indeed a shame for the Congress to allow such Ministers to remain in the Congress.

Even Lord Krishna, Prophet Mohammed and Jesus Christ were opposed in their days. Evil existed and exists Evil opposes me, too. But I do not say kill the evil men. Lord Krishna killed the evil persons with his holy hands. I fight evil and not the evil men. They are diseased persons, sick on account of evil habits or evil associations. Goodness unite ! Let us purify our evil brethren, drunk with power or blindly selfish.

About Our Foreign Policy in Parliament :

I am very sorry to inform my readers that my voice is throttled. The rulers who have the majority in our parliament do not allow me sufficient time to express my views in detail. The other day when the Foreign Policy of the government was presented to the House by Pandit Jawahar Lal Nehru for discussion I was not given time to speak. Communist and Anglo-Indian and many other members got time but not I. I got annoyed. I vehemently protested to Chair, then I got hardly ten minutes while others got half an hour or twenty minutes. I reproduce my speech. I had lot to say more but I was not allowed. I spoke :

> I want that our Hon. Prime Minister must think every morning why he thinks as he thinks. He thinks as he thinks because he got English education. I think as I think because I was for 31 years abroad in non-English countries. I was in Germany, America. Afghanistan, Japan, China and so on. I am influenced by the ideas prevailing in free independent

countries and our friends here are influenced by English ideas because they were under the British. This fact must be understood.

Now, I go further and I say that as regards the foreign policy, I do not agree, I highly admire the Hon. Prime Minister for his energy. I was quite astonished how one day he was in Madras and the next morning here. I admire all this. But, I do not agree with his foreign policy and I present you my foreign policy.

I say, let us be out of the Commonwealth and let us stop this 'Panch Shila' business. I tell you that this was invented by Russia and China to get some time for preparation. Now the US agreed to it because the Generals of the USA told the President: "Sir, Soviet Russia seems to be a little ahead because Sputnik was put in the space; so, let us also wait and let us have 'Panch Shila." For every thought that comes out of the mind there is always a reason.

For instance, I have written in my World Federation circular that a great deal in made of this Sputnik business. Why? It is also a propaganda. It is the propaganda of Soviet Russia to fight the USA propaganda with this idea. I may tell you, my friends, this communism is not itself any danger to anybody. I may tell you what is capitalism?

Capitalism is a system in which a man who is a little cleverer can amass wealth. Communism came out of the minds of Jews, the great Karl Marx and Engels. Because the Jews were suppressed in Russia and in Germany, they said: "What shall we do so that we may also get forward?" As I always say, races, tribes and castes always struggle to come forward.

The Jews found out that the king, businessmen and the priests really rule the society. It is a fact. In our Hindu society also the Brahman, the Rajput and the Bania were in alliance and they ruled the society. So the Jews found out that if they could show something against the king, against the bania or businessmen then they also rule.

I must explain to you that here sometimes our gentlemen, and especially our communist friends do not really realize what is all this business. The business in the word is that there were small States. They fought and fought and bigger States developed. Till before the First World War there were only about 14 big States in the world. After the war several were eliminated. After the Second World War others were eliminated.

Really, the struggle today is between the Anglo-Saxon on the one side and the Slavs on the other side. They use communism and democracy to influence the people and get a big following. I am sorry to say that this very important question is not properly heard in the Parliament. In fact, hours are needed. I will tell you what I have seen in the world in 31 years. You will be astonished, that what you are thinking is nothing but something put into your heads by certain circumstances.

I wish that sometime the Hon. Prime Minister will appoint a day and call a meeting, and let me speak for one hour and then I shall tell you my foreign policy. Sir, in short my foreign policy is this, that we approach the small States of Europe and especially Germany and Japan who are very angry with Soviet Russia and America, and we approach Latin America, and we also approach the independent States of Africa and Asia and have a big following for India. So we defeat the Soviets and America in UNO with our following and outside we make such a big following that war between United States and USSR will become impossible.

Here I am reminded of a joke. Once upon a time USSR said to United States : US (you ass), US retorted : USSR (you ass ass are). (End of my speech).

I must add here that there is no other remedy to save humanity but my plan of World Federation with unity of religions and economy of joint family every village and town become joint families.

Surrender to UNO. If the rulers really wanted peace they would surrender themselves to UNO There would not be wire pulling. Why deceive the citizens of your own States by the false harangue of peace. You are rulers and you want to rule, by deceiving your own people and the peoples of the world.

I know UNO is very defective. But it is better to have a defective world organization than no organization. We can later improve it. But once you must surrender. Surrender your foreign policy, no more your ministers, ambassadors or consuls. Let UNO alone have representatives at all the capitals and trade centres. UNO will see to it that your nationals do not suffer in any way. Their rights will be protected.

You surrender your military might to UNO. Let UNO have world army, world navy and world air force. Why fear? Your men will be taken in the world military force as well as in world diplomatic corps. You perfect your social order. Make everyone happy. Make a family of your country.

Your happy people will be the best guarantee of your safety. There could not be any foreign danger if the people have internal peace, peace of mind and of home.

I say this to all the States, all over the world. It is the right course. But I know it is, as if, shouting in a wilderness. No one listens. All what they say of peace, communism, five freedoms, Panch Shila, Co-existence, democracy or any attractive thing, is a propaganda to safeguard their chairs and rulers and to make their States stronger. And USA and USSR are struggling for world control.

This fact is not understood. People generally are too busy with problems of bread and butter. Personal ambitions or plans put into their heads by education or circumstances of life, environment. A great deal of your propaganda is needed to clean their heads and to put in their heads our thoughts of Federated World State, World Federation.

Rise ! Ye, men and women of world vision ! You have a great responsibility. You have been given birth, you are kept alive, you were given this vision on a plan, with a purpose. You do your duty. Herald around. Enlighten the people.

My Story : Our Parliament Session ended on the 21st of December. During the session I had to attend the parliament daily. I spoke twice. Once in Hindi and next in English I delivered my harangue. I also asked several questions. I gave several resolutions for consideration in the House but none was taken up. With one exception all were rejected. My fellow members admitted that injustice was done to me. The ruling caste does not want me to come up lest I could control the government backed by the Union of martial races. This or any such suspicion is entirely groundless. I stand for the ideal that all work for all to make all happy.

You might have heard that the Parliament members of the British Commonwealth countries gathered at Delhi. They held meetings. I did not attend their deliberations but I was at several tea parties given in their honour. At the Government House, at the tea party given by the Hon'ble President, I met many members from Ireland, Africa and Pakistan. At the tea party given by the Hon'ble Prime Minister I met many members, Ministers and the High commissioner of Pakistan. I put him straight question : 'I am telling that we shall destroy Pakistan, will you arrest me if I go to Pakistan, He said : 'Never ! I guarantee that you would not be arrested !' He added that he would give me visa.

On the 8th Dec. I presided and spoke at a peasants meeting at a village near Qutub Minar. That day I spoke at the Central Hall of our Parliament and at Dr. Ambedkar's death anniversary. Here five to six thousand persons were present. I attended twice Mongolian meetings.

On the 21st Dec. I addressed and presided another peasants meeting at another village, several other M.Ps. were also present and spoke. This evening the Hon'ble President Babu Rajendra Prasad heard my prayer and history of the Religion of Love.

In Parliament

The Speaker of Lok Sabha, after great difficulty gave me a little time to speak. I stood and said : I rise to speak on the general budget and so I shall be speaking on general points. I say that members of the House and members of the Government are moving in certain ruts of Ideas. My concern is that they should get out of this rut and see around and have general view. I want that we should make a new society. With new ideas. These ideas, as they are prevailing now, make us fight and they divide us. I say that we must have ideas, but at the same time, we should keep our old culture. On the basis of our old culture, we should build our future.

Now, I call the present ideas as ruts of Ideas. For example : They speak a great deal about public sector, of private sector, nationalization, and all these things. These ideas grew during the last 50 to 60 years and they have captured the minds of our members, and they do not vet us of those ideas. They do not know why these ideas were created, how they developed; they have no knowledge of it. They find themselves midst of a stream of certain ideas and they go on.

I say that people should get freedom which they are not getting now. They are hampered at every step, every where. I do not mind if people make money; I do not mind if they start new industries. But I would certainly mind if they do some thing in which time is wasted or energy is wasted. I shall mind if they will enjoy life in a way that they spread diseases and make people idle or anything of the kind. So, what I think is, we should not mind if some people make money. But we should see that they do not enjoy in a certain way which means waste of time and energy.

I want, Sir, that we should change the system of the Government. This system of Government was started by the British for the British, with the aid of those people who took bribes from the British against the interests of the country. Thus this machine was built up. So I say we must change this entire machine; the rule of the collectors and of captains, the rule of the baton and the rule of the police. We should realy give freedom to the people. The people have not got freedom yet. It is Government by the Government officials.

I wish that people have freedom, there should be only one tax, and that tax should be on property, land, houses or factories. But there should not be tax on our walking, on our motoring or on our daily life.

Now a man thinks he can make a little money by trading. But you tax him, you stop him. I think this system should go. I would suggest that the object of industry should not be profit, we should produce for our own use. This is a system which was introduced in certain parts of the united States-production for use. That is to say, we build factories, not to sell the products but to provide ourselves with those articles which we produce.

Here I will also speak a bit about Pakistan. I was recently there. We make big budgets. What for? To make our lives better. We build houses, we make cities, we make roads and canals. But if unfortunately a war comes. And if Americans give A-bomb or H-bomb to Pakistan, and if they throw one bomb on Delhi, our Delhi will be finished. Now we have to consider the situation. I say that there is a method by which there will be no Pakistan and this fact I said in Karachi and Lahore, their papers reproduced my statement. So, I say, there is a way of saying things. I honestly believe that it is possible that there will be no Pakistan, but only we shall have Aryan from Iran to Assam and Himalaya to Ceylon. If we can bring it about, there will be no danger of war. There will be no question of Kashmir. So, I beg you that my plan of Aryan may be adopted officially. Our Aryan is not also an isolated unit. Our Aryan will be only a district of the province of Asia of world's federal government. If such an Aryan is created, it will be secure. There can be no security if countries prepare for war here and there.

Here I come to the most important point. Our people here and our people abroad, and humanity in general have not understood how humanity has developed so far. There were small States. They were fighting and fighting and bigger States came into being. Then the bigger States were fighting and fighting and still bigger states came into being. Now only two are left in the field – USA and USSR – and without knowing we have become part of one.

We might say that we are quiet neutral, we might say that our policy is independent. But when we are a part of the British Commonwealth, and when this Commonwealth is a part of the USA group we are not neutral. I think such a lie should be stopped, facts must be faced. So the question is: what are you going to do under the circumstances? Are we to remain in this British Commonwealth and when war comes between USA and USSR, we also become the victims of the war and aggression of USSR? Are you satisfied with this situation? I am not. I consider it very dangerous. What are we to do then? I say, and I repeat it in this House also that we should boldly go with a new plan and programme, the programme of World Federation as our cread.

Mr. Deputy-Speaker : The hon'ble Member's time is up.

Raja Mahendra Pratap : Please excuse me. After four days of penance, I got this opportunity. I also dare to say to the Chair: Please do not promise, if you promise fulfill it.

Workers should be declared half partners in all factories. If we could do that then there will be no more strikes. We should take representatives of workers in the Board of Directors and when the profit comes, we divide with them half and half. In that case there will be no strikes.

Now, I would just read the points and would not enlarge on them. The evil of selection in the services is very great. For instance, there are 200 persons to be taken and 18,000 people apply. Now, is the Government for 200 people or for 18,000 people? This has to be considered.

Then there is the evil of courts. Some Hon'ble Member has just now said and he has truly said that the courts must be finished immediately. These courts are a nuisance for society.

Shri Naushir Bharucha (East. Khandesh) : What will happen to the lawyers?

Raja Mahendra Pratap : Lawyers will become leaders of the people.

Then there is the evil of hospitals, I hear people say that even the compounder wants some bribe to give medicine. This is a very serious question. So I also say that there should not be many hospitals. But there should be moral institutions to stop people from doing things which create diseases.

Mr. Deputy-Speaker : The hon'ble Member's time is up.

Raja Mahendra pratap : There are still two or three very important points.

Mr. Deputy-Speaker : I would advise the hon'ble Member that he should reserve his remarks for some other opportunity. If the House will feel interested, perhaps hon'ble Members would attend his lecture. But he should conclude here.

Raja Mahendra Pratap : I would say only one thing more.

We should establish this principle that any and every idea, which creates friction and struggle, should be suppressed and any idea, which makes us friendly and brings us together, should be accepted.

Pakistan : It is itself a problem. There is no Kashmir question at all. Let us go back and see why Pakistan was created. Quarrel was for leadership. The British were leaving. Brahman, the leader of the Hindu world, and the Arab stock in India, leader of the Muslim world, both wanted leadership. Two kings could not rule in a single kingdom. They divided the country. In Pakistan the Arab stock leadership is overthrown. The Hon. President of Pakistan is of Moghul Blood. The Prime Minister is Jat. Afghan or Pathan blood is ruling Pak Punjab. This new leadership of Pakistan is naturally favourably inclined to my plan of Aryan. Brahman leadership in our country feels uncertainty of its position in Aryan Federation. But I say that if foreign interests make Pakistan fight India, one day Brahmans will be the worst sufferers. Let us see far into the future. Remedy is Aryan with local liberty but unity in Federation. In my plan we shall have respect for spiritual leadership, Brahman or Syed. We shall respect the Gurus. All castes or tribes will be secure. There leaders shall rule villages and towns. Religions and our ancient culture will form the foundation of our future. Prevailing tension can undo our progress through ages past. Pakistan will equally suffer in an Indo–Pak war. They will get benefit only who would make us fight.

German Unity : East and west are equally responsible for German disunity. They both fear united Germany. Program feeling expressed in both the camps is only to deceive the German people. Germans themselves will have to bring about unity. Form a Nordic party to unite the Nordic district of North Europe from Norway to Austria. Insist that the capital of Nord will be at Copenhagen. It should disarm the anti-German elements in the East and the West.

Japanese Liberty : Japan is not entirely free yet. Japan has to be liberated. Japan herself can do it best. Japan's plan of the Asiatic unity made her an enemy of Europe and America. My plan of World Federation is such that it gives complete autonomy. To every land and makes all countries secure in one world government. World capital will be at Honolulu. Japanese form a great part of Hawaii population.

Indirectly Japan could influence world opinion through world capital. World Government will stop production of A and H bombs. Atomic energy will be used to travel to other planets. Let Japan take up World Federation movement. It will give her liberty.

My Story : I left Delhi on the night of the 27th March 1958. As an M. P. I am fully entitled to get first class free on all Indian railways but I started on a short notice and there was not a single first class berth available, I travelled in second class. You do not know what it meant, a crowded compartment, not a place to lie down. However I got a chance to preach. As soon the fellow passengers found my identity they wanted to hear some stories of my 'exile.' One said, another repeated, they heard my name when they were young. Now I found that there were some military officers equally entitled to travel first class but were travelling second, not getting a first class berth.

I spoke on travels, I spoke on politics. I brought in religion. One passenger at last made room for me to get a nap. It was midnight. Next morning I reached Pathankot. A bus brought me to Jammu. Here friends led me to the house of Shri Om Prakash

Saraf, P.S.P. Jammu leader. He himself had come to the bus stand to receive me.

Another trouble was brought to my notice. Four Harijans were on hunger strike. I went to visit them. Soon after we left by car. Motoring through wide valley, racing along a dangerous narrow mountain road, we reached Sunderbani, a beautiful spot surrounded by green hills.

I was taken to the Dak-bungalow, the comfortable resting place. Here was also staying Mr. Omar, the president of Kashmir PSP. Students came and continued to come the gentry of the town, I talked, took dinner, talking to the assembly.

Next day in the afternoon was held the public meeting. But just as we started to lecture, rain came. It thundered menacingly. I told my audience that I am at war with the rain god, it seems, My meetings are often disturbed by rain. I spoke of my plan to give home-rule to every village and town and hurriedly ended. We returned to our car.

Now the rain ceased. People flocked to us once again and asked us to speak a little more. Mr. Omar gave the message of P.S.P. I repeated that you should get power. Only change of leaders would not help you much. Some youths had danced for us. I said there leaping showed their enthusiasm for freedom, to get true liberty.

We returned to Jammu but here again started rain. Another meeting could not held. The host gave me fine dinner and quiet room to sleep.

On the 30th March morning a very crowded press conference was held. I reviewed the international situation and showed the danger of Indo-Pak tension over Kashmir. My plan, I explained, would solve every problem of the world, including that of Kashmir. I proceeded further to preach Religion of Love. One Pandit Yogeshwarji was so much impressed by our prayer that he immediately promised to open a centre of the Religion of love. My friends saw me off at the bus stand. At Pathankot I found my berth reserved in a first class compartment. Another M. P. was also there.

On the 1st April about sixteen members of the Defence Committee of the Parliament were taken to Ambala by a Viscount plane. We were shown Air show. It was the Silver Jubilee of our Air Force.

Third Sputnik : It is also very big news. Russia could send out into the space her third Sputnik. It is much larger and very heavy. Some communists are very proud of this achievement but it has nothing to do with communism. Czarist Russia built St. Petersburg and Trans-Siberian railway. German mind co-operated with Czarist Russia and it is cooperating with Red-Russia. Capitalist USA have highest houses. It has nothing to do with capitalism. It is the Race which races on the road of progress. It is the Race which creates all kinds of ideas, known as religious, political, social or economic. We want to see the human race developing as one unit and all the races functioning as organs of one body. Russians have to be awakened to realize their real self and all the races of USSR have to be inter-woven in Turan of World Federation.

My Speech in Parliament on 26th April 1958

I thank you for the opportunity that you have given me. I have to say that according to the rules of the party, I should denounce every word of Shrimati Uma Nehru, and I should support every word of Shri Naushir Bharucha. But I felt that when Shrimati Uma Nehru was speaking, she was speaking for me, and when my Hon. friend in the opposition was speaking, he was speaking something against my sentiment.

I believe that there should be no Bill, because the more the bills are made, as I said once, the more work we make for the pleaders. I have always said, and I repeat it–that what our Parliament should do is that we should evolve a system to make our people moral. I said, and I repeat it, that we should take into service of the State all the Mullahs, all the Pandits and all the priests. I mean the good men out of them and see that they form certain observing units in different parts of the cities and in different parts of the country: they should watch who is inclined towards crime, and they should check it immediately by bringing that fact to the notice of the society that this man has got to be improved.

In some cases a man is very much inclined to anger or gets easily agitated. We know this by experience. Under these circumstances, the doctor should find out what the defect is with that person. There must be some defect in him. It might be sexual defect. And medical service can be utilized to cure him of that.

So, I mean to say with all respect to the House that the House should not think that its only business here is to discuss Bills and bring forward more laws. I think we should devote more time to see how we can change the system, as Shrimati Uma Nehru said. The system is wrong. It is the system which creates or which develops criminals. This system is wrong, and I believe that this system can be changed. I can understand the feeling of my fellow-Member that the victims suffer, and we should have some sympathy for these victims and also with the families of these victims who suffer as a result of the murder etc. But, as Shrimati Uma Nehru has said, if there is a criminal, it is society which is responsible for that criminal. It is society which is responsible for having developed him into a criminal. If there are robbers, again, society is responsible. There should be some system whereby there should be no robbers and no thieves in society. And how can have that system?

I say that we should have every village as a joint family, and every town as a joint family, and the principle should be 'No one without work, and no one without bread'. I do not say that this system should be evolved through the Congress or through the Communists or through the SP or PSP But I say that this should be evolved through pure and simple religion. Religion tells us that all human beings were created by one God. When we believe in that, we believe that God wants the well-being of all. These petty spiritual leaders who only quarrel for their religious groups have forgotten the universality of God. So, I say, that through God we can so evolve our society that there will be no criminals in society; and if there is a tendency on the part of anyone to become criminal, then it can be checked from the very beginning.

As I said once, I am not very anxious to tax riches or control riches. I am not very anxious about it. But I am very anxious that people waste their energy and time. For instance, a lot of dancing is going on. In the name of culture, our girls are made to dance. This should be checked. Than, for instance, there is horse-racing. This should also be checked. Again, gambling should be checked. If the people who have money are prohibited from doing things which make our society ugly, the people will be more spiritual and moral.

As you, Sir, know, I was going to speak on the Demands of the Defence Ministry, and I had some new ideas about that; but I was not allowed time. Again, I was going to speak on the Demands of the Finance Ministry...

Mr. Deputy-Speaker : That should not be a complaint that time was not allowed. Now time is allowed.

Raja Mahendra Pratap : I just want to explain that I was waiting for a week to get my chance, because there might be some misunderstanding that I arrived just fifteen minutes before and I was not waiting for a week.

I mean to say that my proposals as they are such that these laws as they are passed today will not be necessary. For instance, if I had been allowed to speak on finance I would have presented my programme, which I presented to Comrade Lenin in 1918, that we do away with gold and silver. We should have, for instance, the notes where Government say "We promise to pay the bearer on demand one mound of wheat, or ten sears of butter or a ton of coal etc."

Mr. Deputy-Speaker : But here we are concerned with doing away with the criminals and not with gold and silver. So, the Hon'ble Member should devote himself to that.

Raja Mahendra Pratap : I only mean to say that if my whole programme for society is adopted, there will not be any need for passing such laws showing some sympathy to those criminals or that kind of probation and all that.

My Story : On the 9th May 1958 I inaugurated All India Urdu Conference at Bareilly. I spoke long in favour of this beautiful language. It some how happened that the policy of our government entirely changed, as if, simultaneously in regard to Urdu. It was so to say my miracle talk. Two nights in the train were not in vain. 21st May. I inaugurated the large birth day festival of Maharana Pratap at the Roshanara Park Delhi. I said, I try to do what Maharana did. I fought against the British and I am trying to bring complete freedom to our country, remaining within the British Commonwealth is not freedom.

I left Delhi on the 22nd May by car, passing night at Muzaffarnagar, I came to Rajpur on the 23rd. On the way I visited the college which is named after me. 25th, Sunday, I held prayer meeting at noon, at Dharm, Dehradun. I and my daughter, we brought Saint Nihal Singh to our residence and had lunch together.

In the evening I held our prayer meeting at Pratap Kothi, Rajpur. Prof. Ahuja was present. At Mussoorie, walking on the Mall I met many friends, Sir Sitaram, Thakur Satyanarain Singh, Union Minister, Babu Chandra Bhanu Gupta and many others.

Single Tax Bill

I produced a Bill in the Parliament for tax-structure of Free India :

A Bill (By Raja Mahendra Pratap M. P.) To free the people from numerous taxes, Be it enacted by parliament in the ninety year of the Republic of India as follows :

Chapter I

1.

   i. This Act may be called Single tax Act.

   ii. It extends to the whole of India.

   iii. It shall come in to force at once.

2. In the Act, unless the context otherwise requires,

   a. 'Tax' means money collected by Panchayats, Municipalities, Corporations or by Provincial or Central Governments.

   b. 'Single tax' means only one tax.

Chapter II

3. There shall be single tax all through.
4. Only land, houses, money and jewellery in banks shall be taxed.
5. Land occupied by fruit trees shall be taxed according to the income from fruits.
6. Canal or tube-well water using land shall be taxed, according to the income of the land.
7. Land having mines shall be taxed according to income from mines.

8. Houses having factories shall be taxed according to the income from production.
9. There shall be no restriction on bringing in gold, silver or jewellery into the country.
10. Gold, silver, jewellery or wealth could not be taken out of the country, without Government permit.
11. Customs shall continue to function as hither to.
12. There shall be no taxes on cars, trucks, tongas, carriages or rikshaws.
13. There shall be no octroi or any road side taxes or tolls.
14. There shall be no tax on cows, bulls, goats, camels, dogs and other animals.
15. There shall be no death duty.
16. There shall be no income tax.
17. There shall be no water tax, canal or tube well tax.
18. Taxes on land, houses, accumulated wealth in banks shall be increased to cover all the village, town and government expenses.
19. There shall be no fees in schools and colleges.
20. Land and houses not able to pay taxes shall become government property with due compensation to the owner.
21. Excise department shall cease to function.
22. Moral societies shall be formed to dissuade people from using intoxications.
23. Harmful drugs and strong intoxicating material shall be seized and burnt.
24. Moral societies shall keep watch, on habits of people and report to authorities cases inclined to crime.
25. Money shall not be allowed to be used for wild pleasures.

Statement of Objects and Reasons

People are too much hindered and tortured by numerous taxes.

Movements grow in opposition to government, dislocating administration.

The single Tax will give the general public great relief.

The Bill seeks to make the general public free from taxes on every step.

Home Rule Bill 1958

A Bill (By Raja Mahendra Pratap M.P.) To give Home Rule to every village and town.

Be it enacted by parliament in the ninth year of the Republic of India as follows:-

1.

    i. This Act may be called Home Rule Act.
    ii. It extends to the whole of India.
    iii. It will come in to force immediately.

2. In this Act, unless context other wise requires,
    a. 'Adult' means a person who has completed twenty one years.
    b. 'Village' means collection of houses in rural areas.
    c. 'Town' means town areas, Municipalities, Towns, Corporations, Cities.
    d. 'Profession' means a group of people following the same kind of work.

Chapter II

3. Every village and town shall be given Home Rule.
4. Professions in every town and village shall be organized by all the adults of those professions.
5. Elected leaders of the profession (Number) form village and town governments.
6. Village and Town governments shall appoint judges to hear and decide all the complaints of the citizens.
7. Villages and Town governments shall appoint village guards and shall organize a police force to keep law and order.

8. Village governments shall elect members of the District Boards.
9. District Boards and Town governments shall elect members of the Provincial Legislative Assemblies of their Provinces.
10. Legislative Assemblies shall elect provincial cabinets.
11. Provincial Assemblies shall elect members of the parliament.
12. There shall be no upper houses in the provinces and at the centre.
13. Parliament shall elect the President of the state and the central cabinet.
14. Parliament shall make laws for the whole country.
15. Parliament shall appoint judges of the Supreme Court.
16. Provincial Assemblies shall appoint judges of the High Courts.
17. District Judge shall appoint punches to hear the Appeals from villages.
18. Appeals from District Judges and Town Judges shall go to High Courts and appeals from High Courts shall go to the Supreme Court.
19. In all cases decision shall be swift; no case could hang on for over a year.
20. Village and Town governments shall appoint a moral Board of Sadhus or religious leaders of all religions to make people moral.
21. In all schools and colleges farms and factories shall be established, so that students and teachers produce their daily necessities.
22. In every factory and mine workers, managers and proprietors shall share profit among them.
23. Net profit shall be divided half and half between workers and share holders or proprietors.
24. Representatives of the workers shall sit on the Board of Directors of the factories and mines.

25. The principle shall govern all the village and Town governments that not one shall remain without work and without bread.

Statement of Objects and Reasons

Government has been monopolized by a single party and government officials. People are ruled, exploited and oppressed.

The Bill seeks to give home rule to the people.

Commodities Notes

Resolution : This house recommends to the government to form a committee to study the possibility to introduce Commodities Notes, such as, wheat, rice, dal, meat, ghee, coal, charcoal, wood, iron, cement, lime, etc. Notes, or Notes of cloth, shoes etc. in place of the present gold or silver notes.

And if the committee favours the idea it should present to the house. Its plan to introduce commodities Notes. It should also tell the House what expenses will be incurred by the state in storing the commodities.

These commodities of course will come as taxes from land and factories or mines.

My Story : On the 25th June I was at Rajpur, in my Himalayan home and remained there upto 23rd July.

On the 24th July I arrived back at Delhi. The newly elected independent M. P. Mr. Prakash Vir came with me from Hodal. On the 26th July I left Delhi by the Mail train. One Minister of Rajasthan and another M.P. were with me in the couple.

On the 27th I arrived at Howrah. Mr. Sanjib Choudhuri and friends came to receive me. Some children with flags welcomed me. One World ! One World ! And greetings to me were shoulded. I was given a stay at Ambassador Hotel.

The same day from 4 p.m. conference for reunion of India and Pakistan was held at the Great Eastern Hotel. In the evening Choudhuri brothers. brought me to their home, gave dinner and made me at home in this garden house, with lawns and pond of water, varandah with marble floor.

A film on Me : 28th July. I had lunch with Shri Somen Tagore Sahib in his artistic home. In the afternoon I was taken to a film in which I appear on horse back leading soldiers from Kabul. It was a reference to our raising an army among the Afridis. I was ascend to speak before the picture. I said how we formed the first provisional Government of India. I was its president, Moulana Barkatullah was prime minister, Moulana Ubaidullah was home minister but the expenses of our Afridi army were paid by Sardar Nasrullah Khan, brother of Amir, from his personal account. I added our work in not yet finished. We have to take out our country from Commonwealth and reunite it in Aryan. There was enthusiastic cheering.

In the evening yesterday, I and Mr. Sanjib Choudhuri visited Mr. Chatterji, Hindu Maha Sabha leader. The present president of Sabha, Mr. Banerji was there and couple of more friends were present. I spoke on my plan. I showed how Hindu leaders had blundered. Caste-wise or race-wise approach should be made. Moghuls fraternized with Hindu Rajputs and invited Hindu Jats to settle around Delhi for their protection, Now Mr. Noon is Jat and General Mirza is Moghul. Afghans are extremeely sympathetic. It is good opportunity to realize Aryan.

Lecture In Parliament (19-8-58)

This was an important speech of mine about the tussle with Pakistan I quote :

Raja Mahendra Pratap (Mathura) : Today our Hon'ble Prime Minister began with two points, that is raids on our frontiers and the situation in west Asia. I shall also deal with these two points.

As regards the raids, I think it is just natural. And these raids will continue till either India and Pakistan go to war or till India and Pakistan get reunited. There is no other third way. We people have studied this question thoroughly. Great barristers and philosophers and political leaders gathered together on the 27th July at the Great Eastern Hotel, Calcutta. I was presiding over the meeting. There it was decided that we should all work so that India and Pakistan get united. Bengal-Bengal will be one, Punjab-Punjab will be one. Then, of course, there will be no raids.

Now, as regards the situation in West Asia I have to submit our Hon'ble Prime Minister saw the situation very well, sees the situation very well. It is just as he describes, but he did not, I think, go to the background of the situation. In this world of ours, there were small, little tribes here and there, and these tribes were struggling and fighting. Then, out of these small tribes, bigger tribes rose. Then, these bigger tribes fought and the nations came into being.

Before the First World War, there were only about 14 great States in our world. They again fought. It was just natural, natural growth. They all wished to grow. They fought and fought, and several big historical States were eliminated. Turkey, Austria and Germany were eliminated as big powers, and we saw at the end of the First World War that Japan grew into a powerful State, more powerful than before. England retreated a bit, Russia advanced a bit. This was the situation. And we saw that Germany rose and Japan rose, and they wanted to expand, spread, in this world. Another war came. I have lived through both these wars, and in fact, I played a little part too in the First and Second World Wars. So, I know a bit as to how they developed and how they ended.

At the end of the Second World War, only two powers remained in the field–Russia and the United States of America. Now they are struggling as to who should rule the world.

Here I must also explain one thing, which is not understood even by some, so the greatest learned people that Communism by itself is just a group of some ideas. Communism is not by itself a powerful force. These are ideas. In the same way, democracy is also an idea. Unfortunately, our people here have got converted to democracy through British education. Democracy has captured their brains, and now every time they speak of democracy. Why do they speak of democracy? Because democracy has taken possession of their minds. They themselves do not know why they speak of democracy.

In the same way, my Communist friends must also admit that Communist ideas have taken possession of their minds, and these two great racial groups of Slavs and Anglo-Saxons are trying to rule the world, and they are utilizing these ideas as they are trying to utilize the atomic bombs and the hydrogen bombs. This point must be understood very clearly.

Here I may say a word about the mental condition of the people. My experience is that every man is living in a certain stage. Just as in schools some children are in the second class, some are in the tenth class, some are in B. A., in the same way, religiously, spiritually also, some are better advanced, some are highly advanced and some are only playing with idols. So, we find that spiritually they are in different stages.

I might say here that politically also these people are in different stages. Some may be old, I mean in years, but in politics they might be only children. This must be understood that some people are living in a tribal atmosphere, and even some of our greatest statesmen speak of our country and their country, of our boundary and their boundary, and our canal and their canal. They have no absolute outlook.

In our world today, we need the absolute outlook. It is very difficult, but you can understand this point very easily....

Mr Deputy-speaker : It is not so easy for me to understand.

Raja Mahendra Pratap : I did not mean the Chair. But I meant that it could be very well understood. If a professor of B. A. class goes round to the third class and delivers the same lecture as in the B. A. class, the third class students would be thinking that this man seems to be mad. What is he speaking about? We cannot understand a bit.

What I mean to say is that when I speak of world federation, some who are children politically cannot understand it. That is what I mean. It is very clear. I mean to say that political development must come to this House. Of course, it is a very respectable House. Some greatest learned people are here. But one thing is also very clear. Suppose a very honest and very learned Hindu gentleman is here, and if I speak something about Islam, he will say, 'What does this Musallah mean? What is he speaking to us?' He is one of the greatest learned men of the greatest tradition; and there is no doubt that he is learned, but he does not know anything about Islam. So also, let Islam, coming right from Mecca, and suppose we speak to him about Gayatri, Banaras, Sandhya etc, he will say, 'This Kafir will be going to hell to be burned for all time, and he dares to tell me all these things. It is quite wrong.'

Now, this is the situation. So, those people who are influenced by Democracy or those people who are influenced by Communism cannot realize the fact that if there is no world government, countries will fight and no army can save any country.

My conception of world government is this, our capital will be at Honolulu in the Hawaii islands, and all the five continents will be self-governing provinces.

Shri C. D. Pande (Nainital) : And the Hon'ble Member will be its president.

Raja Mahendra Pratap : And in Asia, there will be Aryan Federation from Iran to Assam and from Nepal to Ceylon; there will be no trouble then of Ceylon, it will be part of our Aryan Federation.

I propose the same thing for Arabia. I say that from Oman to Morocco, there will be Arab Azam (Great Arab). Arab azam can be created and it will be created, and then there will be no such trouble in west Asia.

With all respect to our Prime Minister, he is very sincere, and he is very honest, and he honestly wants peace, I would say that he does not know the way how to have peace in this world. Peace can only be there if there is world Government; otherwise, there can never be peace. This State will prepare for war, and there will arise some small States as in west Asia, and there will be no peace.

All religions should unite to fight evil and promote goodness. There is some such thing as evil. Islam has called it as Satan and Hinduism has called it as Indriyas. This evil gets into head sometimes, and it makes very good faces and very good out garbs.

Mr. Deputy-Speaker : The hon'ble Member's time is up.

Raja Mehendra Pratap : Now, I shall stop. I would only say this. My slogans are three. The first is that all the world should be united into a world federated State. Secondly. All religions should unite to fight evil and promote goodness. The third is in relation to the economic situation. Our economy should be that of a joint family, every village should be a joint family, and every town should be a joint family. There should be respect for elders, love for children, and all healthy and strong should work for community.

Remarks in Parliament (11-27 Aug. 58)

During this Session of our Parliament from the 11th to the 27th August I have been making remarks in place and out of place. What else I could do? My questions are not admitted. My resolutions are rejected. The only way left for me is to interrupt and exclaim.

They were speaking of facilities which are given in different colonies of the capital of building cinemas and parks. I asked what facilities were given to the workers of Electric Power House? These men who give light to Delhi have no electric lamps in their dirty huts.

They were discussing that the permits which the Government gives to some people they sell them at much higher prices. I exclaimed : 'There is a general rush for wealth and only teaching of morality can stop such things.' The discussion was about the great agitation at Jaipur. I shouted : 'This is due to misjudgement of the government that such things are happening at Jaipur, Ahmedabad and Kerala. Government should reconsider this and the steps they take.'

Pandit Jawaharlal Nehru got eloquent pleading for 'Panch Shila.' I exclaimed, 'World Federation will be better policy.' He replied: "I am in entire agreement with Raja Mahendra Pratap for once..."

Today the 27th August, the topic was about Sheikh Abdullah. I asked : 'In view of the fact that Sheikh Abdullah agrees with my plan for Kashmir, may I know, when he will be released?' I got no answer. These remarks are sufficient as specimens.

My Story : On the 29th July I was at Calcutta. I had lunch with Messrs Chaudhuri. They kindly gave me a car and I set out to see my friends. I saw Dr. Bhupendra Nath Dutta. Shri Barindra Kumar Ghose was not at home. I spoke to the members of Shri Somen Tagore's party. I had dinner with Shri Debnath Das. Several I.N.A. officers were present. I took train at night. I reached Delhi on the 31st July at about six in the morning.

From 7th August till today the 27th August, these twenty days, I am here at New Delhi. Only on Sunday last I went to Niloha via Meerut by car. Pt. Sunderlal ji accompanied me. Ch. Yadram ji gave us lunch at Meerut. Shri Mahender Singh took us to Niloha. We addressed a large meeting there.

On week days my routine work is very regular. Every day I go to the parliament. I receive many visitors with different kinds of requests. My time is taken up by writing my papers in Hindi, English and Urdu. I have to attend to my correspondence too.

Yesterday I was invited to a tea party at the President's official residence. I met the Hon. President, the Vice President and numerous friends including the Ambassadors of Iran and Afghanistan. Our Hon. Speaker and many fellow members were present.

There was yet another tea party at the Presidential Palace on the Independence day, the 15th August. On that day a photo was taken as I shook hands with Hon. Pt. Nehru ji.

I receive many invitations but I can not go to all of them. This evening there was a function of some Martyr's Day, to my regret I could not go there.

I Said in Parliament

1. The question was asked, how many Muslim University, Aligarh students went to Pakistan, I had to say :

   'Is it not a fact, many of our freedom workers were educated in England? So, if these people go to Pakistan, they will bring Pakistan and India together. Where is the harm?'

2. When the, opposition was walking out, calling "shame" at the Government food policy, I shouted loud addressing specially the Hon'ble Prime Minister.

   'Sir, Impression should not be created that we are very kind, opposition is very kind-hearted but the Hon'ble Prime Minister is hard hearted. I beg Hon'ble Pandit Jawaharlal Nehru ji also to leave, I ask Congressmen, too, to leave the House.'

3. There was a discussion about some dishonesty of some people. I said : 'There is a general rush for wealth and only teaching of morality can stop such things.'

4. They were speaking about Kerala and some got very critical. I said : 'This is due to misjudgement of the Government (central) that such things are happening in Jaipur, Ahmedabad and Kerala. The Government should reconsider this and the steps that they are taking in these matters.

5. When they were talking about West Asia and our government's policy, I said, 'World Federation will be the best policy !'

6. Now please read as the Secretariat reports. I said : May I know whether other governments did not object to this? Did they not say : 'How is it that you are speaking of peace and you are also speaking of neutrality, but your Navy took part in the exercises with the British Navy?' Did any country object to it?'

7. I asked Sheikh Abdullah agreed with my plan for Kashmir. May I ask when Sheikh Abdullah will be released?
8. When a member was speaking about monopolies of some companies I asked, 'My hon'ble friend forgot that the worst monopoly is of the Congress party?'
9. When they were speaking for and against Kerala's communist government, I said, 'I have an important submission to make to the House. I say that this matter should not be discussed in the way that parties get more and more consolidated and fight more and more and disrupt the country more. I beg to say that this question should be discussed and considered only from the standpoint of absolute justice. That is what I have to say.'
10. When the government was reporting on ejectment and demolishing unauthorized house, I asked, 'May I know how many houses have been built? It is better to construct first and then demolish the houses.'
11. When they were discussing some kind of common market for the East. I asked, 'I should like to have a common market for the whole world but may I know if there is any plan to have a common market for Iran, Afghanistan, Pakistan, India, Nepal, and Ceylon?'

A member said : 'Aryan'.

'Yes, this is Aryan.'

12. The question was about Indo-Pakistan frontier, discussed between two Prime Ministers, I asked, 'May I ask why did not the hon'ble Prime Minister take advantage of this opportunity to settle the boarder question, and do away with the frontiers altogether?
13. The socalled opposition got enraged over food situation and was delivering hot speeches. I asked, 'You have not given me an opportunity. I have to say something very important. I say re-thinking is necessary. Some people think that by this method our Ministers have become Ministers, and they should adopt the same system of strikes and hungerstikes in order to become Ministers. This is the whole trouble. We need re-thinking. This method of strikes and hunger strikes should

end for all time and we should all co-operate. I say that our first principle is, all to work for all to make all happy and to have a frictionless society. This should be the ideal. Then all this agitation will cease.

Note: *Agitation is going on all over U. P. Over six thousand persons are in jail for defying law under Mahatma Gandhi pattern! I say, Mahatma Gandhi age is ended, World Federation age has begun, now all struggles should cease.*

14. A little later during the discussion :

I said : I have to explain something which may not be misunderstood, I am only opposed to bloodshed.

Shri Braj Raj Singh : There is a bloodshed.

An Hon'ble Member : Don't worry.

I said : I am a revolutionary. I want revolution, but I want revolution in a way that there will not be bloodshed. Some hon'ble friends are rushing for this agitation and when these friends come against the Government there will be no end to bloodshed. I as an experienced revolutionary, having experience of four revolutions want to conduct a revolution in way that we shall transform the Government, so that there will be a real, moral state where all will be happy and not one will be dissatisfied.

15. When air was surcharged with emotions and passions, I said, 'Let us all from a harmonious group so that friction may be removed. We can all sit together and try to come to one point. Let there be harmony'.

16. The question was of anti-social gangs in the capital, I said, 'You should see that a moral front is built. I have a moral front. Perhaps, the Hon'ble Home Minister knows that. So I say why it is not introduced.'

Pandit G. B. Pant. (Home Minister) : I think the suggestion is worth considering.

I said : Thank you, very much.

17. The members of all the parties in parliament got excited on the report that some Indian gentleman was refused admission the Ashoka Hotel in an Indian dress.

I said : I demand a division on this.

Mr. Speaker : Order, order.

I said : I demand a division on this un-Indian thing in India.

The Home Minister had to declare–Indian dress would be allowed.

18. My adjournment motion presented on the 17th September 1958.

'I come from Braj, the heart of Indian Culture of Vaishnav Faith. I come to the court of Indraprasth to relate the plight of Brajbasi, it is very urgent matter, thousands of Brajbasi are badly suffering and no proper arrangements are made.'

The motion was disalowed on the ground that it was state question. I had to make the following observation:

I said : I have given notice of an adjournment motion, and you have refused it. I want to say that Braj is not a State question.

Mathura teen lok se nyari- Mathura is separate from Heaven, hell end earth. So, that is a common problem for all of us. There are thousands of people suffering because water has destroyed many villages.

Mr. Speaker : It does not arise out of the question.

I said : I say that every Hindu here, and even Muslims, because Braj was respected by the Mughal emperors, should join me in this question that Braj should be helped by all of us and the people there who are suffering. Their suffering should be removed. The army can help to take out the water, and the people who are suffering on account of bad wheat can be helped by giving good wheat. This I want to present to the whole House.

I will demand division on this, to see whether our Hindu brethren are for it or not. Or, say you are not Hindus.

19. The five year plan was under discussion. I asked for time to speak. The Hon'ble Speaker said I could go for lunch and return.

I asked : You had promised me time. I went for lunch and returned.

Mr. Speaker : The Hon'ble Minister.

I said : Braj is a holy land, it should also have a voice.

I again asked : Will Braj get time or not? I did not get time that day.

20. Old famous leader Acharya Kripalani and young leader Mr. Masani were attacking Kerala.

I had to say : I have received an invitation from the Chief Minister of Kerala to go there. I shall be going to Kerala and shall see the situation there. I request that a debate on this be allowed after I come back from there.

21. The planning was discussed. The Hon'ble Home Minister Pandit Pant was speaking.

I : On a point of order, Sir.

Pandit G. B. Pant : We will have our chat later.

Mr. Deputy-Speaker : What is that?

Raja Mahendra Pratap : The point of order is that we should build men. You are planning and planning.

Mr. Deputy-Speaker : This is rather a point of disorder.

I said in hindi : *Mein Braj se aata hun, Indraprastha ke darbar mein. Meri baat nahin suni jati hai. Panch hazar saal pahle bhi ek Brajwasi yahan aaya tha, uski baat nahin suni gayee thi to Mahabharat hua tha.*

Pandit G.B. Pant : I entirely agree with him. Our method of approach takes the whole man into account and not a part of it.

I had to repeat : I come from Braj to the court of Indraparasth (Delhi) My words are not heard. Five thousand years before came another man here from Braj. His voice was not heard too. The result was the Great War.

The reference is the coming of Lord Krishna to the court of Duryodhan at Delhi of those days.

22. Some people died of gas poison in a well.

I asked : May I know whether the families have been fully compensated?

23. Today Kerala was under fire.

I said : It is not morally correct. They slander us and we slander them.

24. The question was of rare manuscripts.

I had to ask : May I know whether any particular investigation has been made in our Braj, because in Braj there are very valuable manuscripts?

25. Equal pay to Indian engineers.

I asked : With all respect to the Hon. Minister, may I know whether he means that Indians are less qualified and Britishers are better qualified?

Sardar Swaran Singh : Certainly not.

26. The question was being discussed what about beggars in the capital. I had to say.

'I am the president of the Yogies. My friends ask me how are we to be protected, in Hindu religion beggary is allowed.'

27. A question was asked about the Nepali Military Mission visiting India, I had to say:

On a point of order, Sir, it must be made clear that this question does not create the impression that we did not like the delegation's coming here. We would have been very glad if it remained here for months.

My Story : You read my numberous remarks in our Parliament. They tell indirectly my complete story of these days but still there remain some other details which my dear friends want to hear. For their sake I do not drop the column.

I start by telling you the story of yesterday. At 10 a.m. I went to oblige a friend and follower of Religion of Love Shri Bhagwandas living about eight miles from my residence. Now the car could not proceed further. For three furlongs I walked through mud and water. I remained at the house for only two minutes. I took leave to reach the Parliament. To day was the last day of this session. I could take part in the hot discussion on Kerala. I said: Passions should not be aroused. Let us have peace. Let us have calm discussion. It was the spirit of my counsel. I took my meal at about 2.30 p.m. At 4 p.m. I rushed to all India Railways Commercial Clerks Association. There I was enthusiastically received and my speech was warmly listened to. I received applauded-ovation when I left. I hurried and reached the meeting in memory of Raja Ram Mohan Roy, founder of Brahmosamaj, Lady Mayor was in the chair. When I arrived a Christian Bishop was speaking. As soon as he finished I was asked to speak. I mentioned, how I spoke about Brahmosamaj in my book of the Religion of Love. After me spoke the Chief Justice of India.

At the invitation of a high officer I went to see Army production exhibition on the 9th September, he also kindly gave me lunch in his family. This day in the afternoon was the grand reception given by Pakistan High Commissioner to the Prime Minister Malik Firoze Khan Noon. I attended it. It was here that Noon Sahib said that he knew me since 1918.

Historical Document

Our friends will highly appreciate this historical document of great value. Former Governor General of India the Hon. Pandit Rajagopalachari ji himself gave me this document, when I visited Madras. He presided at the meeting called by L. Y. M. A. Lakshmipuram to hear me on the present situation and World Federation. The president introduced me to the audience, he also read this document, I give it here in full, just as I received it. I may tell my readers that 'Young India' was the paper of Mahatma Gandhi and our Raja ji was the editor then.

Young India, August 24, 1922.

Kaka sends me a letter from the Sabarmati Ashram from which the following is taken.

> 'I send you herewith a leaflet under the caption India people purporting to come from Raja Mahendra Pratap. I think similar proviolence and revolutionary leaflets must have been sent to all parts of India. Such literature is likely now to unsettle men's minds. I think we should codemn it as being detrimental to the best interests of India, Islam and the world.
>
> 'I do not know whence this pamphlet has come. It is just possible some mischief-maker or some unscrupulous Government officer might have circulated this pamphlet in the name of Raja Mahendra Pratap.
>
> 'Let me here tell you what I know of this Mahendra Pratap. He was the Raja of Hathras, a small principality near Brindaban. He dedicated a large portion of his property to a technical institute known as 'Prem Mahavidyalaya'. I saw this Raja in company with a friend at Brindaban. We talked for some ten minutes on the need of technical education.

The Raja looked so very kind, nonaggressive and earnest. I have the sweetest recollection of the visit. The problem of the poor was all-in-all with him.

'When the war broke out I read in the papers, I suppose it was in Swami Shraddhanand's 'Saddharma Procharak', that the Raja has left for the west and was suspected to have slipped into Germany. During the war many rumours were current about his having approached the Kaiser, the Ameer and other big persons. The last rumour I heard about him was that he was arrested and shot by the British in Mesopotamia.

'The present pamphlet may or may not be from Mahendra Pratap, but it is mischieveous enough in as much as it bears his name.'

No apology is necessary for 'Young India' to condemn violence. Our brothers who love the country no less then we do, but who believe that the only way to freedom is through the sword know that the life-purpose of this journal is to fight brute-force, no less it is from the people than if it is from the Government. I have read the sheet sent by Kaka with the above letter. I have not seen more conclusive arguments for quiet concentration on the constructive programme, than in the implications of this foolish sheet written though it is, for an entirely different purpose.

After calling upon the people to seize and imprison the present officers of Government, the leaflet emphasizes that 'There should be no civil war. All must obey him whoever moves first.' It enjoins on the people to have patience with evil people. It asks men, not to get impatient in any case. The discipline and patience, and the spirit of organized obedience implied in this proposal can never be possible unless the nation is purified and organized. No programme for the achievement of liberty, either by violence or by non-violence is possible without the essential preliminary requisite of strong, disciplined, and thorough organization. And this is just what is known as the constructive programme. 'There should be no civil war.' 'All must obey the leaders.' 'Have patience with evil people', 'Don't fear, 'Don't get impatient' are words which literally express the present Congress programme regarding Hindu-Muslim unity, untouchability and organisation of villages.

Not even Mahatma Gandhi more emphatically preached non-violent unity, tolerance and love in spite of differences, than Raja Mahendra Pratap in the following passages :

> 'Extremists or moderates, national volunteers or the present police merchants or labourers, Zamindars or tenants–all shall be brother workers in a common cause. Do not distrust Eurasians or Christians. Know Sunyetsen, a Christian has made China free'.
>
> 'Protect foreigners in every case. It is extremely dangerous to create an international ill-will against your cause. Your cause is a private quarrel between yourself and English Imperalism. 'It should be made clear that we war only against the English Government. We have no quarrel with the English people.' 'India is a land of sages. India is a home of religions. India will protect English ladies and children.' C. R.

Let me explain Further that 'C. R.' stands for C. Ragajopalachariji. People shorten his name and call him 'our Rajaji'. He is now seventy nine years old but is keeping good health. His one son is a Member of our Parliament.

My Story : On the 28th Sept. I spoke at the opening ceremony of the office of the Republican party. It is the party of the late Dr. Ambedkar. Scheduled Castes are its main supporters. I related the need of cooperation among all the groups for the welfare of the people. I arrived at Delhi on the 11th Oct. I held prayer on the 12th and reached Vrindaban by train on the 14th where I presided at our School meeting and spoke at our public meeting. I told the Vrindaban people the story of our parliament.

On the 15th I returned to Delhi, I left at 5 p.m. for Madaras.

I could not get first class berth. I had to travel in second. But I got full berth to sleep. Another passenger slept on the floor. Next day from Nagpur I got a comfortable berth in a first class compartment. In forty eight hours we reached Madras. Chowdhri Partap Singh Daulta, Communist M. P. from Punjab was travelling with me. I am an independent M. P. A friend and a professor met us and guided us to another railway station. Our train left at 8 p.m.

The scenery in Kerala is superb, green dense forest and high hills. We reached Trivandarum on the 21st October at 7 p.m. We got a room at the Rest House.

On the 22nd we met the Chief Minister and the finance minister. Another M. P. guided us and showed a bit of the Capital.

On the 23rd we saw the P. W. D. Minister Mr. Majeed, a Muslim. A State car was given to us and we visited Cape Kumari, one hundred and eight miles, going and coming.

On the 24th we went to Cochin and Ernarkulam. We were in the car for nearly three hundred miles. I have never seen in the World this astounding continuous habitation for two hundred miles on both the sides of the road. There were all along houses, shops and at short intervals villages and towns, and behind these houses dense forest extended. At some places rice fields were visible. We talked to students, teachers, priests and laymen. We did not see any trace of lenguidness. P. S. P. Leader and former Chief Minister Mr. Thanu Pillai was of course very angry. He denounced all the Communists as 'scoundrels'. I said that Communists too, let all the good people of all the parties unite to fight evil but he vehemently said that 'no Communist can be trusted. Every Communist is a liar'. I met a fine Muslim gentleman who said that there was no question of Hindu-Muslim here. There were four communities and they divided power among them. It was a chance, we saw Mr. Nair, M. P. at the same restaurant where we took meals at Alleppey. At Ernakulum we had a talk with Mr. and Mrs. Udaya Bhanu, Congress leaders. They talked sense. They would not prefer President's rule. Comrade Gopalan, M. P. warmly received us. We were back at Trivandrum late at night.

At 8 a.m. on the 25th Oct. we left the capital of Kerala and reached Madaras on the 26th morning. My friend Ch. Partap Singh Daulta went back to Punjab. I took a room at a hotel. My new friend Mr. Vaidya Nathan showed me round Adyar, the famous Centre of Theosophy. In the evening I lectured on World Federation at the Crescent Club. Mr. Allapichai, advocate, presided at the meeting. One scion of the great Moghuls, Mr. S. M. Fossil was the host at tea. Mrs. Rood too spoke in favour of

World order. The moving spirit of Mr. K Vaidya Nathan organized this function. He is working for World unity, World Federation.

Next day I visited Mr. R. S. Santanam, a leading lawyer and secretary of L. Y. M. A. and the famous leader, the Hon. Pt. C. Rajagopalachari ji, once the Governor General of India. In the evening I addressed the large audience of L. Y. M. A. and the Hon. Pt. C. Raja Gogalachari ji presided over. I spoke for fifty minutes. The president kindly admired my talk and said some highly complimentary words. I am naturally very grateful to his very valuable regard for me. When he brought me to my hotel in his car I told him : Every thing is possible by your blessings.

I left Madras on the 28th and arrived Delhi on the 30th noon, in a bit over forty eight hours. I attended to my heaped up mail. My daughter came from Rajpur. She came to mourn at the death of a relation. We had lunch yesterday, the 31st October at the residence of Sardar Baisakha Singh with family members.

I was busy with Parliament from 17th November to the end of the month. What I could do there is most revealing from a part of the official report I give herewith.

Debates in the Parliament

17 November 1958

Raja Mahendra Pratap : May I make a statement, Sir, and then the Prime Minister may make a statement after hearing me. I have something very important to say. I say that Pakistan is in such a condition that any day Delhi may be bombed. The danger is there. I say that dictators are of this nature. Leader Hitler attacked Czechoslovakia, attacked Poland, attacked France thus there is a danger. I say with my own experience that we can come to terms with Afghanistan and Iran. Afghanistan is Sunni Muslim. Iran is Shia Muslim; and if we come to terms with them, then, in case Pakistan does something wrong to India, Afghanistan and Iran will consider that they are attacked. I am prepared to go to Kabul and Teheran and arrange such a treaty with Afghanistan and Iran.

19 November 1958

Raja Mahendra Pratap (Mathura) : Sir, I have to draw the attention of the Hon'ble Minister to a very serious point. Perhaps you know, Sir, that there was a great strike by electrical workers. I intervened when they were on strike. When they went on hunger-strike, I went to the Hon. Minister, Shri Patil, who was at that time in charge of this ministry. He agreed that he would do everything to help those workers. I went and told that to the workers and they agreed to call off the strike. After that the Committee was announced.

I want to know whither these people who have been recommended as members of this committee know anything about this strike... Do they know anything of this new fact that a strike might be declared and then the whole of Delhi will be in darkness?

27 November 1958

Raja Mahendra Pratap : I told the House in the last session that I shall be going to Kerala and it would be better to discuss this question when I come back. My friend Shri Daulta and I, we two went to Kerala. We were there only for three days. But we toured 400 miles in Kerala, and we did not see anywhere any trouble of any kind. I asked some people here on the road, I asked some people there on the road; I asked one Muslim gentleman, 'What is the condition here? Are you suppressed by the Hindus here?' That Muslim gentleman said: Here are four communities– the Nairs, the Ezhavas, the Christains and Muslims.

Mr. Speaker : The Hon'ble Member will kindly resume his seat. I have no intention to avoid any statement by the Hon'ble Member who has taken all the trouble to go there and study the conditions by himself. But if I allow the Hon'ble Member to go on saying what happened in Kerala, another Hon'ble Member, who possibly has got a different impression on the same subject, may say : what he says is wrong.... So, leaving all other topics, let hon. Members address themselves to this simple point... I submitted to the House that such controversies relating to what is happening in Kerala need not be brought in this discussion.

Raja Mahendra Pratap : That is my preface. I am coming to the point. I must also explain very clearly before this House that I am a religious man. I decided even to convert Comrade Lenin to religion.

An Hon'ble Member : Did you succeed ?

Raja Mahendra Pratap : Anyhow, I was really very greatly distressed this morning when I saw a lot of shouting in this House. I quite agree with the hon. Prime Minister that in this House there should be a kind of decorum, this is very unfortunate that Shri Masani and Dr. Menon brought these resolutions, these suggestions. What they really want is not served by these resolutions. I am not a Communist. Therefore. I can say without any fear that they are helping the communists by the resolution. You know in every country when some people are prosecuted or persecuted, then those people are very much liked by the people.

Now, if such a resolution is brought here, the result is that people will like the Communists more. I say that such a resolution is very unfortunate even for that object for which they meant it. I want to say that now when there is a danger on the border, there should not be brought such questions in the House which divide us more and more, because then a day will come when all the parties are dissolved, I do not wish that then there may be a certain dictator who may dissolve all the parties.

What I saw in Kerala was quite peaceful. I asked all kinds of people. We were both together and I think he will bear with me when I say we were always together. One gentleman Shri Thanu Pillai, who was formerly the Chief Minister there, said that all the Communists are scoundrels and no Communist can be believed.

Mr. Speaker : The Hon'ble Member is referring to some statement of some Hon'ble Member there. It will give opportunity to others to say all sorts of things. I want to avoid that.

Shri P. S. Daulta : I just want to submit that every word of what he said is true.

Raja Mahendra Pratap : I am giving an eye witness account before the House as to what I saw in Kerala.

Mr. Spaker : That is not relevant.

Raja Mahendra Pratap : We asked certain principal of the school. This gentleman was with me.

Mr. Speaker : All that is not relevant.

Raja Mahendra Pratap : That principal said : we are very satisfied.

Mr. Speaker : That information may be useful elsewhere, but not in this context. Let the Hon. Member confine himself to this resolution.

4 December 1958

Raja Mahendra Pratap : I just want to explain that this trend of discussion is wrong. Of what use is production if we cannot produce for our own use? This should not be the discussion. We are competing with China, Japan or with this and that. Why not make our own home very happy? Let every one get what he wants.

I beg to say that this whole thinking is wrong. You want to export. Why do you want to export? You want to export to make money. I think some intellectuals are conspiring to make themselves very happy and are not thinking of the common man.

Mahatma Gandhi said that every village should be made self supporting. If every village is made self-supporting and if our country is made self-supporting where is the necessity of all this talk of export here? So, I say that the whole thinking is wrong. Even the discussion is wrong. Some are speaking of millowners' conspiracy. Another is saying something of the labourers. Why not say that according to our culture the whole society is one? All humanity is one. We want good of all. We want that not one man remains without bread and without work. I think this should be the principle.

8 December 1958

The Hon'ble Pandit Jawaharlal Nehru was speaking.

Raja Mahendra Pratap (Mathura) : May request him to say a World about World Federation, World Government a word?

Shri Jawaharlal Nehru : May I say the Hon'ble Member is often referring to world government, but I cannot imagine any time where people's opinions psychologically are farther away from world government than today? Of course in theory we all agree. In theory, of course, that in the only thing one can work for ultimately, but one must have the environment in people's thinking. The Hon. Member is always talking about it, as if by repeated questions here he can establish world government.

Raja Mahendra Pratap : I have received a letter from London saying that Mr. Macmillan is for world government and only Mr. Nehru is not for world government!

Sir, I feel that the fundamental problem has not been understood by this House. Through centuries humanity has been growing, States have been growing, and we have reached a point when out of these States two great States remain, the USSR and the USA. Now, the struggle is as which one of these will rule the entire World. That is the question. They have allied themselves with or have made other countries as their followers including the Great Britain, which was ruling yesterday half of the USA. The great China, the historical China, which has a long history and was once a celestial empire is today an appendage of the USSR. Therefore, today, Sir, in this World there are only two States which are struggling for World control.

Wherever the people may be, whether in India or in Europe or anywhere else, they are really followers of the USA or the USSR. If my friend speaks of very great kindness of the USSR, it means that they wanted to convert him to their following; if some one made a speech that he was very kindly treated in the USA, that means, that the USA converted the person to the USA's thinking. So, today, the problem is, who is to rule the World the USA or the USSR. If the USSR rules the World, the World will become red, pale or some kind, of reddish colour, and if the USA rules the world then there will be a strong caste system in this World. The Whites will be considered the Brahmins (holy men) the Chinese and the yellow people will become the Kshatrias (warriors) of the World; the Indians and the Arabs of a little brown people will become the Vaishyas businessmen of the World. And the Negroes will become the Sudras, the menial Servants.

So, for me, the future picture is very clear. That is, if the USSR rules the World, we will all be under the Moscow rule, and we shall be trained in communism. We will be divided this way : you are of this caste and you are of that province, etc. We will be used by Moscow. If the USA rules, then of course, as I have explained, there we will be. Now, the question for us is, what do we want. Do you want to be a follower of Moscow or do you want to become Vaishyas in the new World? I do not want that we be Vaishyas and I do not want that we be followers of Moscow.

I have great respect for my Communist friends. But friendship does not mean that my friend becomes a member of my family. I mean to say that we should see the future in its right perspective. I say that the only remedy for us, for the World, for Russia and for the USA is that we should accept one World Government, or World Federation, with local liberty but all the countries are to be united and there must be unity in federation. We accept that principle. We accept the principle that there are certain qualities of humanity: beauty, strength, intellect, morality and enlightenment. We respect the qualities, whether they are in England or in the USA of in the USSR or in Africa, among the Negroes. We are prepared to respect the quality and we can give those people some better opportunities to develop themselves to a greater extent. But the World must be united.

There should be no more war between nations. I would accept a bed World Government, a savage World Government, but I will not accept very great, divine people in different counties fighting in name of Christianity or Islam or in the name of Hinduism or Communism or Congress.

I would not accept them they may be very divine personages, but I would not accept them if they lead us to war. We know what war means today destruction of countries and destruction of the future. With great respect for our Hon. Prime Minister, I must say that unfortunately he has not understood yet the necessity of World Government. As I said, this noon I received a letter from London, in which it was stated that today even Mr. Macmillan and the Foreign Minister of England accept the principle of one World Government, but 'your Mr. Nehru does not see that it is possible in the near future.'

So, with all love and regard for our Hon. Prime Minister, I ask him to change his ideas and to accept the World Federation as a creed of India. Then we will proceed to approach all the nations of the World. We will approach the Eurpean countries, the Latin American States and the free countries of Asia and Africa. We will be in a majortity in the U.N.O. and in the World and the USA and the USSR will not be able to fight any more. So, I request our hon. Prime Minister to consider this programme. He can settle all his questions and problems if he accepts my World Federation.

In my World Federation, in Europe, there will be a large Nordic district in the north of Europe. It settles all the questions from Austria to Norway and from Germany to England. Of course, we give the option to England either to join this or the English group of North America. It is quite free to choose. In my programme, everything is settled. We make a state of South Africa. I am not a white man, but I will teach the Negro friend like this: 'These

Brahmins in India did a great service to our country and they remained a little higher up. So, my friend, black man, accept the qualifies of the white man. Let him do the service of helping the country. These whites have invented these engines, radios, etc. Use them; where is the harm? Why consider them as aggressors? Love them.'

If our Prime Minister accepts my programme, I settle every question through the World Federation. I can go to Ceylon and say to the Ceylonese, 'Dear Ceylonese, you become part of Aryan from Himalayas to Ceylon and from Iran to Assam. Friends, where is the harm, whether you come to us or we come to you? We came some ten thousand years before. Our Rama came to you and our Buddhists came to you.'

So, I have a method. In the end about Pakistan, there will be no Pakistan if Aryan is established. My friend got very eloquent about some little pieces. What is that piece? We shall take the whole of Pakistan tomorrow. I can assure you, if I am given a free hand, I can finalise Aryan and I will ask the Prime Minister to allow me to do it.

We have been very often talking that Pakistan is attacking here or attacking there and the Hon. Prime Minister says : 'I have no other method but to make protests.' I give a good method. You say, 'I accept Raja Mahendra Pratap's Aryan programme and I shall help him.' Then what will happen? They have made a Baghdad Pact. I will make a Kabul Pact. I will make a pact with Iran and Afganistan. Punjab shall make a new pact with Kabul and that will give us strength. Iran, I may tell you, will be very pleased. Our capital will go there and our capitalists will have very much to do to develop Iran. And Iranese will be quite protected from the USSR. Because we will be one, and we are friends of the USSR. I accept the Hon'ble Speaker's advice that the simile was not good. I would say my girl or my sister. I say, you live well in your family and I live well in my family, and we all join hands together for common welfare of humanity. God is good and if God has created humanity that God wants the good of all. He created all the religions in different parts at different times. Men foolishly did not understand this fact. God meant only good of all. All religions are good for all of us. We will go to a Muslim and say, 'Oh yes, you are a Muslim. You have a God-given divine religion. But Sir, some wrong ideas, through foolishness of man, have also come to your mind. You remove them.' I will say the same thing to the Hindu.

19 December 1958

A debate was going on cinema. I said that our cinema does not show reality. The actors of cinema live very bad lives and from them only evil idea can come out.

Mr. Speaker : Order order. The Hon'ble Member ought not to make such sweeping remark about all persons who are engaged in the cinema enterprise or the cinema industry. Of course, there are bad people in every matter. Possibly, there may be a greater tendency in this industry more than in anything else. But, on that ground, let not everyone be tarnished with the same brush.

Raja Mahendra Pratap : Good, not all of them. I was in Hollywood also. I saw how people are living there. They live in great luxury. Ordinary people, our own people from India were living as some princes, I was their guest. They were very kind to me. But, I knew, behind them there was a lot of sexual love affairs.

What I say is this. We have to take into consideration what kind of people are making the films and what is the object in making these films. They make films only to make money and, therefore, they appeal to very low emotions of the people, because only by that method they can make more money. So, we have to consider what kind of people are making the films and what is the object in making them.

Then, we have also to consider, when people are appointed as Censors, what kind of life they live. Because if these people who are appointed as censors are people who are drinking or who are only going to the cinemas, they are not the fit people to be censors. So, I say, in all cases we have to consider what kind of life our people are living. I have always been insisting on it of course, I was not allowed to speak about the rent question.

But there also I wanted to say that the object should be to make a healthy and happy society.

Now, in this film business, we can give the right kind of education. But, it is not given. For instance, there are many subjects which the common people do not know. For instance, in these films pictures of different countries can be shown. For instance, there are expeditions sent to the South Pole. They can show some things which cannot see here. Through films we can see those things. What I say is this. In this film business new thought should be brought in; and that new thought should be that we teach morality to the people.

I may also say that sometimes falsehood is brought into these films. I went to Calcutta. A friend insisted that I should see a certain film. I said, I never see films. He said. 'Your are shown in that film'. 'When' I asked him, 'Yes'. I asked, 'What is that film?' and he said 'Bagha Joytin.' I was shown there with a big turban; I was shown in a German office.

Of course I could not recognise myself in that film. Then I was shown with a big sword in my hand and a lot of soldiers behind me, fighting the British troops. The object of the film may be very good. Perhaps these people are very kind to me, but historically the film in not correct. So I have to say that very truthfull films should be produced. If they had only asked me to appear in that film I would have agreed, but what was the use of making a substitute like this when I was here?

Mr. Speaker : The Hon'ble Member is not willing to see a film, but is prepared to act in it!

Raja Mahendra Pratap : I say that the theme of the films must be correct. I only formed an army composed of Afridis and these Afridi soldiers fought at my bidding, but I was not there.

Every story in the film must be very correct and if, for instance, it is only an imagination then that imagination should not show some great personalities like Rama, Krishna, Radha and such great historical and religious personages in a false form. You perhaps know that sometimes pictures of Budhha and Krishna are made. They also import into it love affairs which really should not be there, because we respect Shri Krishna and it is a very wrong thing to misrepresent him. I am a Brijbasi; I feel shocked when they show that Shri Krishna and Radha had certain love affairs and sexual connection. It is quite wrong. Our Lord Shri Krishna lived only for twelve years in Braj. A twelve year child cannot have sexual instinct. What is the idea of showing these pictures? It is a shame for our country. So I say that these people who are making films should not depict our great religious lords in such a way that is creates a very bad impression upon the people.

I am a Brajbasi; I come from Vrindaban. People wrongly believe that Shri Krishna indulged in sexual love and they make all kinds of sexual love in our town. Poor Bengali women come to Vrindaban. Our people say that Shri Krishna was in love with Radha, so we may also love in the same way. This is very wrong. We should show proper respect to our great personalities of the past and we should not show them in a way that they are rather degraded in our imagination.

Our films can do a lot of good if they are properly directed. How to direct them in the correct way is a very important question. I have always been impressing on our Government that we have no lack of good persons in our society. We have very honest, sincere and nice sadhus. Some of them are in Rishikesh, in Mathura, in Hardwar or elsewhere. They are very good people; they are honest people and lead very pious lives. They can be asked to come here to censor these pictures and they should readily do so, not these government officials who are sometimes going to cinemas, sometimes going to tea parties and sometimes indulging in heavy dinners. These are not the right people for censoring our films.

I myself see that there is corruption every where. There is corruption in courts; there is corruption even in elections and there will be corruption in films also, if you move this manner. I would request the Government to invite those Sadhus; we can give them good quarters and ask them to show us how to make our society moral. We can even ask them to enter the film business along our line of thinking. When I say film business, I do not mean it in the ordinary sense, not with a view of making money, but with a view of making society more moral. I am never tired of repeating that in every aspect of our life we should insist on morality. There is no question of party in this matter Congress, Communist or any other. We want a moral society, to achieve which we should come together.

We should see to it that no member of Parliament indulges in anything which is immoral, because it is we who make the laws for the whole country, for the whole society. If we do something immoral, if we do something against the laws, how can we make laws for the country? How will they be obeyed? Why will they we obeyed, if people see that those who make laws are not observing them. If we ourselves do something against the laws, against eternal moral laws, how will people in the country obey the laws?

I say let us combine all our forces. Our country is in danger. There is danger of war with Pakistan. There are so many dangers. I spoke in the Defence Committee and I asked Pandit Nehru to allow me to undo Pakistan; I can undo Pakistan.

Mr. Speaker : Order, order. That has nothing to do with cinemas.

Raja Mahendra Pratap : I have finished. I will only say this. Let us combine all our forces to safeguard what we have got and proceed further along the line of progress, progress in the line of morality, this is not progress in making big houses and big hotels and making all kinds of comforts for the few. That should not be the progress we make; we must insist that not one individual should remain without work and without bread.

My Story : This is the story of December 1958. On the 1st of December was my birth day. Our school and college celebrated it with pomp and fanfare at Premnagar and Vrindaban. I went there from Delhi. I addressed the students at the Technical Institute and attended their light refreshment party. Sardar Bajewala of Patiala took me in his car to Vrindaban. I attended the school function and spoke for a few minutes. At Prem Nagar was dinner, I stayed with my grand niece.

From 2nd December to the 20th I daily attended our Parliament on all week days. What I did there is stated at length. I tried to serve all who came to me seeking my aid. I brought all the deserving cases to the notice of proper authorities. They take lot of my time. I attended to my correspondence. And I edited my five circulars as usual.

On Sunday the 7th Dec. we held the meeting of the Executive Committee of All India Jat Mahasabha. I am its president. I have nominated a brother of H. H. Maharaja of Patiala and Sardar Habibullah Khan, Barrister, living at Lahore, Pakistan, as two vice presidents besides several others. Thakur Jhamman Singh, Advocate of Aligarh our General Secretary, Kunwar Kalyan Singh, veteran Jat leader and members from Jodhpur and Jabalpur besides others attended. As this meeting ended we held our weekly Prayer. I delivered the main sermon. Some friends also spoke. In the evening I went to the late Dr. Ambedkar's anniversary. Here gathering was very large. I spoke for just ten minutes. People highly appreciated my talk.

On the 9th I presided and addressed a meeting of the Union of workers of the military workshop No. 505 at Delhi Cantoment. In the night I left for Lucknow. In my coupe, as my companion, I had one great leader of the Congress, Mr. Algurai Shastri.

At Lucknow I was the guest of the University Students Union. They gave good break fast and good lunch, They led me to the Hindu College where I addressed the students. Principal Mukerji kindly endorsed my talk. I spoke long at the University Union Meeting. Pandit Sitaram Shukla M.L.A. gave dinner and invited famous singers to entertain us. Raja Jagmanpur M.L.A. Raja Singramau and a couple of more M.L.As. were present. Next morning I was back at Delhi.

On the 12th I attended two marriage functions. Marshal of our parliament had invited to one, to the other our advocate at Dehradun had called me. I could not refuse them.

In Our Parliament

Now I give you official report of my speeches in the Indian Parliament.

Raja Mahendra Pratap (Mathura) : I some times feel very disgusted that my suggestions and my submissions are not followed and attended to. I said that these two things do not go hand in hand-on one side we speak of socialist pattern and, on the other side we see the president coming right royally. I wish that there will not be contradictions in the statements of our great leaders. I will speak now of my principle, my principle is : all to work for all to make all happy. I do not regard these different parties as different. I only believe that they are all my countrymen and we are all trying to make our country prosperous and happy. I have said in my amendment :

> 'but regret that the Government has failed to frame the Budget so as to avoid the necessity of raising loans'.

When our Government speaks of Mahatma Gandhi they praise him very much. They make memorials for Mahatma Gandhi. But they do not act according to the ideas of Mahatma Gandhi. Mahatma Gandhi, when he introduced Charkha, meant people will make everything they need in their own country by their own hands. That is what he meant. But it is not followed. Our Government is taking loan after loan and burdening our generations to come with a heavy burden. So, I have said : let us follow a system by which we make all that we can with our own resources, even if we cannot make very rapid progress.

Then I have said : 'but regret that the President's Address does not recognize the labours right to an equitable share in the profit.'

I am very glad indeed that the President's Address has accepted my long heralded plan that labour should be associated with the management. Labour also be given I say, full half share of all the profit.

Then I have said ; 'but regret that the Address does not suggest the formation of a World Federation to reduce the tension in the international sphere.' I honestly believe that the only way to stop wars between nations is a World Government, World Federation. Now very important people, Ministers, Prime Ministers, Prime Ministers sometimes, of defferent countries speak of the necessity of a World Government. But, unfortunately, our Hon. Pandit Jawaharlal Nehru, though he admits that a World Federation should come, but does not work for World Federation. I have said, and I repeat, that we should take world federation as our creed, as the Slaves of Russia adopted communism and the Anglo-Saxons adopted democracy. This fact has been repeated by a very important newspaper, 'Asahi' of Japan. Asahi has asked Mr. Kishi, the Prime Minister of Japan, to adopt World Federation as the creed of Japan and to invite all the nations of the world to co-operate on the plan for a World Federation.

I cannot help repeating this too often, I want to repeat it always whenever I get an opportunity that : 'speak not please of this danger and that danger; speak not please that there is danger in the Middle East and we have sent the people to Indo-China, we have done this and we have done that.' I say that these partial patching methods do not succeed.

The only way is World Federation. Of course, I have a plan of World Federation with the capital at Honolulu and every community to be a self governing province.

Shri S. M. Banerjee : Why Honolulu ?

Raja Mahendra Pratap : If such a plan is adopted and if Asia is one of the provinces of the world federated government then in that there will be a district from Iran to Assam and there will be no Pakistan. There will be the principle of local liberty but all unity in federation. In such a case there will be no danger of war between Pakistan and India.

Shri V. P. Nayar (Quilon) : You can step in the Prime Minister's place in the world government.

Raja Mahendra Pratap : Then I say that adequate steps be taken to check the waste of time and energy and on this I can say a lot. I say that the principle should be that all should be employed. There should be work for all and bread for all. Once when I was speaking in the United States of America I said that for 2,000 years we have prayed : Give us day by day our daily bread. Now let us take spades in our hands and work and so be sure that every one gets his daily bread.

Unfortunately in our country when my Hon'ble friends speak of welfare of all and of very good plans and programmes, what they are doing? They have developed a band of intellectual workers. They tax the people and divide the money among themselves. That is what they are doing. They are not thinking of the common man and the man in the street. How many people are there who are unemployed today, without their daily bread and without their right spiritual, moral and political? So, I say that we should remodel our whole plan and programme and re-organise and overhaul the Government. This system of Government made by the British for the British was only to suck the blood of India and take money to England to build great palaces. This system of Government is wrong. This system of Government bribes our intellectuals or well educated youngmen to work for this system and not care for the people below.

Now I must say a few words about some of the speeches which I have heard here. One Hon. Friend spoke a great deal against co-operative system and its methods. I beg of my hon. friends to realies as to what all this is about. You have not understood how the mind works. Why it works and for what purpose it works. I will explain it to you.

When some people get hold of the Government, whatever they be, it may be a caste; it may be a tribe or he may be a dictator, when once they are in command of the Government and hold the reins of the State, then they always try to make their own chairs secure. That is what is always done. Now, what did these Hon'ble friends do? There were Maharajas in the country. They realized that there were some people called subjects. So they thought of arousing the subjects against the Maharajas. They aroused them and the Maharajas had to run away. Their States were taken over. They saw that these zamindars also have great power because they have wealth. Now what to do? They thought of arousing the peasants and they aroused the peasants. They did away with the zamindars. Next what do they find? They find that a well-to-do peasant is also a danger to their Government; so, let him be put down. This is what the co-operative system is. Now they are trying to arouse the landless people against the peasants who are well-off. These are all tricks which should be known. What is behind them? It is always the blood current. There are always some caste, there are always some tribes, there are always some national blood currents which govern the country or the larger areas. Our Communist friends do not know this. I want to tell them that it was the Jews' great brains, that of Karl Marx and Engels and others, which found out as to what was the matter in Russia and in Germany and who were ruling. They found out that the Czar was ruling, the priests were ruling and the businessmen were ruling. This is natural. Brahmins did the same. That I have told you before. The Brahmins, the Rajputs and the Banias made an alliance and ruled. This is natural. So, when the Jews found that out they said, 'Down with the king, down with the priests and down with the businessmen.' They could develop a revolution and turned out the king, they turned out the priests and they turned out the businessmen. Then what happened? What happened was that all the great posts and important positions were monopolized by the Jews. I was in Soviet Russia in those days.

An Hon'ble Member said to a young Communist, who here spoke some thing, 'You were not born then.'

Raja Mahendra Pratap : Mr. Trotsky, Mr. Lunacharsky, Mr. Radek, Mr Kamenev and all these were Jews. They held the most important places. In Soviet Russia, of course there was great hatred against the Jews. I was there in those days and I saw it myself and heard it myself. The Russians called these Jews as Judas. They said, 'These Judas have taken our country. These Judas have done this and that'. There was a great commotion in the people. They thought as to what to do. Then the Russian mind found out a good leader in Mr. Stalin. He was not a Russian and so the non-Russians could be satisfied. Mr. Stalin was only a leader of a small community, a blood current, the Georgians, who are called Gurji in Turkish language. He was made the leader.

Mr. Deputy-Speaker : The Hon Member's time is up.

Raja Mahendra Pratap : I am saying something historical. I am sorry that you are not paying attention to that. I will tell you very briefly in a few minutes.

They did a great deal of nationalization. What is nationalization? I said before also and I say again that nationalization is nothing but a system of certain intellectuals to control wealth. This is what is nationalization. I say: Give people liberty. You may make money as much as you like and by any means we do not mind that but we shall control as to how you spend the money. If a Czar indulged in naked ballet it is a kind of dance in Russia then what is the difference if Mr. Stalin also indulged in naked dance? So, I say that there should be a moral system for the country. We want you to spend your money in schools, in colleges, in service to the people and in uplifting the common man. But we will not allow these dancing parties. It is a shame for the capital of India to see in the newspapers advertisements of dances in the Imperial Hotel.

Pictures of seven or eight women are given and advertisement reads that there will be a performance by those women at midnight in the Imperial Hotel. Is it not a shame? I believe our Government officials should do penance for that. They should go on hungerstrike.

Mr. Deputy-Speaker : Therefore, I am going to put a stop to that. (Rings the Bell).

Raja Mahendra Pratap : Sir, our Hon'ble President has not kindly taken notice of my five points. I want that India should be out of the Commonwealth. There should be Aryan from Iran to Assam and Nepal to Ceylon. The workers should be given half share in the management and in profit. There should be self-Government, home rule in every village and town. Still these Superintendents, collectors and thanedars are ruling the country. I want that every caste, every profession should be organized in every village and in every town, and the chaudharies or the leaders of these castes and professions should rule the town and village. The police should have with it factories, farms and fields. There should be no fees for students. The students should work and produce their necessities of life.

Speech on Railway-budget

Raja Mahendra Pratap (Mathura) : To begin with, I congratulate the Hon'ble Member in the Chair for the quality that he has shown today as a good administrator. He called out not names but constituencies in several cases, and he announced the names so that we could go out and come back. Very kind of you, Sir.

Then I congratulate the Minister too, because I believe that the railway department is the best managed department of all the departments of the Government. And I believe that in the railway department, the reservation department is still better managed.

I happen to be the patron of the clerks of the reservation department. They had asked me to bring some of their demands before the Minister. I wrote about them to General Shahnawaz Khan, and he promptly replied. This is also very good of the railway department, they immediately pay attention, but I must say that our Minister and our Deputy Ministers are not properly supported by their staff, and it would be better if some Jatav is put in a high position in the railway department and some Pathan is also included. I believe also that the Anglo-Indians should be given special consideration in the management of the railways. Of course, I believe, all to work for all to make all happy. Brahmans can go to the law department and Baniyas can go to the finance department, but let this department be managed by Harijans, because they also should have some place.

I am not claiming any place for the martial races in the railways, for the martial races is only our army, there, they will have monopoly.

Now, I beg to say that we want a railway line from Vrindaban to Aligarh. Our Braj wants it definitely and seriously. If there will be a bridge at Vrindaban, most of the flood difficulties will disappear there.

We also want a small railway line from Dehra Dun to Rajpur below Mussoorie. So that passengers going up to Mussoorie will have much more convenient journey. If the budget does not allow it, let us give to the private sector the building of these two railway lines. I believe there is no harm in giving the private companies a chance to build some railway lines. I think there is a certain prejudice which has come into the minds of our high leaders that only with the public sector, they can better manage. But what is the public sector, only some people monopolies the financial side of these companies and these departments. This should not be so. After all, man is man whether he is working as a government servant or he is working in a company. So I suggest that the private sector can be given some chance.

I may also say that some people are punished in the railway department, because they have some quarrel with the higher officer. I think it would be better if this matter is looked into in a little more kindly way.

One Mr. Rawat, ticket collector was degraded and transferred from Mathura, to Jhansi, and one coolie Munna is suffering for about a year and in not being given a chance to work as only a simple coolie at our Mathura Junction.

I may also remind the railway department that during the last three years, they have often promised me that they would provide seating arrangements for the first class travelling during nights. It is very difficult sometimes to get into the compartments, because the compartments are locked up, and a first class passenger who is going to a nearby station, two or three stations away, does not find a place to sit. They had promised me, but somehow, that has not yet been fulfilled.

I must say that there is a great improvement in the restaurants. Formerly, I used to see that these bearers used to charge four annas or eight annas more. I must congratulate the railway department for this great improvement.

I must also mention here that some of our railway clerks, and also reservation clerks, have taken an oath that they would not take any bribe in future. It is a very good sign, if it is backed up.

There is a complaint that some ticket collectors are asked to realize so much fine. I think this is absurd.

An Hon'ble Members : Rs. 500.

Raja Mahendra Pratap : It is absurd that a ticket collector must realize so much fine. I think we should be glad that he realizes, less because nowadays there are less number of ticketless passengers.

Sometimes, some of our departments say, well, this does not concern us, this belongs to the other department, or this belongs to that office and so on. I think this is not very good. All offices and all departments should closely co-operate for the betterment of all.

Then there was the question of the beggars on the railways. This is a problem neither of the railways nor of any other department. It is the country's problem. I think that every beggar should have shelter and should have daily bread; and you can use him for some work too; and he can produce something. We must calculate how much time and energy are lost in different pursuits, and then put everyone to work.

Now, I must say a word about morality also. After all, if a man who is serving somewhere, who is working for the country, and who is living in the country is immoral, then he can do nothing good; he will spoil everything. So, I propose that my Religion of Love should be introduced all through. We should pray every morning and every evening. We must see how we spend time, whether we waste time or spend it usefully. If we have misused time, then, we must, of course, ask God : Pardon me, Sir, and then use the time rightly. I shall not go further into that.

I shall not speak long. I have got only two or three points more. And I shall just point out some defects.

An Hon'ble Member : What about world federation?

Raja Mahendra Pratap : It is a political question. Here It was the question of morality which I was discussing.

I am told that some instructors are paid only according to the scale Rs. 60-150, while other instructors are receiving Rs. 300 to Rs. 400. I think justice should be done to all. I do not say that the higher-ups should be pulled down, but I say that the lower-downs should be brought up.

In the end, I am very sorry to say that some high officers are still travelling like the Nawabs of the old days in big bogies with a big following.

An Hon'ble Member : Like Moghuls.

Raja Mahendra Pratap : What is this? On the one side, we speak of the socialist pattern of society, and on the other, we make the officials live like Nawabs. I think a better example should be set.

My Story : I am writing these lines sitting in my flat No. 105, South Avenue, New Delhi.

From 1st April to the 9th May 1959 our Parliament was in Session. Many times, during this period, I spoke on different questions.

On the 1st April and the 8th May I had to speak on Tibet. First April proved a really Fool's Day in our Parliament. There was quite an uproar, short of giving blows, in such a storm my suggestions created complete calm and the House burst into laughter. I said why quarrel here, communist members can go to Peking and Jan-Sanghies can proceed to Kalimpong and work for peace in Tibet.

During these two months I went to two distant places, On the 25th and 26th I presided over the Urdu conference at Vijaiwada. It took thirty six hours to reach the place by an express train. On the 3rd May I presided at our Reunion Meeting held at Calcutta.

Trip to Namli, Ratlam was very tiring. It took me nearly thirty hours in trains, going and coming. I arrived back on the 25th May. There I inaugurated a new party. I do not like that parties are multiplied. But what can we do. We do not want the over growth of population but the people do not stop giving birth to children. I spoke long and explained my plan of World Order. I hurried to Ratlam and got into express train. Friends saw me off.

Gwalior is not far. Mail train takes only about five hours. A jeep took me and friends another twenty four miles. But the last four miles were terrible, there was hardly any road and it became dark. Our meeting started at ten in the night. I finished my lecture just before midnight. Then supper was served and we left the village at 2 a.m. I got into train at 4 a.m. on this 18th of May.

It was a great pleasure to meet H. H. Nawab Hamidullah Khan Sahib at Bhopal. But it was equally painful to see some parts of three Mosques broken and hear the stories of some Muslims, how they were robbed and beaten. I visited Bhopal on the 28th of April. My adjournment motion on the subject was rejected by the Hon. Speaker of our Parliament.

I Proposed in Parliament

1. Need to give family quarters to all soldiers
2. Need to give free education to children of all the soldiers.
3. Need to reduce the gulf between officers and soldiers.
4. Need to abolish the system of non-commissioned officers.
5. Need to establish farms and factories in all the cantonments.
6. Need to give land to soldiers on retirement.

I Got Sick : I am sick. I am still in a hospital. Today is 30th June 1959. The pain was so sudden in stomach that operation had to be advised by Dr. Gopal Singh and Dr. Goel. It was on Saturday night, 20th June, that my daughter and Maharaj Kumar Limbdi together with Dr. Gopal Singh brought me to this Community Hospital and left me in charge of the local doctors and nurses.

In great agony night was passed but the attending nurses did their best.

In the morning friends gathered. Consultations were held. More relations came. By the time that I was taken to the operation table Maharani Jind, Jind Princess, Chowdhri Hyder Hussain, well known Maharaja of Limbdi, my daughter, Mr. Pandhi, the House agent and Dr. Gopal Singh were all here. A Sardar of Jind gave me two pounds of his blood. Dr. Bushby prayed. And I was made unconscious by an injection.

I did not die. I am alive to tell my tale. The credit goes to Dr. H. Aldreich and Dr. R. Bushby. The first is from U SA, the second is also foreigner. This is a Mission Hospital, much better fitted than the government hospital, Mussoorie. I am told, my intestines got twisted.

I have passed ten nights in the hospital. There were moments very painful and I sang: Death is dear, death is sweet but I hate this dreadful pain. Maharaj Kumar of Limbdi has been very over kind, my daughter daily visited me. Friends kindly came and sent wires and letters. I felt, I was not alone. Doctors come. Nurses attend day and night. And I get very good food. I cannot, however, yet eat all that I get. With a word of sincere gratitude I end this story here.

Holy Interview : I was received by H. H. Dalai Lama on Sunday the 14th June at noon, at the Birla House, Mussorie. I saw him standing in the middle of the room. I greeted him. He greeted me. And we both sat together on a sofa. The interpreter stood behind. My daughter, grand daughter and a princess Limbdi who accompanied me sat in chairs in front.

I showed H. H. the letter I received from the late Dalai Lama in 1926. H. H. read the whole letter and was greatly pleased.

He asked me to advise him with vast experience in making India free. I told him, he could ever count on my service in need. And I said, I could return to India after thirty one years of exile, he will surely return to Tibet one day. I advised him to tour the world.

I revealed to H. H. that in 1925 I was helped by China to go to Tibet. I had goodwill of the USSR, too. I wanted to open another route to India via Tibet and Nepal. In my plan it was necessary that China and Tibet were best Friends.

I told H. H. how the then Prime Minister of Tibet came to see me and met me when I was returning to China. H. H. repeated the name of the Prime Minister. I took leave. He stood up and said, 'I only want freedom of my country.'

Here I am meeting our Hon'ble Prime Minister Pandit Jawahar Lal Nehru. We meet. We exchange letters too. I give here my speech in our Parliament. I delivered it on the 26th November 1959. In this connection I have to say with regret that while other members were given half an hour or fifteen minutes I was allowed to speak for only five minutes. In this speech I read my letters to the Prime Minister and I quoted in full his reply.

My Speech at Parliament

Raja Mahendra Pratap (Mathura) : I have some important points to say.

I beg to say here that we have been talking of peace, but we have been fighting here in the house. If we are fighting here, how can we make peace in the world. I beg to say that we show to the world some very good example of our behaviour.

Today we are discussing about a letter which the Hon'ble Prime Minister sent in reply to the letter which Mr. Chou-En-Lai sent. I beg to bring to the notice of the House what I wrote to the Hon'ble Prime Minister, Pandit Nehru, and what he replied in this connection.

I wrote to him sending an express letter on the 6th November, as follows :

Hon. Friend Pandit Jawaharlal Nehruji,

I did not want to trouble you, you do not seem to value my opinions. But I felt obliged this morning reading your war-like statement at the press conference yesterday.

Your attitude towards China needs complete overhauling. I beg you in your interest and in the interest of our country.

Chinese people are very stubborn. Your war-like statements will make them furious. They will create more incidents. We will find it difficult to resist their further aggression. A situation may develop when you may be forced to seek Anglo-American aid. Things will slip out of your hands.

I am prepared to go to China to propose a treaty among China, India and Japan to sent out our overflowing population to vacant southern islands and thinly populated Africa. Believe me, it will be a master stroke. Tibetan problem will automatically disappear. If you like to discuss the matter I am prepared to run to you at your leisure.

Yours sincerely
M. Pratap

This was my letter. I am very thankful that the Hon. Prime Minister immediately replied and sent it by special courier with quite a big seal. This is how the letter reads :

New Dear Raja Sahib,

I have your letter of the 6th November. I am sorry I am not in agreement with you about various policies. I do not think it will serve any useful purpose for you to go to China at this stage.

Yours sincerely
Sd/-
Jawaharlal Nehru

Since we are having a discussion on the correspondence between the two Prime Ministers, I thought it right to bring this also to your notice.

I beg to say that neither Panchsheel nor the declarations for peace will establish peace in this world. The only way is world army and world court of Justice. If we insist on this programme you will find very soon that the world follows you. Some people think that I am a rival to Shri Jawaharlal Nehru. I am nothing of the kind. The other day, that is the day before yesterday, in Moradabad, there was a huge meeting of world federation.

Mr. Speaker : All that is not relevant. Now, Shri Brajeswar Prasad.

Raja Mahendra Pratap : The day before yesterday, there was a huge meeting of world federation at Moradabad; and I addressed about three thousand people. I said that even if the military made me the dictator of India, I would still insist that our Shri Jawaharlal Nehru should remain our Prime Minister.

I wrote that I wanted two hundred and sixty votes of our Lok Sabha to form a new government. I also stated in that connection that if I formed the government I would not allow elections for the next fifteen years and these parliament members would continue for that period. I also added that these members would also get pension for life. Some members considered it a big joke and laughed at it. Some members paid no attention to what I wrote. A few thought, it was impossible. A couple of members considered it was worth trying and asked me to form a shadow cabinet. I told my friends that to begin with they should kindly start discussing the matter at their private parties.

My tour : Since 3rd of January I am on tour. Today is the 30th January 1960, I am sitting at our estate office at Aligarh, the town of Muslim University.

I toured through my constituency of Braj, Mathura District. I lectured in a day at three or five villages to twenty miles apart. I went to Lucknow, Rae Bareli, Lakhimpur and Oel. Raja Yuvaraj Dutt Singh asked me to distribute prizes at his college. I also spoke at a public meeting there. At Agra I also had five engagements in a day. Major Dr. Chauhan arranged this tour of Agra. I also spoke to the workers of the Electric Power House. I did this tour of Mathura and Agra on Jeep Car.

On the 27th January I went by Jeep to Dehradun one hundred sixty miles and returned on the 28th covering the same distance. Yesterday I arrived at Aligarh. I am here busy with our estate affairs. Though not a yard of land is in my name yet have to manage this property in the name of my minor grandson. Our benevolent national government did not reinstate my name in the property confiscated by the British Government on account of my taking help from Kaiser's Germany to liberate India from the British Empire. The nationalists kindly say that it was a shame for the government not to pass an official Bill to reinstate me but our government is shame proof. I do not mind. God knows best.

Official Report of Parliament

I am a quoting here what I spoke in the Parliament last week.

Raja Mahendra Pratap (Mathura) : I am very thankful to the Deputy-Speaker for having kindly allowed me so early to speak on this important subject. I first want to read out the substance of my amendments.

First of all, there is no reference in the President's Address against the pomp and show indulged in by our Government. I withdraw the harsh words which I used in the very beginning of the first session that a four-anna cap is sitting under the canopy of a Rs. 2000 umbrella. I withdraw that. But I beg to say..

Mr. Deputy-Speaker : By saying it again the Hon'ble Member withdraws it?

Raja Mahendra Pratap : But I beg to say that it is very unfortunate that our Government is indulging in pomp and show and in dancing and in music and all that kind of wasteful acts.

Mr. Deputy-Speaker : Does the Hon. Member attend all those functions and see them with his own eyes?

Shri Radha Raman : He enjoys them.

Raja Mahendra Pratap : When people are hungry and when the workers of the Electricity Department and the work houses who have there small little huts have not got any light in their houses, we see that millions of lights are used in Delhi all over the place. That is very unfortunate, and that fact is not mentioned in the Address by the Honourable President.

Shri Raj Bahadur (The Minister of State in the Ministry of Transport and Communication) : My Hon'ble Friend wants darkness all around?

Raja Mahendra Pratap : My second amendment seeks to point out that there is no mention in the Address about complete employment of all the people in the nation. We hear a great deal about the Government servants. We hear a great deal that people should have more salaries, but we do not see that in our country there are millions of people who have no livelihood and who have no employment. I think Government should adopt this principle namely 'that in our country not a single person will remain without work and without bread'. That can be realized if we accept the principle that every village should be a joint family and every town should be a joint family, and that there should be respect for elders, love for children giving them good education and healthy and strong working for the community.

I now come to my third amendment. I regret to find that the Honorable President spoke in a way about China which would create more international friction. The only remedy is World Federation. I beg to say that our honorable benevolent national Government exaggerated a great deal this China affair, and I must congratulate them that they got three great benefits out of this exaggeration.

One is that the people began to say : 'let us make our Government's position strong.' Secondly, they also defeated the Communists in the country. Thirdly, they succeed in winning over the sympathy of the USA, so much so that President Eisenhower spent only two days in Pakistan but stayed in our countary for four days and a half.

Shri Jhunjhunwala (Bhagalpur) : Ours is a big country.

Raja Mahendra Pratap : That is a very great success for our Government.

Raja Mahendra Pratap : My fourth amendment is that the elections in Kerala created trouble in our society. I cannot congratulate our Congress on winning these elections. They have created more trouble. People are divided. Factions are created. The principle should be : all should work for all to make all happy. Friction in the nation should be eliminated. We should adopt this principle: Any thought which divides us is bad and every thought which unites us is good.

They speak a great deal of corruption. But I beg to say that it is not the fault of the Government that there is corruption. The fault lies with the people. If there is any fault with the Government in this matter, it is that they are not trying to teach morality to our people. There should be one ministry for teaching morality. If it is not possible to create a Moral Ministry at least the Home Ministry should have a department to teach people Morality.

Shri M. P. Mishra : There should be a Minister in charge of Morality.

Raja Mahendra Pratap : Some friends speak of raising the price of sugarcane and the like. I beg to say that we should insist that labour will have half the benefits of the factories. That is, they should be made half partners in all the factories including sugar mills.

Some friends sometimes speak of Universities and say that they are not running well and so on. I beg to say that there should be reorganization of the Universities in such a way that the representatives of the students and the representatives of the guardians of the students should co-operate with the managements of all the Universities.

They also speak about Goa. I have often said and I repeat that it is a very small, little, matter. We can very easily settle it with a treaty with Portugal. We can open up vast lands of Portugal in Africa and we can have a treaty to the effect that our people can go there and colonise. That will help Portugal and it will help us also.

In this connection, I can also suggest that we can have a treaty for inter-marriage between Indians and Portuguese on a very large scale. That will also help us; it will help the Portuguese too.

Mr. Deputy-Speaker : Would the hon'ble Member do some pioneering work in this respect?

Raja Mahendra Pratap : As regards Pakistan, I am very glad that Marshal Ayub Khan has come to believe in my opinion. He suggests : let us have common defence. I have been speaking about it for the last three years. I believe at this moment our Prime Minister is failing in his duty in this connection if he would extend his hand and grasp the hand extended by Marshal Ayub Khan, I think so far as Pakistan is concerned, our problems will end.

Of course, I say, we shall have Aryan – from Iran to Assam, from Himalayas to Ceylon – and then there will be no question of Pakistan at all. We shall have local liberty, but all unity in federation. Aryan will be a district of the province of World Federated State.

The Minister of Parliamentary affairs (Sh. Satya Narayan Sinha) : Now there is Mars and Moon also.

Raja Mahendra Pratap : Our friends also speak of over-population. Here again, I beg to say that the best solution will be for our people to go to Brazil and all the vacant lands of the south sea and Africa. That can be arranged. I know from my own experience, Japan was sending missions to Brazil and the Brazilian Government agreed to the principle. In fact, thousands and hundreds of thousands of Japanese went and colonized there. I believe that this can very easily be settled, if I am given a free hand in the matter (Interruptions).

I also beg to say that Government is very much interfering with the people. People do not feel that they have got swaraj. Police have got swaraj, high officials have got swaraj; the great leaders of the Congress have got swaraj; But the people have not got swaraj yet.

I believe that every village should be turned into a self-governing unit. Every town should be turned into a self-governing unit. Our friends here may like it or not but I beg to suggest that as castes are there, we should organize all the castes from the Brahman to the Bhangi and from Syed to Mehtar and their leaders should from the village government and the town government. If you do not like caste, I do not mind, but what to do? Take the name of Pandit Jwaharlal Nehru. If he is a Pandit we know he is a Brahmin, if he is Jawaharlal, we know he is a Hindu, and if he is a Nehru we know he is a Kashmiri. So, in our names there are province, religion and also caste. What to do? Supposing you do not like castes, let us have occupations. All the occupations should be organized and their leaders should form the village governments and town government.

We speak of the Third Plan and the Fourth Plan; we may speak later on of the Fifth Plan also. But the most important point is this. We should give the people complete swaraj; and let them make the plans for themselves. We should not interfere with the people. Of course, as regards big factories and canals they are very good ideas and I congratulate our Hon'ble Prime Minister for suggesting that we should have big industries.

But, I beg to say one thing. We shall have big industries, and big canals; Pakistan will also have big canals and industries. China has big canals and big industries also. If we shall fight one day, we shall destroy Lahore and they will destroy Delhi; we shall bomb Shanghai and they will bomb Calcutta. What is the fun of it ? We build and build and then destroy everything.

I saw how France and Germany made great progress. I saw also China and Japan. They had made great progress but when war came then all was destroyed. Having had that experience I beg to suggest that we should always insist on world unity and world government (Interruptions).

Sir, I only want to touch upon a few more points before I finish. I say that the people should always realize this, that whatever they believe in is nothing but what has been filled in their minds from their childhood. If some one says that he is a Hindu, he is a Hindu because he has been brought up in a Hindu home. If someone says that he is a Sikh, he is a Sikh because he has been brought up in a Sikh home. This fact should be realised. If a man is born in Bengal, he will speak Bengali. If a man is born in the Punjab, he will speak Punjabi.

What I want to say is, it is very important that our Government should have laboratories to find out the origin of all thoughts, find out how these thoughts develop, how these thoughts capture our minds and how these thoughts sometimes drive men as you pull an ass with a rope. It is very unfortunate that we do not know this.

Another thing is, there is the blood current; that is to say, blood current coming from parents and foreparents. Blood currents some times make people very stubborn, sometime they get easily agitated, and this is all the fault of blood. I lectured about this in the United States also. This fact should be realized as to how blood currents effect society, how thought currents effect society. Hinduism is some thought, Islam is some other thought. Congress is some thought, Communism is some other thought. PSP is some thought and SP is some other thought. These are all thoughts and our people are fighting for those thoughts. If our benevolent Government will take into consideration these facts, I hope we shall be able to do away with all friction.

In the end, Sir, I only want to say this. I believe in this great principle that all should work for all to make all happy. One should always examine one's thoughts every morning and evening or pray according to my Religion of Love. One must find out what thoughts make one fight. If some thoughts make one fight, one must eliminate those thoughts.

Again in Parliament

On the 9th March 1960 I delivered my second speech of the current Session. During the course of my talk of fifteen minutes I said these points :

Central government should not tax directly. Allow the States to tax and the Central Government should take a certain amount from every State.

The system of taxing should be changed. Tax not at every step. Tax only land, property and money in banks.

Government should never trade. Full freedom should be given to the people. Leave the initiative to the people. Government should only advise. Let the people have as much money as they like but government should not allow the people to misuse the money. People should not spend money in shows, wrong enjoyments and in actions wasting time and energy of the nation.

Government should help people to go out and settle in vacant lands of our world.

Our embassies and consulates should set examples in simple life. It is not enough to put on home spun cloth, they should also have simple furniture and cheap cars.

Government should not burden the country with foreign loans.

I am glad to see that government discourages drinking and harmful films.

Age of Mahatma Gandhi has come to end, age of World Federation has begun.

There should be no more strikes or hunger strikes. There should be no more demands for higher salaries, so long as there are beggars and roofless people in the country.

Gambling of all kinds is bad. Speculation in shares should end.

Print not too many notes, printing of too many notes produces inflation.

Stop not gold from coming in. You tax the exports, it is not good.

Work for World Government. World order alone can establish permanent peace. If there will be a world Government then we need not spend a lot of money on defence.

Ban litigation, intoxication, shows, expensive sports, dancing of girls before men. Make moral society.

Defence Budget

I have put forward the following points for proper consideration :

A. The problem of ex-soldiers and ex-officers should be considered with sympathy.

B. Ex-soldiers should be given suitable work.

C. Ex-officers should be given farms.

D. In every Cantonment there should be farm and factories.

E. Military organization should be utilized for social welfare.

F. Strong drinks should be prohibited in army messes and clubs.

G. Family quarters should be provided for all the soldiers and officers.

Aryan New Year : Our Meetings were held on three days : 20th 21st and 22nd March. Hundreds came. The hall was packed beyond its capacity and on one day hundreds were standing down below on the lawn and were hearing speeches and music from our loud speaker. Members of Parliament came, the Hon. Speaker addressed one day, Hans Maharaj and Pandit Sunderlal spoke on all the three days and many friends showered fine thoughts to the tune of our principle, Universal Unity. I declared, we fight evil, we want to eliminate all kinds of friction, we want all to work for all to make all happy.

A Bill in Parliament to Release My Property

My well wisher Members of Parliament, who wish that my estate, which was confiscated by the British Indian Government should be released by the Government of India in my favour, they brought a Bill for it.

Mahendra Pratap Singh Estates (Repealing) Bill

Mr. Chairman : The House will now take up the consideration of Mahendra Pratap Singh Estates (Repealing) Bill.

Shri P. R. Patel (Mehsana) : I beg to move :

> 'That the Bill to provide for the repeal of the Mahendra Pratap Singh Estates Act, 1923 be taken into consideration.'

Before I speak on the Bill I must thank my Hon'ble Friend, Shri Ram Krishna Gupta because he has permitted the House to curtail the time allowed for the consideration of his Bill. At the same time, I must also thank the Hon'ble House for being so good enough to grant the request made by me.

An Hon. Member : Specially Shri D. C. Sharma.

Shri P. R. Patel : When I speak on the Bill, before my eyes is Mahendra Pratap, a young man of 29, who was fired with patriotism, who thought that whatever be the sacrifices, the country must be freed from the British rule. With this view, with this determination, he left his young wife and two children to the care of God, left the country and outside the country he tried in his own way to free our country.

We know that at that time to say 'Swaraj is my right' was an offence. We know that our Leader of the House was tried and sentenced for commiting certain offences, which were offences against the British rule. Most of us, including myself, have also committed offences. And our offences, what were they? Our offences were to free our country from the foreign British rule.

Mahendra Pratap left India, went outside, had been to Germany and Afghanistan. The Britishers did not like anybody working against the British rule, working in a way that the British rule may end in India. So, the British Government was prompt in taking action against him. His estate was attached under the Bengal State Prisoners Regulation, 1818 very well. So many citizens of our country who dreamt of freeing our country, who did something to free our country were put behind the bars. Many great men of our country have been put behind the bars under these Regulations. His properties were attached and his only offence was his patriotism for the motherland, his determination to free the country from British rule. His properties were attached in 1916 and then the British Government thought it proper at that time to forfeit his estates.

They brought a bill before the Central Legislature in the year 1923 and passed an Act under which they forfeited the property and declared that it vested in His Majesty. The property included agricultural land as well as other movable and immovable property, like shops etc. If we see the Schedule we find that there are as many 79 or 80 shops forfeited to Government along with agricultural land and other property

The question will arise as to who is the authority to repeal this Act. I submit that this is a Central Act and unless this Act is repealed, I do not think any provincial government can return the property. Unless this Act is repealed, I do not think the provincial government would be even competent to pass any order regarding other property except agricultural land. So, my submission is that as the property was forfeited and vested in his Majesty under this Act passed by the Central Legislature, this House is the only competent body which can repeal it. To keep this Act on our statute book is a black spot on our statute book. This Act is the Blackest Act that the British legislature, I would say British legislatures and not Indian legislatures, have passed.

At the time of discussing this Bill, which became law, the Home Member I think it was Sir Malcolm Hailey, who moved the Bill for the consideration of the House, said :

> 'The Bill of Attainder not only attached the property of the offender but attached it in perpetuity. Here we are attempting to meet the problem of applying more modern methods and ideas in regard to the State's claim on the property of a fugitive rebel, accused of what would once have described of treason and felony.'

It was the birthright of every Indian to commit the offence of felony against any foreigner. I think if he committed this, it was an offence under the British law but it would be an act of virtue after independence. If we do not repeal this law and if we keep this Act on our statute book, it would be a shame to us and we do not deserve to live in Independent India.

Later on, Sir Malcolm Hailey says :

> 'That my description of him is accurate. I hope that no one here will harbor any doubt. In the other House my friend Mr. Crerar gave a complete history of the career of this misguided and mischievous man.' 'I do not wish to repeat those details here.'

After that he has said many things. I do not want to take up the valuable time of this House. But I would say that if to rebel against foreign rule was mischievous, every Indian was entitled at that time to do mischief of that type, it was the privilege and birthright of every Indian to rise against British rule and try in all possible ways to drive out the Britishers. There was nothing wrong.

The methods may differ. Our Rashtrapita, Gandhiji had certain methods. He taught us nonviolence and satyagraha, and we fought our battles under his leadership. There were others who believed in violence, and they used bombs and all other things, but their intention was to free the country. We might differ on the ways adopted, but it was a patriotic act.

The great leader of our country, Subhas Babu came with his army. What for?... to free the country. I think that was the best bravest act on the part of an Indian, a great son of the country. So, there are different ways and methods to free the country, but the intention, the ideal, was one, and that was the freedom of the country, to drive away the Britishers from the country.

While discussing the Mahendra Pratap Singh Estates Bill in 1923, I was pained to read, the then Indian Members praised the Government for bringing it.

An Hon'ble Member : Who were they?

Shri P. R. Patel : What is the good of reading the names? But that shows the mentality of the country at that time, that show what a hazard it was to speak against the British rule or do anything against British rule, because, after all, educated persons sought safety by just praising the Government for introducing and bringing forward such a Bill.

Later on, the then Foreign Secretary, Mr. Denys Bray said :

'Sir, after this chorus of approval, no further words on behalf of the Government are really required. But like my friend Mr. Agarwal, I too have had some acquaintance with Mahendra Pratap, though my acquaintace has been of a very different kind. Ever since the day he embarked on his career of high treason, it has been part of my duty to follow him very closely... As the Honourable the Home Member says, on very long and very laborious journey... which is not yet over. I propose simply to take one episode in his career, and to bring it into somewhat sharper relief by means of certain documents in the archives of the Foreign office. Mahendra Pratap was sent by the German Government as one of the members of its mission under Von Hentig to Kabul. At the time it struck me as a somewhat incongruous membership; indeed I think it was not until I was able to peruse this booklet now in my hand that I realized what great store the German Government set by his presence on that Mission. It is a German diary kept up by one of the German members on that mission depicting the long journey from Berlin through south-east Europe, across Asia Minor, down the Euphrates to Baghdad right across the breadth of Persia into Afghanistan and the many references in it to 'our Indian Prince'... For as such Mahendra Pratap appears to have imposed on the German Government... and the great solicitude set up through out the whole of the mission whenever our Indian Prince went down with a touch of fever on the way make it quite clear that the German Government attached the utmost importance to Mahendra Pratap's presence on that Mission and expected great things from it.

Then describing Raja Mahendra Partap's activities, he says, that letters were written to Nepal. Regarding that, he says,

'Of these two, one reached us as soon as postal arrangements between Kathmandu and Simla could bring it. I am not able to display the house the original, for his highness the Prime Minister of Nepal in sending us the letter and the two covering letters of Mahendra Pratap requested that they might be returned to them as an interesting, if some what amusing souvenir of the Great War. But I have in my hands photographic copies. There are first, two letters from Mahendra Pratap both signed M. Partap, for the time being President of the Provisional Government of Hind.

Then, at that time, there was laughter in the House.

The Provisional Government of independent India was established by Raja Mahendra Pratap in 1915 in Afghanistan.

He foresaw all things at that time that India was going to be free. He did all these things, not for himself. If he meant anything for himself, he would have been happy with his estate, and he would have been happy with his wife and children. Why should he have left all these things and gone to Germany and Afghanistan? He went because at that time our patriots thought that to free our country foreign help must be sought and at that time since the Germans were at war with Britain, it was thought that some help might come from them. So, in order to get some help from the foreign powers, he' and like him, others also, had been to foreign countries, seeking help, and tried to free our country.

Raja Mahendra Pratap had been outside, from December, 1914 to 1946. He returned India after we had the interim Government here. He could have returned earlier, and in fact, a resolution was moved on the House, perhaps in 1937 or so I do not remember the year well... and some hon'ble Member desired that permission be given to him, but then the British Government said that if he entered, then he should be prepared to bear the consequences, which means that he would be put in jail and be tried for treason and all those things. But, throughout his life, whether he was in Russia, or in Germany or in Kabul or in Japan or in America, his endeavour was just to help the country to be free. But the British Government had penalized him for this.

Now, the question before us in whether we should do justice to him for the patriotic act done by him, which was considered as treason by the Britishers, I am glad that only the other day, I read in the newspapers that the Congress Party was very sympathetic and might also support the Bill. But as I read in the newspaper, the question that was put was........

Mr. Chairman : May I know whether the Hon. Member will take some more time.

Shri P. R. Patel : Yes.

Mr. Chairman : Then, he may continue on the next day.

Mr. Deputy-Speaker : The House will now resume further discussion of the motion moved by Shri Purushottamdas R. Patel on the 4th March. 1960 :

> 'That the Bill to provide for the repeal of the Mahendra Partap Singh Estates Act, 1923 be taken into consideration.'

Out of one hour allotted for the discussion of the bill, 20 minutes have already been taken up on the 4th March, 1960 and 40 minutes are now available. Shri P. R. Patel may now continue his speech. He has already taken 20 minutes and now he will try to conclude.

Shri P. R. Patel : Mr. Deputy-Speaker, Sir, the other day I was saying that the Act of 1923 was passed and under that Act the properties of Raja Mahendra Partap were confiscated to His Majesty and vested in His Majesty and that by the some Act properties were to be given to his son on some condition. It would be interesting to know the conditions. The conditions are :'That neither he nor his heirs shall during the life time of Mahendra Pratap Singh alienate any of the said properties, that is to say, either the estate right title interest, claim and demand etc. without the sanction in writing of the government of the United Provinces of Agra and Oudh.' Then another condition is : 'That neither he nor his heirs shall render assistance or support to the said Mahendra Pratap Singh either pecuniarily or otherwise in any manner whatsoever.'

So the properties were given to his son with the condition that he should not help his father by a single farthing. Furthermore, one condition is that he must remain loyal to the government then. So these are the things to be taken into consideration.

The point before us is whether this black law should remain on the statute book because in the bill that I have moved in clause (2). I desire that the Act of 1923 should stand repealed. So the House shall have to consider whether this black Act would be an ornament to us and should be kept in our statute book or would it be proper to repeal that law. That is the first question that the House should consider.

Then the second question will be that the properties have been attached and confiscated to His Majesty. Then the government for the loyalty of his son has given it to his son. But now the question is whether the properties should be devested and given over to Raja Mahendra Partap. That is also a matter to be considered. Naturally, any man may feel that after all the properties are with the grandson today and why it should be devested and given over to him. That is not the question though. The question is that the properties were confiscated from him for what. It was for the act of patriotism, and nothing more. Now if we return the properties to him, we amend the misdeeds of the Britishers. That, I submit, is the only point. I will not take more time.

Shri Jawaharlal Nehru : Mr. Deputy-Speaker, Sir, I should like at this early stage in this discussion to state the government's view point with regard to this bill. With the basic object of this bill, that is, to remove from the statute book a measure which we consider objectionable and certainly which cannot be approved of by any national government in this country, with that basic object we are in entire agreement. Broadly speaking, therefore, we agree not only with that object but the consequences of this bill. What we have been considering is the proper way to bring this about. We referred this bill to the Uttar Pradesh Government. They expressed their general agreement with the objects of the bill. So there is no argument necessary on the merits, I might say. But certain difficulties have arisen about the Constitutional procedures which are feasible. Normally speaking, anything appurtenant to land is obviously in the purview of the State Government and not of the Central Government. It is in the list attached to the Constitution.

If it was only land, I would normally say, I do not speak with any absolute certainty, that this should be for the State Government to take up and deal with. This bill, however, deals with not only immovable property but also movable property. That again introduces an element of confusion, because movable property might be dealt with in one way and immovable property possibly in another.

On the other hand, it might be argued that this being a statute of the Central Government. It can only be repealed by the Central authority not by a State authority.

In spite of my effort and my colleague's effort to get a very precise and clear decision on this subject, I mean to say, advice on this subject, a measure of doubt remain as to what the proper procedure is, which might not be challenged later, because we should not take a step which might be challenged on constitutional or legal grounds.

There are one or two other smaller matters too, that is, possibly, some small amendments might be more helpful and might improve bill, again, so far as the law is concerned. But the basic question is what I have just stated and I want to place before you and the House.

I should like, perhaps, that other Members can throw some light on this as to how best to proceed, because we obviously are in favour of the bill but we are anxious that what is done should be correctly done, according to the Constitution and should not be challengeable in any court of law later on.

Mr. Deputy Speaker : If some time is required, then perhaps, we can postpone the further discussion of the bill, till some future time, and then we can take it up. Meanwhile, these things can be thought out and some way found.

Shri P. R. Patel : That would be proper. I agree to the proposition.

Mr. Deputy-Speaker : Then, a regular motion might be made by the Hon'ble Mover or some other Member.

Shri P. R. Patel : I beg to move : 'That consideration of the bill be postponed till government consider the matter and come before the House.'

Mr. Deputy-Speaker : That might not be proper from of the motion. He should not say 'till government cosider' etc. He might merely move that the further consideration of the bill be postponed till, say the, 15th April or any other date he may like.

Shri Khushwant Rai : He may say, till the first day of the next session.

Shri Ansar Harvai (Fatehpur) : Yes till the 1st day of the next session.

Mr. Deputy-Speaker : I have no objection.

The Minister of Parliamentary Affairs (Shri Satya Narayan Sinha): We have no objection.

Shri P. R. Patel : I beg to move : 'That further consideration of the bill be postponed till the first day of the next session.'

Mr. Deputy-Speaker : The question is : 'That further consideration of the bill be postponed till the first day of the next session.'

The Motion was adopted.

Mr. Deputy-Speaker : So, the further consideration of the bill is postponed. Now, we shall take up the next bill. But there is one thing that I would like to mention. The motion that we have adopted is to take up further consideration on the first day of the next session. That would be a government day. It would not be necessarily a non-official day, but it would be a government day. Therefore, we shall take it up on that day.

Note: *The bill was postponed, and never got passed. I regret not. Not much is left of the property. Villages are taken over by the government of all the landlords to do away landlordism, but it is good in any case to cancel the order of the British Government. If our government had done it when I arrived back in the country in 1946 unnecessary loss of half million rupees could have been saved. Better late than never. I am anxious to satisfy my daughter, grandson and granddaughter in a way that no litigation in the family ruins them. I also want to create Trust to have a Centre of the Religion of Love, a Centre of World Federation and a Prem Vihar permanently.*

Hyderabad and Back : Travelling two nights and a day in a fast express train I reached Hyderabad in the morning of the 22nd May 1960. Nawab Nazir Yar Jang and more than dozen friends received me and profusely garlanded me. I was taken by car to Jiwan Bhawan. I stayed here for four days, as a guest of Seth ji.

After my arrival the first meeting was held at Aivani Urdu. Nawab Zain Yar Jang was in the chair. I spoke at length.

In the afternoon I spoke at the Theosophical Society. The speaker of Andhra Assembly was in the chair. I spoke on World Unity. At night Love Centre was established at Jiwan Hall. I prayed and explained the need of the Religion of love. Some important persons were present.

I visited the University. It has beautiful Library and several colleges. Buildings are grand. Next day 24th May, I visited the famous Salar Jang Museum. On 25th May friends took me out to show the beautiful picnic spot by the Usman Sagar, an artificial lake of a great size. I with friends visited Udasi temple. At 6.30 p.m. we went to the Ritz Hotel. Here I was the speaker of the evening at the Rotary Club. I addressed the audience and answered some question.

Friends saw me off at the station and once again profusely garlanded me.

A night and a day brought me to Bhopal. Here I was a guest of H. H. the younger Begam Sahiba. I saw her on the 27th morning and expressed my hearty sympathy for her. She wept remembering the late His Highness. Evening I reached Ujjain. I was a guest of the Martial Races Union. Nobles brought me to the Grand Hotel.

28th forenoon we visited the Jat temple. In the afternoon I attended the reception of the Daily Bhaskar. It was a pleasure to meet the editor and friends. The procession was a grand affair, the President of the Union and myself rode an elephant. H. H. Doongarpur and several Maharajas, Rajas, Thakurs walked with three to four hundred persons for about two hours through streets of the town. Then a large meeting was held. A couple of thousand persons were present. I was asked to inaugurate the function. I gave a blue print of my programme. The President read his address.

Taking dinner at our hotel I boarded a train for Bhopal. In the morning I changed the train and arrived back at Mathura in the afternoon of the 29th May 1960. Visiting my grand niece and Sardar I came to Vrindaban. 30th May I returned to Delhi by my jeep. I must here thank Mr. Manohar Prasad, Seth Jiwan Lal and Nawab Karmullah and friends for making my Hyderadad trip so successful. Maharao Krishnpal Singh insisted and at his bidding I attended the Martial Races Union. I thank the Union workers for the hospitality.

Correspondence : Pandit Jawaharlal Nehru Sahib kindly took the trouble to answer immediately my recent letter. I had written him that he may take the first step to declare that India was prepared to surrender her army to UNO and our Hon'ble Prime Minister as the apostle of peace may request all other weak, small or neutral States to surrender their armies to the United Nations. I give his answer in full :

No. 399–PM/60, New Delhi, 20th June 1960

Dear Raja Sahib,

I have your letter of the 18th June. I am afraid the proposal you have made of various countries surrendering their armies to the U.N.O. is not feasible. Yours sincerely Jawaharlal Nehru (to) Raja Mahendra Pratap, M.P. Rajpur, Dehradun.

I am very thankful for this prompt reply. It is in a way negative but his kindness is clear in finding time to attend to my proposal.

In any case, some such plan is bound to come. Lord Attlee said, the other day, practically the same thing, he said that U.N.O. must have its army.

Recently in some cultural meeting held at Berlin some Spanish leader and our Babu Jai Prakash Narain said that U.N.O. must have an unarmed police to keep watch all over the world and that it could go freely to all the countries.

U. N. O. Answered : I am very glad that U.N.O. has cared to send an answer to my letter. I very thankfully print it in full.

United Nations, New York, 24th June 1960

Dear Sir,

This will acknowledge the receipt of your letter, with enclosure, addressed to the Secretary-General of the United Nations and referred to me for reply. As you may know, the United Nations is an organization of States and its various organs act upon proposals brought forward by governments under the terms of the Charter of the United Nations rather than by individual citizens. In order to best support the aims and principles of the United Nations it is suggested that you direct your proposal to the appropriate department within your own government. Your interest in the United Nations and its activities is appreciated.

Yours very truly,

Mrs. Josephine Frank
Chief Public Inquiries Unit Visitors' Service
(To) Raja Mahendra Pratap M. P.
105, South Avenue, New Delhi, India.

My Trip to Kabul

Last year when I wanted to go to Afghanistan I got sick. This year my trip to Kabul materialized rather suddenly.

I was talking casually with Afghanistan Ambassdor at the annual function of Pakhtoon about someone going to Afghanistan, was it possible, how one goes. I was told it was very easy and that was the best season.

Then, a few days later I heard from Mr. Jamal Khwaja that he had just returned from Kabul and that the uncle of the King lovingly remembered me. I decided to visit Kabul.

On the 27th September I got visa and I bought a return air ticket to Kabul. On the 1st October I departed and the same day in the afternoon I was at the royal capital. One my old friend Sardar Abdul Wahab brought me to Ariana.

On the 2nd October morning H. E. The Indian Ambasador called on me. He invited me for lunch. There came too H.R.H. Marshal Shah Wali Khan with his two princes. Another Afghan Minister and a high official were also present.

We talked of things old and of things new. It was my great pleasure to meet once again Aala Hazrat Shah Wali. He told me that His Majestry the King had ordered that I was to be royal guest for ten days at the Hotel Kabul.

A secretary of the King was deputed to look after me and a car was placed at my disposal. I was taken round and shown several factories. It was now quite a modern city with very wide well paved streets and large buildings flanking both the sides.

Sardar Sultan Ahmad Khan and Sardar Abdul Hadi Khan, former ambassadors and minister called on me and gave me banquets. Several great personalities were present at these occasions.

I was invited to tea by the princes, son of the former Crown Prince Sardar Inayatullah Khan. We talked long and sipped tea. The eldest prince Khaliullah Khan remembered my Seven Points written on yellow silk, the Crown Prince had framed them and hanged them on a wall in 1916.

H.R.H. Prince Shah Wali kindly called on me at the hotel. On the 9th October my Mehmandar Sahib took me to Paghman at the summer residence of H. R.H. the Marshal H. E. the court Minister, Royal Chief Secretary and princes were also present. It was more a dinner than tea. So much and so many delicacies were offered, we remembered how it was at this very place that His majesty Amir Habibullah Khan received me and our Indo Turco-German Mission for the first time in October 1915. Dreams of the past floated in our hazy memories! And I rejoiced.

It was significant that I arrived at Kabul for the first time on the second of October 1915 and I arrived this time on the first of October, exactly forty five years after. On the second October this year I visited the same pretty villa in the Bagh Babar where I stayed in 1915-16. I paid homage to the tomb of the emperor Baber. The marble tomb built by Emperor Shahjahan was being rebuilt. Two large swimming pools were constructed. The garden, however, had lost its former beauty. The Harem Sarai now had a school of Pakhtooni children. It was very appropriate as it was from here that four Provisional Government of India worked among the frontier tribes. Sardar Nasrullah Khan, the prime minister raised and financed twelve thousand strong Afridi army on behalf of our Government.

In the night of the 9th October I was received by his Majesty the King Zahir Shah. Right royality my car drove to the palace gate through guards who saluted. Here I was received by three men in black unifrom. The secretary of his majesty accompanied me, I was led to the chief Secretary who then took me to the king. He was standing. We shook hands and we sat down. I presented to the King my six booklets and seven hand written points. His Majesty very keenly read them. He started talking in simple clear Persian.

His Majesty deplored the present condition in the world. 'Our Foreign Minister also spoke for Peace at U.N.O. but it seems that they go their own way, heeding little for universal desire for peace...' His majesty desired closer relation between Afghanistan, India and Pakistan. He appreciated my work and said! 'you are sowing seeds, one day they must grow and flourish...' At present some rulers do not mind inflicting wounds, the King added. I highly appreciated the royal opinions, I heartily thanked his Majesty and took leave. He stood up. We again shook hands. The chief Secretary who was standing at a distance followed me and saw me off at the car below.

Sardar Abdul Hadi Khan had given me lunch on the 7th Oct. On the 10th Oct. Sardar Sultan Ahmad Khan gave lunch. H. R. H. Marshal Wali Khan, the Court Minister and Prince Asadullah Khan were also present. In the afternoon Indian Embassy gave me tea. The Ambassador had to join some other tea party of some departing diplomat but he returned and we chatted till 8 p.m. Shrimati ji is from Kapurthala family and it was a pleasure to hear her religious trend. The Ambassador was all for renunciation at an early age but then he was persuaded to enter life with a zest. In the position where he is, he naturally admires the foreign policy of our Hon. Prime Minister. The Ambassador kindly saw me off at the airport on the 11th October and I also took leave of Janab Olomi Sahib the royal secretary and thanked the driver too who drove me around.

In the afternoon of the same day at 4.15 I reached New Delhi. During half an hour halt at Amritsar we served tea.

I should also mention two other visitors at Kabul. Sardar Habibullah Khan Tarzi, once Ambassador at Kabul called on me and was kind enough to say that I helped him in Japan. He added that I was helping everywhere the cause of Afghanistan. I thanked him for his continued goodwill.

Another visitor was Molvie Abdur Rab, son of the famous Haji Abdur Razik. Haji Sahib was asked by the Prime Minister in 1915-16 to help the freedom movement of India. At his house long Indian meetings were held and secret plans were discussed. Molvie Rab thought that he and I yet could do something on frontier. I however said that as I was now a royal guest I should not do any thing without the formal permission of Afghan Government. I hinted at the same time that if I could stay at Kabul with a friend I would earnestly work for unity of Aryan with local liberty.

Justice demands that I should mention that my Life Story does not mention very important meetings held at the residence of Sardar Mahmud Beg Tarzi in 1915-16. He was keenly interested in Jehad. We talk long about Turkey and Arab. Moulana Barkatullah and Captain Kazim Beg always accompanied me when I visited Tarzi Sahib. He had an independent view point.

When I arrived at Kabul a Trade Mission from India was there, I also Joined the dinner party given to this trade Mission. I also took part in the tea party given by the Indian traders of Kabul. It seems that they do brisk trade inspite of Pakistan in the middle of two countries.

I stated how H.R.H. Marshal Shah Wali Khan was kind to me, how old friends gave me lunch and tea parties and how I was the Royal guest of His Majesty. I also described the great progress of the capital city. It is now modern in every respect, with very wide streets and large, high buildings flanking on their two sides. Parks are beautiful. Two visits were not, however, mentioned in the story. I visited Dr. Mhd. Asaf Sohail, President of the Press Department in the morning of the 5th October. He is a Medical Doctor and author. He gave me several books in Persian, one of them was written by himself. He is a personality of his own type and very interesting to talk to. In the afternoon on the same day Mr. Olomi, appointed by the Royal Court to look after me, took me to H. E. The Minister of Education Dr. Ali Ahamd Popal. He was very much interested in my fromer visits to Afghanistan. Twice when I wanted to take leave, fearing that I was taking too much of his time, he asked me several more question about the past. I took this opportunity to tell him some thing about my present plans. He kindly kept me with him for over an hour though the time fixed for the interview was only for fifteen minutes, I thank him here once again.

In Parliament : In the present Budget Session I have already spoken twice, once on the 23rd Feb. 1961 and next on the 16th March.

Both the times I spoke in Indian Language and published my speeches in my Hindi paper.

My more important work in this Session has been my constant appeals to fellow members to get together 255 and to form our government on my plan. We mean to postpone elections for fifteen years and to bring home rule to every town and village. I mean to turn the entire nation into a family.

Government and people have accepted wrong ideals. They want to build great cities, powerful army and big industry. I say, all this progress is destroyed one day. States make progress and then clash and ruin each other. The ideal should be to make man care-free!

I want to form a government which will see to it that not one remains without work and bread and see to it that One World Government is founded with World Army, World Court of Justice and World Religions Board.

I can understand that long established habit of thinking makes man a slave to his thoughts A Hindu will not like to pray to Buddha. I mean to liberate Man from the slavery of thought.

My Tour Abroad

I left by air on the 8th of May this year and returned to Delhi on the 19th of July travelling by train from Calcutta.

It took me only twelve hours from Delhi to Tokyo. In fact the actual flying time was only ten hours. The plane stopped at Bangkok and Hongkong for two hours. I went by a jet of the Air France. Service was superb. Flying was very comfortable. Old friends greeted me with flowers. I was their guest for night at a Japanese hotel.

From the 9th May to 30th May I was guest of the Congress for Cultivating Human Spirit. We were one hundred and four from many different countries. More than half were Indians.

Best hotels were provided. Entertainments were given. Meetings, receptions and discources were arranged from Tokyo, the Capital, to Kyoto and Fukuoka in the south.

At some out of the way places country folk received us very enthusiastically, to shake hands with us was their hobby. Some of us, I saw, enjoyed this hand shaking.

We were shown a motor car factory. People of that town hoped to develop it into a Detroit of Japan. We were received by the ailing founder of Ananai Kyo and in fact the organiser of all this wonderful movement to develop Human Spirit. He was lying on bed. One by one some of us shook hands with him. His followers worship him along with God of the universe and god of Japan.

From 30th May to the 21st of June I was the guest of my old Japanese friends. Welcome meeting was arranged. I spoke and heartily thanked my friends. I could speak at many different meetings. The Asahi News Paper took special interest in my visit to Japan. I met the Prime Minister for two minutes. I had a long conversation with the former Prime Minister Mr. Kishi. He said that World Federation was the right way for Japan.

The Hon'ble Speaker received me and introduced me to the Parliament. Members cheered me.

My chief host, I should say, was Mr. Juntaro Imazato. He got some friends together and got up a reception committee. In the end they also gave me farewell, at a farewell meeting. Some of them saw me off at the air port.

Our World Federation Centre which I founded in 1937 was not in good shape. My cottage was in ruin. I made a new committee to look after it. Count Sakai kindly agreed to be its President. Indian Ambassador at Tokyo gave me a dinner. I called on Afghan Ambassador. Japanese friends gave me lunches and dinners. Three friends gave me also Japanese currency for daily use. I thank them heartily.

Government Guest at Taiwan

At Taipei, in Taiwan, I was a Government guest. Ministers received me and gave lunches and dinners. I was very glad to see the Grand old man General Yu Yu Rin, my old friend, now 82 years old, he is still the President of the central Yuan. President of the Legislative Yuan Mr. Hwang was very sympathetic. Mr. Lo, the Chinese Ambassador in India till 1949 had some bitter tales to tell. He had to leave India when our Government recognised Red China. But above all the most important was my interview with Marshal Chiang Kai Shek. He was very cordial and took photos with me.

I think, it is in the best interest of Peking to give up the territory which Indian Government thinks China has wrongly occupied. Taiwan has very similar views about Tibet as India has. It is not wise for Peking to force India to combine with those who are opposed to Red China.

Visit to Five Port Cities

I visited Hong-Kong, Singapore, Bangkok, Rangoon and Calcutta on my way back

At Hong-Kong I stayed for five days. Sardar Pritam Singh found for me a nice hotel room. Seth Hari Lila and Thakur Rathor gave me dinner and lunch. Mr. Ma, Chinese friend showed me the entire Kowloon territory driving me in his car for over eighty miles. I spoke at the Hindu temple and Gurudwara.

At Singapore I stayed seven days. I was a guest of our Indian Assistant Commissioner Sardar G. J. Malik, Sardarni Sahiba made me feel quite at home. I had the pleasure of meeting some important personalities of Singapore at the reception given by our naval ship Trisul and at the national function of Philippine Republic. I could speak twice at Gurudwara, twice at one Hindu Society and once at Arya Samaj. I found among the Sikhs a great enthusiasm for Punjabi Suba. One Chinese friend took me to a spiritual temple and give us rich Chinese lunch.

At Bangkok I stayed with our Indian ambassador. He, Sardarni Sahiba and their two daughters made me very comfortable. I lectured at the Gurudwara. I spoke at the large meeting of Arya Samaj. I preached at the Vishnu temple. The meeting held at the hall of Hindu Samaj was attended by all the sections of the Indian people. Pandit Raghuath Sharma of the cultural lodge had called it. The Ambassador presided. I was the chief speaker. I spoke on Religion of Love and World Federation. The audience, I was told, was highly pleased. I saw different Buddhist temples. Sardar Sahib, our Ambassador, gave a dinner party inviting Indian leaders to meet me.

At Rangoon I was a guest of my old friend Mr. Bashir, now a Pakistani. His son-in-law and Mr. Dubey, his manager, made my stay at Rangoon very pleasant. I saw temples. I paid a visit to the tomb of the last emperor of India Bahadur Shah. Mr. Iqbal helped me to see several former I.N.A. Officials. I also visited former president Mr. Ba Maw. I expressed my views to a small group of Hindu Mandal.

16th July was a very busy day in Rangoon. In the morning I spoke at Gurudwara. At noon, at the tea party given by Northern Indian Association, I gave short outline of my plan. I had tea with Dr. Ba Maw. In the evening I delivered a long address at the Gandhi hall. It was a crowded meeting.

Mr. Sanjib Chaudhri Advocate, General Secretary of the world Congress for World Federation with a few of his followers received me at the Calcutta Airport. He took me to a batch of Hunger Strikers. These poor people are being removed by the Government from their homes. I sympathized with them but asked them to give up the fast and to work as our volunteers to remove all the troubles of all the people, to make happy human society. I stayed at Calcutta only one night. I reached Delhi on the 19th July by train.

My Story : 7th October 1961 suddenly brought a great change in weather. It became cold enough to discard electric fan.

I have come to my constituency to work for election campaign. I have not however started touring villages. Only once I inaugurated cattle show in Khapparpur. Advocate Mr. Gurdatt Singh arranged meeting for me. I spoke at length.

I had resigned but as my friends insisted I agreed to work on as the President of All India Jat Maha Sabha. It may be interesting to know that besides Hindu Jat Vice-Presidents we have one Sikh-Jat Vice-President, a brother of H. H. Maharaja Patiala and another Muslim Jat Vice President, Sardar Habibulla Khan, Barrister, Lahore, Pakistan.

I stand for universal unity. Different parties from Swatantra Party to Communist Party, including honest Congressmen are helping me. Only most selfish, narrow minded and anti-social element can think of opposing me.

12th November. I presided over Jat Mahasabha Executive Committee at the residence of Ch. Birendra Singh Vakil, Mathura. In the evening I attended Saudi Arabia Function at New Delhi. Here I met many friends, including ambassador. When I arrived at my flat I found that it was opened from behind and theft was committed.

13th. I went by jeep to Dehradun and Rajpur, arrived there in the evening. I had asked H. H. Maharaja Sirguja that 14th Nov. being birth day of Pandit Jawaharlal Nehru, he may ask his son-in-law to sent sagai (first ceremony of marriage) for my grandson Kumar Amar Pratap. Ceremony was duly performed, on that date. My daughter, I and Kumar Amar came to Delhi on the 17th in our two cars. It was a pleasure to meet Maharaja Sirguja on the 19th. We also have dinner with our one relation.

On the 20th Nov. started our Lok Sabha. 8th December it ended. On this or that I asked questions. I spoke whenever I got opportunity and once again I upset the Hon'ble Speaker. And I walked of the House on the 30th November.

Four speeches I delivered in Parliament. Twice I spoke on this last day. I attended three embassy function, once a wedding celebration and I addressed ten thousand people gathered in the meeting of Hans Maharaj. My time is very much taken by visitors. Many came to get some kind of recommendations. My daughter remained here for eighteen days. I also remained busy with Parliament. I am sorry I could not attend to correspondence properly. My secretaries are in my constituency.

Correspondence : I feel it my duty to quote the letter of Pandit Jawaharlal Nehruji. It is dated 26th November 1961.

Dear Raja Saheb,

I have received your letter of the 24th November as well as your previous two letters. I am sorry I could not reply to them as I have been very heavily occupied.

I am afraid it is not possible for us to accept your suggestion that you should be sent to various foreign countries. As you know, your views differ from those of the Government here. We can hardly send someone who represents a different policy. If however you wish to go to any particular country at your own instance, I imagine there will be little difficulty in your doing so.

Yours sincerely
Jawaharlal Nehru

I wish I could go and try to do what our Government is unable to do. I think that it is surely possible to have a treaty among China, Japan and India to sent our over population to vacant lands. I think, it is also possible to combine China, Russia and India to promote world order. I also believe that Pakistan and Afghanistan can join hands to promote Aryan of my plan of World Federation. If I can lecture in USA I am quite sure that Americans will appreciate my plan of World Government with world army, world court of justice and the unity of religions.

In Parliament

When the Prime Minister was replying to the External Affairs debate, I interrupted and said : 'What about my three peaceful solutions?'

At the end of his long speech. I remarked : 'Why not try my peaceful methods ?'

Mr. Speaker : The Hon'ble Member wants to go to China.

Shri S. M. Banerjee (Kanpur) : He has the passport.

Mr. Speaker : If he has, let him go.

Thus I Spoke in Parliament : Supposed to be the defenders of the Hindu Faith were attacking the Christians in the Parliament. Thus I spoke on the occasion: I give you here official report.

After this speech in the Parliament I am giving many other items or paragraphs showing my activity in the House. You will see that on several occasions my fight for my cause annoyed our Hon'ble Speaker. I believe that I did my duty as I must.

Raja Mahendra Pratap (Mathura) : Sir, I stand to oppose this. I am in a very unfortunate position that I opposed something which was supported by many of my friends. But I oppose this with tooth and nail, because I believe this is very wrong. I beg to say this is nothing but undue Hindu defeatism, which is apparent in every action of our Hindu brethren. If money comes, where is the harm? Let money come. Let more money come and if we are strong enough, we will utilise that money in the interest of our people.

Shri Raghunath Singh (Banaras) : A beggar can not be strong.

Raja Mahendra Pratap : I may also point out that it is something against Hindu religion itself. Our Lord Krishna has stated in Gita that whenever there is evil in this world, I appear. Why do we not accept? Lord Buddha, Jesus Christ and Prophet Mohammed and Lord Krishna himself coming to destroy the evil of this world ? I am from Braj and I must support what Lord Krishna said.

Shri Raghunath Singh : Shri Krishna said, Religions of other are dangerous (Translation).

Raja Mahendra Pratap : There are some wrong ideas which have taken possession of the minds of our fellow brethren here. They do not get angry.

Shri Raghunath Singh : You were quoting Lord Krishna; therefore I am saying this.

Hon. Deputy Speaker : (Translation) I want to draw the attention of the Hon. Member to the rule that there can be only one speech. He can ask one or two questions. He can not take much time.

Raja Mahendra Pratap : I only beg to say that we should not create more divisions in this country. When we oppose Christianity, we create division ourselves. I am working for the unity of religions. God has given me Religion of Love and I preached this Religion of Love all over the world. I even presented my book 'Religion of Love' to Comrade Lenin, who had got it engraved at Moscow that religion is opium.

I am for unity of religions. I am for unity of races. I am for unity of countries. I am for one world, for world federation, for world government, for world army, One God and one people. All are brother.

I got Defeated in Election

My well-wishers compelled me to fight Lok Sabha election again from Mathura Constituency. I fought, but I learnt that Congress candidate is spending lot of money. Same thing with other candidates. Jan Sangh, Swatantra, Hindu Mahasabha, Republican, PSP, all six parties are fighting election, and all are attacking me in their campaign. I tried to my election committee made me run about a great deal in my constituency. It often happened that I left after breakfast and unturned to dinner, late at night. On certain days I had no lunch.

I went by car or jeep. I spoke to the village folk. On some days regular meetings were held. My life story was recited in songs. Large audience heard me speak. When Raja Man Singh of Bharatpur came to speak for me, in one meeting there were over ten thousand men. Pandit Sunder Lal, all world peace leader, came twice with friends. A couple of thousand men were charmed with his eloquence. Hundreds greeted me, scores touched my feet in many villages where I went. At the end it was painful surprise all round how I got defeated when I was so popular with the general public. Money did the trick.

I left Delhi on the 23rd December 1961 and I returned Delhi on the 6th of March 1962. I shall be here during this month. It is the last Session of our Parliament.

Future Uncertain : I got defeated in election. I had not money enough while Congress candidate spent more than three times of what I could spend. Congress men have become expert in making money. Congress party rules the country. Officials fear the party bosses. They can be demoted, transferred and harassed in more ways than one if they dare to disobey the wishes of the party members.

I do not know where these conditions will lead the country? Having had experience of four revolutions I can say that the situation is developing in favour of revolution.

I am not sorry. I equally wanted to examine the condition of our public in my constituency. It is considered holy among the Hindus, as the birth place of Lord Shri Krishna. His Maternal uncle Kansa ruled in this district. He wanted to kill Shri Krishna in this Braj, as our district is called in holy books, are surely some descendants of the soldiers and servants of Kansa. They must naturally oppose me.

Pure simple religion is for purification of thought. As some exercise is necessary for the body, some daily exercise is necessary for the mind, it is the prayer.

Evil misleads men to hate this or that from or religion advocating cunningly anyone special religion. Evil creates friction in society. Recently Evil is teaching fanaticism of political parties. Man gets charmed by the charming arguments of evil and fights for some ideas.

Will the public help me to continue my preaching work, it is a big question. Today I can not promise continuation of my English, Hindi and Urdu publications.

In my constituency the successful Congress candidate got less then half the votes of all the votes polled. Opposition votes were divided into six parties or independents. Over eleven thousand votes were rejected. If I had only received all the votes polled by the Jan Sangh candidate I would have won by ten thousand votes. These are facts revealed by the official record. What more happened behind the curtain God alone knows.

Unbelievable Facts : President of Jan Sangh lost the election and his security was confiscated. Presidents of Hindu Mahasabha, Swatantra Party, Republican party and S. P. could not be elected to the Parliament.

The leaders in Parliament of P.S.P. and Jan Sangh were defeated at the polls.

The Chief Minister of Madhya Pradesh who is Congressman and Kashmiri, thus related to the Hon'ble Pandit Jawaharlal Nehru, was badly defeated.

In all, thirty four Ministers of the ruling party could not be elected. They lost their legislature seats to the opposition.

I happen to be the president of Prem Maha Vidyalaya which I founded in 1909. I am also the President of All India Jat Maha Sabha and I am the President of World Federation and Founder of the Religion of Love but with all that leadership I lost the election.

It may be interesting to know that Lord Shri Krishna of this district was defeated in battle at Mathura legendary date five thousand years ago, and had to leave Braj. He founded his state at Dwarka.

The Congress successful candidate of my district is also Jat but he has one non-Jat wife and another Jat wife. Sardar Pratap Singh Kairon, the Chief Minister of Punjab, and Shri Devilal, opposition leader are also Jats. Clanish unity is shattered. But there is still such love for the Jat clan among the Musalmans that at Lahore Sardar Habibullah Khan, Barrister and Sir Zafrullah Khan, Pak representative at the UNO are proud to consider themselves Jats.

Maharaja Ranjit Singh founder of Punjab kingdom, was Jat. Rulers of Patiala and Bharatpur were Jats, so are the present Maharajas of those states. But most of the ruling princes in India, nearly five hundred out of five hundred sixty were Rajputs.

Our present government denounces castes but elections were fought mostly along the caste line. Party candidates appealed to caste affinities.

I wish, our present rulers see the facts and organize castes and give them power to rule village and towns and suppress these fighting parties altogether.

We should help the natural trend of unity among castes. For example my nephew late Raja Bahadur Mursan was married to a Rajput noble lady and his son was married to a Rajput princess of Rajputana. The invitations were sent out in my name, as his grandfather.

I was married to a princess of Jind state, younger sister of Late H. H. Maharaja Ranbir Singh of Patiala. Nabha, Jind and Faridkot rulers are Sikhs but they intermarry among Hindu Jats on account of common clan, religion counts less than blood relation.

The last session of the last Parliament had ended on the 30th March. In it my first and last speech was delivered on the 15th of that month. I asserted that if corruption and nepotism were not suppressed we would have either Revolution or military rule.

The prevailing system of election in the so-called democratic countries which gives equal vote to a prostitute and a saint is responsible for this situation. Would be legislators have to seek aid of the worst evil characters and when they enter legislative assemblies they have to satisfy those thirsty and hungry for wealth and position who supported and arranged votes for them.

Among nations and religious groups, too, bad characters show themselves fanatic nationalists and extremely religious, of course, outwardly. The same evil can be seen in all the political parties. Evil characters make themselves most conspicuous by denouncing other parties.

The only hope lies in world consciousness. Arise and Unite, Yes, world workers everywhere! Now or never is written on the wall of destiny. Not a day is to be lost.

My Story : I, my daughter, grand-daughter and grandson are at the Bhakti Bhawan, Mussoorie on the first of June. Grandson returned to our Himalayan home at Rajpur, fifteen miles down the hill. We mean to stay here till rains set in and make Rajpur cool. Then we also go down to our Pratap Kothi or Pratap House, at Rajpur which is six miles up from Dehradun. It is called Doon Valley.

On the 18th June, I inaugurated a grand cycle feat. The rider, Shri Babu Ram, rides the cycle day and night, twenty four hours, without sleeping, eating and attending to natural call on the cycle.

It became cloudy and foggy and rain also started from the 25th June. I caught cold and was not well for a couple of days. Visitors started leaving the hill station. Dr. Mohan Singh came to see me and showed me too much respect. He told me that he received messages from highly advanced souls and he could transmit thoughts thousands of miles away. Sardar Amar Singh Khalsa visited me and related how he met me at Kabul, he was disguised as a Muslim. He is a prominent leader of the Sikhs. Swami Satya Bhakt met on the road. He has very similar ideas of the unity of religions. He later came to see me. He is an author of numerous books. Two Nepali noble men took me to see another Swami, far up Landhour hill. He related his experience of deep meditation. I told him that my Mission was to liberate man from the slavery of thought. All religions, all parties and all philosophies are only thoughts. They have captured human mind.

Prosecution or Persecution : On this last 20th September I was summoned to the court at Dehradun and asked questions about a small piece of land. It was alleged that I had forcibly taken its possession.

I told the court that my advocate informed me that the Police Superintendent had ordered the Sub-Inspector of police, he would send two police constables and give me the possession of the land. Police was not under me. If the police gave possession, the police should be asked, not me.

I added that at the age of twenty two I gave away five villages with the net income of rupees twenty seven thousand per year to found a school and a college. I left all my land, property and family in 1914, at the age of 28, to free India, this little piece of land could not have any value for me.

Legally it belongs to my grandson and not to me. Both the Lok Sabha and the Rajya Sabha praised me but did not give back my estate to me, confiscated by the British in 1916.

I may give the background of this prosecution to my readers to better understand it. Several years back an old man come to me. He said that being a refugee of Punjab, he was a very poor man and needed a job. I appointed him as a clerk in my office. He asked me to write to Mr. Khanna, the Minister, that he might receive some money for his claims, for property left in Pakistan. I wrote to the Minister who kindly immediately sent him one thousand rupees.

This clerk without my permission allowed one neighbour to plough and sow a piece of land of one of our houses at Dehradun.

All this trouble is about this piece of land. A court at Dehradun ordered my prosecution. My advocate appealed. Now Justice Broome, the only Englishman left in the service of the Allahabad High Court, ordered that prosecution should be carried out. He also refused permission to appeal to the Supreme Court of India. My friends think that it is not prosecution but persecution.

Another Persecution : Believe it or not, just when I had finished the last paragraph a postman handed me a registered letter from Japan from Mr. Sheth. He threatens Prosecution.

It is very strange that he on one hand, calls World Federation Centre in Japan a public institution and on the other hand, he wants to prosecute me for returning money, he says which he gave to the institution.

I have not sold the property. I do not mean to sell it. Legally it belongs to me. I keep this legal ownership to safeguard it from anybody's usurpation. When the World Federation Centre Committee is legally registered I shall, of course, transfer legal ownership to it. If Mr. Sheth accepted my request to act as General Secretary it does not mean that I asked him to act for life.

My friends who also kindly agreed at my request to act as president and other office-bearers found Mr. Sheth extremely opposed to co-operative action. He wanted to act as absolute dictator. Under these conditions I had to request Mr. Dhana Singh to act as General Secretary. He kindly agreed.

I want Mr. Sheth to reflect. He should ask pardon of God for being obstructive in the repairs of the Centre and Count Sakai, Mr. Imazato, Mr. Dhana Singh, Mr. Nanjo, Mr. Kinoshita, Mr. Nakatani, Miss. Futami and Mr. Takeda who are all honourable persons, let them repair the Centre if they do.

Why give me bad names, why threaten to prosecute me? My friends will surely say that it was perhaps a design to stop me from coming to Japan.

I consider Tenno Heika the rightful, all powerful and spiritual ruler of Japan. If I come to Dai Nippon, I shall come to His Imperial Majesty's land of the rising sun.

Letter : Most heartily I thank our Hon'ble Prime Minister Pandit Jawaharlal Nehruji for sending me this valuable opinion: 'I have read through your Primer of the new Science of Thought. With much that is in it, I agree. With some parts, I do not agree. Any how it was good of you to send this to me.'

I received the following letter from H. R. H. Maharajadhiraj of Sikkim :

My dear Raja Sahib,

Thank you for your letter of January 8th, 1964. We are conscious of how you have devoted your life to the cause of better understanding among people and the extensive travel you have undertaken for this aim. We are, however, a small country and our funds are fully committed. However we have established certain institutions for the dissemination of knowledge and research of the great thoughts and philosophy that went from India to Tibet. I refer in particular our Namgyal Institute of Tibetology, Dr. Nirmal Sinha, perhaps we could arrange for you to give us a talk or two. The audience will be small but earnest. This Institute would look after your needs in Gangtok.

With best wishes.

Yours

(Signature) The Denjong Chogyal

Death of Thakur Jhamman Singh : He was an advocate at Aligarh. He was my legal adviser. He was a faithful follower of the Religion of Love. He, at the same time, had great respect for Vedas. He sent me a translation of a couple of Mantras. He passed away on the 13th of October 1963. I express deep sympathy with his family.

Shame ! Shame ! : I was shocked to hear this news. The socalled patriots broke the statue of Lord Irvin ! If they had shot him dead when he ruled the country I could have called it patriotism but today it is an act of cowardice.

I fought against the British empire for over three decades but I can not kick a dead body.

If these patriots who oppose the English language would oppose the Commonwealth I must support them. No clogs can be tolerate in all world order.

These quarrels, shouting and opposition in the law making bodies to break the law where laws are made, must be condemned as vandalism.

Sheikh Abdullah

I welcome. We welcome. It as a landmark along the path of progress of our country. He has been released after the hard trial of ten years. Conspiracy case was brought against him by the Kashmir Government. A few millions of rupees were spent on the trial. And now the cases against him and his colleagues have been withdrawn by the present government of Kashmir.

Such is the world. Many strange things happen in this world. We see men ascending the thrones and next we see them running away or arrested and beheaded !

All is well which ends well. We are glad that after all sense prevailed. Foolish and mischievous charges have been withdrawn. I always stood with Sheikh Abdullah, in my opinion he was an honest servant of his people and home land.

I well remember that day. I was still a member of the Congress party. Meeting was held at Delhi. I entered when session was in full swing. I recognized Mr. Purushottam Dass Tandon on the platfrom. I went up and sat with him. Sheikh Abdullah and the late Pandit Pant were near us. I asked the Sheikh Sahib to carry out my plan about Kashmir. He said, he agreed but ask him and pointed to Pandit Jawahar Lal Nehru. He was addressing the meeting and his back was on our side. Bakhshi Ghulam Mohammed who was standing came too near us hearing our enlivened talk.

At the end of this meeting when Pandit Nehru ji came to us he told me in Urdu: 'You are writing, as if Nehru is dead. Congress will not allow him to die.....' I was, in those days, supporting Mr. Tandon, he was the president but Mr. Nehru deposed him.

The Government of Mr. Nehru got Sheikh Sahib arrested for indulging in 'Conspiracy' against India.

Now what? Who is to be blamed? Can any compensation on earth make good the suffering of ten long years behind the Bar ? I was put behind the bar, as a war criminal, by the American army in Japan. Five months were sufficient to find me innocent. Here it took over ten years to release the leader of Kashmir, beloved of the people, Sheikh Sahib.

Just during these days, I am writing these lines on the 9th April 1964, discussion is going on between the Home Ministers of Delhi and Rawalpindi. They are talking about ways and means to stop murders of the innocent people in Pakistan and in India. How best to stop destruction in the names of race and religion, is the burning question of the day. As much more they talk so much more they confuse the issue.

Sheikh Abdullah can best solve this complicated problem. He can carry through my programme regarding Kashmir, Aryan and Asia.

'Ask him', asks Pandit Jawaharlal Nehru Sahib, the same situation remains. Mr. Nehru has invited Sheikh to Delhi. Mr. Abdullah has accepted the invitation. Let us hope for the best.

Nehru Passed Away

This is heartbreaking news. Pt. Nehru passed away. I pay hearty condolence at the demise of the Hon'ble Pandit Jawaharlal Nehru, the late Prime Minister who led India the present stage of independence during the last seventeen years. I pray for his soul and present best sincere sympathy to his family members.

Our Hon'ble President, Rashtrapati Pandit Radha Krishnan ji writes :

My dear Raja Mahendra Pratap,

Thank you for the message of condolence which you have so kindly sent on the tragic passing away of Shri Jawaharlal Nehru.

Yours sincerely
S. Radhakrishnan

Shrimati Indira Gandhi, also cared to thank me for the sympathy I expressed at her great sorrow, at this bolt from heaven. I opposed the policy of the late Prime Minister but I wept when the Radio confirmed the news of his death.

Letter from the Prime Minister, the Hon'ble Pt. Lal Bahadur Shastri wrote :

My dear Raja Saheb,

In the present day conditions when the parties have basic differences in the approach to the various political and economic problems, they may not find it easy to work together. I am not opposed to united action. However, in a democracy, there is a place for party system. It is at the same time essential that all parties should preserve certain standards. If we understand this and work accordingly, both the Government and the opposition can serve the interests of the country very well indeed.

Yours sincerely
Lal Bahadur

They Want Me, President

Once when Maharao Krishna Pal Singh M. P. told two other members of the Indian Parliament that Raja Mahendra Pratap should be a member of the Rajya Sabha, the upper house, Mr. Yajee M. P. and Mr. Paliwal M. P. a former Minister of Rajasthan, said 'No ! We must try to get him elected as the President.'

I took it as a big joke because I knew that inspite of their goodwill for me it was beyond their power to get me elected as the President when I was no longer a member of the Congress Party.

I have no ambition. I am now 78 years old. I was the first President of the Indian Government abroad. The second President of Azad Hind Government, our government in foreign countries, was the famous Netaji, Babu Subhash Chandra Bose. We both did what we could to liberate the country with foreign help. What more honour I need !

I am also the founder of the Religion of Love and World Federation. I preach Unity of Religions and work to hasten a world government. There can not be any man than to be the founder of a new Religion for the salvation of mankind. So why to be elected as the President of India?

Letters : Shrimati Indira Gandhi ji writes :

Dear Raja Mahendra Pratap ji,

Thank you for your letter and for giving Rs. 5000/- to the Nehru Memorial Fund. I have been deeply touched by the many tributes paid to my father by people of all sections from all over the world.

With regards.

Yours sincerely
Indira Gandhi

I did nothing thank for. I just paid my offering to my friend whom I loved but always differed with his political and religious views.

There are several more letters deserving honourable mention but I am unable to quote them as I am very busy with the preparation of my grand daughter's marriage on this 1st of May. Reception is on the 2nd May when three hundred guests are expected.

Hon. President, Rashtrapati who always acknowledge the receipt of World Federation circular, kindly writes :

My dear Raja Mahendra Ptatap ji,

Thank you for your kind letter of the 20th of April 1965. I am glad to know that your grand-daughter is getting married on the 1st of May. My best wishes to the couple for a happy home life.

With the best wishes,

Yours sincerely
S. Radha Krishnan

He also kindly sent me a copy of his Geeta. He took great pain to edit this famous book. In Roman script he has given the text and English translation, with full of wisdom comments. I am very thankful for this precious gift and his loving message. He is a great supporter of World Unity. He has been always extending moral support to me in this work of World Federation.

The Marriage of my Grand Daughter : 1st, 2nd and 3rd of May, 1965 were the days of great joy, delight, festivities and feverish activity in Pratap Kothi, Rajpur (Dehradun) as Kumari Sarla Pratap, grand daughter of Raja Mahendra Pratap was given in marriage to Kunwar Rajendra Singh ji, son of Rai Bahadur Sardar Singh ji. Landlord and Rais of Moradabad.

Pakistan Attacked India

After a handful of skirmishes in June-July, on 5th August about 30,000 Pakistani soldiers crossed the Line of Control and attacked Kashmir. Indian Miltary resisted and tipped off by the local populace crossed the cease-fire line on 15th August. On 1st September Pakistan launched attack to capture Akhnur town in Jammu, which would sever communications and cut off supplies routes to Indian troops. Attacking with tanks Pakistan made gains against Indian forces, who were caught unprepared and suffered heavy losses. India responded by calling in its airforce to blunt the Pakistan attack. Next day Pakistan retaliated, its airforce attacked Indian forces and air bases in both Kashmir and Punjab. India decided to open up the theatre of attack into Pakistan Punjab. Pakistani army remained unable to capture Akhnoor.

On 6th September India crossed the International border on the Western front, marking the official beginning of the war. The 15th infantry Division of Indian Army battled a massive counter attack near the west bank of Ichhogil canal, which was the defacto border of India and Pakistan. Indian troops crossed Ichhogil near the village of Barki, just east of Lahore. Pakistan took Khemkaran from Indian forces, Pakistan attacked by Air Force Jets on Indian infantry, as well as on civil area, hit a railway train coming from Barmer with reinforcements near Gadra railway station. India destroyed about 97 Pakistani Patton and Sherman tanks at Khemkaran and nearly 100 at Chawinda. The war was heading for a stalemate with both countries holding territory of the other. We suffered 3,000 battlefield deaths while Pakistan suffered 3,800. By 22nd September both side agreed to a U.N. mandated cease-fire.

Ceasefire between India and Pakistan : Exactly. It is ceasefire. No more. It is neither peace nor truce. Hearts are on fire. Minds are burning. Blood is boiling. It is a temporary patch up.

We remain where we were at the start of the hot war. Thousands of soldiers died, Indians and Pakistani. People died of air bombing. Houses have been destroyed on both the sides. What for? Both said that Kashmir was their personal property.

Poor Kashmir, people of Kashmir suffered most. Poor Punjab, Punjabies were killed in the struggle of the two. Pakhtoon and Rajputana were not spared. Lord Krishna's Dwarka was bombarded. Frontier of Bengal got blood bath, too. Blackout made nights miserable.

And now when our government agreed to ceasefire there are some shouting leaders who oppose the ceasefire. They do not realise that not one country in the world showed any sympathy with India. China and Indonesia openly supported Pakistan. Iran and Turkey sided with it.

I openly blame our government for this situation in the diplomatic field. China repeatedly requested us to have round-table conference for last five years. Hon'ble late Pandit Nehru insisted that China first must agree to the proposal of Ceylon group. Hon'ble Mr. Shastri never seriously tried to make peace with China.

For over one year our relations were deteriorating with Indonesia. For last two years Pakistan was coming closer and closer to Iran and Turkey but India took no steps to improve friendly relations. India with its vast resources can easily make better economic conditions of the country which need new industries.

I always offered my services to Indian Government to bring peace with China and Pakistan but they never paid any attention to my suggestions.

During the long centuries of the Muslim and British rule in India passion of love and hatred have been developed among the different sections of the people. Selfish and short sighted leader to collect their following play upon wrong love and wrong hatred.

I seek not immediate gain. I am doing my God given duty. Jesus Christ preferred crucification than the leadership of the Jews. I prefer to die unsung than get some official honour by joining thir chorus of war and hatred.

Lal Bahadur Shastri Passed Away 11th January 66 :

We mourn for demise of Mr. Lal Bahadur Shastri. He did not say what I wanted him to say but he acted as I wanted him to act. His talks on Kashmir that he would never discuss Kashmir and then his agreeing to consider the question of Kashmir peacefully gave him a shock which killed him.

The air is thick with all kinds of conjectures: Who will be the prime minister? To me it is immaterial whether A rules or B rules. When I had written so far I heard the radio news that most of the Chief Ministers favour Shrimati Indira Gandhi.

When I heard the news that the President had appointed Shri Nanda, I wired to the President 'Glad for peace, Sorry for demise. Wish Shri Nanda success.' And I wired to Shri Nanda: 'Congratulations. Wish success in keeping peace.' Just now the radio announced that Shrimati Indira Gandhi will be our new Prme Minister. I wired her-Congratulations.

The radio also announced just now that the army had taken over the government in Nigeria and that the Prime Minister was arrested. The other day he presided at the conference of Commonwealth, today he is under arrest. Such is the fate of passing phantoms in this ever changing world.

Letters : H.E. the Governor of U.P. writes from Lucknow :

My dear Raja Sahib,

I acknowledge your letter of 28th January with thanks. It is always a pleasure and a privilege to address a conference of the type you have mentioned and invited me to inaugurate. Unfortunately I am busy with certain other programmes. I propose to visit Dehra Dun about the month of May and will be glad to spend some time with you then. Hoping this finds you hale, healthy and active, I remain,

Yours sincerely
Biswanath Das

Account of Tour : Left Delhi in the night of the 20th April 1966. I was accompanied by my secretary Mr. Akbar Khan and a servant. Arrived in the early morning at five on the 22nd. Many friends received me at Dadar, Bombay at that early hour. I was taken by cars to Khursil Naz where I stayed three days as a guest of Mr. S. C. Singh.

I visited Mr. Ismail at the Consulate General of the Dominican Republic. In the evening I addressed a fine group of persons at Tilak Mandir of Vile Parle. Here this Institute is doing great Social Service.

24th April, Mr. Ismail took me out to Nhava island, It was a big picnic party, vice Consul of Germany and the owner of island together with many notable friends were present. Naval School honoured Mr. Ismail. In the afternoon a tea party was given at Khursil Naz. In the evening I spoke at the same Arya Samaj which was founded by Swami Dayanand in 1875. From here Arya Samaj spread through out the Country and abroad.

On the 25th, Mr. Thakkar took me to the railway station. This time I was the guest of Mr. Kabali at his residence at Lonavla. On the 26th I was received by Major Dr. Chauhan and friends at Pimpri. The host was Mr. Moorjani. Rich lunch was served. At. 6 p.m. a selected group of friends gathered to hear me. Later a large public meeting was held. On both these occasions I delivered long speeches. At night dinner was given by Mr. Mullru, a devoted worker.

On the 27th, Pimpri town was visited. It is a pity that sanitary arrangements in the town are in deplorable condition. At Poona in the Mira Hall I delivered a long lecture. It is the institution founded by Sadhu T.L. Baswani. Reception was very friendly and enthusiastic. I returned to Pimpri and passed there this night.

On the 28th, I visited Carve Institute. The youngest son of Maharishi showed it round. Next day I visited Vidyarthi Graha. Here friends were very much interested in my views. I visited Kesari office where friends garlanded me and showed me my signature of 1948. I spoke on Poona Herald office and Sindhi Panchayat and at night I delivered a speech at Poona University Staff Club. This night I was the guest of Mr. Atur Samgatani, a very prominent pushing business man.

On 29th I spoke at a public meeting at Dehu, Poona. I also spoke at the mosque, Buddha Vihar and Gurudwara. In the evening I attended the party of R.S.S., Pimpri. Here I also spoke. At night I was the guest of Seth B. Narain Das. On the 30th Seth Sahib gave me a purse and bought tickets from Poona to Bombay. I was received at Bombay by Mr. Kabali, Mr. Thakkar and Mr. Pillai. I also visited Shrimati Shila Azad. In the evening I was seen off by Mr. Thakkar, Mr. S.C. Singh and family.

On the 1st of May it was very touching scene founding my identity a military officer touched my feet and said that his fellow officers highly honoured me. At Badnera I was received by the representatives of Literary Conference and taken by car to Amravati. I took lunch with Mr. Humaun Kabir, a former minister of the Central Government. At night I presided at the Literary Conference, organized by the well-known advocate and leader Mr. Jodh.

On the 2nd May 1966 I took train once again changing at Wardha reached on the 3rd May morning Agra. Joined Sahanpur Barat and attended the marriage party of Rajkumari of Mursan, sister of Raja Gopal Prasad Singh Bahadur.

I Suggest : July 1966. I suggest that the leaders of the different parties meet at 2 p.m. at South Avenue M. P.'s Club on Sunday the 28th August, i.e. next month.

Let us decide on a common plan for the coming elections. I propose that we divide India among all the parties minus the ruling party. This division should be made according to the strength of the members. If the leaders honestly want to depose the rulers then this is the only way leading to sure success. In this case there will be only one person to oppose the congress candidate. We can allot some places to some independent candidates to avoid a triangular contest. We shall also decide at this meeting who and who will form government when we succeed at the polls. A regular shadow cabinet will be formed. We must include Acharya J.B. Kripalani, Professor N.G. Ranga and Mr. Sripad Amrit Dange in our cabinet.

I think, we should not entirely disappoint persons of integrity whom circumstances have brought into the ruling party. We can appoint for instance as ambassadors Messrs Kamraj, S.K. Patil and Y.B. Chavan, and such, others can be sent abroad on important posts.

Mr. Namboodiripad can best serve India in China. Dr. Syed Mahmood can go to Ankara. General Shahnawaz can help us at Teheran. It is not a complete list. It is only a roadway post to show the way.

We shall bring Swaraj or Home rule to every village. Local laws will be made by local people. There will be indirect election and election will be by common consent. Villages will form District Council. Districts and towns will form Provincial government. Provinces will send representatives to form Central government.

I think that only fifty persons at the Centre are sufficient to run the country. Today administration is very expensive.

My Diary : 21 August 1966. I am on tour. I left Rajpur on the 13th of August. Two days I stayed at New Delhi. I had a talk with Dr. Ram Manohar Lohia. I attended Sunday meeting of Diwan Shimbhu Nath Chopra Ji, Editor of 'Swaraj', Delhi.

I presided at the Executive Committee of All India Jat Maha Sabha at Mathura. I stayed, as usual, at Prem Maha Vidyalaya, Vrindaban, founded by me in 1909.

On 26th August, afternoon I invited some friends and gave a tea party at the Wengers Restaurant. Maharao Krishnpal Singh M.P., Pandit Sunderlal and friends were present. Mr. B.P. Maurya M.P. and Kunwar Yashpal Singh M.P. called on me. It was decided that every effort should be made to avoid triangular contest in elections.

I also visited Shri Anand Swami and had a talk with Jan Sangh leader, Mr. Balraj Madhok.

Election Campaign

My friends decided that I should contest Lok Sabha Election. Therefore my well wishers printed this appeal :

Dear friends ! The beginning of next year will bring a new test for our country as we are facing horrible dissatisfaction in our society. Strikes, lathi-charges by police, murders etc. are the common themes of this day. Members in assemblies and parliament fight like bulls and rams. General public is frustrated. Disruption in society rules supreme. Oppressed masses feel helpless to face the corrupt government. Government feels pleasure in crushing the interests of people. Present rule is utter failure in maintaining peace and order. Our neighbour countries are at daggers drawn with us.

Let us think with cool minds and try to amend matters in time. As citizens of this country it is our sacred duty to find out ways and means for permanent peace here and abroad.

The only remedy is to elect honest, sincere, and right persons for legislatures. We must bow before better qualified persons and help them in elections. It will end the corrupt rule of India. A handful of persons led by narrow selfish thoughts of party-love and self interest dominate the government and misuse their power for selfish ends. Let us end this state of affairs and establish a moral government consisting of all the honest persons of our land.

Appeal to Mr. Mao (October 1966) : I wrote a letter to chairman Mao of China : You are not realising what you are unconsciously doing. You are degrading the Celestial land, destroying its glory and blunting the high sense of humanity of your great ancient people.

China gave birth to the great philosopher Kung Futzu. China embraced holy Buddhism. It shows the high standard of development of the Chinese people.

Tiger eats raw flesh. Cow eats grass. Man likes to drink milk or drinks tea. Men of animal nature like war. Man of divine nature like live happy peaceful life.

In the same year 1925 I and Chinese Vice Chairman Madam Sun lectured from the same platfrom at Peking against the atrocities of the British Police at Shanghai.

Now in India I have been heralding that China and India must be friends. Indian leaders to please US rulers are not shaking hands with you.

So far as this socalled cultural revolution by the red guards goes against luxuries has a divine impulse but cruelty, disregard for fellow men and fanaticism are the work of devil himself you are untaken in lauding them.

In Russia and USA there are many true friends of China and humanity. Poor Mr. Johnson does not know why he is working as an agent of devil. Poisonous thoughts have entered the head of Johnson.

Mankind stands at a cross road. One leads to destruction. The other leads to unimaginable progress. Man can colonise planets.

I appeal to you to discard all those thoughts which create friction. I have discovered a New Science of Thought. I show how to clean the minds of all the friction thoughts and how to establish happy world peace.

Religions should fight evil and promote goodness. World State with world army and world court of Justice should be established. All should work for all to make all happy.

General Information : November 1966. The political situation within our country is worsening day by day. Mr. Kamraj, Congress President ran away from his house and our Prime Minister saw danger to democracy when cow protection rally was held in New Delhi on 7th November. This shows the weakness of our Government to control the matters. Several other unwanted things are happening. Every true citizen of India is shocked to see unrest all over the country. A very strong All-Party Government at the centre is needed very soon to save the country and its freedom.

Realising this I am contesting next general election from Aligarh general constituency. I aim at establishing a very strong government at the Centre and to give home rule to every village and town.

Now-a-days I live at 51, Mitra Nagar (Near Raghuvirpuri), Aligarh. My election campaign office is the same building.

Friends are organizing tours and meetings for me. It is the duty of very right citizen living in my constituency to help me in winning in the General election. It will save the country from further catastrophe.

This Election System : It is a wonder of wonders. How and who invented this system of elections? And how the most advanced nations with the best brains, yet developed in our human race, adopted and continued this system? It appears, they realized that it is the best system to keep the masses satisfied.

I think that the masses were deceived and the intellectuals deceived themselves. They did not realise that it is great waste of time and energy. In this system evil easily comes up and gets leadership. Best and honest intellectuals have no chance to get their right places.

Any one comes up, advertises himself and if he has money enough he has every chance to get elected. And if he is elected he gets a good salary. People get nothing. People even lose their liberty. These elected persons make laws. I should say, make chains to bind the people.

They say, it is democracy. It is the government by the people. We also heard of the dictatorship of the workers. But what we see in the so called capitalist and communist countries? Intellect with some qualities of attracting people and of deceiving people rules.

I want peoples of India, Russia, China and America know that they are in all cases treated as beasts of burden. Yes, some kind masters give better food to their horses and cattle. Some rulers give more conveniences to their subjects.

Power of propaganda is wellknown to the rulers and business men but the masses who are deceived do not realise that they are deceived by the power of propaganda. They do not know that a lie uttered one hundred times is taken as truth.

I am sorry to admit that in religion, clever religious leaders have written false stories to impress the masses about the vast powers of their incarnations or prophets. It is the weakness of human nature that once a man begins to believe something as absolute truth, he argues and discusses with great vehemence and comes to blow in many cases.

In case of parties we see the same phenomenon. Cleverness produces such convincing arguments that people get deceived and begin to follow some leaders.

In heat of election people are swayed this way or that way by power of speeches, propaganda and money. It is my duty to expose these facts.

I am contesting in these elections to end this system of election. I may not succeed immediately but succeed I must. Sixty or sixty five years back when I spoke of making India free my elders thought to think of freedom was utopean. But this freedom come. As I am still alive and healthy I want to enter the fortress of this system of government and try my best to break it up from within.

Under the present circumstances when leaders and the masses are equally slaves of these ideas, elections and this parliamentary system, for us there is no other way. We are not taken seriously if we remain outside. During five years when I was in the parliament my voice echoed and reechoed through out the country. This I want to repeat.

I Am Defeated Again

Feb. 1967. I have been defeated at the polls. There is, however, another way to get justice. The opponent used very unfair means to misguide the voters. He called me Musalman before the Hindus. He said I wanted to give away Hindu girls in marriage to Musalmans. And gave me some names.

Musalmans are also our countrymen. They have as much right to get elected as the Hindus. If Musalmans will call me Musalman I shall be very glad. But calling me Musalman to influence the Hindus against me is a crime in the eyes of the law. It is raising communal feelings. It is creating strife in society. I mean to file petition on this ground in a court.

Let me speak my mind now. Once the matter goes to the court my mouth will be shut. Writing about the case becomes contempt of the court.

Poor Judges can not always do Justice. They are obliged to follow the letter of the law. Knowing the facts they can not follow the known truth. They must accept the truth as proved by clever lawyers. I say, therefore, that generally money and the head of a clever lawyer win.

Speeches delivered before thousands of people are no secrets. Thousands of persons can say on oath that I was called Musalman by the opponent and his friends and supporters.

Thousands of men can equally say on oath that the voters were brought by trucks and rickshaws and carts. Such facts widely known still need proofs as law requires. In any case, I refused to get voters brought by my agents.

This system of election in very wrong. Poor persons cleaning the streets, or peasants of the villages hardly know anything about international politics. It is, as if the school children are given the task to examine the graduates.

Should I be President of India : Some friends suggest that I try to get elected as the President of India. They say that Mr. A.P. Jain, who was defeated at the polls, was appointed Governor of Kerala. There is no reason, they insist, that I do not try. The election of the President, I am told, will be held in next May.

When I am the founder of Religion of Love and World Federation I do not need any more honour but to further the cause of unity of religions and Word Government it will be helpful if I become the president of India.

It is not, however, for me to try. It is for the leaders and members of the parties to decide. I do not belong to any party. I have my own views about administration. I want people to rule.

To me they are all fine phrases that 'people's government for the people' or 'proletarian dictatorship'. In all cases some clever heads rule. In religions also clever heads built their big followings.

I only want that cleverness is coupled with honesty and not with cunningness. People should insist on honesty. They should not be misled by fine faces, speeches and castles in the air dreams.

Poor people, simple people and ignorant people have to be liberated from the clutches of selfish leader. Do not form parties. Do not join parties. Selfish people form or join parties. Natural groups of families should work for common welfare. In all cases a village, a town or parts of big cities should develop home rule.

We should study Laws of Nature and nature of Man. We should realise the duty of individuals.

Creator or laws of creation having developed mankind on this earth work for preservation and continuation of our human race. We should learn to distinguish between the laws governing the universe and thoughts and wishes coming out of narrow human mind, selfish tendencies and ignorance.

Confusion is born of ignorance and of the desires of the flesh. Sages taught us long how to control our wrong desires and how to organize society and carry on our government but the history is our witness. Evil continued and wars devastated cities and killed multi-million of people on this earth. War in Vietnam continues.

Not filing Petition : Last time, I filed petition to get justice. But now as my young grand daughter only twenty four years old lost her husband, I am not in a mood to go to the court.

Poor grand son-in-law, Kunwar Rajendra Singh committed suicide by on 6th March, taking overdose of sleeping capsules. What a pity. His family is rich. His eldest brother was married to a sister of H. H. Maharaja Sahib of Bharatpur, who in the last general elections defeated a Union Minister by ninety five thousand votes. He was happy with his charming wife. Some thing about property upset him.

Kr. Rajendra Singh, wrote to me on the 1st March, 'We were shocked to hear the result of your election. I am sure there is some mischief somewhere. The report we got from Aligarh was from a reliable man and so we were confident about your victory. My brother-in-law defeated Health Minister by over thirteen thousand votes.......' It was his last letter. I hope his family and my young grand daughter will submissively bow to the Will of God. He who gives us birth has every right to take us back at His sweet Will.

Letters : Hon'ble President, Rashtrapati Dr. Zakir Hussain kindly write :

Dear Raja Mahendra Pratap ji,

I write this to thank you for your letter of the 11th instant..............in regard to your suggestion to start a class for parliamentarians, I am afraid, I don't find myself in a position to do so. This seems to me the rightful domain of religious and moral preceptors like you.

With my warm regards,

Yours sincerely
Zakir Hussain

I am very thankful for the message. He kindly kept up the tradition of the Hon'ble Pt. Radhakrishnan who for years kindly sent, practically every month, his good will for my work. Now he is retired but still he writes : 'I have read your latest issue, as usual your interest in world unity is unabated.'

I had written him and I repeat people who glibly talk of abolishing privy purses do not realise that in our army Rajputs, Jats, Marathas and Gorkhas have real power. And among princes Rajputs, Jats, Marathas and Pathans rule supreme. If the army will get the idea that their princes are being ruined, unity of the Indian nation will be shattered.

Our Defence Minister is a Jat and Sikh, I hope he will bring my views to the notice of his colleagues. I am very thankful for his answer.

H. H. Maharaja Sahib of Baroda who is a congressman and a minister in Gujrat cabinet writes :

My dear Raja Sahib,

Thank you very much for your letter of June 27. I certainly remember you very well and have happy memories of our association in the Lok Sabha. I have made a note of your comments and we will have to see what happens now.

With personal regards.

Yours sincerely
Fatehsinhrao Gaekwad

H. H. Bikaner, Maharaja Karni Singh M.P. writes :

My dear Raja Mahendra Pratap ji,

I have received a copy of your letter dated the 6th July to Sardar Swaran Singh ji on the subject to abolition of privy purses and wish to thank you for the kind sentiments expressed there in. With regards......'

He also sent me a copy of the note he prepared on the subject of privy purses. I thank H. H.

My Tour : I left by my Jeep on the 11th of August and returned Dehradun on 27th of August. I visited Aligarh, Hathras, Mathura, Vrindaban and Delhi. I stayed four days at Aligarh, one night at Hathras, six days at Vrindaban and five days at Delhi.

News : October 1967. My Grandson Kunwar Amar Pratap Singh was married first according to Civil Marriage Act with Kumari Balbir Kaur B. A., later according to the Religion of Love.

Letter : Sheikh Abdullah c/o Deputy Commissioner, Delhi, writes :

My dear Raja Sahib,

May peace of Allah be upon you. I have always considered it a privilege to fight for the cause of justice and the cause of the oppressed. As Gita says: "Action alone is the province, never the fruits there of." In the second letter he writes, 'I have been transferred from hospital to a bungalow on the Kotla Lane. My previous restrictions, however, continue. My health is good and I am carrying on as best as the circumstance permit. I hope you are doing well. Please accept feelings of my highest regard.

Yours sincerely
S. Abdullah

My Film : I do not see cinema shows but all of a sudden I have become a film Star. Mr. Yavar Abbas of 'India My India' fame started last year to make a film of my election, an election where I failed. I do not mind failure. I succeeded in showing the hollowness of this election system. Qualities or service to humanity are not respected. Ignorant masses are influenced by big lies, propaganda, money and connections. Sentiments carry them away. My opponent went to Delhi, did Satyagrah for cow protection and was jailed for fifteen days. On his return to Aligarh he was carried in a big procession. He become a great hero overnight. Fanatic Hindus supported him. A Congress millionaire Muslim bought Muslim votes. I was defeated. Congress candidate got much less votes than me.

Now Mr. Abbas, founder of Face Film Co. affiliated to CAP organization of London sent a car with a very good driver on the 5th late at night.

6th April. I left by the film car. I took two servants with me. In four hours and fifteen minutes covered hundred fifty miles. I met Pandit Sunderlal and in another two hours and a quarter reached Prem Maha Vidyalaya Vrindaban. Next day in another car Mr. Abbas arrived with Madam Wordsworth, Mr. Langley, film expert, and secretaries. I was filmed walking along the Jamuna river.

8th April. I took lunch at Delhi with film friends and arrived in the evening at my residence at Dehradun. Credit goes to the driver for quick and comfortable journey.

Late at night on the 9th film party arrived. At midnight they took supper. I took them to Rajpur where are our guest rooms.

10th. In the afternoon was the main shooting. At Love Center a meeting was called. Friends came. Tape recorder was taken when I initiated Mr. Narang into the Religion of love. Gathering was also filmed. Next day I brought documents from my bank locker. They were filmed and shooting went on the afternoon. My would be grave with grey stones were filmed.

12th. Mrs. Wordsworth, Mr. Langley and companions took me to Haridwar. My photos were taken on the road. I inaugurated the function of the Kanya Gurukul, Girls School. Next day I inaugurated the building of Jat Dharm Shala. Here lot of shooting was made. I was brought back to Dehradun. Mr. Abbas had left for Chandigarh.

My Tour : I made a tour of twenty two days. I left Dehradun in the morning of the 1st of August and returned to Dehradun late at night on the 22nd August 1968.

At Aligarh I had to attend to some business of the Hathras Raj. It was a pleasure to have a rich lunch with the Khwaja family. Prof. Jamal Khwaja who appreciates my ideas can spread my views in the Muslim University. It is a shame that the students struggle and fight in the elections of the office bearers of the Students' Union.

Letters : Hon. Prime Minister, Lady Indira Gandhi :

Dear Raja Sahib,

Thank you for your letter of August 11. It is good to see that you are as tirelessly active as ever. I should very much have liked to have a long discussion with you but I have many Independence Day commitments tomorrow (15th August), and I am going to Gujarat on Friday (16th) to visit the flood affected areas there. I hope you will forgive me. With all good wishes,

Yours sincerely
Indira Gandhi

Mr. Mitrokhin of USSR Embassy came to Dehradun on the 3rd Sept., and took my interview again record for Moscow Radio.

Mr. Yavar Abbas and Mrs. Wordsworth of a London film company visited Dehradun on the 7th Sept. for only four hours to take my more pictures whose coloured documentary film they have been shooting for one year with gaps in the middle.

Pandit Sudarshan Chakra and his son both poets, arrived at Dehradun on the 18th Sept. to write a long poem in Hindi depicting my life. They are to stay some days with us.

My Education System

I went to Aligarh to support Shrimati Gayatridevi, wife of the BKD leader Chaudhry Charan Singh in election. I spoke at Iglas and Gorai. After me Ch. Kumbharam Arya M.P. spoke at length. People were very impressed.

I also spoke at Hathras, at Upper Court I presided. After midnight I could come to my residence at Aligarh. Next morning I cought cold and cough. I am still ill to this day the 5th of Feb. 69.

I spoke at Hathras. I had earlier supported Ch. Digamber Singh in three large meetings in Mathura. Illness could not hinder me. I went to Delhi. Stayed as guest of Lajpat Bhatia. Received Dr. Von Hentig and family at Palam Airport.

Dr. Von Hentig came to Vrindaban on the 1st Feb. He was shown round High School. Reception was given to him. Later he visited polytechnic. He went round workshop and class rooms. In the afternoon Ch. Dharam Singh gave him tea at his Mathura residence.

Taking breakfast at my residence in the boarding house we all saw him off. He went to Aligarh and Agra.

Jesus Christ : That son of a carpenter, whose mother was a jew lady, was the most honest communist. Rulers of Red Russia could not recognise him, misled by the gorgeous robes of the Christian priests. They denounced that Christianity which supported the degenerated Zar.

Jesus did not serve the roman empire. He denounced the traders who were trading before the Synagogue where he prayed. He was living with his disciples sharing equally meals and drinks. For communists he is the ideal to be followed. Western Europe and America are no longer true Christians. They fought battles killing fellow men. They who wage war or prepare for wars can not be called, should not be called Christians.

Elder brother of Jesus, more than five hundred years older, was Lord Buddha. Jesus followed him. Chinese, Korean and Mongolian Communists have discarded Buddha due to lack of knowledge of that great renouncer of wealth. Lives of some modern Buddhists were not according to his teachings. Buddhist temples hoarded wealth. Some priests began to live in pomp and in luxury.

Buddha taught Man receives reward or punishment according to his deeds. Buddhists and Christians were punished according to this Law.

Communist States have become more nationalistic. Race consciousness got the upper hand. For true communists there is no frontier. Communists cannot fight each other. Communists should be true Christians. They can never use Nuclear weapons. Atomic war may kill rulers of London, Paris or Washington but alongwith them multi million workers and peasants will perish.

Soldiers of all the countries, including those of France, England and United States come from the poorer families. Comrade Lenin said : 'Workers, Peasants and Soldiers unite. You have nothing to lose but your Chains.' How can than any communist State kill soldiers of any country.

They may be hired men, hired by the rich. But they are sons of poor people. Circumstances of life made them sell themselves for daily bread. They must not be killed. The rich people became richer in the game of gambling. It is not their fault that they became rich. It is the fault of the gambling system. Now we shall develop towns and villages into joint families. It can not be done, however, by force. Force develops rule of the rod. We shall develop it through my educational system.

My Education System

I make it very clear that if a man is born in Russia he will speak Russian. And if a man is born in China he will speak Chinese. If a man is born in a Christian family he becomes Christian. If a man is born in a Muslim family he becomes Musalman.

In the same manner if a man is given education and educated in a French school he will speak French.

If you will dip a white kerchief in red colour it will become red and if you dip white kerchief in black ink it will become black.It must be clear to every person that education colour man. Present condition of our world is simply due to the education given so far.

Every religious group and every national State educated their people in their own ways. 'Our religion is the best and our nation is superior to all other nations,' people were taught. Now communism has become a kind of religion to most communists. They guard their dogmas with the fanatic faith of a Catholic, Hindu or Muslim. You will often hear communists saying: 'It is a bourgeois thought.' 'He is reactionary.' Compare it with what a Musalman says: 'He is Kafar.' Christian will say: 'He is heathen.'

Thus they make airtight compartments. It has gone on through out the past ages.

I suggest that every school should study for three hours and work for five hours to produce daily necessities.Their minds should be daily cleaned of all the friction thoughts. They should know that all religions are different thoughts. Communism, socialism or nationalism are based on some other thoughts.

It should be clear, we do not want a nation to rule other nations. We do not want to impose any faith on our students. Nor we want to teach communism with its prophet Karl Marx or Lenin as its first Khalifa.

We shall, however, make students joint proprietors of all the school property when they grow up. It will be a commune without any dogma. Morality will rule the community.

Qualities will be respected. Five Qualities are beauty, strength, intellect, morality and enlightenment.Enlightenment will be respected most. Enlightenment sees the entire universe governed by the same Laws. It sees Man is given birth to serve the creation. All should work for all to make all happy. It knows that in the welfare of the entire human race is the best welfare of all nations and individuals.

Situation in India : Today 15 June 1969. Our Country's situation is not less alarming. Congress as a party got charge of the Indian Government formed the British Parliament. Leaders of the Congress formed the Government in 1946.

Twenty three years have passed by. Kerala, Bengal, Punjab and Tamil Nadu have non-Congress Governments. In Bihar is a coalition of the Congress and some other parties. At the centre majority of the Congress is greatly reduced.

Struggle is going on. There are parties which expect to form the Government at the Centre if not today, surely tomorrow.

Our leaders have learned this democracy from their British tutors. They are discarding the experience of their old civilization and culture. They have learned to hate their best due to some nasty experience of the political slavery.

Strikes, breaking of heads by the unruly mob, firing by the police, killing of fellowmen, destruction of public and private property are the treat news of every day.

Today is 19th of June. Only today's I give here some news. At New Delhi, one Shrinivasan was murdered last night. Police guard Gurdwara after clash. State Bank strike at one thousand branches. Three cheats were members of a gang operating in the walled city of Delhi. 164 arrests were made in Hyderabad and Secunderabad and many more arrests were made in some other district towns. Madurai firing now toll two. Doctors on strike reject talks offer.

Such are news in the English press. Vernacular papers of Agra, Mathura, Aligarh and Bulandshaher report daily robberies on a large scale. For instance, it was reported once that not far from Delhi forty loaded trucks were stopped and goods carried away by armed robbers.

Hearing and seeing still worse things I suggested that the Home Minister of India should be a retired general and under him should work one thousand retired military officers. But the Government does not listen to my advices. For last nine years I have been proposing ways and means to make true friendship with China and Pakistan but nothing has been done.

Now Mr. Kosygin proposed a closer understanding among India, Afghanistan and Iran. Is it not my plan for the last twenty years of Aryan Federation, Iran to Assam?

Kerala and West Bengal are supposed to be red. What kind of red they are? They also introduced lottery. Inducing millions of poor people to buy lottery tickets they made a few rich. Undeserving persons became rich. Nation became gambling minded. People became gamblers.

In hill stations, hotels make money by arranging shows of girls. They crown some as Miss May or Miss by some name. Girls make display of their beauty. Our ancient culture taught modesty. Islam introduced veils for women. I insist on decent life.

People are talking of Red Revolution and Military rule. They think revolution will be supported by Russia or China or by both. And Military Rule will be supported by the USA.

I wish our rulers take early steps to satisfy the discontented people. There is no harm if small States are created. Only make administration less expensive. If Nagas and Telangana had been given home rule, loss of life and destruction of many millions of property would have been avoided. Vishal Haryana, Hill State of Garhwal etc. should be formed.

My Tour : I started this campaign on the 2nd Oct. 1969, birthday of Mahatma Gandhi. I shall be to touring till 1st of December, my eighty fourth birth day. It is to see the pulse of the Indian public and to change the trend of thoughts.

On the 2nd October I addressed a Harijan meeting at Dehradun and another meeting at Roorkee forty two miles away. Next day I left Dehradun and arrived Bombay on the 5th Oct. Friends came. I was profusely garlanded. I stayed with Mr. S.C. Singh. Mr. H. H. Ismail took me out. I met Mr. S. K. Patil. Lunch was given in a Hotel Restaurant. I returned to Dadar. Friends and visitors came. This noon I also addressed a meeting at a Islamic School.

6 Oct. Mayor came to see me. Reporters of Newspapers asked me many questions, Mr. Silam, former Lt. Governor of Pondicherry came and took tea with us. In the evening I spoke at the Muslim students Hostel. Next day I called on Mr. K. M. Munshi. I was

sorry to see that he was too sick. A Trade Union leader took lunch with us. In the afternoon Mr. Lachhman Singh took me to Sindhi colony. Here I spoke on Religion of Love at Sadhu Bhavan. Afterwards I spoke at Marathi Hindi School.

The other day Governor of Bombay received me. Lord Mayor gave me welcome in a reception meeting at the corporation. I addressed the councillors. I was very glad to see the Mayor of Honolulu with the Governor. I told him that Honolulu will be the World Capital when my plan is realized. I must thank all important persons who came to see me and my host Mr. S. C. Singh who made me comfortable at his residence.

On 13 Oct. I arrived at Ahmedabad. I stayed with Mr. Quraishi at the Sabarmati Ashram where Mahatma Gandhi lived for fifteen years. In the afternoon I was received by the Chief Minister of Gujarat. I had to tell him straight that it was the fault of administration that riots and distruction occurred at Ahmedabad. Hundreds of persons were killed. Houses, shops and Masjids were burnt. Next day Mr. Bashir Quraishi took me round in his car. I saw burnt houses and shoes of Muslims seattered and three damaged Mosques. In two camps I heard sad stories of men and women who had lost their children and husbands.

On 15th I met Mr. Moraji Desai. He said that he was telling the same thing for last twenty years that instead of secularism we should advocate unity of religions. Daughter of the late Sardar Patel was also present, spinning thread. The other day Ex-Speaker, a member of the Parliament and the Vice-chancellor of Gandhi University came to see me. On 17th, I spoke at the training school. I visited Jagannath Temple whence riot had started. Arrived at Rajkot in the evening. Friends welcomed me.

18th Oct. I am staying as a guest of Mr. M. Ubani, Advocate and former administrator of several States. I spoke at two schools. Mr. Purushotam Gandhi took me to Rashtriya Shala where Mahatma Gandhi stayed and went on famous hunger strike. It is now the centre of many activities of social service. In the afternoon I addressed the students of the Science college. Two sons of Mr. Udani and Mr. Gandhi saw me off. It proved long journey.

24 Oct. I visited a colony and took train, friends saw me off.

My Story : I am writing this at Delhi on the 24th November 1969. Friends received me at Bhopal railway station and brought me to the hostel of the members of the Legislative Assembly. Here I got a comfortable room.

The function at Bhopal was supported and financed by the Government of Madhya Pradesh. I spoke thrice at meetings. Governor and the Chief Minister addressed. Delegates presented their views. Specialists of several Indian languages were present. The object was unity of all the peoples speaking different languages. I was also photographed with the Governor and the chief Minister. Governor gave us tea party.

In the evening of the 28th October 1969 a meeting was held to officially present the Biography of Maulana Barkatullah, my Prime Minister. Author Mr. Irfaq was highly praised and congratulated for writing the book and for getting it printed in Urdu.

The M. P. Government's Minister for Education Mr. Avasthi inaugurated and I presided at the meeting. Several fine speeches were made honouring the memory of Maulana Sahib. I spoke at length about the noble services of my late friend and colleague.

At the end of this function enthusiasm ran high. Several gentlemen came up and kissed my right hand. Many more shook hands.

A.D.C. of H.H. Begam Sahiba Captain Assadullah Khan Sahib took me to the palace where I stayed for the night. It was right royal guest house, very comfortable.

Next morning I took the early train. Friends saw me off. In the evening I reached Kanpur and stayed with Dr. Kalka Prasad Bhatnagar, Ex Vice chancellor of Agra University. His wife is a prominent follower of my Religion of Love. Here I may also mention that ten Musalman gentlemen of Bhopal told me in writing. 'We are the followers of Religion of Love.'

I felt here at home. I stayed at Kanpur three nights. Mrs. Sumati Devi Bhatnagar showed me the wonderful temple built by one rich family. Mosaic work, pictures in marble pieces of different colours is a very rare art. I spoke to the staff of D.A.V. College. At length I explained the plan of Shadow Government. The Principal gave tea.

On the 1st November I arrived at Lucknow. Sardar Shamsher Singh took me to his residence where I stayed. Sardar sahib is a son of my late sister.

A letter from Dehradun giving me the news that thieves entered the store room of my residence and removed some valuables, upset further plan of my tour. I met some friends, Choudhri Akhtar Hussain, Raja of Kotwara, Mr. and Mrs. Gandhi and returned Dehradun.

I found eleven boxes were opened and some valuables were stolen. Raja and Rani Charat Singh Sahib, Kumar Devendra visited me. My daughter came from Mussoorie. On the 9th Nov. I presided at the Old Boys annual function of the Muslim University at Aligarh. I gave some facts of my tour, sad story of Ahmedabad and presented my suggestions. Aryan is the remedy.

On the 15th Nov. I arrived at Chandigarh. I was the guest of Mr. Pratap Singh Daulta, Advocate. We were together in the Parliament. Mr. Bhatia, Advocate gave a tea party. I could speak to some advocates at the Bar of Punjab Haryana High Court. They all seemed to be interested in my programme.

I returned Dehradun on the 18th. My grandson and his wife came from their farm. My daughter again came from Mussoorie. Friends came to my small tea party.

Progress of Shadow Government

Our Shadow Government is progressing. It is great success that it is starting with four Ministers and four prominent Advisers. About a dozen more friends have also agreed to be Advisers.

In 1915, I started the Provisional Government of India with only two ministers. Secretariat had about two dozen persons. Later more ministers and workers joined.

Pandit Sunderlal, well known author and liberal leader, Dr. Syed Mahmood, former Foreign Minister in Nehru Cabinet, Rao Birendra Singh, former Chief Minister of Haryana and Raja Bahadur Kamakhya Narain Singh of Ramgarh State, president of Janta Party, are our Ministers.

Four prominent Advisers are : Mr. Sanjib Chaudhuri, Advocate Supreme Court from Calcutta, Mr. M. Udani, former administrator of States, now advocate, Rajkot, Mr. M. R. Bhatia, Advocate High Court, Sardar Narotam Singh, Advocate High Court, Chandigarh. To be short only four names are mentioned.

Every Advisor can enlist ten to ten thousand volunteers who will be trained in social service. In famine and flood they will serve society. They will try to help every needy person so far it will be possible in each case.

There should be supporters in millions. Any body, every body, who agrees with the object of the Shadow Government can become supporter. In every town and village supporters should multiply in large numbers.

Every Minister and convener can appoint collectors of funds. Each one will be responsible for the right use of public money. Receipt books will be printed and given to collectors. For twenty five paisa also a receipt will be given. In boxes for collection even a paisa can be dropped.

Supporters can start clubs or meeting place. They can independently preach the ideal of the Shadow Government.

The object is to change the system of the government peacefully. Ideal is to remove friction from society. My 'New Science of Thought' will remove friction from minds of all persons in the world.

Shadow Government when can drop off shadow and becomes Government, it will make a family of the Indian nation.

Letters : General Habibullah, writes from 11, M. Gandhi Road, Lucknow :

Dear Raja Sahib,

I am very sorry, I was not here when you came. I was laid up in Military Hospital at Delhi.........Please do let me know when you next visit Lucknow so that I can be of some service to you.

With kind regards.

Yours sincerely
E. Habibullah

Hon. Shri Morarji Desai writes :

'India is passing through very critical position unprecedented in the history of the Congress organization. I trust, a good and sober sense will prevail on all those concerned and they will realize that country and the Congress organization are supreme and are above personalities.

With regards.

Yours sincerely
Moraroji Desai

I wired :

'Messrs Ramsubhag Singh, Morarjidesai and Patil, without attacking any section or party please decide to form National Government'.

I am wiring :

'Messrs Jagjivanram, Subarmaniam. Please give up name Congress, just call National Party or Social Democratic Party'.

Friction thoughts are misleading leaders. They know not that they are sick, sick of friction thoughts. A T. B. patient vomits blood. They vomit fire.

Tavarish. L. V. Mitrokhin, Deputy Head of the Information Dept. of the USSR Embassy in India, wrote : 'Dear friend, After serving my country for five years in India I am now leaving for my home. I take this opportunity to thank you from the bottom of my heart for your kind cooperation, and guidance in my work. I hope that you will continue giving me advice in future as well. As I leave India I carry with me memories of love and affection shown by all the people with whom I came in contact. I will always cherish these memories. With kindest regards, yours sincerely L. V. Mitrokhin.'

My Diary : On 18th March 1970 I went to Budaun, spoke at the Bar of the Court. At Dabra I was the guest of Raja Mirendra Singh. I spoke at the College. At Gwalior, Raja Sahib Pahargarh took me to Adhyatm Niketan.

I addressed meetings at Bhatona, Gesupur, Lakhota and Sardarnagar. The last mentioned village is one of the five villages I gave to Prem Maha Vidyalaya Technical school named after me.

On 20th, 21st and 22nd March 1970, Aryan New Year function was held at Love Center, Rajpur. Tibetan students made it lively. Local leaders addressed meetings. Sadhu Ahuja was the chief organiser.

Letters : Rastrapati. Hon. President writes :

My dear and esteemed friend,

I am glad to go through your letter of 23rd April, I saw some write up also in the newspaper describing your meeting with Lenin. Hope you are keeping fit.

Yours sincerely
V. V. Giri

It is our paper's crown.

Honorable Minister of Education writes :

Dear Raja Mahendra Pratap,

The Lenin Centenary falls on 22nd April 1970 and a Committee has been set up under my chairmanship I shall be happy if you could participate in the function. It would be nice to hear your recollections of Lenin. I do hope it will be possible for you to come to Delhi to attend this function.

Yours sincerely
V. K. R. V. Rao

I went, I spoke at the function. I described, how Comrade Lenin brought small chair and put it near his chair. I sat on it. I presented my book of Religion of Love. He said, he had read it, It was Tolstoyism. I also presented to him a plan to do away with gold and silver. Notes only to be printed for the daily necessities, what, rice or butter.

I thankfully must mention that the Ministry of Education paid all my travelling expenses to Delhi and back to Dehradun.

General Cariappa, former Commander-in-Chief of Indian Army wrote :

Dear Raja Mahendra Pratap Sahib,

I have just received your letter of the 19th April ....Raja Sahib, I have never 'retreated' in my life and in this case it has been quite wrongly reported, all out of context. I stick to what I have been saying in this respect for over 3 or 4 years in my articles and in my public addresses ......Your printed circulars contain convincing evidence of your undiluted loyalty to motherland and your intense and most sincere wish to ensure that our dear motherland remains intact and truly democratic country, unfettered by strangle holds of outside overlords. It has always been my cherished wish too and it will be so until I die.

With best regards,

Yours sincerely
K. M. Cariappa

He is the Head of five million ex-servicemen or retired soldiers. He has a very good name in the army. General Ayub Khan of Pakistan worked under him. He could have brought Indo-Pak armies under one command. Pandit Nehru did not agree.

Rao Birendra Singh Sahib writes :

Respected Raja Sahib,

I am in agreement in your views. I hope the people in general would soon appreciate them and a favourable atmosphere would be created. Just now the masses are playing in the hands of selfish, corrupt and hypocrite politicians. I hope to be able to see you soon one day to get your blessings for the cause of Vishal Haryana.

With regards

Birendra (Rao Birendera Singh)

Vishal Haryana or Maha Braj is exactly the same. I am with you. You are with me. I am sure; we shall together save India from chaos.

Great Shock : Raja Kamakhya Narayan Singh Bahadur of Ramgarh passed away. Only eleven days before his death he wrote me in Hindi that he was entangled in many kinds of troubles but my letter very much comforted him. He hoped that I would continue to show him the right path.

He was also a minister of our Shadow Government. It is a great loss to our young movement.

He was a natural leader of men. Mr. Sanjib Chaudhary, Advocate of the Supreme Curt, wrote to me that the Raja Bahadur of Ramgarh should be the Prime Minister of India.

He gave away his vast land to the peasants. He was the founder President of Janta Party.

General Cariappa : General K. M. Cariappa, former Commander-in-Chief of Indian army, today advocated President's rule in the country as a temporary measure and handling over the administration to military authorites in a few states where lawlessness and disorder were known to be rampant.

General said, India should not go in for costly nuclear venture. On the contrary India should make every effort to win over China's friendship.

There had been more police firings in the country in the last 22 years than there had ever been during the 200 years of British rule.

India should have honoured place in family of nations.

General P. P. Kumarmangalam : Former Chief of Army Staff General P.P. Kumarmangalam yesterday accused politicians of encouraging youths to violence and indiscipline for their own selfish ends.

The General said the politicians also encouraged youths to factionalism and communalism and were not in the least worried about what was happening to the country provided they could stay where they were.

Letters : Hon. President writes :

My dear and esteemed friend,

Thank you for your letter of the 14th July and a copy of the July issue of 'World Federation'.

With kindest regards

Yours sincerely
V. V. Giri

The letter is dated 16th July. It is very prompt response. I am heartily grateful. In this issue are my important suggestions.

General Cariappa writes :

My dear Raja Mahendra Pratap Sahib,

I thank you for your letter of 5th June with a copy of your June issue of World Federation. I have the May issue also. I have read both with interest. You have quite rightly said in your letter that we have talked enough and now we should act to change the system to establish peace in land. In this action we naturally would not talk of toppling any personalities, we only want to see that our Democracy in its purest form remains for ever with. No intervention by or influence of any foreign 'ism'. Our own ism Indianism must remain Supreme at all times.

With best regards,

Yours sincerely
K. M. Cariappa.

July 1970 : At Mussorie, every Sunday, prayer meetings were held. I addressed. Friends spoke. Three ladies were initiated in Religion Love.

At the invitation of Swami Bhajnanand ji I went to Mainpuri Ashram. Babu Chimanlal took me there. I spoke four times. People seemed very impressed. They liked also my literature.

Congratualations : Twenty fifth anniversary of the united Nations is on the 24th of October. I heartily congratulate it. It is a long forward step to the World Federation for which I have been working since 1970.

I said, Earl Russell said and Lord Attle said, UNO should have permanent strong army.

I suggest, U. N. O. army units should be stationed at Gibralter and Singapore. Suez canal and Panama canal should be under the direct control of UNO It can alone have atomic bombs. Its head office should be shifted to Honolulu in Hawai.

U. N. O. should be free from Veto. Its executive committee should be the cabinet. Assembly should be its Parliament.

Conversion of Indian Rulers : You can well ask me, when I want to go to Peking to convert President Mao why I do not try to convert rulers at Delhi. There are good reasons for it.

Firstly, I tell you what happened when I, defeating the ruling party member entered the Parliament. My speeches were considered very interesting and hitting by the leaders of the different parties. I was told by several members that Pandit Jawaharlal Nehru did not like me to come forward. He considered me his rival. I shall not be a rival to Leader Mao. I want to see him still more secure.

Secondly, people in India are fanatic Hindus, Muslims and Sikhs. They hate the idea of a new religion. I am already back in India these twenty four years, after an exile of thirty one years. My experience is that I have been hampered all along. In China and Japan it is different. A religious current flowed from India to those countries. Many persons in Japan and China considered me Buddha. Hindus turned out Buddhism from India. They can not tolerate another Buddhism appearing in the country.

Letters : Hon. President, Rashtrapati writes :

My dear and esteemed friend,

I have gone through your letter of 2nd November and the enclosure.

Yours sincerely
V. V. Giri

I am very thankful to our President who has loving regard for me.

The Chief Minister of our province U. P. writes :

My dear Raja Saheb,

Many thanks for your congratulations. I shall always cherish your good wishes in the difficult and complicated task that faces me.

Yours sincerely
T. N. Singh

I thank him for the answer. The difficulty is, he leads a combination of five parties. One of which believes in creating trouble. In any case I am prepared to try to clean the minds of all members of friction thoughts. They need thoughts of unity.

The great poet and the leader of Tajikistan writes :

Dear Friend,

I wish to express you my gratitude for your letters. Our meetings and conversation as well as your hospitality will be ever in my heart. I would like to inform you also that my poem dedicated to the V. I. Lenin' Centenary was published in newspaper and magazines in Moscow and Dushambe. Soon it will be edited as a book in Russian and Tajikistani languages. In your last letter you expressed the wish to visit Moscow. If you are well we will be glad to invite you to USSR in a time convenient for you. I wish you good health and happiness in your life.

Sincerely yours
Mirzo Tursun-zade

It is for me to be most thankful. He made me the Hero of his poem. It is some plan of Nature that I could develop such close relation with Russia and Tajikistan.

H. E. Dr. Von Hentig writes from 6531, Seibersbach, West Germany :

My dear and highly esteemed Raja Sahib,

It is with the greatest attention I am following your steadily renewed proposals. The Berlin question is extremely precarious. Most of the people will not realize that just in these days the victors are showing us. What I preached for years : We still are the vanquished and victors keep their sovereignty over defeated German. The now concluded agreements are only camouflaging the status of entirely, in all vital respects, dependent and military occupied Germany. This applies to both parts of our country, the one under the patronage of Russia, the other of the U.S. A. Our whole energy has to be concentrated on the aim of getting freedom through a peace treaty.'

Indian Foreign Policy

12 Nov 1970, Dehradun. Though my friend Sardar Swaran Singh is at present the Minister for External Affairs at New Delhi yet our foreign policy is extremely wrong. He is not in the position to set the policy right. Cabinet runs in the rut.

Indian foreign policy should be the spirit of World Federation. Working along our line we can federate with Pakistan, Nepal and Ceylon. Afghanistan and Iran will be in the Aryan Federation.

We go to Africa with our plan. We do not create bitterness against the whites who bought light to Africa. We teach, Africans should take full advantage of the European science. From Hebrew religion sprang Christianity and from both of them sprang Islam.

We can tell China, please forget the past. Our culture teaches humility. Come, let us be dear friends. Fools were talking of land boundaries. Wicked persons to become leders excited the people. Now we are world federationists. We wish, you realise Golden Federation from Tibet to Japan.

We can express warm gratitude to USA for all the help they gave us. We can tell Russia, Russia is derived from Persia. Aryan human current flowed from Persia to Russia, Prussia, Francia and Ireland or Arya land. Aryan current flowed through Afghanistan, Punjab and the rest of India, on to Java, Sumatra and Bali. Another route it took to Brahma, Shiam and Kambhoj. Central Asian Turks and Tajiks and Mughals came to India. Karl Marx can not separate us.

England has been the teacher of the modern India. Our teacher is our Guru. Our culture teaches us respect for the Guru.

We admire the racial liberal spirit of France.

We are thankful to Germany and Japan for the help which they gave us in our freedom movement.

India and Italy are both central penensulas of two continents, Asia and Europe, respectively. Both have two islands at their feet. Both have high mountains at their heads. Historically both are similar in having ancient greatness.

Arabs brought Islam to India. Arabian culture mixed up with our culture.

USA and India were both under the British and both made themselves free. English language is popular in India.

Now we stand for One World, World Government, and World court of justice, World army or World Federation. We believe, U.N.O. is another step to world government. First step was League of Nations.

We can make close friendship with Latin America. We can settle the South African problem by showing the way of racial cooperation through Brahmanic teachings. Whites should insist on morality and qualities and not on the colour of skin.

We can fraternise with Portugal and Spain. They do not believe in racial superiority of colour. Greeks came to India. We have some similarities in philosophy.

Indian Ambassadors abroad should adopt this line of thought. It is the right Foreign policy.

My Diary : World Federation Club, Dehradun, gave a grand reception to Hon. Lady Vijay Lakshmi Pandit at Dharma on the 18th December 1970. Lady Vijay Lakshmi and Mahant Indresh Charan Das are patrons of the club.

On 29th Dec. 70, I gave a tea party to my friends and said : See you again, God willing.

I left Dehradun on the 30th and came to Delhi. I stayed at Delhi Headquarter, founded by Lt. Colonel Satanand at Anand Farm. I stayed at Delhi up to 10th Jan. 71. During this time friends came to see me and I visited friends. 5th Jan. I addressed International Human Relations Society. On the 8th Jan. Pandit Ram Chandra Sharma called a meeting to hear my views. Lord Mayor of Delhi, Mr. Hansraj Gupta presided.

At the invitation of the Students Union of G.S. Commercial College I accompanied by Lt. Col. Satanand reached Jabalpur on the 11th Jan. 1971 forenoon. The journey took twenty seven hours in train. Union meeting was attended by the citizen of the town. I spoke at length. I also addressed Staff meeting and a meeting of Gandhi foundation. Hospitality of the college made the stay at Jabalpur very comfortable. Mr. Shrivastav, the Principal, took the guests to the Fall, a picnic spot.

On 16th January at Vrindaban I acted as the priest of Religion of Love and performed the marriage ceremony of the daughter of Shri Shiv Kumar, the editor of World Federation. Bridegroom is a young well educated person of a respectable family. The hall of the Center of Religion of Love, was full. Enthusiasm prevailed.

I left Vrindaban for Delhi on 25th January 1971. I am staying at my Head quarters at Delhi the capital of India. Lt Col. Satanand is very helpful in Divine Mission to spread the message of love and goodwill in the world. My address of Delhi is: Prem Dham. Patparganj, Phone No. 213357. Government spent nearly ten thousand rupees to extend telephone line to the headquarters of Raja Mahendra Pratap at Delhi.

On 26th January 1971 I took part in the tea party of Hon. President of India, given in honour of Republic Day Celebrations.

Newly appointed Vice Chancellor, Delhi University, Dr. Sarup Singh writes : 'This is a very difficult and challenging assignment, but with the goodwill of friends and elders like you and with the cooperation of my colleagues in the university. I hope I am able to maintain the traditions.'

I was glad to learn the good news that one of the Ministers of our Shadow Government Rao Birendra Singh won in election and is now in Lok Sabha. He was once the Chief Minister of Haryana.

Rajmata of Jaipur and Rajmata of Gwalior have won and entered the Lok Sabha or House of Commons of India with flag flying. Several persons of royal blood are now in the Parliament. Maharaja Karan Singh of Kashmir is a member of the Indian cabinet. He is Minister of Tourism and Civil Aviation.

Lady Indira Gandhi had her greatest success in these elections. She has now two third majority in Lok Sabha.

Next to the New Congress of Mrs. Indira Gandhi, the largest party in Lok Sabha is CPM or Marxist Communist Party. Comrade A. K. Gopalan is the leader of this party. It is a strange phenomenon that CPM is opposed by Naxalites or Maoist Communists and CPM opposes the Communist Party of India.

Old Congress badly failed in these elections. Swatantra Party had her debacle. President was defeated, her strength in parliament dwindled.

All the parties spoke and speak of removing poverty. Leaders, however, live royally. Ministers have luxuries of Maharajas. Most of the plans are on paper. But as we say masses are always led by slogans. It is an art to deceive the people.

Condolence : We have to express our sympathy to Chaudhary Charan Singh who himself failed in the election and his party was routed. Prophesies were made that Chaudharyji would be the Prime Minister of India. Stars however got eclipsed. Now Chaudhary Sahib and Babu Chandra Bhanu Gupta better join the Shadow Government and make common with us.

National Congress

I joined the Indian National Congress in 1906 when Pandit Jawaharlal Nehru was still not in Congress.

I was a member of the Executive Committee of the Reception Committee of the Congress held at Allahabad in 1910. Pandit Motilal Nehru was the chairman.

I remained in Congress till 1952. Since then I attacked the Congress, saying that it is no more Indian National Congress, it is half India congress. It is not national, it is a party congress.

Now when the masses gave verdict in favour of Lady Indira Gandhi, I began to say, I am New Congressman.

There is an interesting story. Once upon a time red rain fell in a kingdom. People eagerly drank this water which appeared sparkling red wine. They all got mad. The king asked his wise Minister: 'What to do now?' 'Sir, now we better also drink this water.' They drank and became like all the people.

I think I should say as they all say I am a New Congressman.

I also got disgusted seeing the apathy of Maharajas and businessmen. I showed the way to my relative Maharajas how to act now. One said the Supreme Court will decide, another said, God will take care of them. Several of Maharajas still believe in pleasures of the world.

Businessmen did not care to understand my Mission. They still believe some saint will protect them. I have respect for saints. They make people pious. But I tell the saints, businessmen and Maharajas that they should see the trend of thought in the world.

Sexual pleasures and intense desire to get more and more wealth made people blind in upper class. Classes are in nature. Nature wants them to cooperate for common welfare. Friction is produced by blindly selfish persons who want to get hold of wealth without working.

I hope, my great Mission is understood, before it is too late. Catastrophe can overwhelm humanity if people do not learn to clean mind of all friction thoughts according to my science.

Letters : From Hon'ble Speaker :

My dear Raja Sahib,

I thank you very much for your letter congratulating me on my election as Speaker of Lok Sabha. I very much appreciate your kind sentiments. I pray that with God's grace I will be able to come up to your expectations.

With regards,

Yours sincerely
Gurdial Singh Dhillon

Hearty thanks for kind response. May a new spirit prevail in the united House? Discuss not to show ability or to get a place in the news. Cooperate for common welfare of the country and humanity.

H. E. Governor writes :

Respected Raja Mahendra Pratap ji,

It appears, that reports published in the press about my speech were not correct. What I said was if the U. N. O. does nothing about East Bengal, it may meet the same fate as the League of Nations. I am convinced that, in the ultimate analysis, each nation must shed a portion of its sovereignty to a World Government which should be able to restrain the nations from indulging in wrong actions either within or without the country.

With regards,

Yours sincerely
Shriman Narayan

I am very thankful for the letter. He has the true spirit of a world citizen. He is a well known follower of Mahatma Gandhi and at present he is the Governor of Gujarat State.

Former Chief Minister of U.P., Ch. Charan Singh writes :

My dear Raja Sahib,

I do not think I committed a mistake in not making a common cause with the Grand Alliance. In fact, members of the grand alliance themselves are now having second thoughts................We will have to take along all the sections of our people and not a selected few.

With regards, I am,

Yours
Charan Singh

I can call him my old friend. He is one of the oldest leaders of the Congress. Now he is the president of Bhartiya Kranti Dal. Translated it is the Indian Revolutionary Party.

Bangla Desh : Repeatedly people ask me to give my opinion on this 'most burning question.' They read not my literature or my articles. Or they forget and ask my opinion.

I told Maulana Abul Kalam Azad in 1948 that longer Pakistan remained as a separate state greater dangerous it would prove for India.

I tried and General Cariappa tried. General Ayub Khan agreed to have common general staff for Pakistan and India. It would have been coming together. Pandit Nehru exclaimed, 'Common Front ? Against whom common front ?'

Now General Yahya Khan said that he would like to meet Mrs. Indira Gandhi. I think, he should have been invited immediately to come to Delhi. Recognition of Bangla Desh, Hon'ble Mr. Rajagopalchari said, would mean declaration of war against Pakistan. Mahatma Gandhi's non-violent India should not want war. I also think that war is a big gamble. Introduction of lotteries in all the States of India has made the nation gamble minded. Beast in man always appreciates war thoughts and war itself. Parties prosper by their fighting programme.

Mr. Chou Enlai always wanted to have a round table talk. India insisted on agreeing first on some Ceylon conditions. I always said and say, we must have most friendly relations with China. Lord Nirvana Buddha built a bond of friendship among India, China,

Japan, Mangolia and Tibet. Great law is man gets what he sows. Nations rose and fell. Empires were built and empires disappeared.

For me, Bangala Desh is a phenomenon. There is a very clear background for it. Islamic brotherhood thought brought entirely different races together in one State of Pakistans.

General Yahya Khan caught hold of the reins of the State, depriving his own master General Ayub. Army first made Ayub a dictator next the same army made Yahya dictator.

Indian rulers quietly saw all these developments. They quietly saw Pakistan army massacring poor unarmed Bengalies. Leaders, not in power, shouted and shout. India must recognise Bangala Desh.

Meeting with Hon'ble Rashtrapati : On the 2nd August 1971 at 10 a.m. Rashtrapati received me, my friends and coworkers at Rashtrapati Bhavan, New Delhi. Dr. M. M. Chopra had arranged the interview.

In symbolic way Rashtrapati embraced me and took photograph with me and my friends among whom were two members of Lok Sabha.

I told the President that complete understanding with Nepal and Afghanistan and very close friendship with China were immediately necessary for India. Delay will prove dangerous.

1st September, 71, Today, I gave twenty minutes interview to Television New Delhi which was highly appreciated. It was all about my life and what I am doing at present, preaching Religion of love, working for World Federation and teaching New Science of thought which cleans the mind of all friction thoughts, the only way to have Universal Unity.

India errs : When I was in Indian Parliament and when some members were talking loud attacking China that she had taken eighty thousand square miles of our territory I said China had only taken steps to occupy the boundry line according to Tibetan maps.

Repeatedly I volunteered to go to China to make peace. Pandit Nehru gave me a written reply saying that my views differed, he could not send me any where.

I believe, India is erring. In twenty three years India fought three wars. As I write these lines danger of war looms over our heads.

Internally there are dissensions. Government talks loud of integrity and of communal harmony but groups in general work for disintegration.

Letters : Right Hon'ble Dr. Seewoosagur Ramgoolam Kt. Prime Minister Mauritius of writes from Government House, Port Louis:

Dear Raja Pratap,

I am sorry I did not reply to your letter addressed to me early this year, but at any time you will be welcome in Mauritius and we would gladly show you whatever is here to see. The best season is between July and September.

With my warmest regards.

Yours very sincerely
S. Ramgoolam

It is right royal invitation. I will surely take advantage of this opportunity.

Hon'ble Minister Maharaja Dr. Karan Singh writes:

My dear Raja Sahib,

The Jawaharlal Nehru Memorial Fund has undertaken two major schemes, namely, the publication of the Selected Works of Jawaharlal Nehru in a series of twenty volumes and preparation of an authentic archival documentary film on Jawarharlal Nehru. The success of these two projects will depend upon the material we are able to collect from those possessing Jawaharlal Nehru's letters, photographs. Film shots and his voice in tapes...........I am writing to you especially as I feel that you are likely to have material relevant to our projects. And am confident that you will extend your cooperation in our effort..............With kind regards.

Surely I will contribute through our opinion but I like that gentleman.

Socialism and I : When I was only twenty one year old I was expressing some views which my friend Sardar Jugendra Singh called socialism. He advised me to read the book 'Looking backward'. I got it and read it. I was astonished to find similarity in my views and the views expressed in the book.

I believed and believe, I received inspirations from Lord Buddha. Compassion for the poor and not the hatred of the rich was the moving force in my mind. At the age of twenty two years I made the Trust of five villages and buildings and founded Prem Maha Vidyalaya, a technical institute where no fees were charged. It was founded at Vrindaban in 1909. It is still there but now it is an Inter College, run according to the laws of the Indian government.

I enthusiastically received the news of revolution in Russia in 1917. I was a guest of the Afghanistan government, staying at Mazarisharief on the Russian border.

I cooperated with Soviet Russia which helped me in my fight against the British empire. I was received by comrade Lenin at Kremlin in May 1919.

I am now eighty five years old. I have studied the world a bit better. I admire the wish to serve society but I condemn the fooling of the people to get power.

I shall do nothing to undermine the governments of Russia, China or the socalled communist countries, but I shall do all what I can that the rulers of these lands realise that no czars or emperors ever tried to control the social and economic life of people. It is the worst despotism not to give freedom of speech to the people and press.

I proposed the German, West Africa may be given to the jews to build their national home. It is far bigger than Palestine. My proposal was discussed in U. N. O. in 1950. I received its report of fifty pages.

No war, no murder, no attack to harm fellow human being should be our slogans ringing round the world.

It is a shame for all of us that we could not stop war in Vietnam, murders in North Ireland and settle the tense situation in Middle East. I believe, if you cooperate with me to revolutionise thinking we shall have a joint family of all mankind.

Eighty Days In Japan

Today is 1st March 1972. I left India for Japan on 20th December last year. I am still in Japan, and staying at Keio Plaza Hotel, Tokyo, Japan. Since my arrival till now friends rushed to visit me at the hotel. I also went to visit friends.

I continue to give my message of universal brotherhood in the land of rising sun. During World War Second I worked for Indian freedom and stayed in Tokyo. I had my own residence there. Now I have sold it to Mr. Dhana Singh Bains, a resident of Japan now.

In Japan Eighty Days : In 1961, I visited Japan after 15 years and stayed 40 days. This time I stayed in Japan 80 days.

Last time I was a guest of Rev. Yono Suke Nakano for 20 days and for next 20 days I was a guest of Mr. Juntara Imazato and his friends. This time for first ten days I was a guest of Mr. Dhana Singh Bains and for 70 days I should say I was a guest of God. I was living in the tallest hotel of Japan, 48 storey high.

My room was on the 19th floor. From my window I could see a panorama of houses. Mostly roofs were seen. Down below motor cars running on broad streets looked like toys. At night glaring lights red and white made a picture beautiful and bright.

This Keio Plaza Hotel is the symbol of the great progress which Japan has made during the last 25 years. Tokyo, which was completely destroyed in 1945, has risen to this great glorious height, broad streets, streets over streets, trains running over and underground. Taxies are air-conditioned and have radio. In my room was radio, television and phone.

Japan is today very expensive country. Thirty five years back for ten cents one could buy ten Sardins. Today a good meal costs about four U. S. dollar.

During my stay in Japan, I addressed three meetings. In one meeting I asked my friends to help me in my divine mission of liberating China from the slavery of Karl Marx. Twenty one persons signed the pledge. In the welfare dinner party friends present sang the song of world peace. The party was arranged by Mr. Matsumoto.

Mr. Nakatani and Mr. Keno Shita who both translated separately my book of Religion of Love into Japanese were very helpful in this visit. Mr. Imazato loaded me with sweets. Mr. Nishimura brought presents. Mr. Dhana Singh made my trip successful.

Political tussel that I saw in Japan deserves great attention. The curse of fighting of political parties in Japan is as acute as anywhere else. What is dangerous is the activity of Red Army and anti-treaty organization. If America does not take early notice and agree to leave Japan to herself, there can be a great bloody war.

When President Nixon came to China, a delegation of Soviet-Russia came to Japan seeking a loan of two billion U. S. dollars and cooperation in development of Siberia. All kinds of wire pullings should end in the interest of world peace. Japan and China must co-operate in their own interest and in the interest of humanity.

My Will : I hereby cancel all the previous Wills. I make this Will considering I am eighty five years old and I have now money in Indian, Japanese and Afghanistan banks. I am of course completely free to give any amount to any body so long I am alive. But as I decided, this money is of Religion of Love and World Federation I shall spend it very conscientiously.

After my death Prem Maha Vidyalaya Association (Trust which I created in 1909) will spend only interest of my money in Indian Banks for Religion of Love, World Federation and my New Science of Thought.

I request the Imperial Government of Japan to form a committee after my death of fifteen persons to spend only interest of my money in Japan for Religion of Love, World Federation and my New Science of Thought.

This committee should include Mr. Juntaro, Mr. Takeo Nakatani, Mr. James Kinoshita, Mr. Chisema Nishimura, Mr. Katsusaburo Mastsumoto, Mr. Dhana Singh Bains, Mr. Toshiro Nakano and Mr. Masaaki Tanaka.

I hope and wish Government in choosing other members will give preference to those who support my divine Mission.

I request Royal Government of Afghanistan to form a committee of fifteen persons after my death to utilize only the interest of my money in Afghanistan bank to promote Religion of Love, World Federation and my New Science of Thought. My book of Religion of Love was written in Afghanistan in 1916, thus by birth it is Afghanistani.

In this committee I wish H. R. H. Prince Shah Walikhan, H. E. Mr. Said Kasim Rishtya, Hon'ble Abdul Hadi, Mr. Ahmad Mahmud and Mr. Janat Khan Grewal are included.

If there is some objection to promote Religion of Love, my soul will not mind if committee pays more attention to realize Aryan, Iran to Assam, Nepal to Ceylon.

I have every right to cancel this Will if I so desire.

My object is to make a family of all mankind.

Current Event : These lines are being written on the 22nd of June, 1972. Our illustrious Prime Minister Shrimati Indira Gandhi has made a very useful trip, useful for India and useful for the cause of peace. She received warm welcome in Sweden, Czechoslovakia and Hungary.

Convention of Freedom Fighters

In the afternoon of the 12th August 1972 convention was held of the Freedom Fighters Samiti. I presided. Pandit K. C. Pant, Home Minister inaugurated. Rev. Sant Kirpal Singh gave blessings and Hon'ble Shrimati Indira Gandhi, Prime Minister addressed it. She said that she had come to receive blessings of the Freedom Fighters. I spoke extempore. I pointed out that in her name my name and the name of Mahatma Gandhi met. From Mahendra or Maha Indira, was taken and Gandhi was added.

When I wanted to open an office of the Congress at Moscow Mr. Sukermanov of the Foreign office said that 'Tavarish (Comrade) Raja (Mahendra Pratap) is our friend but Congress is not'. I did not receive the necessary permit.

In 1927 when I heard at Moscow that Pandit Jawaharlal Nehru had come to Europe and his coming to Moscow was hindered by some Indian Communist, I got for Pandit Nehru an invitation from Foreign Office. I went to Germany, thence to Switzerland and met Nehru and told him that he could go to Moscow. Soviet Government would welcome him. Later he visited Moscow.

On the 14th August, Lord Mayor of Delhi gave a grand reception to the Freedom Fighters. He banded me the address welcoming us.

On the 15th August, we were honoured at the Red Fort by the Hon'ble President Dr. V. V. Giri. Hon'ble Prime Minister Mrs. Indira Gandhi gave us engraved Copper Plates. They were in Hindi. I give below English translation of the plate given to me :

'On the occasion of the 25th year of Independence for taking memorable part in Freedom fight, Hon'ble Prime Minister Indira Gandhi presented this engraved copper plate to Raja Mahendra Pratap'.

During last twenty five years we were not remembered by the government of India. Only now our wonderful Prime Minister, winner of the war of Bengals and maker of Simla agreement thought of the forgotten Freedom Fighters.

On the 16th August 1972 she gave a reception to all the Freedom Fighters at Teen Murti building which was the official residence of Pandit Nehru, her venerable father.

Freedom Fighters of all the states sat in different groups. I was sitting on the only chair in U.P. group. In Indian fashion all sat on ground.

Hon'ble Mrs. Indira Gandhi came to me. I stood up and greeted her. She asked me to sit down on the chair and standing behind me got us photographed.

Presidential Address : Being president of Freedom Fighters', Convention, I had to read the address, so it got printed. But the speech was not read, as it was differ to the views of the Government. It was simply distributed in the convention of Freedom Fighters on the 12th August 1972 and I spoke extempore, as I have already written :

My Dear fellow freedom fighters,

I should thank Dr. Madan Mohan Chopra for kindly arranging this convention. He has worked hard for full one year to make this convention successful.

Members of the Executive Committee, including several members of Parliament have given their most valuable support for the cause of the freedom fighters.

Let me pay my sincere tribute to the memory of our unknown freedom fighters. They suffered and gave their lives without any desire of name and fame.

We all did our best to serve the cause of India's freedom. We must thank our Hon. Prime Minister Shrimati Indira Gandhiji for her plan to help freedom fighters, giving them pension. It is a bit too late but better late than never.

I admire Shrimatiji for her work in Bengal, Bangla Desh, and for making peace with Pakistan. I can not however endorse her economic policies. I know it is not her fault. It is a kind of thought infection. That class war thought has come to our country too. Man does not realise how thought ruling his mind can drive him like cattle.

Now let me tell you about my work and of my friends.

I could establish a Provisional Government of India at Kabul in 1915. We had also an army of 12 thousand Afridis for a short time. Brother of Amir Habibullah Khan, Prime Minister Sardar Nasrullah Khan morally and financial helped our movement. The Afghan government being neutral could not openly support us.

What our provisional government did for the freedom of India is well recorded in many files in National Archives, New Delhi. Files in the foreign office in London also tell stories of our provisional government of India. A couple of historians of America and Russia have recorded many facts which they found in secret documents.

Several books already printed speak of the details of my wok in different parts of the World. An Englishman, who was once resident at the State of Charkhari has published a book in which he speaks of meeting me at Berlin. He also says that he followed my activities up to Tashkent. Kaiser of Germany, Sultan of Turkey and three kings of Afghanistan helped me in my work. Comrade Lenin sent me to Kabul in 1919. I went to Tibet to find another passage to India. If I were to relate at length only one fact of these stories it would make a long essay.

Now I must also refer to the great work of Babu Subhash Chandra Bose who followed in my footsteps 26 years later. He could work on ten times greater scale than me. He had the advantage of full support of Japan which was in war. Ghadar Party and Babar Akali played their roles very significantly. Many members and warriors gave their lives for the great cause.

I should also mention valuable cooperation of Babu Rash Behari Bose, Babu Anand Mohan Sahay, Mr. Deb Nath Das, Sardar Sohan Singh and others who served the cause of India from Japan.

My Prime Minister Maulana Barkatullah and Home Minister Maulana Obaidullah Sindhi deserve our respect, love and regard for all that they did. The body of Maulana Barkatullah was laid to rest at Merrisville, California, USA.

I admit that neither my army nor the army of Netaji could capture Delhi. It was the silent work of Mahatma Gandhi and sagacity of Sardar Patel and Pt. Nehru which made it possible to transfer the administration of India from the hands of the British to the hands of the Congress leaders. Now instead of English rulers we have Indian rulers continuing the same system of administration which was evolved by the British in their own interest through many decades. Now I appeal to my fellow freedom fighters to complete the work of freedom.

Government interference in our day today life must end. All should have freedom to do business. Nationalization is a misnomer. It is governmentisation. Government has no right to make ceiling on land and on property. Laws have become chains which bind the people.

By right teachings and preachings we should make men moral. Not by rod but by thought we can make society happy.

I appeal to all be liberal righteous and God fearing people of India to help me in my work of unity of religions. Religions of Love, World Federation, one world Government and my New Science of thought which cleans the mind of friction thoughts.

I believe I have a God given duty to do my utmost to realize a happy peaceful family of our entire human race. All should work for all to make all happy. It is the way of universal unity.

Eighteen Days at Kabul

I took a servant with me, Shri Gobind Sharan. He is also my driver and photographer.

We left by Ariana Air Lines on the 2nd October 1972. I chose this date because on this date I, at the head of Indo-Turko-German Mission, arrived at Kabul in 1915 for the first time. Later I revisited Kabul several times.

We arrived at Kabul in just two hours. I was received at the airport by Mr. Yakub Khan, the Vice President of Pashtany Tejaraty Bank and Mr. Ali Mohemmad, representing the President who was on tour.

We stayed at Metropol Hotel, comfortable and not expensive.

It was my great pleasure to meet my old venerable friends H. R. H. Marshal Shah Wali Khan and Hon'ble Mr. Abdul Hadi Davi, President of the Senate.

It was a great pleasant surprise when H. E. Mr. Allah Nawaz Khan walked in to my room at the hotel. He was a member of that batch of young students who left studies at Lahore and secretly came to Kabul to fight the British to liberate India. He worked in the secretariat of the Provisional Government of India, which I founded at Kabul on 1st December 1915. H. M. King Nadir Khan appointed him as Ambassador of Afghanistan in Germany. He was at the high post for over a decade. Now he is retired. His one son is a deputy Minister at Kabul. He gave me the pleasure of his company every day or every second day for a couple of hours. He took me to meet H. R. H. General Abdul Wali Khan, son-in-law of the king. He is a very bright, promising young prince. I presented to him my book of Religion of Love, as I saw he was very liberal in his views.

H. E. Indian Ambassador Mr. K. Mehta invited me to tea one afternoon. I was very glad to meet Dr. Balmukand Das who kindly called on me twice and saw me off at the air port. Dr. Ved Pratap Vedic, a promising writer and author, visited me. Kabul Times wrote about him.

I had official lunch with the Vice President and Directors of the Pashtany Tejaraty Bank at the grand Bank building. Once Vice President invited me to lunch at his home. There I also met Hukim Latif Khan.

Climate of Kabul was very pleasant. It was not cold, sun was shining. Only once we had a shower for a few minutes.

Modern buildings have risen. Roads are broad and fine. Hotels are numerous. There is a little inflation. One U. S. dollar is exchanged for seventy eight Afghani. Indian rupee is worth eight Afghani.

H. M. the King was in Europe. My friends told me, I should either stay on for two months to have the audience or I come again. I said, God willing, I might come again.

I came to the airport in the morning of the 20th October 1972. H. E. Mr. Allah Nawaz Khan came with his grandson to say goodbye. Mr. Sarna of the Indian Embassy was also there. He came to see off his son. He also met me.

At 11.35 a. m. plane was moving, at 2.30 p.m. Indian time we were at Delhi.

I should add to the story that I visited Bagh Baber where I started to write the Book of Religion of Love and where I founded Provisional Government of India. Here I also lived for many months. It is greatly improved with two swimming pools. Tomb of Emperor Baber has now a roof.

It was a great surprise. A big Indian delegation going to Russia stayed at the same hotel for a night, where I lived. Mr. and Mrs. Jagdish Gandhi were in the group. Hon'ble Mr. Bibhav, U. P. Transport Minister told me that he was the editor of Prem for eighteen months at our Prem Maha Vidyalaya. At dinner I spoke. Several members of the delegation kindly referred to my 'sacrifices' for the cause of freedom of India.

Great Soul No More : Pandit Rajagopalachariji passed away. He was eight years older than me. He had loving regard for me. He considered my articles in our World Federations as 'Inspiration'. He often wrote me letters appreciating my views, though he had different ideas on some important points.

Our Government declared seven days official mourning at his demise but never cared to listen to his advices. He strongly advocated all parties government, in other words truly national. I also believe that one party government is usurpation of power by a group. It is, as if, a robber band captures a house or a foreign invasion succeeds to establish its own government. This system must end. All should work for all to make all happy.

In India, it is a proverb : Parents are neglected when they are alive and they are worshipped when they are dead.

Self Styled Adviser

I wrote to Shrimati Indira Gandhi that the absolute monarchs also had some advisers who could say some time straight: 'Your Majesty, it is wrong. You should not say this, you should not do that.' I may be considered one such person.

I advised the Prime Minister to divide Andhra and not to say that small states are not desirable.

I can only say. I can not compel any leader of any party to do as I like. I can however tell them and enlighten the public that the desire to become a leader makes them form parties. And the ego of individuals to become some thing makes some people followers of parties. Some persons feel delight in saying, I am president, I am secretary of this or that party. 'I am something different from you' spirit works.

Attraction of personality is also a great force to develop a party or a group. I do not mind if there are numerous leaders. I do not mind if some persons amass wealth. They should not clash. They should not live in luxury. They should not waste time, energy, their energy and time and of the people.

It was a surprise : An Artist came direct from Moscow to paint my pictures and an official from USSR Embassy, New Delhi acompanied him. This official took my several taperecords on different question. They both also took photographs. It shows that inspite of my liberal views, I am rightly considered a friend of Russia and of the present rulers at Moscow.

Russian Friendship : It is proved, proved beyond doubt. The official Russian Organ, Soviet Land, published by the Information Bureau of USSR Embassy, New Delhi has brought out in April issue a great research work about the gold plate letter which I wrote to the Czar (Tsar) of Russia in 1916 from Kabul, as the president of the Provisional Government of India.

It has brought out certain facts which had remained so long in the hidden files of the foreign office of Imperial Russia, now of course in the possession of the USSR.

A photographic copy of the gold plate letter has also been printed in the article. It is also stated that when the Czar was informed by his foreign office that a gold plate letter was received, Czar himself wrote on the report, 'Show me gold letter.'

It is also interesting to read that the British Government tried that the letter and the messengers were handed over to them. Czar did not comply with the request and allowed the messengers to return to Afghanistan.

I remember that morning when the Prime Minister, brother of the king, Sardar Nasrullah Khan, hearing the advance news that messengers were on way to Kabul, rejoined and called me to his residence.

I went as usual accompanied by my prime minister, Moulana Barkatullah. The Sardar was very happy. He told me, "Your plan succeeded, tomorrow they will reach Kabul." He was so happy because he was afraid that the messengers would be killed. They came and told us their story. They gave the name of the Governor General as General Kropatkin, brother of Prince Kropatkin. The name in the article in Soviet Land is different.

Two Russian young men came to see me at Dehradun in April this year. Mr. E. Rumyantsev from Soviet Information Bureau and Mr. G. Cheremushkin, artist, direct from Moscow.

The artist made my sketch and painted a picture, sitting just before me. Mr. Rumyantsev tape recorded my views on several topics including my interview with Comrade Lenin.

Tribune Magazine, dated Sunday 13th May 1973 has brought out a long article by Mr. Rumyantsev under heading 'Unforgetable Meeting with Lenin'.

What I call true Russian Friendship is that Russian friends remember me and bring forth facts of my life before the Indian public, reminding the rulers in India that I was the first Indian who tried to make contact with Russia.

It is also to be noted that my talk of liberating Russia and China from the slavery of Karl Marx did not annoy my Russian friends.

As I said, I am not against the present rulers at Moscow. I admire Comrade Lenin for saving Russia from foreign yoke. He used slogans of Karl Marx because he had no other alternative. Trotsky had started the theme of class war and backward workers of Russia had taken it up.

Now of course, I assert, freedom of speech and freedom of the press should come to Russia. Russian intellect demands it. Changed conditions demand it. It was mischief to create hatred of nobility and the rich. Russians and Russians should now embrace.

Story of Gold-Plate Letter

This article is published in April, 1973 issue of 'Soviet Land' magazine, under the same heading : 'Story of Gold-Plate Letter', By A. RAIKOV, Candidate of Science (History) :

On 14 March 1916, an extraordinary event occurred on the usually quite sector of the Russian-Afghan frontier. Four men crossed it in the proximity of the town of Termez. The Russian frontier-guards looked at the intruders with surprise. Though they presented Afghan passports, the trespassers turned out to be Indians and not Afghans. They were Sardar Samshir Singh and Mirza Mohammed Ali with their servants Aya Singh and Abdul Haq. They handed a letter, signed by Minister Barkatullah, to the officer of the frontier-guards. It said that the bearers were envoys on an important diplomatic mission to the Russian Governor General in Tashkent.

The Russian authorities established that the person apprehended were representatives of the 'Provisional Government' of India which had been set up by the Indian patriots in exile at Kabul in 1915. The government was headed by prominent leaders of the Indian national liberation movement. They were Raja Mahendra Pratap and Maulvi Barkatullah. These men intended to prepare for an armed uprising in North India to liberate the country from the British colonialists.

The Indian patriots took it for granted that the Russians sympathised with the Indians. They realised the importance of friendly ties with Russia for the free India of the future. That was why they attached a special importance to the establishment of contacts with Russia. This was the reason for the arrival of the Indian mission in Russian Turkestan in March 1916. However, Raja

Mahendra Pratap and his comrades-in-arms totally ignored the balance of forces in the international arena during World War I. More than that, they disregarded that fact that in 1916 Russia together with Britain was a party to an imperialist alliance which was at war against another bloc of imperialist powers headed by Germany.

The Russian authorities were quite attentive to the envoys of Raja Mahendra Pratap. Several days later they were taken to Tashkent and were received by Martson, the Governor General. The envoy handed him two letters from Raja Mahendra Pratap. One was addressed to him and the other to the Tsar. In the first letter Mahendra Pratap wrote that he was a friend of Russia. Speaking on behalf of 300 million Indians he appealed to the Russian authorities for aid. The letter contained ambiguous hints about it being possible for Russia to improve its relations with Afghanistan as well as with Germany and Turkey. He asked the Governor General to send the other letter to the Tsar.

That letter was rather unusual. An oblong envelope of thick paper with seals contained a gold plate with a text engraved on it. Mahendra Pratap wrote to the Tsar that the fight for the liberation of India was the purpose of his life. He expressed the hope that Russia would help India to gain freedom from British Colonial domination.

The Tsar gave the following instructions on the report of the Russian Foreign Minister, Sazonov: 'Send me this gold letter.' The photostat copies of both sides of the Raja's gold plate are kept in the archives of Russian Foreign Ministry.

Though Russia was Britain's ally in the war against Germany, the arrival of an Indian mission in Tashkent gave rise to anxiety in London. Soon the question of the Indian mission in Tashkent became the subject of diplomatic correspondence between the foreign ministries of the two countries. In the beginning the British Foreign Minister in its letters to the Russian authorities tried to play down the incident as of no consequence. The British even tried to discredit Raja Mahendra Pratap. However, the British merely camouflaged their real intention in their diplomatic exchange with the Russians. In a telegram to the British Ambassador in Petrograd Sir Edward Grey, the British Foreign

Secretary, suggested to have the members of the mission arrested and handed over to the British. The British Embassy asked the Russian government for the photographs of the envoys and the photostat copies of their passports. The embassy described Barkatullah and Mahendra Pratap as dangerous rebels.

However, the Russian government rejected England's demand. It did not give any official reply to the Indians and permitted them to leave the country and return to Kabul. But before they departed, the Russian diplomat Chirkin, who at one time was Russian Consul in Bombay, had a meeting with them. The Indians told Chirkin that in their view the political situation that had taken shape was extremely favourable for the overthrow of foreign domination in India. They explained that the reason for their visit to Russia was to ascertain whether Russia would remain neutral in this struggle.

Reporting on the talks Chirkin pointed out: "Even our hostility could not stop this irrevocable war of liberation." He further indicated that the Indians were sure of succeed.

Early in May the Indian envoys left for Kabul.

In those days Russia was closely connected with England. Though their plan for winning Russia over to India's side was naïve, the diplomatic initiative of the Indian patriots was indicative of their unshakable faith in the fact that there were greater grounds for friendship between the Russian and Indian people than for the Anglo-Russian imperialist alliance.

It seemed that the February Revolution in Russia and the overthrow of the Tsarist autocracy should have given hope for a change in the attitude towards Mahendra Pratap. On 15 May 1917, he sent another letter to the Russian authorities. But the provisional bourgeois government did not respond to the appeal. In October 1917 a proletarian revolution took place in Russia. The Great October Socialist Revolution brought about a radical change in the situtation not only in Asia but in the world. Soviet Russia was now the main support and ally of peoples fighting for their freedom. Though Mahendra Pratap failed to realise the profound character of the change in Russia, he immediately sensed that it was favourable for the Indian people.

His letter of 29 November 1917, is of great interest. After describing his misfortunes the Raja wrote enthusiatically about the October Revolution. He congratulated India's 'neighbour Russia on the accomplishment of such a change.' His letter read in part: '... I am pleased to learn from the latest reports published in the Indian papers that the Russian government is now under the guidance of Russia's noble sons. ...I fervently believe that my contact with Russia will be of tremendous mutual advantage.... I hope and trust that I could be useful in rendering good services to Russia in the interests of India and the whole of mankind.' Concluding, he wrote: 'As I have invariably stated my aim is to establish close friendly relations between Russia and India. Because we are confident that it is through Russian-Indian friendship that it will be possible to secure the liberation of India and to establish a balance of force in Asia and the whole world.' These words written more than half a century ago are remarkably valid today.

Raja Mahendra Pratap received an invitation to visit the capital of the revolutionary Russia. On 7 May 1919, he was received by V. I. Lenin together with other Indian revolutionaries.

Later he recalled that the meeting with Lenin made a profound impression on him. It put an end to his attempts to ask for aid from the imperialist powers. He got opportunity to work for the freedom of India in Tashkent and Afghanistan in totally different conditions. He was given full support by Soviet leaders. Mahendra Pratap realised that only a socialist state could be a sincere friend of India.

I brought out the entire article as it appeared in the April issue of the Soviet Land.

It shows, I tried to approach Czar to help the freedom movement of India. I solo approached the Kerensky Government. It replied that there was no change in its policy. Commissar at Tirmiz in 1918 invited me. I came in closer contact with Red Russia. The article in the official Magazine proves that the loving contect still continues.

Another article I must paste here, which shows that Russia is truly a friend of India.

Unforgettable Meeting with Lenin

By E. Rumyantsev

In India, there lives a man, who met Lenin and talked to him. This is surprising, because time flows quickly and there are very few people left, who met and talked to Lenin who died about a half-century ago. The man, who met Lenin is Raja Mahendra Pratap. He lives at Dehra Dun.

He is 85, a venerable age. I want to mention, getting ahead of the story, that the atmosphere in his house does not at all carry the impression of senile aloofness. The owner of the house is surrounded by youth. Through the weight of years former active temperament dozes out—in intonation, gestures, an unexpected glint in the eyes, lit up with reminiscences. He continues to lead active spiritual life, and the questions of philosophy, morals, sociology etc. interest him as before. He has written several books. A new book by him will be published soon.

Our interlocutor has a tenacious memory. He knows how to narrate. By listening to him, one automatically goes back to those remote events, which he had himself witnessed, and becomes a witness, rather a participant in them.

Raja Mahendra Pratap has been to Russia several times. His most memorable visit was in 1919.

This was a great and complicated period. The imperialists, counter-revolutioneries, enemies of the young Republic of the Soviets, were trying not only to supress the Russian revolution by the force of arms, they fabricated lies about the Soviet Russia, the Bolsheviks and Lenin. Proletarians and honest people of many countries supported revolutionary Russia. These people came from different countries of all continents to defend the first proletarian revolution in the world, to understand its ideals and to tell the truth about it to the oppressed masses of their countries. There were hundreds of thousands of such people and Raja Mahendra Pratap was one of them. He headed a small group of the Indian fighters for freedom.

The fact that Lenin found time to receive the Indian delegation and to help it, is striking. Lenin was then busy in the gigantic task of saving the Republic, which was surrounded by a ring of the imperialist intervention and counter revolution, the Republic, which was nearly exhausted by hunger, disease and a host of other misfortunes. That despite his busyness, Lenin found time to meet the Indian delegation is explained by the fact that he attached great significance to his great country of the East.

Meeting With Lenin

'I was the first to enter Lenin's room.' Raja Mahendra Pratap remembers. 'Lenin stood up to greet us, he himself brought a small, armed chair from a corner, and requested me to be seated. For the first few minutes I was slightly confused and did not know, where it could be better to sit, in the armed chair or on a small sofa nearby. At last I sat in the armed chair and my comrades sat on the sofa. Lenin asked, 'In which language should I speak : English, German, French or Russian. We decided to talk in English.'

Raja Mahendra Pratap told me that the route of the trip of their delegation, which came to Russia facing great difficulties, its plans and programmes of further actions and also other important questions, were decided with Lenin's assistants.

The guests of India discussed with Lenin the transformation of the society, moral values and philosophical problems as well as problem of fighting for freedom. 'These problems worried us most,' the Raja told me.

A Book Presented

I presented my book '*The Religion of Love*' to Lenin, in which some aspects of my viewpoint were presented. Lenin told us that he had already read that book. I was highly surprised, how and where could Lenin get that book? But afterwards I remembered that the evening before I had sent a copy of my book to one of the secretaries. It meant that Lenin had specially read that book at night before our meeting. Naturally, I asked him about his impressions of the book. The answer was very short: 'It is Tolstoyism'. Here I would like to mention Lenin's regard for Tolstoy and Tolstoyism. Lenin considered Tolstoy as the greatest artist and was proud of his genius. However, he could not share the erroneous philosophical views of Tolstoy and religious and idealistic aspect of his view point and the native petty-bourgeois character of his teachings. As a revolutionary and thinker materialist, Lenin considered them harmful to the cause of freedom of the working class. Lenin's assessment of the book of the young Indian publicist was again principled Leninist view point.

Undoubtedly, Lenin's critical remark could not basically change the views of the Indian thinker, but the meeting with the leader and personal acquaintance with the revolutionary Russia helped him a great deal in analyzing the essence of the events which had taken place there and to understand their world historical significances.

And now remembering his memorable meeting with the leader of the Russian Revolution, the old Indian thinker said, 'I consider Lenin a leading personality. I was lucky enough to meet him in the most difficult period of the Republic of the Soviets, when it was surrounded by a ring of enemies. And only Lenin's genius, which united workers into a single union, helped it to win in the most difficult struggle and to build a new society, unprecendented in the history.'

It was clear that the discussion had slightly tired our host, but he continued to speak. He described his great interest in the USSR, which he has retained all through his life, as well as, how heartily he desired victory to the people of the USSR in their fight against fascism. He also speak about the friendship of our two great countries.

'You have proved this friendship, by your faithfulness to the Indo-Soviet Treaty during the period of hard test for our country in December 1971. And therefore, our friendship, which has been tested for durability has become still more firm, it has a bright future !' He said at the conclusion of our meeting.

There are two small bas-relief of Lenin in the room among memorable and valuable articles dear to him. Apparently they are gifts of his friends from Moscow. Having noticed my interest, our host stood up and showed us a book. 'This is also about Lenin', he said, 'It is his biography' I got this also from Moscow. I get letters from there......'

The threat connecting the Indian philosopher with Lenin's country stretches through distances and years.

Mirzo Tursun Zade the great Soviet poet has sent me his message, his book of poem, 'Ganga to Kremlin', I am made the hero of the story, a robe of honour with Tajik cap and some souveniers as present. Mr. Latif Faiziev and Mr. Dmitrii Bulgakov brought them. Mr. Rumyantsev of the 'Soviet Land' led them. These two messengers are film producers. They are going to prepare a film of the revolutionaries. In it, they said, I shall play very important role.

My Tour to Mauritius

I arrived by plane at Mauritius on the 15th September 1973. Protocol Officer Mr. Allock of the foreign office received me at airport and brought me to the continental hotel, Curpipe. Here I was the guest of the Mauritius Govt. for eleven days. A government car was also placed at my disposal.

I met my host, the Prime Minister. I presented to him some of my books. I suggested, as the population of the island was mostly Indian it may also join, Aryan Federation. I told P.M. that I wanted to preach and speak at meetings. He asked Mr. Navin, his secretary to take me to Mr. Rathi who should arrange meeting. Mr. Rathi arranged Hindu Maha Sabha reception.

I met the Indian High Commissioner. He invited me to the dinner party given on the eve of my departure. He came out to car and promised me to send cuttings of four newspapers which had published my news and views.

Mr. A.C. Misra took me to the Urdu Institute. The secretary is an old Boy of the Muslim University. Several persons, two poets spoke and recited poems. I spoke in Urdu and suggested that they should form Aryan Federation League.

Arya Samaj gave me grand reception. I spoke here at length on unity of religions. D.A.V. Colleges, Gurukuls and Orphanages in India are the great work of Arya Samaj.

Hindu Maha Sabha also gave me a reception. Audience was not large but speeches were very touching. I as a Brajbasi have special claim on Hindus.

I was invited to Seva Shivir of Swami Krishnanand. Here Hindu youths are trained for social service. Hymns were sung. Audience was very large. I spoke on Religion of Love and gave my views as usual, on One World and New Science of Thought.

I accompanied Swami Satya Prakash to Shivanand Ashram and Tagore Club. Young Swami of Shivanand Ashram had seen me when I went to Swami Shivanandji who sang song in my praise. At the club I said, Dr. Rabindranath Tagore was a great phenomenon of nature. Entire mankind was phenomenon. Great teachers were produced by Nature to serve society in a better way.

I attend inauguration of an exhibition at John Kennedy College and World Federalist Youths meeting. At this meeting Mr. B.L. Mallalieu Q.C.M.P. spoke on one World. I proposed to them in writing that he should found a branch of our World Shadow Government. He wrote to me, 'I have been working for this all my life and will continue to do so all my life.'

Mr. Gautam Tilak gave me lunch. He was present at my both receptions. He also visited me at my hotel accompanying Swami Satya Prakash. By the way, his younger brother is a son-in-law of my friend Babu Anand Mohan Sahay.

I must thank Mr. Vijay Kumar for his picnic party and taking me to a sea bathing place. I thank also Mr. Jassodanand for taking me round one day for sight seeing. He showed me big lake of several miles long, took me to Pari Talab which is now known as Ganga. There are temples. At Shiv Ratri more than hundred thousand people gather here. He showed me a beautiful valley and the sea side. I should also thank the driver Mr. John who daily took me to places which I visited.

Protocol officer Mr. Allock, Mr. Jassodanand and a representative of the Indian High Commission saw me off. Arya Samajies had also come to airport. They met me and saw off.

I arrived back at Bombay in five hours and forty five minutes. Flight was very comfortable. Air India gave a good lunch. I arrived at 3.45 P.M. on the 26th September 1973. Two nights I passed at a hotel.

Today, 28th at 8 p.m. I shall leave for Delhi by plane.

Mauritius : It is a small beautiful island, a bit over seven hundred square miles and population a bit over eight hundred thousand.

Over four hundred thousand are Hindus, about one hundred eighty thousand Muslims. About thirty per cent are Christians.

There are big beautiful churches here and there; most of the Christians are Roman catholics.

Arya Samaj claims that the strength of the Samaj is one hundred and twenty five thousand.

Chinese Community is rich and doing good business but they are mostly from South China.

There are several papers in French language, none in English or Hindi. Two French Dailies 'Cerneen' and 'Nation' published interview with me and printed my photo with Shrimati Indira Gandhi.

There are Embassies of France, Russia, China and USA and High Commissions of UK and India. There are many more diplomatic Missions or Consulates.

A French dialect is spoken by the people. French and English are official languages.

There is a Legislative Assembly of about seventy members. Governor is appointed by the Queen of England at the advice of the Prime Minister. At present a Muslim is the Governor.

Island was first discovered by the Portugues. Later it came under Dutch rule. Still later it was ruled by France. Since 1810 it has been under the British. In 1968 it became an independent member of the Commonwealth.

First December : On first December 1973, I shall complete eighty seven years of my life on the earth in this body.

The date is also to be remembered as the birth day of the Provisional Government of India founded at Kabul, Afghanistan in 1915.

Believe me. I never desired to have long life. I say, however, He knows best who gave me birth and keeps me alive.

Important Letters : There are many files about me in National Archives of Government of India. National Archives recently asked me to give some more documents and letters. Some very important letters and documents have been handed over to Mrs. Singh of National Archives who came over to Dehradun.

Among the documents and letters three may be mentioned here.

1. Original letter of the Chancellor of Germany of 1915.
2. Passport given by Mr. Trotski Russia, and
3. The statement or Declaration of the Executive Board of India founded during the Second World War. These are however not even half of the letters which are still lying here at Dehradun.

Letters : Hon'ble Prime Minister writes :

Dear Raja Mahendra Pratap,

Thank you for your letter and good wishes. I do not know what the newspapers reported. What happened was too insignificant to be called accident. I have a small fracture on the third finger of my left hand, caused as I was trying to get off a frisky horse.

Yours sincerely
Indira Gandhi

From UNO :

Dear Mr. Pratap,

On behalf of the Secretary-General I wish to acknowledge the receipts of your letter..........Mr. Waldheim is always glad to be apprised of the views and opinions of private citizens of Member States and he wishes to thank you for writing. Your interest in and support of the United Nations is greatly appreciated.......'

Chaudhari Charan Singh, President of B.K.D. and now president of the union of eight parties writes :

Respected Raja Sahib,

Your letter of 9th July. So many thanks. You have suggested that we should all concentrate at having national governments both at the centre and in the states, but the question is: How ? I am,

Yours sincerely
Charan Singh

It was never tried. Concentrated efforts must succeed. We will go to any length to end one party rule.

My Story : I stayed at Prem Maha Vidyalaya, Vrindaban from 28th July to 12th August 1974.

H.H. Sant Kirpal Singh founder of Ruhani Satsang and Manav Kendra died on the 21st August 1974. It is a great shock to our movement of peace.

If God willing, I will fly to Kabul from Delhi on the 5th September.

Pandit Sunderlal came to me at my flat, 45 Rabindira Nagar, New Delhi-3, and declared that he was hundred percent in favour of Shri Jai Prakash Narain movement and that he, Raja and Mr. Narain should meet as soon as possible. I wired to Babu Jai Prakash Narain to kindly come to New Delhi.

My Eighth Visit to Kabul

On the 5th September 1974 I came to Kabul by the Ariana airline from New Delhi. Dr. Balmukand Das received me at the airport and brought me to Metropol Hotel where I also stayed in 1972 for eighteen days.

Next day in the morning Hon'ble Mr. Abdulhad Davi, President of former Senate came to see me with his one relative. We talked of things passed by and of the new Young regime. He was republican by spirit since decades past.

Next day finding the address of the former Afghan Ambassador in Japan Hon'ble Mr. Said Kasim Rishtya, I went to see him. I told him as I had told Mr. Davi that I had come to Kabul to form a local centre of Aryan Federation as I could form in Nepal.

He told me that Mr. Allahnawaz was living very near. I went and saw him. It was a great pleasure to meet him again. He worked in the Secretariat of our Provisional Government of Hind in 1916 together with other young students who had come from Lahore. Later he was Afghan Ambassador in Germany.

I visited Pashtany Tejaraty Bank and took from them a document showing my balance at the Bank.

I wrote letter and picture cards to many friends in India; Japan, USA, Canada and Germany. I also wrote letters to newspapers in India and at Kabul.

Mr. Allahnawaz Khan and Dr. Balmukand Das kindly visited me several times. Once Dr. Das brought four Indian Professors now at Kabul University.

Professor Bhatnagar arranged a meeting at the Indian Embassy. Audience consisted of the entire Embassy staff including Charge d' Affairs and professors. I spoke at length of my past and present activities. I was glad to see goodwill of the audience.

I reserved my seat to fly back to New Delhi on the 21st September. I packed my things and was in the bathroom when some one knocked at the door. Half naked I opened the door. Two visitors were there, putting on my pant I asked them to come in. It was about quarter to ten at night on the 20th instant.

Smart looking young man told me, 'Please do not leave tomorrow. On Sunday at 11 a.m. the President of State will see you.' And he apologized for the trouble he gave me at this late hour. You have brought very good news, I said and thanked him profusely. The other man was an assistant of the hotel.

On Sunday, 22nd September Mr. Anwar of the Protocol Department of the Foreign Office brought a car and took me to the palace.

We met Hon'ble President, who rose from his chair, came forward and shook hands with me. Then we sat on two easy chairs. I presented to him my three books and three photographs and showed him photos of King Amanullah, Prince Inayatullah, King Nadir Khan and some others and photos of two letters of King Habibullah. I gave him also my plan of Aryan Federation. It was astonishing to me to see that Hon'ble President read every word of letters and what was written on photos. In regards Aryan Federation he said it was the work of the public, if public wanted it would do. He kindly told me that Afghanistan could never forget my services to Afghanistan and that I come and come again and that I was a historic person.

Earlier on the 15th September Hon'ble Mr. Waheed Abdullah, acting Foreign Minister received me at the Foreign Office. I showed him old photographs and letters. He was very pleased and told me that I was a historic person. Same words were repeated by the President too.

Hon. Mr. Rishtya paid me a visit and I visited Hon'ble Mr. Davi at his old home in old town.

Swami Sudhanand, Messrs. Kapoor, Handa, Sharma, Patil, Khandalkar, Surne and Arya visited me.

I should also mention that on the 20th September, I joined the marriage feast of a relation of Dr. Das and Mr. Nandkishore. It was a pleasure to meet here many Hindu citizens of Kabul.

On the last day, 25th September Dr. Balmukand Das gave a feast at his home. In the afternoon Mr. Allah Nawaz and a relation of Mr. Davi came to say good bye.

In the evening Prof. Saksena and Prof. Bhatnagar came. Two more persons came to say Adieu. Two more friends came. Thus from 5th to 25th September I had good time with old and new friends.

It was my eighth visit to Kabul. My first visit was in 1915. Helped by German and Turkish Officer and Moulana Barktullah I arrived at Kabul on the 2nd October 1915.

New Year 1975 : I wished happy New Year to all our friends and to all the rest of our human race.

I wish happiness to one and all but I must add that the signs of times signal Danger.

All is quiet on the front for the moment. But the most dangerous situation remains in West Asia where Israel and Syria are face to face with full preparations for another war.

Once when I compared my life with that of Buddha, saying I was born of a Raja, Buddha was born of a Raja, I left home when I was twenty eight years old, Buddha left home when he was twenty nine years old. He gave Buddhism to the world, I have given Religion of Love, the religion of this age. A friend got agitated and said, "Please do not compare yourself with Buddha, Krishna or Christ, people will hate you for relating such comparisons." Poor friend, he died a miserable death and I am, thank God, still alive and healthy at the age of eighty eight years.

Letters : H. R. H. Chogyal of Sikkim, in this letter stated that in these days Indian Reserve Police was ruling the country. I am extremely sorry to hear it but I am not surprised. Here in India, in a way, we have also Police Raj or Police rule.

Here and there, police makes 'Lathi' charge, attack by big rods, gas bombs are thrown over the crowd, students are killed by police firing. President of India twenty years back said that there was not such firing in British Raj as in Swaraj. Now it is worse.

That letter of Chogyal disappeared from my table. Fourteen years before, when I was in Parliament, letter of Hon. Mr. Atlee was stolen from my office. I had that times three secretaries. I had remove one of them whom I suspected for the mischief.

H. E. Dr. von Hentig, 6531, Seibersbach W. Germany writes :

My dear Raja Sahib,

The saying that having been considered dead predicts longevity seems to be confirmed by us two. So the approaching first of December gives me the great joy to congratulate you at being still strong and incessantly at work. Looking back at your already long life you may be proud of the vicissitudes you went through and the result of your work. Of course we-and I might associate my humbleself to you-were and had to remain callers in the desert but ideas once conceived will continue to work. I read recently the autobiography of the late Chinese Emperor Puyi. He came finally to adopt your recommendation of clearing the mind from evil thoughts........... May God bless you further on and keep you in good health to achieve your high aims to the benefit of coming generations. Be sure of the admiration and collaboration of your most faithful friend,

Werner Oto von Hentig

Dr. L. V. Mitrokhin, Counsellor and First Deputy Head of the Information Department of the USSR Embassy in India writes :

Dear Raja Sahib,

It was such a great pleasure to meet you after so many years. All these years in Moscow I have been looking forward to meeting you and exchanging views with you. But, I am sorry to say, my conversation with you left me convinced that probably you yourself have not been able to liberate yourself from the friction of thoughts.......... As long as you believe in the canard propaganda by anti-Soviet agencies you will remain as far from liberation of friction thoughts as anyone could be....... Any honest man, who has been to the USSR will ridicule the statement that USSR is a huge concentration camp....... If you think that dissidents like Solzhenitsyn and Sakharov are the true representatives of the

Soviet intellectuals, I am sorry to say, you are again wrong. They are nothing but are paid agents of the western monopolistic circles..... I hope you do not mind this friendly outburst of mine and in spite of these differences of opinion our friendship will continue. I can assure you on my part that I have great respect for you, an outstading freedom fighter of India and one of the pioneers who paved the way for the Indo-Soviet friendship. Wishing a long and active life.

Yours sincerely
L. V. Mitrokhin

I sincerely thank you for your friendly feelings for me. I am not 'convinced' that USSR is a huge concentration camp. I only informed you for your knowledge that the Indian press carried a report that one million Russians were kept in concetration camps around Moscow.

I remain friend of Soviet Russia as ever before.

The Emergency

On 25th June 1975 Smt. Indira Gandhi proclaimed the Emergency in the country. It was a shocking news for me. All opposition leaders were sent to Jail. But I am left outside. I wrote to her, why did she felt so much insecure that to save her chair she promulgated the emergency and put all the opponents behind the bar. I expected that she would not reply, and police will come to take me to prison, But she replied :

Dear Shri Mahendra Pratap,

I have received your letter of July 8, 1975. I am sure you would not have written with such vehemence had you been aware how close the opposition had taken the country to the brink of anarchy. The Emergency had to be proclaimed and some civil liberties of a limited number of persons put is abeyance so as to ensure the nation integrity and the people's true freedom. We should also do some rethinking on the political practices we have been following in recent years so that there is a greater sense of discipline all round. We had become far too casual about public responsibility. I hope that on calmer reflection you will agree with the actions we have taken.

Yours sincerely
Indira Gandhi

Again I wrote

My dear Hon. Shrimati Indira Gandhi ji,

I am very thankful that You kindly cared to answer my letter.

I wish that you are soon able to bring about normal conditions in the country.

I take your leave to repeat that National Government with you as the Prime Minister is the best solution.

Yours Sincerely
M. Pratap

On 31st August : Syed Asad Madani, President Jamiat Ulema-e-Hind, made all arrangements to take me by car to Delhi from Mussoorie. At a function at Rashtrapati Bhavan Shri F.A. Ahmad, President of India released the book 'Tahreek Shaikhul Hind.' Book is based on official records of the British Government. My name often appears in it.

Believe it or Not : Today is 2nd October. Country is celebrating birth day of Mahatma Gandhi. I remained whole day in my room, arranging matter for "World Federation". There is a censor in all news papers, pamphlets and periodicals due to internal emergency and it is necessary to send all material before publishing to the censor agency. I sent my material on 1st September 1975 to the censor. Only yesterday I received the entire matter from kindly censor. Chief cut of course here and there by the staff but allowed to publish what bore the sanction seal.

I saw some packet covers. I threw them in the waste paper basket. I noticed however there were some printed pages in English. I took them up and began to read. I was astonished to find, these were torn pages from the autobiography of Pandit Jawaharlal Nehru. On page 352, it was printed : 'Sometimes I would weary of too much reading, and then take to writing. My historical series of letters to my daughter kept me occupied right through my two term and they helped me very greatly to keep mentally fit. To some extent I lived through the past, I was writing about and almost forgot about my goal surroundings....'

What is this fate of a famous book of a famous person ! And began to muse, may be, my thoughts remain vibrating when this paper is torn to pieces ?

In Hospital : I felt stomach upset on 19th October 1975 in Delhi. I came to Vrindaban on 20th and took admission in R.K. Mission Hospital. Operation of Prostet glands was advised.

On hearing of my sickness Hon'ble Shrimati Indira Gandhi, arranged a room at All India Institute of Medical Sciences, New Delhi for my further treatment. My family members arrived at Vridaban and took charge of my treatment arrangement. My grandson Raja Amar Pratap Singh, my daughter and grand daughter and Bahu Rani Balbir Kaur came.

Many important personalities of Mathura district came to see me in the Hospital. Later I was removed to Delhi for my further treatment under medical care. I was operated on 5th Novemeber 1975. The operation was successful.

God still needs my services.

An Important Letter : When proclamation of imposing emergency over India was announced in June 1975. I was shocked and feeling the pinch at my heart, I wrote a letter, printed earlier, to admonish the prime minister of India, Shrimati Indira Gandhiji, advising her to withdraw the fatal law of emergency. The letter was written from Dehra Dun from where I chose to go on self imposed exile to fight for the freedom of India in the early hours of world war first and left my motherland.

The voice of freedom lovers was hushed by the Press Censorship law under emergency. Editors and writers felt the horrible suppression. Our paper 'World Federation', renowned all over the World got suppressed. We could not express our innerself for the interest of the public at large. Our paper was made a puppet in the hands of prevailing laws. No checks were ever put upon my expression of the views during his sojourn in foreign lands for the freedom or mother country. I expressed my thought freely in Germany, Afghanistan, Japan, USA, China etc. and 'World Federation' served the cause of suffering humanity freely. The Government of free India did not allow that much freedom even under emergency law. How shameful it was for our country.

Now, the freedom loving people of India revolted against the spirit of slavery and opposed the black law by defeating the Government in the General Elections proving that Indians value the freedom most.

To our great happiness we heard the radio announcing the lifting up of press censorship law. Now I am releasing the letter written to the Prime Minister Shrimati Indira Gandhi to the Press. It was not possible to print this letter during emergency laws. Now here is the letter in full.

Letter written with Fatherly Love

My dear Hon. Shrimati Indira Gandhiji,

I was shocked to hear of Allahabad judgement against you. I was equally shocked to hear censor of newspapers and that persons arrested can not go to court. It is worst despotism.

I could never believe that you would throw the society to such a depth of slavery.

May God give you light and you may realize that one does not live forever.

For a few years one should not do some thing which will remain a blot on Indian History.

Your saying that you are following democracy is not true under the prevailing conditions. It is Police Raj.

You are being deceived by individuals who want to get rid of you. It is said some one killed his enemy giving him too rich heavy food.

Yours sincerely
(Sd.) M X Pratap

The copies of this letter were sent then and there to some friends including Lady Vijaya Lakshmi Pandit. I wrote many other letters to the then Chief Ministers and Governors of Indian States and friends of Shrimati Indira Gandhiji advising them to persuade Shrimati ji to lift the black law. But my voice was not heard. However the then Government did not order my arrest but I was personally helped and honoured by Shrimati Indira Gandhiji.

But Shrimati Indira Gandhiji could not swallow the bitter but the sure medicine of my thoughts and faced unexpected defeat at the General Elections recently held in the country for Parliament. The old leaders of different parties according to my thinking formed Janata Party, winning the election made Government at Centre under Shri Morarji Desai. I hope they will do a good job to meet out the problems of down-trodden people of this country.

Military Rule : Today is the 5th of July 1977. This morning gave the news that Military Rule was declared in Pakistan. Evening news confirmed it.

Military Rule in Pakistan means rule of Jat Punjabi Musalmans supported by Pathans. In 1959 when I went to Pakistan I was told at Lahore, 'Here we Jats rule.'

I welcome this change. I wanted to help Mr. Bhutto. I wrote to the Pakistan Embassy at New Delhi. It was not against the military but just to avoid turmoil.

Now when Military Rule is established and peace reigns in Pakistan I congratulate the military rulers.

Shri Morarji Desai, the Prime Minister of India, who himself had been a freedom fighter disfavoured the grant of pension to the freedom fighters, which was decided by Indira Gandhi, I wrote to him. He replied :

Letter of Hon'ble Prime Minister

Dear Shri Mahendra Pratap,

I have received your letter dated 27th June 1977 in which you have expressed your dissatisfaction over my remarks regarding grant of pension to freedom fighters.

All that I had said was that while there is no question of withdrawing all political pensions granted to freedom fighters, such of them as were wrongly granted to people who were not entitled to receive them will be withdrawn.

My personal views are, of course, well known. I do not think that it was correct to grant pensions to freedom fighters after 30 years of independence. People took part in the Freedom Movement, not to earn pensions, but to fight for freedom and die rather than live in slavery. Here no body has obliged any body. There is, therefore, no question of giving a reward to any body for what was no more than a mere performance of one's patriotic duty. You are perhaps aware that quite a number of freedom fighters have refused to accept such pensions as being repugnant to their sense of patriotism.

Even so, I would like to repeat the assurance that the pensions legitimately given to bonafide freedom fighters will not be withdrawn.

With regards,

Yours Sincerely
Sd. Morarji Dasai

All India Freedom Fighters Convention : All India Freedom Fighters Convention was held in New Delhi on 8, 9 and 10th of October 1977 under the auspices of All India Freedom Fighters Society. I presided over the meet. Defence Minister Shri Jagjivan Ram and Chemicals and Petroleum Minister Shri H.N Bahuguna addressed the convention. I delivered my sermons. About four thousand freedom fighters from all over the country participated in the convention.

The Delhi Municipal Corporation gave a grand reception to the freedom fighters.

The convention expressed 'grave concern at the growing indiscipline and moral degradation of the present day youth' and urged the government to utilized the services of freedom fighters for curbing this trend.

The convention suggested to the central and state governments to organize functions in schools and other educational institutions highlighting the sacrifices of freedom fighters.

It demanded that 'befitting memorial' in honour of freedom fighters be raised in New Delhi and state capitals. Effort should also he made to write a comprehensive history of the freedom movement.

The convention also wanted an increase in the pension of freedom fighters. The amount be raised from Rs. 200 to Rs. 400. Also the amount of pension given by state governments should not be deducted from the central government pension.

Diary : It was some divine plan. When I was suffering for lack of money, selling of my old things could not make two ends to meet, I received news from Japan that the plot of land, fifteen hundred square metre, which I bought for rupees fifteen hundred was now worth a million rupees. I sold the plot to my honorary manager who looked after it and paid tax for twenty years, at half the market price. I became suddenly rich. In my old age I have not to depend on any body.

Indian Government also started to give me five hundred rupees per month. That old proverb proved correct that pain and pleasure to me always in abundance.

By the grace of God I have six servants including a driver and two at Dharma, our house at Dehradun. My secretary left as he got ill. I have advertised. I hope to get a new secretary.

Only the other day, I was invited to Chandigarh. Meeting was on the 8th Nov. I went by car. I was given a fine room at the Congress Bhavan. Later our Congress friends were sorry to know that now I had joined the Janta Party. I consider myself a man of all parties and of all religions.

I do not recognize frontiers. For me world is one country. However, I move with the current. Our people have accepted Janta Party as their Party. Overwhelmingly they voted for Janta Party. If people can change their opinion we can also change, I say, we should change. We should move with the people. We work for the people.

1978

New Year. Every morning brings a new tiding. We are so used to it that we do not realize its significance.

There can be hundreds of ways of naming eras. In vogue are Hindu, Muslim and Christian calenders. Buddhists and Jains have their own eras. Due to long British rule in India we use generally Christian calendar. In private letter we often use English language.

There are some conservative extremists who insist on using Hindi. In the world English has developed into International language.

Once England had its vast empire. Sun never set on it. English industry and business made learning of English necessity.

We should see facts. We should move with the ride. Prejudice is a curse in itself.

I fought for three decades against the British empire yet I admit that the English men and women had and have noble character. In fact their character developed their empire. I remember, how Indians preferred English judges than Indian judges. I suggest that we resolve to eliminate all kinds of prejudices and hatred.

Prime Minister Writes

Prime Minister's House
New Delhi
March 14, 1978

Dear Raja Mahendra Pratap,

I have received your letter of March 6, 1978. Religion of Love is good and should govern the conduct of men and women. But any effort to propagate such instruction must depend for its success on voluntary effort of people, devoted to this idea. If you can influence people, it should be possible for you to spread this philosophy of Religion of love amongst large number of people both in India and abroad.

With good wishes,

Yours sincerely
Sd. Morarji Desai

My Abhinandan : With the inspiration of Ch. Digambar Singh, Ex. M.P of Mathura, 'Abhinandan Granth' was published under the editorship of Shri Ram Narayan Agrawal. It deals with my life and activities. The book contains more than seven hundred pages and is well-bound. It also brings to light the fighters for freedom of 1857. Life of revolutionaries of Braj is also depicted.

Uniqueness of the book is that it describes Prem Mahavidyalaya College founded by me in 1909 to modernize and start the industrial training of this country.

Ch. Charan Singh ji, Union Home Minister released the book for public view on 26th March 1978 at Vigyan Bhawan, New Delhi by presenting a book to me. Hon. Home Minister spoke very highly of my sacrifices made for the cause of the freedom of our country.

Mr. M. M. Chopra, General Secretary of All India Freedom Fighters' Association was the organizer of the meet. Th. Nawab Singh Chauhan M.P. took pains for the success. The meeting was crowded. Old revolutionaries like Pt. Sunder Lal, Baba Prithi Singh Azad and Pt. Permanand addressed the meet. Some members of Parliament were also present.

People came by cars, buses and trains to attend the meeting from various part of India.

My autobiography '*My Life Story of Fifty Five Year*' throws light on the thrilling incidents of my life—narrow escapes and endeavours to make India free.

Important Message

August 1978.

Dear friends and the trustees of the Prem Mahavidyalaya Association,

Now running in my 92nd year, I see death just round the corner.

Before that I leave this earth I want to see how our papers, English and Hindi, P.M.V. College and P.M.V. Polytechnic will be running after my death. I beg you to write articles in 'World Federation' and 'Sansar Sangh'.

Raja Mahendra Pratap.

Now I Need Rest

Completing ninety two years on the first December 1978 I need rest. As a rule government retires government servants at the age of fifty five years. At the most it allows servents to serve the state up to sixty years. I wish, my friends consider, as if, I am no more on this earth.

Call me not to come to very long distant places. A friend took me recently to Bombay by air. A great show was put up there. Famous artists took part. Seats were sold from rupees twenty five to rupees one hundred. I have just declined to go to Calcutta. I can, however, allow if some one brings car, takes me to Delhi and thence takes me to Amritsar, Bombay, Madras or Calcutta by air.

By air I can also go to Europe or America. I have good health.

To tell the truth. I have now such a state of my mind that I shall welcome death with open arms. One works whole day, gets tired has rest sleep. One works whole life gets more tired, has rest in death. Death is long rest, undisturbed rest. You do not even dream in death. Death is very long rest without any kind of worry.

Ignorance fears death. Death is a phenomenon or life. Death is the destination of this life. Since baby is born, man rushes towards death.

You may at times say, you were very busy but no engagement can keep you busy when the time arrives to leave this life.

I said, I want rest but I enjoy work. With great pleasure I am writing these lines. I call it my message. Message to all those who have any love or regard for me.

I come to Vrindaban to pass winter. Vrindaban has very mild and pleasant winter.

It is nine in the morning of Wednesday the eighteenth October 1978. Sun is shining bright. From my window on my left I see river Jamuna flowing towards Mathura. Mathura is the birth place or Lord Krishna but Jamuna comes first to Vrindaban and then proceeds to Mathura. Vrindaban is the sacred place where Krishna danced with Braj dames, Gopies.

I thank God for bringing me to Vrindaban from Mursan. My childhood and boyhood was spent at Vrindaban.

Though I was educated at the Muslim College, Aligarh, I came to Vrindaban in holidays. My estate was under court of wards when I was minor. An Englishman Mr. Smith was the Manager of court of wards. He gave me fifteen hundred rupees from my estate to travel and see India.

In three rounds I travelled to Calcutta, Jagannath, Rameshwaram and Quetta. Once I went to Badrinath on horse back.

I travelled five times round the world. I was thirty two years in exile. Now I want that I die at Vrindaban.

I am Convinced : I am writing these lines at 7.25 P. M. on Thursday the 2nd November '78.

I am convinced that there is a very good reason to keep me alive.

Some great wise persons said, Man, know. But even today, inspite of great progress, man has been to moon, man does not know himself.

Circumstances of birth, friends and education make men Hindu, Muslim, Christian and the like, make men nationalist or communist.

He sticks to these thoughts, blindly follows them. Highly advanced persons too are not exceptions.

Learned persons can not be easily convinced that they are slaves of thoughts. Now this I alone can say.

I am convinced, I have still some thing to say or do.

Creator is not a fool. Laws of Nature work throughout the universe. Not an atom is without a purpose.

You and I, we all have some duty in the creation.

We are all doing our duty knowingly or unknowingly. We are made to do what we are doing.

If we obey not the law we suffer. It is the meaning of sickness and all worries.

I had my sufferings. I am told that the relatives of my adoptive mother were not happy. They wanted to declare that the younger Rani was pregnant. They wanted to get a baby from somewhere and say baby was born.

One illiterate elderly person, named Jhandu, who looked after me gave five rupees to a Brahman woman to act as if goddess had come in her body, wildly shake her head and say that I was God chosen person, no harm should come to me. The trick succeeded, all got afraid and I was not harmed.

Thrice I was given poison, at New York, Tokyo and Tashkent but I was cured some how.

In my adventurous travels I often narrowly escaped death. In 1915 when I was coming with German and Turkish friends to Kabul, in Iran British and Russian cavalry men tried to capture us but we escaped.

I slept in a deserted tomb. It was also home of a snake. It came but seeing me it ran away. I saw it entering a hole.

Above all, my present good health, is a clear proof that God wants me yet to live. I bow to His will.

Even now, some times, some new thoughts come to me.

For instance, when I read that in sixty years kerosene would be finished a thought came to me, hydrogen gas from water.

Now I am trying, as much as I can, to herald : You do not know why you think as you think. You are all slaves of some thoughts. In these thoughts are mixed friction thoughts. They have captured your mind.

Believe me, these thoughts have come from the enemies of human race.

While it is time, remove them from your mind. They may make you destroy mankind. Clean your mind daily. Always remain alert. No friction thought should enter your mind. If it has entered remove it. Thoughts of Harmony should always lead you.

You and I, we all have some duty in the creation.

We are all doing our duty knowingly or unknowingly. We are made to do what we are doing.

If we obey not the law we suffer. It is the meaning of sickness and all worries.

I had my sufferings. I am told that the relatives of my adoptive mother were not happy. They wanted to declare that the younger Rani was pregnant. They wanted to get a baby from somewhere and say baby was born.

One illiterate elderly person, named Jhandu, who looked after me gave five rupees to a Brahman woman to act as if goddess had come in her body, wildly shake her head and say that I was God chosen person, no harm should come to me. The trick succeeded, all got afraid and I was not harmed.

Thrice I was given poison, at New York, Tokyo and Tashkent but I was cured some how.

In my adventurous travels I often narrowly escaped death. In 1915 when I was coming with German and Turkish friends to Kabul, in Iran British and Russian cavalry men tried to capture us but we escaped.

I slept in a deserted tomb. It was also home of a snake. It came but seeing me it ran away. I saw it entering a hole.

Above all, my present good health, is a clear proof that God wants me yet to live. I bow to His will.

Even now, some times, some new thoughts come to me.

For instance, when I read that in sixty years kerosene would be finished a thought came to me, hydrogen gas from water.

Now I am trying, as much as I can, to herald : You do not know why you think as you think. You are all slaves of some thoughts. In these thoughts are mixed friction thoughts. They have captured your mind.

Believe me, these thoughts have come from the enemies of human race.

While it is time, remove them from your mind. They may make you destroy mankind. Clean your mind daily. Always remain alert. No friction thought should enter your mind. If it has entered remove it. Thoughts of Harmony should always lead you.